# SADDAM'S WAR OF WORDS

SADDAM'S

POLITICS,

RELIGION,

AND THE

IRAQI INVASION

OF KUWAIT

# WAR OF WORDS

JERRY M. LONG

 University of Texas Press
*Austin*

First edition, 2004

Requests for permission to reproduce material from this work
should be sent to Permissions, University of Texas Press, Box 7819,
Austin, TX 78713-7819.

⊗ The paper used in this book meets the minimum requirements
of ANSI/NISO Z39.48-1992 (R1997) (Permanence of Paper).

**LIBRARY OF CONGRESS CATALOGING-IN-PUBLICATION DATA**

Long, Jerry M. (Jerry Mark), 1951–
Saddam's war of words : politics, religion, and the Iraqi invasion of
Kuwait / Jerry M. Long.— 1st ed.
    p.    cm.
Includes bibliographical references and index.
ISBN 0-292-70160-8 (cloth : alk. paper) — ISBN 0-292-70264-7
(pbk. : alk. paper)
1. Persian Gulf War, 1991.    2. Iraq—Politics and government—
1979–1991.    3. Iraq—Politics and government—1991–    4. Arab
nationalism—Iraq—History.    5. Islam and politics—Iraq.    I. Title.
DS79.72.L66    2004
956.7044′21—dc22
                                                        2003022364

For Ahmad

Iraqi Infantry

IN MEMORIAM

Died in the Kuwait Theater of Operations, January 1991,
during coalition bombing

I remember you, Ahmad, and weep

*Allah yerhamak*

# CONTENTS

# PREFACE

Edward Gibbon observed of the various Roman divinities that the people believed them all, the philosophers disbelieved them all, and the politicians found them all equally useful. Such was the case in the Gulf War when Iraq turned to religion as a weapon, seeking to delegitimate the coalition arrayed against it, while appealing to other Arab states to join its jihad.

*Saddam's War of Words* first charts the historical context of the Gulf War and advances specific political reasons why Iraq invaded Kuwait. It also examines the "slow baptism" of the Iraqi Baʻth party prior to the invasion, suggesting reasons the regime modified its secular ideology to embrace an instrumental use of Islam. With that background, *Saddam's War of Words* then poses and seeks to answer these questions:

How extensively and in what specific ways did Iraq appeal to Islam during the Kuwait Crisis?

How did elites, Islamists, and the elusive Arab "street" respond to that appeal, both in and out of the coalition, and why did they respond as they did?

What longer-term effects resulted from that appeal?

What implications may be drawn from this use of religion?

*Saddam's War of Words* argues that Iraq's calculated appeal to Islam was extraordinarily pervasive. It argues further Saddam proved effective in his fusing of two parallel global narrations (Arab nationalism and Islam), eliciting broad popular response. It finds the coalition was compelled to mount a broad countercampaign, focused especially on defending the religious legitimacy of employing non-Islamic forces against an Islamic regime. The result was a "war of fatwas," with a contending use of texts and traditions and countercalls to jihad. The war's end, however, saw a reaffirmation of the Arab interstate system, yet not in such a way that the ideas of an Islamic *umma* or a nation *min al-khaleej ila al-muheet* (from the gulf to the ocean) ceased to carry cognitive and emotive importance.

Moreover, *Saddam's War of Words* argues that neither side in the war constituted a monolithic force; and it finds the employment of Islamic discourse on all sides to be not simply an argument for or against Saddam, but a powerful and often nuanced deliberation on regional and international issues. Finally, I argue, the tragic events of September 11th are, in a significant way, connected to what I have called "the unconcluded *other* Gulf War."

# ACKNOWLEDGMENTS

The process of writing a book leaves any author with a sense of extraordinary debt, for no writer, of course, is an island entire unto himself. The ideas here began to take shape first during the Persian Gulf War, 1990–1991, while I worked as a Mideast military intelligence analyst. The United States Air Force offered substantial funding for repeated travel throughout most of the region, and U.S. embassies and military installations hosted me during my extensive researches there. More especially, I was fortunate to discuss many of the ideas here with well-informed civilian analysts and academicians: Dr. Peter Bechtold of the Department of State; Dr. Phebe Marr, then of the National Defense University; and Dr. John Duke Anthony, President of the National Council on U.S.-Arab Relations. The council provided significant funding after the war for further travel to the most of the countries that I treat in the text. I also wish to recognize four exceptionally gifted Air Force military analysts who invested countless hours vetting the ideas here: Colonel Richard Ayres, Lieutenant Colonel Nabeel Baker (now on the Baylor University faculty), Lieutenant Colonel David Frazee, and Major Richard Krakoff.

After active military service, I developed the ideas, along with additional extensive research, into a doctoral dissertation at Baylor University. I owe profound thanks to my committee. Dr. Derek H. Davis, dissertation advisor, read with an amazing exactness and—as a practicing attorney—challenged me with the *onus probandi* of Saddam's instrumental use of Islam. Dr. Linda Adams encouraged me when I presented many of the ideas here in her seminar on Middle East politics. Dr. Gary Hull set the standard of historical exactness and encouraged conference presentations. Dr. Bill Mitchell led me through many discussions on Islamic fundamentalism and the Middle East, doing so with intelligence, patience, and good cheer.

I would also like to thank my outside reader, Dr. John Esposito, Professor and Director of the Center for Muslim-Christian Understanding, Georgetown University, for his very helpful comments and encouragement throughout. Dr. Mahmood Monshipouri, Professor of Political Science at Quinnipiac University, provided invaluable criticism of the dissertation prospectus and a helpful discussion of the impact of the Gulf War on pan-Arabism and pan-Islam. Dr. John Kelsay, Professor of Religion at Florida State University, similarly offered helpful criticism of the prospectus. Dr. Marc Ellis, University Professor of American and Jewish Studies, Baylor University, offered extremely helpful advice early in the writing process about how to conceptualize a task of this dimension, then continued to encourage me through all the labors of writing.

While revising the manuscript for publication, I had the great benefit of an ad hoc reading group at Baylor, one comprising faculty friends just mentioned (Dr. Bill Mitchell and Professor Nabeel Baker) and an extraordinary group of advanced students in Middle East studies. These approached the task of critical revision with exceptional insight, rigor, and enthusiasm. I will miss Friday afternoons with Khurram Khadimally, John Kent, John Weium, Justin Page, James Saucedo, and Kevin Sheives, my graduate assistant. I owe additional thanks to a particularly well-informed Saudi friend with close connections to the royal family who gave me insights I could not have gotten otherwise about King Fahd, the military establishment, and the difficulty of the decisions they faced. This friend, with others, also reviewed my translations from the Arabic for accuracy.

I would also like to recognize the superb assistance of Wendy Moore and Lynne Chapman of the University of Texas Press. What would have otherwise been an onerous task, they transformed, and I am in their debt for their cheerful and conscientious labors. I also gratefully recognize the work of my copy editor, Kip Keller. His exact and intelligent reading of the manuscript has made for a much better text.

I further extend my thanks to Tim Holden, graphic design artist in the office of development at Baylor University, for his superb maps. Tim drew the maps on short notice and, in the process, graciously accommodated the numerous changes that I requested.

Finally, I wish to thank a host of friends and family for their ongoing support throughout the long process of writing and rewriting. They provided the cups of cold water so essential for any weary traveler. Here I think of Dr. and Mrs. Scott Walker, Dr. and Mrs. Wes Eades, Dr. and Mrs. Pat Pryor, Alan and Susan Nelson, Chris and Lisa Shepherd, Dee Blinka, Wanda Gilbert, Pat Cornett, Janice Losak. More especially, I thank my children—Laura, Philip, and Emily—for taking an active role here. They undertook both to listen to and to read portions of this book when it was yet in the dissertation stage, offering up personal computers for my use and giving unstinting encouragement. They have done this while pursuing their own undergraduate degrees, finishing

Air Force Officer Training School (Philip), and (in Laura's case) presenting us with our first grandchild, Connor Jacob Augustine, while taking her Bachelor of Science degree. But my chief debt is to Judy, my wife of thirty-three years. Were she not my best friend, who took my hand and journeyed as an equal partner through all these days and paths, there would be no book at all.

*Ashkurik alf marra, ye habibti.*

# SADDAM'S WAR OF WORDS

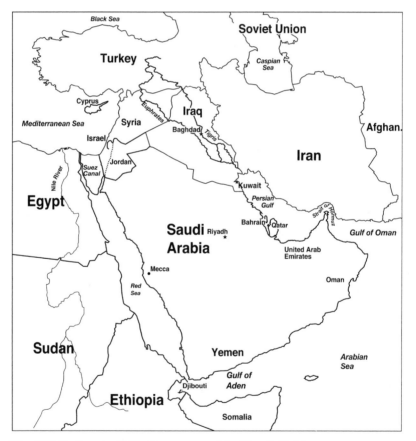

*The Middle East in 1990. Map prepared by Tim P. Holden.*

*In, out, do it, do it right, get gone. That's the message.*
PRESIDENT GEORGE H. W. BUSH, JUST PRIOR TO OPERATION
DESERT STORM[1]

# 1 | INTRODUCTION

The American president had a ghost to fight. He also had a new world order to launch. And when Saddam's tanks rolled across the Kuwaiti border in the early morning hours of 2 August 1990, President Bush seized the opportunity. In his view the opportunity was clear-cut: the conflict, he told religious broadcasters, counterposed "good vs. evil, right vs. wrong, human dignity vs. tyranny and oppression."[2] Thus, determined not to repeat the mistakes of Vietnam, and supported by generals who argued for the importance of decisive force vigorously applied, the president drew his line in the sand and set about building an impressive coalition to liberate Kuwait and inaugurate his vision of a new world order. After the most rapid deployment of military forces since World War II, the U.S.-led coalition accomplished the decisive victory the president desired and that informed military analysts had anticipated.

Most in the West who think about the Gulf War think of it in those terms: well over a half million coalition troops arrayed against the Republican Guards; thousands of air strikes by B-52s; the vindication of PGMs, or precision-guided munitions; the 100-hour ground war; Iraqi capitulation; a victory parade down Pennsylvania Avenue led by the "Bear" himself, General H. Norman Schwarzkopf. "In, out, do it, do it right, get gone." That, the West recalls, was the Persian Gulf War. But the conclusion is too hasty, markedly incomplete. Other factors were at work.

Away from M1-A1 tanks, resupply lines, and ship-launched cruise missiles, other battles were being waged, battles that antedated the second of August and which lasted well after the cease-fire at the end of February 1991. These battles pitted Arab government against Arab government, ruler against ruled, cousin against cousin, rich against poor, mufti against *ulama*. These battles used religion as a weapon, made radio and TV and sermons their venues, and drew their resupply from wells of ancient hostility. Culture and politics were the stuff of these battles. As they raged, they challenged the legitimacy of governments and institutions throughout the region, even as the combatants looked to history and religion for legitimation. For the military historian, the most difficult task in chronicling these battles is that of drawing the battle lines. Unlike Bush's clearly demarcated line in the sand, these lines crisscrossed, weblike, through mosques, bazaars, universities, parliaments, diwans, palaces, refugee camps.

Together, these battles composed a war, a war of which many in the West have been unaware, a conflict that could appropriately be named the "Other Gulf War." The Arab world certainly remembers the Other Gulf War, and it does so largely negatively. In their remembrance, this Other Gulf War was not simply a neat military conflict neatly ended, but an irruption that tore at the social, political, and religious structures of the region. Neither was it a brief conflict that spanned only seven months. The causes of the conflict had long been in the making. Preceding the second of August was an "Arab Cold War," which Malcolm Kerr had written of so eloquently earlier.[3] Only in a quite limited sense, then, did 2 August 1990 mark a strict *terminus a quo* for the war. Saddam himself claimed repeatedly than an economic war had been underway for some time prior. Although the claim was patently self-serving, many in the region could see his logic and agree. And, as will be noted in the next chapter, this was not the first significant border dispute (or even border incursion) involving Iraq and Kuwait. Similarly, the Other Gulf War had no real *terminus ad quem* in spring 1991. The cease-fire might temporarily have stopped bullets and PGMs; it could not erase hostility. It is a war that continues in myriad ways, as the concluding assessments made here will suggest.

Against that background, this work will examine one aspect of the

Other Gulf War, and that is the way in which religion itself (in this case, Islam) became one of the weapons of warfare. The war, of course, was fought for quite secular aims; it was a matter of earthly politics pursued by other means. But by a Machiavellian twist, the combatants resorted to the language of religion to achieve political ends. Indeed, that use was not merely incidental and certainly not ornamental, but deliberate and pervasive. The introduction of foreign troops provided occasions for even more pointed use. The very presence of non-Arab and non-Islamic troops furnished Saddam with pretext. Now, he could defend his actions as building a bulwark against the new Christian crusaders. Religion, then, made sense as a weapon; and by carefully fusing appeals to both Islam and Arab nationalism, Saddam employed a joint discourse—both religious and secular—that resonated with great numbers of people on multiple levels.[4]

To be sure, what occurred in the Gulf War with respect to religion was not unique. Cultures have found multiple uses for religion over the millennia. For the searching, the bereaved, the lonely, and the fearful, religion has been guide, encouragement, and strength. Yet whereas millions have found solace in their various faith traditions, some have used those traditions as the avenue to other, less than heavenly, aims. Of course, intended public uses of religion may be relatively benign, or at least perceived to be in support of the commonweal. But religion is often appropriated in ways more directly self-serving. Edward Gibbon observed of the various Roman divinities that the people believed them all, the philosophers disbelieved them all, and the politicians found them all equally useful. Thus it has been for ages.

Often it is in war that the state looks to religion. Religion can powerfully legitimate policy decisions. If war calls young men and women to make the ultimate sacrifice, religion can supply the ultimate rationale. *Dulce et decorum est pro patria mori*, Horace said; sweet and honorable it is to die for one's country. Religion's role has been to say why that is so. A nation summons its sons to war because an enemy threatens what is most dear. Religion then furnishes ontological grounding for that assessment; it describes why what is considered dear must be considered dear. It supplies, as well, the discourse of war. Religion helps make an enemy categorically different, the anti-nation that malevolently advances against one's own. After making out an enemy to be distinctly and necessarily other and then furnishing the terms of discourse, it can next offer the hope of paradise for those who die. Having depicted the enemy as marching forth from hell, religion can then make the deaths of one's own to be deeply significant for earth, and depict battle-death itself as the high road to heaven.

This analysis will not, however, be an argument against just war or against all uses of religion to describe conflict or for simple moral equivalence. Quite the opposite. The working premise here will be that just war is possible and that a statement like "Germany committed a heinous and unwarranted aggression against its neighbors" carries moral import and intelligibility. Religion may be used to frame the ethical dimension of war and, in my view, to demonstrate why war may sometimes be necessary and the concomitant sacrifices deeply significant and warranted. The book will explore the 1990–1991 conflict as an instance—and it is only one of many—where religion was specifically manipulated to legitimate specifically nonreligious aims. To adapt Milton, one could say religion was summoned from heaven to justify the ways of man to man.

To examine the uses of religion in the Persian Gulf War, this analysis will first describe that region's perspective on the war. This will include looking at the political precursors of the war, Saddam's explicitly political reasons and rationales for invading Kuwait, and the response of the Arab nations both to the aggression and to Saddam's blandishments. The subsequent fracturing of Arab unity and the political turmoil that followed the deployment of outside forces will be taken up next. Politics merged with Islam when Saddam's religious justifications for what he had done, though not unprecedented, increased as the scope of the conflict enlarged. The Saudis also turned to religion—but for different reasons. Their task was both to counter Iraqi religious propaganda and to justify bringing 500,000 non-Arab, non-Muslim troops into lands regarded as sacred to Islam. Islam, then, served both defensive and strategic roles, justifying actions taken and delegitimating the actions of opponents.

These appeals and counterappeals to Islam constitute the principal research area of the present work. The major focus will be on Saddam as a secular Baʿthist who made an instrumental employment of religion in support of his larger strategy. The analysis will next extend to elites, the ways in which they felt compelled to respond, and the reactions of nonelites. Four related research questions will guide:

In what ways and for what reasons did Saddam employ religion during the Gulf War?

How did other governmental and Islamic elites respond?
To what effect did they use religion?
What implications may be drawn from their use of religion?

Regarding the first two questions, the aim is not to evaluate norma-
tively this employment of religion, but rather to lay out as objectively
as possible the ways governments and nongovernment elites sought
to enlist religion to justify policies, delegitimate others' policies, and
respond to others' religious attacks. As indicated earlier, this was not
simply a confrontation of Iraqis and Saudis along a single, neatly drawn
battle line, but a conflict involving multiple, dynamic fronts and changing alliances. Governments convened conferences, sought fatwas (religious edicts by competent authorities) favorable to their policies, issued
calls for jihad, and hosted special media events.

In examining the effects of this employment of religion, I conclude
that the use of Islam proved both profoundly divisive and powerfully
mobilizing. A broad Middle East audience responded vigorously to the
religious entreaties. This, in turn, generated a new level of debate,
prompted marches, and encouraged acts of violence. Religious authorities outside the immediate theater issued more fatwas, and new conferences were convened. It appears that this approach was dramatically
effective, although not necessarily in the ways its employers intended.
The use of Islam by government elites certainly generated considerable
discussion among religious elites about whether religion ought to have
been so used. Those debates have not yet ended.

Of course, this appeal to religion during the Gulf War was not unique
to the Middle East. In describing the line the United States would draw
in the sand—that "aggression in Kuwait [might] not stand"—President
Bush freely and repeatedly made use of religious terminology.[5] And
Arabs noted, inter alia, that the president had invited a religious leader,
Billy Graham, to spend the night at the White House just prior to the
prosecution of the air war in mid-January. This certainly followed the
example set by his predecessor, President Reagan, who unhesitatingly
described conflict with the Soviets as one against "the evil empire."[6]
But to limit the scope of the study, the focus will be almost exclusively
on the use of Islam by leaders in the Middle East and in the larger
Islamic world. The similar employment of religion in the West, and
often with explicitly Christian terminology, merits (and has received)
careful review, but it falls outside the purview of this study.

Although studies have appeared that examine the Bush administration and its appeal to religion,[7] no work has yet appeared devoted exclusively to studying the use of Islam by Muslim governments during the Gulf War.[8] Articles that treat related areas have been published in journals, as chapters in edited works (including volumes of the Middle East Contemporary Survey), in weekly magazines (most prominently in The Economist), and as op-ed pieces.[9] There has been no sustained treatment, however. It is certainly not a paucity of primary materials that accounts for the lack of treatment. The sources are abundant, with much available in translation, primarily through the BBC's Summary of World Broadcasts (SWB), the CIA's Foreign Broadcast Information Service (FBIS), and regional newspapers published in English. The interested scholar may find speeches, interviews, regional news reporting, and other primary sources ready at hand. The supporting secondary literature is also quite extensive. In short, an abundance of research materials awaits treatment.

The importance of such a study may be justified on a number of grounds, but few are as critical as its implications for U.S. foreign policy. Richard Murphy, former assistant secretary of state for Near Eastern Affairs, once wryly observed, "Reading the Middle East is not one of our national skills."[10] Our postwar policies have underscored that lack of skill. The construction of a rigorous sanctions regime against Iraq and the maintenance of a large, visible military presence in Saudi Arabia seemed to have been planned with less than adequate regard for cultural sensitivities; in a sense, the United States continued to prosecute the Gulf War, doing so without taking the proper measure of the Other Gulf War. Although few in the region now regard Saddam as a great pan-Arab figure, there is still considerable resentment in large swaths of the Middle East toward the sanctions regime specifically and much of U.S. policy generally. Understanding the social and political dynamics of the Other Gulf War could help us understand why that is so. It could also afford lessons to apply elsewhere, especially in regions where religion undergirds society and could be manipulated by elites for political aims, whether in war or in peace.

Finally, the perspective of the author is one that supports, insofar as possible, separate and clearly demarcated realms for religion and politics. The interest of this research, however, is not primarily in critiquing governmental use of religion during the Gulf War. Neither is it to hold up the Western pattern as a template which Middle Eastern or Islamic governments ought to follow. The purpose, rather, is to furnish, as objectively as possible, an analysis of the use that was made of Islam and to do so without obtruding normative judgments. At the same time, the author is conscious of differing Muslim sensibilities about both the role of Islam and the proper ordering of church-state relations. It is worth underscoring, however, that while some Muslims may espouse an integrationist paradigm, many do not. And many of those who do, have nevertheless acceded to a de facto recognition of an autonomous sphere for politics, a point that James Piscatori has made with considerable force in his *Islam in a World of Nation-States*. During and after the war, Muslims made their own informed assessments, recognizing that Islam had been a tool of policy legitimation. Yet Eastern and Western perspectives still differ. This study, then, will seek to explore with sensitivity and objectivity the ways in which religion was politicized in the Persian Gulf War and the effects that followed, bearing in mind differing perceptions between Western and Middle Eastern cultures about faith, authority, society, and war—yet finding a common hope for a broadly shared peace in East and West.

*The Arabs are the least adapted of all people for empire building. Their wild disposition makes them intolerant of subordination, while their pride, touchiness, and intense jealousy of power render it impossible for them to agree.*

IBN KHALDUN (D. 1406), ARAB HISTORIAN[1]

# 2 | HISTORICAL BACKGROUND AND INTER-ARAB POLITICS PRIOR TO THE INVASION OF KUWAIT

In a moment of cynical historical reflection, one might be inclined to blame the British for the Persian Gulf War of 1990–1991. After all, they had held the mandate over what became Iraq. They had shuffled about members of the Hashemite clan, creating facts of geography and monarchies. Modern Iraq, it is fair to say, is the product of British plans more than the logical and natural expression of local geopolitical affinities. T. E. Lawrence made that clear when he described the famous Cairo conference of 1921. "The decisions of the Cairo conference," recalled Lawrence, "were prepared by us in London over dinner tables at the Ship Restaurant in Whitehall." And of the rather odd borders, Sir Anthony Parsons, long a British diplomat in the Middle East, observed, "Woodrow Wilson had disappeared by then, and there wasn't much rubbish about self-determination. We, the British, cobbled Iraq together. It was always an artificial state; it had nothing to do with the people who lived there."[2]

Iraq does look cobbled together, and not especially skillfully. Fashioned from part of the Ottoman Empire after World War I, Iraq comprised three of the old empire's vilayets: Mosul in the north, Baghdad in the center, Basra in the south. The Ottomans had made the region three administrative areas for good cause: Mosul was Kurdish and Sunni; Baghdad, Sunni but Arab; Basra, Arab but Shiʿi. Basra had also earlier included what became Kuwait, but the British who dined at the Ship Restaurant—and Sir Percy Cox, who later drew lines in the sand—did not have as their first concern whether there might be an invasion seven decades later.[3]

What is clear is that Iraq was artificial, an ethnological patchwork designed to suit British interests. It is also clear that Iraq was destined for problems, for, as one remarked, "Iraq was created by Churchill, who had the mad idea of joining two widely separated oil wells, Kirkuk and Mosul, by uniting three widely separated peoples: the Kurds, the Sunnis, and the Shiʿites."[4] When, in 1979, an enterprising member of the ruling Baʿthist party, Saddam Hussein, took control by pushing aside Hassan al-Bakr, the elder statesman of the party, in Iraq's thirteenth coup since 1920,[5] the new ruler found the country practically ungovernable. Some exterior crisis, Saddam realized, was needed to focus the potentially self-destructive energies of the disparate groups. For eight years, war with Iran served did just that. But peace, alas, was finally brokered, and something else was needed.[6] For several reasons, Saddam began to look south.

This chapter and the next will sketch some of those reasons and look at both the immediate context of the war and the fractious inter-Arab politics that followed the invasion on 2 August 1990. The aim is to give a point of reference for the succeeding chapters: to show the strictly secular nature of the regime and the invasion and to indicate issues that Saddam exploited in the name of religion, thus compelling others to respond in kind. It may be helpful to consider reasons for the invasion under these three heads:

- *raisons d'état*
- media reasons
- reasons of self[7]

That is, Saddam's calculated invasion reflected needs of the Iraqi state, at least as the president himself perceived them. But having invaded, Saddam was then forced to offer an apologia to the world audience he suddenly drew. Thus, he retooled the brute needs of the state and presented them to the world's media in a way he thought palatable: the media reasons. At some points these overlap; at others, they diverge.[8]

*Raisons d'état* are taken up here, and media reasons in the next chapter under "Iraq." Reasons of self, which reflect Saddam's personal interest, are addressed at length in Chapter Four.

## RAISONS D'ÉTAT

To begin, Iraq had (as it still does) a pronounced geographic need: access to the sea. It is, as one specialist has described it, a state similar to "a man with huge lungs and a tiny windpipe."[9] A country of almost 170,000 square miles, it is virtually landlocked and has but two rivers that empty into the sea. Its coast stretches only twenty-six miles.[10] (Kuwait, a country of 7,000 square miles, has, by contrast, a coastline of 156 miles.) The Shatt al Arab, which leads to the main port of Basra, fifty miles inland, must be frequently dredged to remove silt. The other port, Umm Qasr, is reached by the Khor Abdullah waterway, but the Kuwaiti-controlled islands of Bubiyan and Warba stand at the entrance. Thus, Iraq lacks what the other gulf states have: deep-water portage on the gulf itself.

Because of this lack, the Shatt has been an important, ongoing, and contentious issue. In 1980 Saddam ostentatiously tore up the Algiers Accord, a 1975 agreement with the shah establishing the *thalweg* (the deep-water channel) in the Shatt al Arab as the border with Iran.[11] When the war ended in 1988, precisely nothing had been gained and much had been lost. The need for gulf access remained. As an alternative to the Shatt, Iraq needed, at the very least, control of the Khor Abdullah waterway. And that necessitated—in Saddam's view—control of the islands that offered the deep-water anchorage Iraq so badly needed.[12] If the Shatt played a part in the decision to launch war with Iran, Bubiyan and Warba drove, in part, the decision to invade Kuwait.[13]

The economy presented a more egregious need.[14] The cost of reconstruction following the war with Iran was estimated to be some $230 billion.[15] A year after the cease-fire, Iraq's oil revenues, which accounted for 95% of its income, amounted to $13 billion. But its expenditures came to about $23 billion, covering civilian and military imports, debt service, and third-country national transfers (primarily to Egypt). At the same time, external debt soared to an estimated $65–80 billion, almost half owed to gulf states. In fact, debt had increased around $10 billion since the end of the war. Aside from what was owed in the gulf, Iraq's debt was mainly for military acquisition and development, amounting to $20 billion (owed primarily to the USSR and

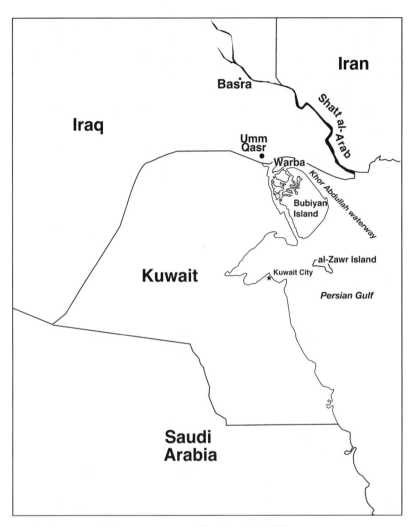

*Iraq/Kuwait in 1990. Map prepared by Tim P. Holden.*

France). Debt service in 1990 came to $6–8 billion annually. Iraq was compelled to seek, again, new lines of credit and extensive restructuring of its debt.

Although it did not have a one-cash-crop economy like the other gulf states, Iraq did have considerable concerns about its oil industry and the revenues it generated. During the war with Iran, the value of its non-oil exports amounted to less than two percent of the total. That imbalance had been ameliorated slightly through attempts to diversify, but Iraq had remained almost entirely dependent on oil for export earnings. The government watched with dismay as prices fell to about $14 a barrel in the first half of 1990 and then rose to only $18 a barrel in the summer. And Iraq fell victim to stagflation. The moribund economy, coupled with an estimated inflation rate of forty-five percent just prior to the invasion, took an enormous toll on the population. The sacrifice of scapegoats, in this case the ministers of finance and agriculture who were sacked, did nothing to help. Iraq was desperate for financial relief. In this light, the accusations about OPEC overproduction (and Kuwait's siphoning of Rumailah, the oil field that straddles the Iraq-Kuwait border) had merit, and were the basis of serious Iraqi worry.

Another concern was the military.[16] Napoleon's remark that one can do anything with a bayonet except sit on it is pertinent here. By the end of the war with Iran, Iraq had close to one million men under arms in its regular army, and roughly a quarter of the Popular Army, which numbered over 600,000, was mobilized. Demobilization on a massive scale would have wrecked the already reeling economy. In the year after the cease-fire with Iran, the government nevertheless tried to demobilize an estimated 200,000–300,000. The government called a halt to demobilization, however, because of the inability of the economy to absorb the new workers and because of clashes with the Egyptian expatriates who had filled jobs during the war with Iran, but were now being displaced. But an unoccupied army posed considerable danger to Saddam's rule; he knew the coup-replete history of Iraq only too well.

By conducting purges for "incompetence" or venality, Saddam ensured there would be no war heroes to displace his image as leader and brilliant military strategist.[17] Sometimes, doing this required unfortunate accidents. The most pointed case was that of his cousin and brother-in-law, Adnan Khairallah, who died in a mysterious helicopter crash in May 1989. But even after the purges, the military was yet seen as a threat. Maintenance of control was paramount. When Ceauşescu was executed in December 1989, Saddam is reported to have distributed pictures of the Romanian dictator to his subordinates and to members of the intelligence service. The message was clear: failure to control rival sources of power can be fatal. Saddam, then, faced a profound dilemma. He could not demobilize for economic and social reasons, but neither could he leave the army idle. He must keep it to ensure his own power, but he must keep it safely away. The army, in a word, needed new employment.

These various internal needs thus generated another need for Iraq, that of "discovering" an external crisis to divert attention away from home. The external crisis could also justify the continued active military service of 5–6 percent of its population (almost 10 percent when the Popular Army is included). Totalitarian regimes have generally used the threat of "enemies" to justify the most abusive of domestic policies as well as continued calls for national sacrifice. Of course there were the usual external suspects to be rounded up: the other wealthy gulf states, Zionism, and imperialism. And there was a growing sense of beleaguerment, in any event, issues to which the government could point for substantiation of its manufactured *diaboli ex machina*.[18] Saddam could point to the Arab world itself. For instance, the Arab summit in May 1989, in Casablanca, checked Saddam's bid for leadership. The Syrians, inveterate enemies, were able to block the Iraqi president's proposal that an Arab League force replace the Syrian military in Lebanon. Saddam could also increasingly point to Iraq's economic enemies (detailed below), whose oil policies constituted an attack on Iraq's vital interests.

Outside the region, the assassination of the Canadian scientist Dr. Gerald Bull in Brussels in March 1990, marked a significant setback for weapons development. The attack, widely attributed to the Israeli Mossad, helped block further development of the "supergun project." In effect, if not in scope, the killing of Dr. Bull paralleled the Israeli bombing of the French-built nuclear reactor at Osirak in 1981. Yet this setback could also serve Saddam's domestic concerns. The West (Saddam would argue), through the instrumentality of the Zionists, was seeking to ensure Arab weakness. As further "proof," at the end of that month a joint British and American customs team at London Heathrow Airport seized forty electrical capacitors that could be used as nuclear triggers.

Yet some further enemy was needed, one whom Saddam could not only threaten verbally, but also engage militarily. He could rail against Zionism or imperialism; he could not attack them directly. Another enemy was required, one which Iraq could attack—and could attack profitably. Iran had served the *diabolus ex machina* role for eight years. Now, as Iraq sought rapprochement with its erstwhile foe, another enemy was wanted.[19]

So Kuwait, as it had before, looked only too inviting.[20] Saddam, of course, had repeatedly proclaimed his intention of not attacking, a position he had publicly maintained even prior to becoming president. Five months before shunting President al-Bakr aside in 1979, Saddam told Francois Deneux, the French minister of foreign trade, "There is no danger to the Gulf states. You know we have no expansionist ambitions. If we did, we would now be able to achieve them, but we do not."[21] Speaking with considerable ideological conviction before crowds at the People's International Stadium in Baghdad in February 1980, Saddam proposed a National Charter to serve, not just Iraq, but the entire Arab nation.[22] Among other points, it would forbid "the use of military force by any Arab state against any other Arab state, and [called for] resolving any conflicts that might arise between Arab countries through peaceful means and in the light of joint national action and the higher Arab interest." Days before invading Iran, Saddam declared:

The Iraqis are now of the opinion that Arab unity can only take place after a clear demarcation of borders between all countries. . . . The question of linking unity to the removal of boundaries is no longer acceptable to the present Arab mentality. . . . The Arab reality is the Arabs are now 22 states.[23]

Several months after the conclusion of the war with Iran, and less than two years before invading Kuwait, Saddam stated again his intentions of nonaggression. "Instead of occupying a sister country, our existing relations should be based on dialogue, affection, and interaction." Then, to reassure his neighbor to the south, Saddam added, "How will it be possible for us [Iraq and Kuwait] to live together . . . if the minimum mutual trust is lacking?" If Arab leaders armed themselves and lived without trust, they would be no better than "Chicago gangsters."[24]

Even in July, just prior to the invasion, some of what Saddam said both to President Mubarak of Egypt and to U.S. Ambassador April Glaspie indicated the possibility of rapprochement. Most of the transcript of the Glaspie talks is filled with bombast and considerable threat (as indicated below), but Saddam did say, "When we meet and see that there is hope, then nothing will happen." And in his 23 July Revolution anniversary speech in Egypt, Mubarak was able to offer some reassurance. He had just met personally with Iraqi Foreign Minister Tariq Aziz and spoken with Saddam by phone the day before. On that basis he could say the problem was but "a passing cloud among brothers." He added, "I want to say briefly, without mentioning any details, that with his wisdom, Iraqi President Saddam Husayn is capable of bypassing this problem very calmly and objectively in order that we may avert obstacles, tension and possible fragmentation in Arab solidarity."[25]

But public relations aside, there apparently had been a plan to attack Kuwait some months before the CIA noted the marshalling of troops in July 1990. Saad al Bazzaz, an Iraqi writer with access to a number of elites and a "close companion" of Saddam, maintained that a "strategic punch" had been planned for months.[26] Writing in *harb taled okhra: al-tariq al-sirri li harb al-khalij (War Begets Another: The Secret Road to the Gulf War)*, al Bazzaz maintained that, while the economic conditions were the primary cause, a longstanding vendetta against the Kuwaitis also played a part. The Kuwaitis came to Iraq and spent prodigally in the cheap markets, flaunting their wealth, in the Iraqi view. Further, al Bazzaz wrote, the Kuwaitis failed to render proper "homage" for Saddam's "victory" over Iran. Elsewhere, the Iraqi Communist Party, in its annual meeting in March 1990, warned of Saddam's schemes for Kuwait.[27] In fact, Iraqi foreign ministry officials had indicated to an American scholar a year before the invasion that they expected to "persuade" Kuwait to give them Bubiyan and Warba.[28]

## INTER-ARAB MEETINGS

More ominous developments were to come. One indication of what lay ahead came during a meeting of the year-old ACC, the Arab Cooperation Council, on 23–24 February 1990.[29] All the participants shared a pronounced concern about Soviet Jewish immigration. Indeed, by year's end some 200,000 Jews would emigrate. This was the largest number since 1951, and Israel would have to budget $2 billion for immigrant absorption.[30] But apart from that shared worry, the meeting was a fractious one, made more so by Iraq's and Jordan's proposal to give the ACC a military dimension.[31] The deep dissension between Saddam and Mubarak was also portentous.[32] In effect, the two leaders had placed themselves on quite different political trajectories, and were following different leadership styles as well, one haranguing for financial support from the gulf states and the other urging tractability.

Speaking at the meeting, Saddam warned his audience of the dangers of living in a one-superpower world.[33] The Soviets were no longer available to counterbalance the United States. Now, using its navy, the United States would seek hegemony in the Gulf. This was a day for Arabs to stand in strength. Were they to do so, they would "see how Satan will grow weaker wherever he may be and the evil will depart our homeland and our nation."[34] Saddam also had a pointed warning that he wished Mubarak and King Hussein to pass on to gulf rulers. If they were not forthcoming with considerable aid, then his fellow ACC leaders should "let the Gulf regimes know that if they do not give this money to me, I would know how to get it."[35]

More significantly, Saddam provided a tentative answer to a question that many would ask five months later: Did Saddam think the United States wouldn't respond to an invasion of Kuwait? Before concluding at the ACC summit, Saddam observed, "All strong men have their Achilles' heel. . . . We saw that the U.S. as a superpower departed Lebanon immediately when some Marines were killed [in 1983]. . . . The United States . . . has displayed signs of fatigue, frustration, and hesitation when committing aggression on other people's rights."[36] And more recently, Saddam had observed the rather muted response to several of his egregious acts, including his use of poison-gas attacks against the Kurds in Halabja in 1988 and the hanging of Farzad Bazoft, an Iranian-born, London-based journalist.[37] In both instances, the West lodged its usual round of strong diplomatic protests, and London briefly withdrew its ambassador for "consultations." There were few repercussions, however, to trade or arms sales, although alarm was growing in the West at Iraq's nonconventional weapons program.[38] Indeed, the Arab League and the ACC defended Iraq, criticizing Western criticism and stating their "complete solidarity with Iraq in the defence of its sovereignty and national security." This "bolstered Saddam's view that confrontation with the West was the road to leadership of the Arabs."[39] Thus, Saddam's "Achilles' heel" analogy was a good observation for a leader who had traveled very little outside his country.[40]

In the meantime, Saddam enjoyed his expanding role as the voice of a proud and hard-line Arabism. He seemed to believe, as his use of chemical weapons and the hanging of Bazoft demonstrated, that bellicosity and severe measures produced political capital, at least as he vied for leadership in the Arab world. Thus, in early April came *the* announcement: Iraq had developed binary chemical munitions, weapons whose "fire could eat up half of Israel."[41] Saddam was not bluffing, and to the consternation of many it became obvious that he possessed the ability to make credible at least some of his expansionist rhetoric. Yet Saddam exercised some caution. In his "fire" speech, he added, "Everyone must know his limits. Thank God, we know our limits and will not attack anyone." A few days later, to reassure wary Western governments, the president continued, "Iraq does not want war. It fought for eight years, and it knows what war means."[42] This combination of bellicosity and tractability surfaced repeatedly in Iraqi public statements after the invasion of Kuwait.

Events in Israel soon provided the next occasion for a meeting of Arabs, one in which certain of Saddam's ideas about regional readjustments would surface. On 20 May, an Israeli soldier who had been discharged from the military attacked Palestinians outside Tel Aviv. A jilted lover, the former soldier killed seven Palestinian laborers. Over the next three days, Palestinians defied a security curfew and rioted. Fifteen more were killed and hundreds injured as the Israelis sought to bring the riot under control, in a situation described by the *Jerusalem Post* as "pandemonium" throughout the Gaza Strip.[43] Outraged Arabs called an emergency Arab League summit in Baghdad, 28–30 May, to discuss what should be done. At the conclusion, the league's communiqué condemned the Israelis for the massacre and the United States for supporting its "aggression, terrorism, and expansionism." Two things make the summit interesting. First, it gave Saddam another venue for voicing his ambitions for his country and for pan-Arabism. But it also revealed grievances in the larger Arab community, showing proleptically how various Arab leaders would respond post-invasion.

After the Taif Accords in October 1989, inter-Arab focus could shift from Lebanon.[44] Saddam's speech thus featured reinvigorated anti-American and anti-Zionist diatribes, along with ongoing concerns about the immigration of Soviet Jews.[45] As he had the previous month with his "fire for Israel" speech, Saddam returned to this theme. He promised that if Israel used weapons of mass destruction against "our nation," the Arab nation would retaliate in kind.[46] Ann Mosely Lesch puts it nicely: Saddam simply articulated "the regional equivalent of MAD, mutually assured destruction."[47] But he sounded two more ominous notes. He reminded his Arab audience yet again of his efforts in "Qadisiyya II,"[48] which was "their" battle. He implied that since he had fought it on "their" behalf, "they" owed him something in return. He would subsequently make clear, as he had intimated at the February ACC meeting, that their obligation included canceling his war debt.[49]

But he also belabored the point that pan-Arab security demanded a strong, united front. Deviation within the ranks by a member pursuing its own "whims and policies" could not be tolerated and would lead to disciplining by the other twenty states. The summer would make clear whom he meant by "deviants"—in this case, those who did not follow oil production guidelines. In sum, the speech was as strident as it was wandering, and as menacing toward those who listened as to those not part of the league. As Fouad Ajami has described Saddam's approach elsewhere, "This [was] pan-Arabism with a bayonet, chemical weapons, and a whip for all those who [would] not submit."[50] Thus, a summit convened to berate Israel furnished Saddam with an opportunity to seek to intimidate wayward Arab brothers.

Mubarak's speech followed. Emboldened by renewed diplomatic ties with Syria and by the decision of the Arab League two months before to return its headquarters to Cairo, the Egyptian president set a different course in his presentation. Beginning with the expected platitudes and expressions of thanks to his Baghdadi hosts, Mubarak then made a subtle but unmistakable right turn. Those who were listening carefully to the president heard a nuanced rebuttal of the previous speaker's tirade. Mubarak appealed to a "long established Arab tradition," a tradition that valued law and negotiation over the use of force. The Arabs should present a united front to the world, but theirs should be a message of reason and flexibility. He concluded with an obvious retort to Saddam. Above all, Mubarak said, the Arab message must be "free of exaggeration and intimidation." Now, two were vying for leadership and offering quite different visions.

Then, the president-to-be of the country-in-waiting, Yasir Arafat, spoke. Arafat was there mainly to remind his hearers of the continued sacrifices and struggles of the Palestinian people. That done, he turned to two other topics. In a glowing peroration on Iraq, Arafat enthused over the new development that Saddam had touted the previous month. Iraq had provided a new military capability, one that would give the Arabs "an opportunity to have an equal weight in the calculations of the new international forces." The language coincided with Saddam's. The weapon, not specified, was for the nation, not just one of its member states. It is highly unlikely that Arafat had any idea of Saddam's invasion plans, but one detects a kind of exultation: here, at last, was someone who could achieve social dignity—by military parity—for the Arabs in general and the Palestinians in particular. In effect, Arafat had opted to support Iraqi militancy over Egyptian diplomacy.[51]

Arafat declaimed on another issue, and that was Jerusalem. The fate of Jerusalem was routinely part of the Palestinian's speeches, but here he was particularly exercised over the nonbinding U.S. congressional resolution to recognize the city as Israel's capital. "How does the U.S. Congress give itself the right to issue [such] a resolution? This . . . constitutes an attack against Arab pride, Islamic pride, and the international will . . . and against . . . its sacred spiritual and cultural position in the hearts of Muslims and Christians." Arafat was not alone in the sentiment. For much of the Arab world it was seen as an audacious attack and one that would reverberate in the coming war.

The conference closed with Jordan's King Hussein. Concerned for his people, who had already borne so much and had faced such economic distress, the king described a new worry. He recalled the Israeli prime minister's unsettling remarks about the need for a "greater Israel." King Hussein reminded his hearers that this conjoined with the massive influx of Soviet Jews. He wondered where the Palestinians in the West Bank would be "pushed" as the new arrivals settled. Land to the east could be the only answer. This, the king declared, was "Israeli irredentism," an "aggression against Palestine and Jordan." One finds little to call hyperbole in the king's speech—only aggrieved worry, the concerns long carried by a ruler genuinely concerned for his people.

## THE SUMMER ROAD TO WAR

More threats and warnings followed. In June 1990, Iraqi Ba'thists had the honor of hearing the supreme Ba'thist speak at a symposium to honor Michel Aflaq, who had died the year before. Reflecting on the need to forward the cause of Arab nationalism, Saddam once again spoke ominously of those who had wasted billions of dollars of Arab resources. If it were in the good cause of Arabism, those who listened would have "nothing to fear from waging [their] struggle under the precept of Islam and its benevolent principles" to rectify the problem.[52] The threats continued during the summer.[53] On 16 July, Tariq Aziz sent a lengthy memorandum to Arab League Secretary General Klibi protesting oil overproduction by Kuwait and the United Arab Emirates.[54] Using strongly pan-Arab rhetoric, Aziz described how Iraq had been "obliged" to defend the eastern flank of the Arab homeland, along with Iraqi sovereignty, in its war with Iran. The gulf states had ignored that, and had deliberately adopted harmful policies toward Iraq. The memo accused the Kuwaitis of encroaching on Iraqi territory, siphoning oil from the Rumailah field (which straddled their shared border), and disingenuously insisting that wartime aid was really a loan. Aziz declared further that the gulf states were part of a larger "imperialist-Zionist plan against Iraq and the Arab nation." In addition to his warnings, Aziz called for an Arab version of the Marshall Plan for the reconstruction of Iraq.

The next day, Saddam continued the same themes in his 17 July Revolution Day speech.[55] The gulf states were agents of imperialism (i.e., of the United States and western Europe) who had thrust a "poisoned dagger" in Iraq's back by keeping oil prices low. Like Aziz, Saddam charged that this brought harm both to Iraq and the Arab nation. Iraq's National Assembly immediately echoed its leader, warning of a "grand conspiracy" against Iraq and the Arab nation. For their part, "Iraqis [would] not forget the proper saying that cutting necks is better than cutting the means of living." But the rhetoric was not just rhetoric, Saddam declared. "Raising our voice against the evil is not the final resort." Kuwait was unmoved. In a counter letter to Klibi on 18 July, Kuwait vigorously denied the accusations. Calling Iraq the border transgressor, it called for the Arab League to appoint a special panel to investigate and demarcate the proper boundaries. Defiantly, the Kuwaiti response declared, "The sons of Kuwait, in good as well as bad times, are people of principle and integrity. By no means will they yield to threat and extortion."[56]

Saddam continued the mortal-danger-to-Iraq analogy a week later in his meeting with U.S. Ambassador Glaspie. He had spoken with President Mubarak, he relayed to Glaspie, and had assured him Kuwait had nothing to worry about, provided they could meet and find that "there was hope." But, he continued, "if we are unable to find a solution, then it will be natural that Iraq will not accept death." The "oil people" are "mean beyond belief," Saddam told the ambassador. Indeed, Kuwait and the UAE had declared an economic war against Iraq, although Iraq had given "rivers of blood" in a military war defending Arabs.[57] "We do not accept that anyone could injure Iraqi pride. . . . [W]e are determined either to live as proud men, or we all die." Saddam had made it categorical. The ambassador, without clarifying instructions from Washington, did not offer a strong remonstrance.[58] Saddam could only interpret this to mean his earlier description of the United States and its Achilles' heel was true. As Amatzia Baram of Haifa University described it: "In Saddam's world, when you issue a threat, you expect to get a counter threat. If you don't, it means weakness, appeasement, and eventually retreat."[59]

But sometimes it seemed to suit Saddam's purpose to appear to be the magnanimous gentleman from Baghdad. He gave several interviews over the summer with the Western press in which the bellicosity was set aside temporarily, and an image of sweet reason put in its place. In an interview with Diane Sawyer just a few weeks before the invasion of Kuwait, Saddam stated:

You know that the Arab land . . . is the cradle of religions. The Arabs worship God alone, but they also appreciate leaders who serve their countries. . . . As for Saddam Hussein, he is to be found in every quantity of milk provided to children and in every clean new jacket worn by an Iraqi. . . . Consequently the Iraqis put up [portraits of me]. . . . If we were to remove their portraits, we would hurt their feelings.

In a gushing moment at the close of the interview, Saddam told Sawyer, "I hope [the Americans] will always remember that God is the mightiest, that the real strength of the powerful always lies in their values and [in] good, humanitarian behavior toward others."[60] For many, the interview was simply gruesome and tawdry. Rather than coming across as a bearer of sweetness and light, Saddam seemed like nothing but an inflated ego tricked out as the maximum benefactor of his people. Ironically, he returned to the "quantity of milk" theme the following January.

Most of the region's leaders disregarded such shows of tractability. Rather, the intensity of the Iraqi rhetoric prompted considerable inter-Arab efforts at mediation, particularly by the Arab League, King Fahd, and President Mubarak, who began his own shuttle diplomacy. Mubarak met in Cairo on 23 July with both King Hussein and Tariq Aziz. The next day, the Egyptian president flew to Baghdad to attempt to defuse the developing inter-Arab crisis. In his visit, Mubarak raised the issue of troop movements. Was it true that troops were moving south and massing at the border? Saddam assured him they were routine.[61] Mubarak's concerns were only partially assuaged.

Efforts at mediation continued in the closing days of July. The Saudis, in concert with Osama al-Baz, President Mubarak's chief political advisor, attempted to arrange an emergency meeting in the kingdom, which was finally held on 31 July.[62] By that point, the Kuwaitis were willing to make some concessions, which included, according to Foreign Minister Shaykh Sabah, writing off $14 billion in wartime debt and allowing Iraq access to Warba for oil operations. However, the Iraqis, making only a pro forma appearance at Jeddah, failed to negotiate, and after two hours the Iraqi delegation, led by Izzat Ibrahim, left the meeting. By that time, an estimated 100,000 troops were massed at the Kuwaiti border.

And one final irony, one further melodramatic but disingenuous touch before 2 August. Earlier in the year, Shaykh Jaber of Kuwait had invited Saddam to visit his country, an offer of fraternal rapprochement. Perhaps a face-to-face meeting between the two leaders could defuse the continuing hostility. Saddam is reported to have replied, "I will visit you and I will surprise you with my visit."[63] And so he did, showing up for breakfast unannounced early on the second of August. But Saddam had given hints for months, and there were those who were not entirely caught off guard when the West was called for help in this, the next Gulf War.[64]

*Politics in Iraq is no longer an avocation of gentlemen.*
BAʿTHIST PARTY MEMBER, 1972[1]

# 3 | HISTORICAL BACKGROUND AND INTER-ARAB POLITICS AFTER THE INVASION OF KUWAIT

In the early days of the invasion, two crises shaped and reshaped Arab political alignments. The invasion itself precipitated the first crisis, and the Arab League meeting in Cairo on 3 August reflects that. The introduction of non-Arab forces five days after the invasion began caused the second major crisis, one that dramatically altered the debate in the next Arab League meeting on the tenth. As the anti-Iraq coalition grew throughout the fall, the agenda of that second Arab League meeting dominated the political battles of the Gulf War. Thus, the debate moved from a focus on Iraq's invasion to the legitimacy of the West's deployment. We will look first at initial responses to the second of August, then at the two Arab League meetings. We turn, then, to a country by country survey to see how battle tactics evolved, looking especially at Iraq, the Palestinians, Jordan, Egypt, Syria, and Saudi Arabia.

## INITIAL RESPONSES TO THE INVASION

Saddam's invasion brought visceral and radically varying responses from the Arab world. In Amman, Jordanians and Palestinians signed up for military service in Iraq. In Egypt, on the other hand, an estimated 5,000 Egyptians sought out the gulf embassies to volunteer for service against Iraq. In Sanaa, Yemen, an estimated 10,000 demonstrators stood outside the Saudi and U.S. embassies chanting, "Fahd, atheist priest / Saddam lives and you must die."[2] In the gulf countries, the usually somnolent press found its voice by vigorously attacking Saddam. Algerians, Tunisians, and Moroccans shook North Africa with demonstrations in support of Saddam. Saudi Arabia began expelling Yemenis and Palestinians. But for most Arabs, the initial reaction was shock, and disapproval of the invasion. The Egyptian paper *Al Ahram*, one of the largest dailies in the Middle East, captured their distress: the invasion was a "terrifying Arab disaster . . . the blackest day in the history of the Arabs, which has made them regress to the pre-Islamic days of barbarism when the sword was master."[3] And most rulers shared that horror; Mubarak and Fahd proved typical.

Egyptian President Mubarak was among the most shocked and devastated. A week before the invasion he had traveled to Iraq, Kuwait, and Saudi Arabia to attempt to resolve the crisis diplomatically. Mubarak felt that Saddam would not do something precipitous without further consultation. And Mubarak had assured the West of his confidence; his personal credibility was at stake. But now Saddam had proved perfidious, humiliating him before a global audience. In a nationally televised speech six days after the invasion, the Egyptian president declared that the initial news "paralyzed his thoughts."[4] Mubarak continued, telling his country, "I am afraid of the consequences of this. It will be destructive and will put the Arab world on the spot." Lamenting Arab governmental fecklessness, Mubarak spoke with accuracy and candor: "The [UN] Security Council met and condemned the Iraqi invasion. . . . They were ahead of us, as though the Arab crisis was not Arab, as though the Arabs were a dead body which does not want to move."[5] The president announced that he had called for an emergency Arab League summit, "not to exchange curses . . . but to solve our problems in the Arab framework, which is more honorable to the Arab nation." Then, in a striking, direct appeal to Saddam, Mubarak remonstrated, "You cannot put me in a bind like this. You cannot commit such a crime and then ask me for the impossible. Don't embarrass me. Just like you have interests, I have interests. I am trying as much as possible to protect Arab honor."

In Saudi Arabia, Fahd was genuinely surprised, later stressing that this was a "tragic event . . . unparalleled in history." Like Mubarak, Fahd had strenuously sought to avert conflict.[6] He felt he had taken extraordinary steps, and was reasonably certain, based on Saddam's assurances, that disaster had been avoided. And like Mubarak, he felt that the invasion, besides being a surprise, was an affront to his honor.

His surprise was echoed in other gulf states that, like Saudi Arabia, had for many years paid billions in what amounted to protection money to poorer, potentially problematic regimes and to certain radical groups. The Iraqis, as well as many others, had received Saudi largesse; this was their thanks. The Saudis had generously supported Iraq, the Arab's "eastern gate," during its war with Iran. But the policy failed dramatically here. One senior official in the Saudi defense ministry wryly observed, "Some of our officials who opposed this policy used to joke that the Arabs of the Gulf region, when hit on the left cheek, turned the right pocket. This isn't happening any more. This era is over for good."[7] The Secretary General of the Gulf Cooperation Council (GCC) was blunter: the Gulf would "never forgive and never forget the betrayal."[8] Saddam's invasion was power politics of a sort the gulf countries were not accustomed to. They played a game called "Finesse," and their manner of play prized subtlety, quiet diplomacy, the art of the cultural deal. Saddam's surprising manner of play was to shove pieces off the board.

## THE ARAB LEAGUE MEETINGS OF 3 AND 10 AUGUST

Already in session in Cairo at the time of the invasion, the Arab League meeting had convened at the ministerial level. Not until the day after the invasion did the foreign ministers act. The league's council, by a yea vote from fourteen of the twenty-one member states, adopted Resolution 3036 that condemned the Iraqi aggression. But more importantly, it also *"categorically rejected any foreign intervention"* (emphasis added). The fourteen included Algeria, Djibouti, Egypt, Lebanon, Morocco, Somalia, Syria, Tunisia, plus the GCC states. Jordan, Mauritania, Sudan, and Yemen, as well as the PLO, abstained. Libya walked out. Iraq rejected 3036. Those who abstained apparently believed that the resolution would hamper efforts to broker an Arab solution if they issued a collective condemnation.[9] The Islamic Conference Organization (ICO) also happened to be meeting in Cairo at the same time. Like the Arab League, it condemned the Iraqi aggression, calling for immediate withdrawal.[10] But beyond its declaration, the ICO would play only a small role in the months to come.

When heads of state from the Arab League met on the tenth, in response to president Mubarak's emergency request, they had to face the excruciatingly difficult question of which specific security measures to adopt. Mubarak's burden at the summit was to somehow find "effective Arab action" that would obviate the need for foreign intervention, which would be beyond Arab control and inimical to Arab interests.[11] Jordan's King Hussein continued that plea. If the Arabs failed to broker a solution, he warned, the "world will handle our problems as it pleases." Reflecting his own existential crisis, Hussein pointedly asked, "Do we grasp the seriousness of what is happening? Are we in touch with the Arab individual's aspirations and the hearts and minds across the Arab homeland, or are we living on a planet other than the one where our Arab people live?" As the king continued, he offered a kind of apologia for Saddam, maintaining that it was he who had defended the Arab nation in eight years of war with Iran and that the crisis stemmed directly from the borders colonialism had imposed.[12]

Mubarak and Hussein were right, of course. The Arab street was volatile from long years of pent-up frustrations; foreign intervention would move key decisions out of Arab control. But by that point, the league had little choice. U.S. troops had begun to arrive by C-141s three days earlier.

So the league patched together decisions that offered the semblance of control. It adopted Resolution 195, drafted by the Egyptians and the GCC, which did several things. It endorsed Resolution 3036, adopted by the League's foreign ministers a week prior, as well as approving UN Resolutions 660, 661, and 662, which called for Iraq's withdrawal, imposed sanctions, and declared null and void Iraq's annexation of Kuwait. But Resolution 195 reversed a key component of 3036 (that which "rejected any foreign intervention") by approving measures taken by Saudi Arabia and the other gulf states in "implementation of the right of legitimate defense." Because gulf countries were turning to the West, 195 offered implicit, rather than overt, endorsement of using U.S. troops. Thus, the league's decision obliquely blessed decisions taken by the Saudis and the Egyptians. Additionally under 195, the GCC countries, Djibouti, Egypt, Lebanon, Morocco, Somalia, and Syria voted to send troops. Jordan, Mauritania, and Sudan approved 195 "with reservations." Algeria and Yemen abstained; Tunisia was absent; Iraq, with Libya and the PLO, rejected it.[13]

Clovis Maksoud, the scholarly and urbane Arab League observer at the UN, provided a kind of wrenching postscript. Maksoud saw clearly that the invasion was a "wound in the Arab body politic." But he also understood that their collective inability to act, when the international community did so decisively, had "marginalized" the Arabs. "The Arab house has fallen in on itself. . . . These deep splits have dealt a grievous blow to the prevailing legitimacy of the Arab order. Our sense of Arab unity has been fragmented and its first casualty is a common national discourse." Seeing the disarray, Maksoud resigned his UN position in despair.[14] The Other Gulf War, begun months before the invasion and fought as a low-intensity cultural combat, now began to claim casualties both inside and outside Kuwait. With that background, we look further at individual states and the "blackest day in the history of the Arabs."

## THE VIEW FROM THE STATES

### IRAQ

One must give credit to Saddam and his regime. With considerable creativity, the Iraqi president rapidly fashioned and refashioned rationales for his invasion. The best way to respond to charges of his egregious abridgment of Arab loyalty, he seemed to think, was to keep talking. To the West his *raisons d'état* in the invasion were transparent enough: this was a way of stamping "paid" on a multibillion-dollar war debt to Kuwait as well as an opportunity to double his proven reserves of oil, assuming that the West would not come to the aid of Kuwait. But Saddam tailored his explanations to his various audiences, looking to see which might prove persuasive. Initially, he suggested, some Kuwaitis themselves, part of a theretofore-unknown revolutionary group, had overthrown the sheikh and appealed for Iraqi help.[15] Thus, the second of August was the *yaum al-nida'*, the day of the call.[16] This, in turn, became the name of a new newspaper in Kuwait City. On the day after the invasion, Iraq announced, in concert with the provisional government, that it would begin withdrawing its troops on 5 August, a day that saw instead the arrival of reinforcements. On 4 August, the provisional government announced the formation of a popular army, a force that, it said, immediately drew 100,000 volunteers. On 6 August, Saddam duly declared he had no designs on Saudi Arabia and would honor his earlier nonaggression pact with it. And then the Rubicon statement two days later: the announcement of the "merger" of Kuwait with Iraq.[17] Because U.S. troops had begun to arrive the day before, and in view of UN Resolution 660, the merger statement was intentionally confrontational. Such were Saddam's media reasons, the public explanations to justify what he had done and to seek support. But apart from these realpolitik responses, he tried another approach, and it proved his best.

As other leaders in the region had done during crises, Saddam turned to history. He spoke of "the Arab nation." Fouad Ajami has observed, "Not the most articulate of leaders, Saddam found his themes as he went along. He annexed the dreams and resentments of other Arabs, appealing to their atavistic impulses. Hurriedly he rolled out his own map of a phantom Arab nation . . . [and] acted out their rage."[18]

The idea of one embracing nation reaches back to 622 when the prophet Muhammad and his followers migrated, under duress and threat, 300 miles north from Mecca to Medina. There, Muhammad's organizing genius was such that he was able to transform the older desert pattern of *asabiyya*, loyalty to a kinship group, and give it a new center, that of Islam. He transferred the loyalties that inhered in the older group to a new one, not based on blood ties, with supreme authority. John Esposito observes that the older pattern of tribal order and loyalties was not replaced but "Islamized."[19] Hereafter, this new Islamic community would be called the *umma*. As the Quran puts it: "Thus have We made of you an Umma justly balanced, that ye might be witnesses over the nations, and the Apostle [i.e., Muhammad] over yourselves."[20] It became the word that the nuclear group Muhammad established in Medina used to describe itself, and would come to mean the "single universal Islamic community embracing all the lands in which Islam is established and the Islamic law prevails."[21]

Beginning in the nineteenth century, the word has also been used in a secular sense (although the religious component is not entirely absent) to indicate simply the "Arab nation."[22] Pan-Arab Ba'thists have often employed it in that way. But whether the religious or mundane sense predominates in a given usage, umma comes laden with compelling connotations of an in-group, a group different from others who are often implacably hostile. It is a group united by the Arabic language, and artificially divided by colonial borders it is one day destined to overcome. Or at least, that is the umma mythos. The reality more often involves separate nationalisms and distinct national agendas. But the ideal, the idea of attachment to the umma, remains powerfully connected to the Arab soul. Saddam knew that; and even while acting as an arch-statist, he found a way to feature himself as the great transnationalist, the supporter of the umma.

At first, Saddam's challenge was to present himself as the protector of Arab unity against internal dissent. This required rather extensive manipulation of political rhetoric as well as an appreciation of double irony. The double irony was this. First, there was no overarching, politically viable Arab nation needing his protection. Second, even if, say, the twenty-one countries of the Arab League could have been construed as one "nation," Saddam was the one who had driven a wedge in it.

But Saddam was not daunted, either in telling the most unctuous, absurd fabrications, or about proclaiming his own role in restoring unity to the Arab earth. The Arabs were one, he solemnly observed; and if there were disunity, it was in large part because of the niggardly ways of the gulf states that had failed to share their largess. The Arab nation, Saddam declared days after the invasion, "will return to its rightful position only through real struggle and holy war to place the wealth of the nation in the service of its noble objectives."[23] And all through the spring and summer, as noted above, Saddam had been laying the groundwork for this, reminding hearers that certain Arab brethren had not been paying their fair share. The Saudis and other gulf states realized their vulnerability at that point. This was, as many realized, an Arab *thawra* (revolution) against Arab *tharwa* (wealth). One Saudi businessman admitted, "We are wealthy people in a neighborhood of paupers. The world around us is getting poorer and poorer and more resentful."[24] Thus, according to Saddam, he was not initiating a war by invading Kuwait, but (the logic was not particularly tight) quelling an economic civil war launched by the "oil emirs."

With the arrival of U.S. and other coalition forces, Saddam was able to extend his rationale for the war.[25] No longer was this simply a civil war between fractious members of the Arab nation. Now Saddam could portray himself as averting an onslaught of new crusaders and could depict their deployment as yet another invasion of the Arab nation by the West. He inaugurated this approach on 8 August, the day of the merger, which was also the day after the first U.S. troops arrived in Saudi Arabia. Iraq's Revolutionary Command Council signaled the great shift in the character of the Gulf War with its "annexation" statement, mentioned above. "One of the most egregious acts of colonialism," the council intoned, "was its partition of the homeland, which was a single homeland the day Baghdad was the capital of all the Arabs. Colonialism divested Iraq of a dear part of it, namely Kuwait." (Here we have a sort of historical shell game. Baghdad had ceased being the capital of the Abbasid Empire in 1258 under the devastations of the Mongol military commander Hulago; there was no "Iraq" then. And colonialism had divested the Ottomans, not Iraq, of Kuwait; it was Istanbul that was aggrieved.) The council went on to warn the "evildoers, conspirators, and criminal force" that all of its "fleets, planes, and centers of oppressive forces in the world . . . will not shake the palm fronds in Basra, Qadisiyah, [nor in] Kuwait. . . . The blood of our martyrs will burn you."[26]

Saddam had still other battles to fight. Besides being a battle to defend the homeland against a foreign incursion, this was a battle for Palestine. In Saddam's rhetorical dictionary, that meant fighting Zionists, liberating Palestinians, and retaking Jerusalem. Six weeks into the war, an event occurred that enhanced his role as a new Saladin. On 8 October, twenty-one Palestinians were killed on the Temple Mount area in Jerusalem. The occasion was a riot over a misunderstanding about the intentions of an orthodox Jewish group that wished to rebuild the temple. The net effect was to garner yet more support among Palestinians for Saddam the liberator.

Three months later, when Saddam launched Scud missiles against Israel, that was precisely the agenda he wanted to underscore. He knew that little real damage would accrue since the warheads carried high explosives only, not chemical or biological payloads. Rather, the missiles served political purposes. On the one hand, the Scud launches demonstrated that he was the one Arab leader willing to unambiguously confront the Israelis on behalf of the Palestinians. That established his bona fides as Saladin redux. On the other, the missiles might have brought the Israelis into the conflict, which would certainly have fractured the coalition and dramatically altered the scope of the Gulf War.[27] One ugly point of irony overlooked or ignored by those who compared Saddam to Saladin is that the twelfth-century military genius was a Kurd.

Saddam chose his words and historical references to evoke a maximum visceral response, as was evident in his "jihad speech" (discussed in more detail in Chapter Five) on Baghdad television on 10 August. Typical of Saddam's turgid rhetoric, it described how the oil emirs, who "pushed women into whoredom," were "servants of the foreigner and Zionism," and had called in the "imperialists, deviators, merchants, and political agents" to attack Iraq.[28] Warming to his subject, Saddam averred that the reason for the attack was clear enough: Iraq "represented the conscience of the Arab nation and [was] safeguarding its honor." He continued: "Iraq, O Arabs, is your Iraq. . . . It is the candle of right to snuff out darkness." In words reminiscent of his April "fire speech," this voice of conscience and right called on all Muslims and Arabs to "burn the land under the feet of the invaders" and to save Mecca and Medina from infidels, rulers without honor, crusaders, and Zionists. But Saddam took one more step.

Although he pitched his message to the Arab street generally, Saddam wished to appeal to Egyptians in particular (and to challenge Mubarak, with whom he had vied for leadership for a year and a half): "To our brothers in Egypt . . . to the sons of Gamal Abdel Nasser, it is your day to prevent the foreigner and his fleets from passing through the skies in Egypt and the Suez Canal. . . . Your brothers in Iraq are determined to continue jihad without hesitation or retreat." To Western ears, this type of speech chews the scenery. But Saddam had touched on all the right themes: the selfishly wealthy, the honor of the Arab male, the dignity of the Arab woman, the sanctity of the holy places, the perfidy of Zionism. And although the Suez remained opened, Saddam's appeal to the street, as opposed to governments, began to drive a wedge in deeper throughout the Arab world. The appeal forced leaders, in the days that followed, to offer various justifications to their people, hoping not to have to lead from behind.

As the coalition forces grew, Saddam's rhetoric found an increasingly receptive audience. The military disproportion between the sides in the Gulf War gave Saddam increased prestige in the Other Gulf War. The West viewed him as unstable, someone with a death wish. Many in the Arab street saw him as exceptionally bold. The West thought any sane man would retreat. But those in the region, and a handful of Western analysts who had studied Saddam, knew that would not occur. Life was at stake in one Gulf War; honor was at stake in the other. Saddam stated just days after the invasion that his country would "prefer death to humiliation by foreigners,"[29] a remark that should have been more instructive to the West than it was. We look now at the Palestinians and other countries to see their response.

## PALESTINIANS

One laments, especially in the Gulf War, the torn allegiances of the almost hapless Palestinians. The use of the Palestinian issue has been as ubiquitous as it has been cynical or self-aggrandizing. The formation of the Palestine Liberation Organization (PLO) itself was a recognition by Palestinians that they were the verbal cause of many, but the focused, practical cause of none. The second of August offered new hope to a people whose fiery earthquake of resistance, the intifada, had become merely routinized. Saddam promised to strike a blow against their chief enemy, Israel, and he appeared to be the only Arab willing to champion their hopes, defy the West, and uphold Arab honor. Yet while Saddam touted the Palestinians as his special interest, the invasion did nothing to help them, and much to hurt. Most Palestinians supported Saddam, particularly in the territories and in Jordan. But not all did; there was clearly division in the ranks. Their challenge was to maintain unity, which they did not, and to persuade others into taking up their cause, which they could not.

After Saddam's invasion, the Kuwaitis and other gulf Arabs characterized the Palestinians living in Kuwait as fifth columnists and collaborators. These were declared *personae non grata* throughout the gulf and forced to emigrate, leaving behind most or all of their possessions. Arafat's declaration of support for Saddam was taken, wrongly, as indicative of the attitude of Palestinians in Kuwait and elsewhere. These expatriate Palestinians were angry with the Kuwaitis, of course, for they had helped build their country, and knew they were wrongly suspected. But these were also among the bitterest when Saddam declared that the invasion was conducted on their behalf. They were the first to know that the invasion could not possibly benefit them.

Thus, although some Palestinians collaborated (they maintained they were forced to do so to avoid certain death), most did not. Kuwait had become home; and though they did not enjoy full enfranchisement, their lives were markedly better than what they would have had in Gaza. A number of Palestinians joined the Kuwaiti resistance. Others offered shelter to Kuwaitis seeking to elude the Iraqi occupiers. Palestinian youths carried the intifada to the streets of Kuwait City, throwing stones at the Iraqi soldiers.[30]

Palestinian intellectuals were also among those who opposed Saddam. They saw clearly enough that the moral and political syllogism they had used for their own situation would be subverted if they did not also apply it to Kuwait's. The syllogism looked like this:

The acquisition of territory by war is inadmissible. (major premise)
The Israelis have acquired Palestinian territory by war. (minor premise)
Ergo, Israeli action is inadmissible (conclusion)

This, of course, is the very language of UN Resolution 242. In baldest terms, Saddam had acquired Kuwait by war, a new minor premise.

If Palestinians failed to draw the appropriate conclusion—Iraqi action is inadmissible—it could only mean they had either forsworn logic or abandoned the major premise. And to do either of those would mean giving up all the legitimacy of Palestinian aims. Hanan Ashrawi understood that. "We do not condemn occupation in one area and condone it another. We do not condone the acquisition of land by force. We do not have double standards," said the articulate Palestinian spokeswoman. The Palestinian National Fund, based in Abu Dhabi, understood that too, and its spokesman agreed with Ashrawi: "[We do not] support Iraq in occupying and annexing Kuwait by force . . . because this is an illegal measure."[31] And Faisal Husseini, later prominent in the Madrid talks, concurred; he opposed occupation "anywhere in the world." But the deployment of coalition forces prompted him, like many others, to qualify his response. This dispute was one Arabs could have solved. Putting troops under "an American umbrella" was a "sin."[32]

Arafat himself stood in an excruciatingly difficult position. Alone among Arab political leaders to offer unambiguous support to Saddam, Arafat the desperate had gambled. Yet his decision is explicable, even if foolish or blameworthy. The intifada, just over two and a half years old, had little to show for all the stones that had been thrown and re-thrown.[33] Demolished homes, high unemployment, border closings, a growing list of martyrs—all these had brought the intifada to a critical juncture. Many had begun to demand guns. Worst of all, the intifada was no longer prominent news, which was bad news indeed for Arafat. The early pictures of stone-throwing teenagers confronting Uzi-carrying Israeli soldiers in riot gear legitimated the Palestinians' (and Arafat's) cause. It kept the world talking. Now, fewer were talking.

The president-in-waiting had other problems. One was an issue he had not created but that he made worse. The Palestine Liberation Front (PLF), responsible for seizing the *Achille Lauro* cruise ship in 1985, struck again on 30 May 1990. The PLF launched a failed attack by speedboat against the Israeli coast. Arafat disavowed any official link with terrorism but refused to condemn the attack.[34] President Bush, in turn, broke off the U.S. diplomatic dialogue with the PLO.

Arafat found his problems compounded further in early June. On the eighth, Yitzhak Shamir announced formation of a new, Likud-led, coalition government. Whereas the Likud under the maddening National Unity Government had been effectively temporizing, this would be worse. Shamir quickly announced in a policy document his support for the Jewish right to settle in all parts of Greater Israel. His appointment of David Levy as foreign minister and Ariel Sharon as housing minister made Shamir's position crystal clear. In his post, Sharon would also oversee Soviet Jewish immigration. Arafat found that there was nothing he could do to block either settlement expansion or the flood of immigrants. And in this hour of crisis, Arafat received very little real support from his Arab brothers.[35] In this desperate time, Arafat's desperate measure was to turn to the leader on the Tigris. Many in the PLO opposed Arafat's decision, decrying the "very negative" repercussions it would have. One lamented that Arafat had put them "in the worst position of all . . . [with] no way out of this mess."[36]

In the streets of the country-in-waiting, the feeling was overwhelmingly pro-Saddam. The massing of coalition forces intensified it. Early in the deployment such sentiment was already evident. Typical are these voices from the West Bank town of Beit Fajar (House of the Dawn).[37] A painter observed, "Saddam is our leader, and I'd go fight for him to remove the Americans and the traitor King Fahd." The owner of a stone quarry, sensing an elaborate plot, concluded, "What these other Arab leaders are doing is selling cheap oil to America so the Americans can improve their economy and support our enemy Israel." And a science teacher: "This is an Arab problem; America has no right to be here. Saddam is not Hitler; he's the second Saladin." But sixty-year-old Musa Muhammad Hussein, more realistic and reflecting insight mixed equally with despair, lamented, "The prophet Muhammad said the people should share three things: fire, water, and grass. It is true the Kuwaiti emir should have shared more. But Saddam is not Saladin. We are like people drowning, trying to grab any straw. Saddam is our straw." And those leaders close to the street knew Musa was right. However much Saddam might appear to be a hero to the young and angry, those who had endured over the years could see only evil days following 2 August. The concern of Elias Friej, the mayor of Bethlehem, captured that fear: "We the Palestinians are now entering a deep freeze of minus 60 degrees."[38]

## JORDAN

The view from the East Bank was equally bleak in the Gulf War. Although Saudi Arabia perhaps faced the most inter-Arab political pressure, King Hussein confronted the greatest pressure domestically and (except for Iraq) internationally. Marvin Feuerwerger captured the king's dilemma in early August: "The king is now trapped between his

Arab obligations, his international obligations, and his desire to survive. . . . [He] hopes he will be at the bottom of Saddam Hussein's enemies' list. This is not a good time to be a traditional monarch on the border of Iraq."[39] Indeed it was not. The king had to balance competing potential disasters. Better than most, he saw what the presence of the Western coalition could mean. "I can only say that any foreign intervention, be it Israel or otherwise, in the Arab world will [cause] a very, very bad reaction and set the whole area ablaze."[40] But the king's more immediate concern was at home.

To begin, over half the population comprised (as it still does) Palestinians, as both citizens and refugees. Seeing the rallies at the amphitheater in downtown Amman in favor of Saddam, the marches on the U.S. embassy, the rallies after Friday noon prayers, and the gifts of food for Iraqis collected by trade unions and charitable societies, the king realized he had no political capital to spend on categorically opposing Saddam.[41] The king also realized that Jordan had much to lose economically, a fact that only exacerbated the domestic dilemma. Iraq was Jordan's principal trade partner, taking about 23 percent of the kingdom's exports at the time of the invasion, and supplying 95 percent of its oil. Additionally, Jordan faced losing almost all the remittances from its expatriate workers, over $700 million annually at the time. Even more troubling was the flood of refugees. In the five weeks following the invasion, an estimated 470,000 refugees crossed into Jordan. When Jordan reluctantly agreed to support the embargo, it did so while facing a forecast of some $4 billion in lost revenue.[42] To declare himself solidly for the coalition meant risking crown and life.

Another critical worry was Ariel Sharon's concept that "Jordan is Palestine." Sharon's "solution," no matter how bizarre or deplorable the idea may have seemed to the United States, had been taken quite seriously in Jordan and other Arab states. Now, with the surging influx of Soviet Jews, the fear no longer seemed so remote. Sharon's appointment to the housing ministry that June further heightened the alarm on the East Bank. Crown Prince Hassan, no demagogue, expressed precisely that concern two weeks after the invasion. Reflecting on both the number of Soviet immigrants and the instability in Jordan, Hassan worried that Israel could use the opportunity to destabilize Jordan and make it an "alternative homeland" for the Palestinians.[43] Palestinians had come in great numbers in 1948 and 1967. They could come again in 1990.

One measure of the king's precarious position and his urgent search for a solution from inside the region was Jordan's hosting of a pan-Arab conference in September, a rather risky "safety valve," but not unlike his appointing Islamists to the Jordanian cabinet; people must be allowed to have a voice. The conference included such Palestinian notables as George Habash of the Popular Front for the Liberation of Palestine and Nayif Hawatmeh of the Democratic Front for the Liberation of Palestine. True to form, Habash summoned the "Arab masses and all its nationalist, democratic, and progressive forces to resist the American invasion of the Arab region."[44] Twenty years before, in another September, these counted among Hussein's bitterest enemies. Now, the king cast about for any way to head off the disaster he felt would undoubtedly follow Western deployment.

This does not mean Hussein ignored the West or was simply obtuse. In fact, he launched his own shuttle diplomacy, traveling throughout the region, Europe, and North America. The king made clear his commitment to the principle of the inadmissibility of the acquisition of territory by war, using exactly those terms. But he hoped the West could see the predicament from his perspective: he must consider his domestic constituency, and he must consider the threat from Saddam. *The Economist* was accurate in its description of Hussein's efforts. Compelled by his concern to protect "his country from economic collapse, predatory neighbors, self-destructive citizens, and a flood of refugees," the king tried to find "a grey area where others saw black and white."[45] But the West was in the mood for coalition-building, not for searching out nuances of Arab culture or deliberating on threats other than those to Kuwait, Saudi Arabia, and the oil fields.

## EGYPT

A different situation presented itself in Egypt. In August Egypt emerged as the strongest supporter of the Saudis and the coalition efforts, a position it maintained throughout the conflict. This was particularly true of the palace and (generally) the street, although the views of the media and intelligentsia were rather more mixed. For the palace, support for the coalition reflected, in part, Mubarak's bid for Arab leadership, or at least an acknowledgment of his *primus inter pares* status in the Arab League. Saddam, by attacking an Arab brother, was committing a "sin" that rivaled Egypt's own, that of signing a peace treaty with Israel in 1979. The return of the Arab League headquarters from Tunis to Cairo in the spring marked Egypt's reentry into the fold. Additionally, Egypt renewed diplomatic relations with Syria and Libya. At the same time, it currently held the rotating presidency of the Organization of African Unity (OAU). Disastrous as the invasion was, it afforded Egypt opportunities for better things, most especially a reinvigorated leadership role.

But Egyptians in general also had practical reasons for opposing Iraq. Thousands of Egyptian expatriate workers returned from Iraq with stories of horror.[46] Iraqi soldiers, home after the 1988 cease-fire with Iran, reclaimed their jobs, reportedly sometimes murdering the Egyptians who had replaced them. Others who were forced to flee were stopped at roadblocks as they left, and stripped of money, gold, and consumer goods. Additionally, they claimed the Jordanians charged exorbitant prices for food and transportation. On the other hand, the United States generously wrote off $7 billion in military debt; the gulf states, $4 billion. The Saudis extended an additional $1 billion in grant aid, and the United States promised to help secure more-sympathetic treatment from international lenders.[47]

In the media and among various elites, early opinion strongly supported government actions against Iraq.[48] The secular Wafd party newspaper called the invasion an "ugly crime." The left-wing Tajammu party condemned the invasion for having "unraveled Arab solidarity." The pro-government papers condemned Iraq even more strongly in their various editorials. But that view began to change after large numbers of Western forces arrived in Saudi Arabia, and articles increased in stridency as foreign forces increased in numbers. Now the Wafd found a plot. The United States had intervened to "redraw the map of the Arab homeland," attacking Iraq because it posed a threat—not to Kuwait— but to Israel. Even the semiofficial *Al-Ahram*, Egypt's largest daily, wrote that Egyptian forces sent to the Gulf were there *not* as "part of the U.S.-European armada, but to prove to Arab brothers and friends alike" that Egypt was able to take a leadership role. Cognizant of its potential liabilities as part of the coalition, the government began to downplay its posture in the Gulf War. It emphasized its role among Arab forces rather than coalition forces, and clamped down on demonstrations of any sort, even those that were pro-government.

SYRIA

Syria's support for the coalition paralleled Egypt's. Egypt's support signaled its return to the Arab fold; Syria's, to the international. At first such Syrian support seemed extremely improbable. This was the Syria of strident Arab nationalism and its own version of Ba'thist socialism. This was the Syria that feared entanglement with the West. For years Damascus had established its bona fides as the frontline confrontation state, what Augustus R. Norton has described as its "role as the militant standard-bearer of Arabism and self-appointed protector of Palestine."[49] But Damascus had little to show for its confrontational posture, and now there were inducements for adopting a more pragmatic posture. Such miracles of political rehabilitation were among the wonders to emerge from the Gulf War.

Like Mubarak, Syrian President Assad remained steadfast in his support of the coalition. Several issues compelled him to do so. A strategic link at this moment with Saudi Arabia and Egypt meant improved ties with both the United States and the gulf region. That, in turn, could help negotiations with Israel regarding the Golan Heights. It could also mean removal from the State Department's list of state sponsors of terrorism. And there was money. The Saudis and Kuwaitis reportedly extended some $5 billion in grants in addition to direct loans.[50]

Unfortunately for Syria, it got back none of the Golan, and remained on the State Department's list of the unsavory. But the money from the gulf states was welcome. Syria was able to project a tractable, more moderate image. Best of all, President Assad had a photo opportunity in November with President Bush in Geneva. At a time when Syria's relationship with the Soviets was showing signs of strain, especially in acquiring military hardware, Assad found the tentative rapprochement helpful.

Syria had another interest in joining the coalition. In many ways the conflict simply continued a proxy war Syria had been waging with Iraq for years. Syrian complicity had helped keep the Kurdish pot stirred in northern Iraq. Syria had sided with Iran during the previous Gulf War. The Iraqis, for their part, had resupplied Michel Aoun, the dissident Maronite general in Lebanon. Joining the coalition gave the Syrians an opportunity both to fight against Iraq (something it could not do alone) and to press irredentist claims to a greater Syria by establishing virtually uncontested control in much of Lebanon. When Syrian attacks forced Aoun's capitulation in mid-October, the international community said little in protest.

Although the official Syrian position supported the coalition, there was considerable unrest from others (notably the Islamists), and even reports of riots, for many saw Saddam as pan-Arab hero.[51] Assad, however, allowed little political dissent, including any from radical

Palestinian groups in Syria. Yet the president also felt compelled to legitimate government cooperation. He offered a fourfold rationale to assuage the various constituencies he faced.[52] First, he told his citizenry that he had promised Fahd during the Arab summit on 10 August that he would assist. Honor demanded fulfillment. Second, the Syrian military, being Muslim, would help protect the holy places of Mecca and Medina, since the non-Muslim West could not. Third, to appeal to the Ba'thists, he stressed that his opposing Saddam was part of a pan-Arab action that would protect the Arab umma. But then he added, as a crowning fourth point, that Arab troops would be replacing, not simply augmenting, foreign forces. This last point was the most disingenuous of the four. But on balance, Assad fared reasonably well on the home front during the Gulf War.

## SAUDI ARABIA

We turn finally to the country that had the key role of political opposition in the Gulf War. The Arab world watched Iraq with horror on 2 August, and at that point the political lines were pretty neatly drawn: support Iraq or condemn the invasion. Most condemned. But five days later, the arrival of the Americans smudged those neat lines. Now the Arabs watched the Saudis and the oil emirs. To the chroniclers of the Gulf War, the decision to appeal to the West for assistance must have seemed straightforward, especially with the barbarians crowding the gate. But that emphatically was not the case for the Saudis.

Inviting in the West was Fahd's second-worst option. He could see the implications. Naturally cautious in any case, he knew the pan-Arab front of the war would now be dramatically broadened. But the worst option was not to exercise the second worst, in Fahd's view. Not turning to the West meant risking his kingdom. Analysts may debate, until all the sand in the *al-rub al-khali* (the "Empty Quarter," a vast desert in southern Arabia) turns to glass, whether Saddam would have continued down the coast from Kuwait. But given all the indications the king had—the Iraqis had made several incursions of up to five miles into Saudi territory just after the invasion—he had every reason to believe that he had only a couple of days to decide what to do. After looking at satellite photography and listening to the urgings of his nephew Bandar and the American secretary of defense, Fahd decided.[53] He made the second-worst decision possible.

Hours after Fahd gave the go-ahead, 2,300 U.S. paratroopers, AWACS aircraft, and other support equipment headed to the kingdom. But Fahd himself had to fight a different war, one that required different weapons. In part, that meant taking retaliatory measures against neighbors that temporized in the Arab League meetings on 3 August and 10 August. The kingdom cut off oil supplies and other aid to Jordan, a devastating blow to the Hashemite kingdom's fragile economy. Suspecting the Yemenis of being potentially subversive, the Saudis expelled an estimated one million expatriate Yemeni workers.[54]

But the Saudis had a more important battle, and that was seeking to legitimate its actions both at home and in the inter-Arab world. One of the earliest attempts to fully justify inviting non-Arab, non-Muslim troops to come to Saudi Arabia, and one that became the template for ensuing position statements, was offered by Fahd on 9 August in an address to his nation.[55] Describing Saddam's invasion as "the most sinister aggression witnessed by the Arab nation in its modern history," Fahd announced that Arab and "other friendly forces" had been invited to the kingdom. Their mission would be purely defensive, one designed to safeguard Saudi Arabia. Their mission done, those troops would leave immediately at the kingdom's request.

Prince Sultan, the defense minister and second in line (after Abdullah) to the throne followed suit. In a prepared statement issued on 21 August, Sultan framed his response by recalling that the Iraqi invasion was "the most horrendous aggression known by the Arab nation against a sister Arab country."[56] Sultan was careful to stress that the government had taken its decision as a *defensive* measure. He then offered a fivefold justification of Saudi Arabia's right to defend itself, citing various documents:

- The Islamic *shari'a,* which—following the Quran—authorizes the use of force in self-defense
- The UN Charter, Article 51, which stipulates the right to collective self-defense
- The Arab League Charter, Article 6, which stipulates that the league may determine measures to be taken against an aggressor
- The Treaty on Joint Arab Defense
- The Arab Summit decision of 10 August 1990

Sultan closed by assuring his listeners that the presence of foreign forces was strictly temporary and that those forces would leave as soon as their "task" was done and the Saudi government requested them to do so.

Fortunately, the king had an ally in the Saudi press, as did the gulf emirs in theirs. Of course the government exercised great control over the never very lively media (the contrast, say, to its Egyptian counterpart is stark). But after the invasion, the gulf media began to speak with a great deal more vigor. They accepted—they believed—that Saddam was a genuine menace, and had to be dealt with by the ship's main battle guns, even if that meant foreign forces. This was not the usual stuff that might pander to government directives. Writers expressed vigorous, personal antipathies, matching the Iraqis insult for insult. Typical of the exchange was this from the Saudi's *Al-Bilad* newspaper. The writer warned fellow Muslims against Saddam's "shameless and flagrant prattle." It found the Iraqi leader's discussion of Islam to be "very funny," in view of his having "inflicted a treacherous and perfidious stab in the back." "Saddam Hussein," it concluded, "is a hypocrite."[57] Most Saudis reading that would have agreed. For unlike in Morocco or Syria, for instance, the street in Saudi Arabia largely aligned itself with the palace and the elites.

Despite having generally popular support, King Fahd knew that one speech about the large American presence was not enough. He gave many, whether speaking in person or by way of statements read on his behalf. In November, Fahd gave a particularly detailed account of the invasion, one reflecting the increasing pressure he felt because of the foreign troops.[58] He reiterated how exhaustive his efforts had been to dissuade Saddam from attacking Kuwait, and then to compel him to withdraw. He stressed that this tragic event, "unparalleled in history," was certain to have led to an attack on Saudi Arabia itself had he not taken extraordinary measures, and that turning westward was the only option left. His brethren must understand that the response of the United States was one of "God's gifts," that the "power of Almighty God had made the West respond" as it had. Of course, Fahd also emphasized that as soon as the war was over, "every army [would] return to its nation." He had every reason to want the process to move along quickly. The longer the negotiations, the more restive his fellow Saudis—as well as other Arabs in the region—would become.

Nadav Safran, who has written extensively on Saudi security concerns, said early in the deployment that an assault was preferable to a siege because the latter generated much greater risks from the "prolonged presence of culturally alien foreign forces."[59] His closing warning was especially prescient: a permanent American presence in the region would be detrimental to both the Saudis and other gulf rulers.

Quite apart from their numbers, those culturally alien forces were a real problem for the king. The Saudis had spent more than $100 billion in the preceding twenty years on defense.[60] Their pilots had been trained at Tyndall Air Force Base in Florida to fly F-15s. Their ground forces had worked with specialists handpicked from the United States Army. Saudi AWACS, purchased with political capital dearly spent, sat alert at Riyadh Air Base. And the Officers' Club, a block away from the headquarters of the Ministry of Defense and Aviation, had (as it still does) the ambience of an exclusive country club. So what had all that money really purchased? Not to belabor the point, very little. The Saudis had spent billions and yet had to call for non-Arab aid because the Saudi military still proved inadequate to confront the impending Iraqi threat. One Saudi critic complained, "The fact that this once fierce warrior society was suddenly reduced to a bunch of women who needed to summon a man to defend us is definitely offensive."[61]

To be sure, the Saudis—with the Americans—stressed the role of the Arabs among the coalition forces. The Arabs, ostensibly, operated under the command of Lieutenant General (Prince) Khalid bin Sultan bin Abdul Aziz. Daily press briefings from Riyadh featured both Western and Arab spokesmen. Briefing graphics prominently displayed the positions of Arab forces. Debriefs stressed Saudi (and Arab) achievements. And Saudi publications about the war highlighted in a special way the Arab role.[62] But again, the Saudis called on the West only because it was *vital* (in a diplomatic sense) to do so. It bears repeating that this was Fahd's second-worst option.

All of this underscores where Fahd's real problems lay. The Saudis knew the threat was real. They knew livelihoods and lives in Dhahran and Jubail were at stake, even if the Asir in the far southwest was reasonably safe. They accepted the king's justifications, and most offered their support. But something deeper, almost visceral was at work. Saddam had violated the cardinal tenet of loyalty to the kinship group. He violated another critical tenet in holding hostages; that cut against the grain of traditional hospitality, the responsibility of the sheikh. But Saudi actions ran perilously close to violating what Arabs term *maru'a*, or manliness.[63] The ability to defend one's clan held a paramount place in this culture. Yet they had been forced to turn to the West, whose culture they considered inferior, to protect them. To put it bluntly, that was extremely dishonoring in the eyes of many Saudis. Thus, the monarchy's extraordinary defense of its actions.

But King Fahd also had to be concerned with justifying the deployment to the inter-Arab community. He could watch CNN and see the demonstrations in Sanaa, Amman, Tunis, Jerusalem, and Rabat. Fahd knew of the antipathies of the poorer countries toward the wealthier. The Arab League meetings showed how those who opposed the invasion could also oppose foreign intervention. As the prominent Palestinian Faisal Husseini had put it, occupation was wrong, but putting Arabs under the American umbrella was a sin. So the monarchy, which had extended the invitation to the West and in whose kingdom the preponderance of the half million pitched their tents, had to fashion the primary apologia. The Saudis had to demonstrate that theirs was not a dishonorable, but an essential, step. And in offering the repeated *raisons de guerre*, Fahd was helping other Arab leaders in the coalition face their own constituencies.

## POLITICS, IN SUM

Such was the political context as Arab governments confronted it: the various grievances, the fault lines, the disputes, the rhetoric, and the pleas that characterize the Other Gulf War. Here was the concern, voiced again, that the United States was the guarantor of Zionist expansionary plans, indifferent (or hostile) to legitimate Arab concerns, rushing to protect only its national interests, and defiling the holiest places of Islam while doing so. Here was the Saudi king, faced with having to make the second-worst possible decision (appealing to the West) to avoid the consequences of the worst (not appealing to the West). Here were two Arab presidents, Saddam and Mubarak, two men with dramatically different styles, both vying for leadership. One spoke of fiery strength; the other, of reason. Both were concerned with honor, but they had very different ideas about how it should be gained. Both wanted the Arab "message" made clear, but had opposite ideas about how to tell it. Here also was Arafat, who called for justice for his people, and the monarch of a poor kingdom who sought economic relief. Both wondered how policy decisions in Jerusalem and Washington would affect them. One wondered if his state would ever be created; the other, if his would be lost. These issues were not new, but they were about to have the acid of war poured over them and their toughest points made to stand out in sharp relief. Well before 2 August, the outlines of the war had been visible.

In that context, Saddam turned to Islam. Religion offered both a rationale and a weapon, an explanation for the seemingly inexplicable and an offensive tool to try to fracture the coalition. Because the coalition comprised "instrumental" allies and because governments had concerns about constituencies, Saddam recognized important vulnerabilities. The employment of Islam, then, seemed plausible. The introduction of culturally alien forces in such massive numbers made it seem more so. The next section will look at how Saddam had treated Islam before the war, then turn to his use of it after the invasion.

*This knight, not yet forty-three, speaks profoundly, discusses wisely,
and acts with pride, as if Tito had left him his experience, Nehru his
rationality, and Gamal abdul Nasser his Arab decisiveness.*
A BIOGRAPHER OF SADDAM[1]

*Kill them. Kill everybody who went into the mosque. And kill
everyone who identifies with them. . . . Kill all the male relatives,
too. That way, there will be no one to take revenge.*
SADDAM ON THE GRAND MOSQUE TAKEOVER IN 1979[2]

# IRAQ, DEEP CULTURE, AND THE
# EMPLOYMENT OF ISLAM BEFORE
# THE INVASION OF KUWAIT

On 8 August 1989, almost a year to the day before the Iraqi invasion
of Kuwait, the people of Baghdad witnessed a parade whose elements
were as incongruous as its symbols were significant. This was, in fact,
the solemn dedication of a new national monument to the heroes of
the recent war with Iran. Duplicated along the parade route, the tower-
ing monument stood, in Saddam's words, as an "arch to victory and a
symbol to this Qadisiyya [where] brave Iraqis have recorded the most
legendary exploits in their defense of their land and holy beliefs against
the Persian enemy."[3] The arch itself is formed from two swords crossed
over the roadway, and stands some forty meters at the apex. The swords
point, the artist tells us, toward Iran and Israel. A monument four
years in the planning, workers forged the metal swords by reusing
melted down weapons from Iraqi "martyrs." At the base of each sword,
nets hold helmets from the vanquished Iranians. Here, the details matter. The huge forearms, which thrust up from the earth and clasp the
swords, are modeled from plaster casts of the arms of the president himself; it is Saddam, hero of the new Qadisiyya, who wields the blades.[4]

The parade as well as the monument furnished details that merit
consideration. Saddam led the entourage. Riding a white stallion, the
president wore a white jacket with gold epaulets and a white helmet

trimmed with an ostrich feather. Older observers could not have missed the import: Saddam's regalia were that of the discredited monarchy, just what Iraqi King Faisal would have worn in formal ceremonies. And the Shi'a would have immediately recognized the symbolism of the horse. Every year in the festival of Ashura, commemorating the death of the Imam Hussein, the revered leader is shown riding a white horse into the fateful battle at Karbala. Another detail of the parade, one of distant history: a miniature ziggurat and a replica of the famed Ishtar gate had been rolled into place.

The features of that August 1989 dedication seem oddly discordant, juxtaposing Babylonian history with the Iraqi monarchy, pan-Arabism (or at least secular Iraqi statism) with Shi'ism. But our view is that they have everything to do with a reasoned and coordinated ideology of power; the features were hardly accidental or—on a deeper level—discordant. The various elements of the parade, included for the depth and power of their symbolic resonance, addressed needs of the Iraqi state. More importantly, they served the interests of what Chapter Two terms "reasons of self," the interests of the president himself. Exploring how that is so provides a crucial context for understanding the Iraqi employment of religion in the Gulf War. Saddam staged the dedicatory parade to serve the interests of both the state and himself, and he would employ Islam in the invasion of Kuwait the same way. But this sort of hybrid practice developed over some years, and we trace that here in order to make sense of Saddam's religious discourse in 1990–1991.

## SOMETHING OTHER THAN A NATION

In a confidential memo in 1933, the Hashemite King Faisal, whom the mandate-holding British had imposed as leader of the newly formed Iraq, lamented:

There is still—and I say this with a heart full of sorrow—no Iraqi people but unimaginable masses of human beings, devoid of any patriotic idea, imbued with religious traditions and absurdities, connected by no common tie, giving ear to evil, prone to anarchy, and perpetually ready to rise against any government whatever. Out of these masses we want to fashion a people.[5]

Divisions abounded, partly as a result of Churchill's conference work in Cairo, and the king saw them: various kinship groups, ethnicities, mercantile stratifications, propertied and nonpropertied classes, and religious confessions. The Ottomans, with their millets, had allowed disparate groups a degree of autonomy.[6] But what was appropriate for empire maintenance could hardly suffice for nation building.

The Ba'thist coup makers of 1968 confronted the same challenge. From the diverse pluribus within the state borders, the Ba'th party sought to construct the more tranquil unum of a nation. Ba'thist ideology, however, was strongly pan-Arab, stressing *qawmiyya,* the larger unity of all Arabs, rather than the more immediate dimension of *wataniyya,* that unity which adheres in patriotic attachment to one's country.[7] As Saddam gradually accreted power at the expense of President al-Bakr, the problem that had confronted Faisal became more particularly his own, and he met it in ways that changed over time. Indeed, his task resembled that of his sometime mentor, Gamal Abdul Nasser.[8]

Saddam's challenge was to use ideology to overcome the enervating and potentially devastating weaknesses arising from the primordial divisions throughout Iraq. In Abbas Kelidar's apt phrase, Saddam (and others) "perceived Iraq as a kind of Arab Prussia awaiting the emergence of its Bismarck."[9] Initially, he presented Ba'thism as such an ideology, a system whose supranational tenets could weld the country together. The work of the Syrian Arab nationalist Michel Aflaq seemed to offer such politically curative powers. "Nationalism (*qawmiyya*)," wrote Aflaq,

is the same sort of affectionate attachment that ties an individual to his family because the homeland (*watan*) is a large house and the nation (ummah), a wide family. . . . The one who sacrifices on behalf of his nation defending its past glory and future prosperity is truly a more elevated soul and a flourishing life than one who limits his sacrifice to one person. . . . [Nationalism] is spiritual and generous in the sense that it opens its heart and shelters under its wings anyone who has shared with the Arabs in their history and lived in the environment of their language and culture.[10]

Saddam followed Aflaq's reasoning. In 1975, while addressing Iraqi ambassadors to Europe and Japan as the deputy chairman of the Revolutionary Command Council (RCC), he espoused the true pan-Arab line:

We do not consider the patch of land (*ruq'a*) on which we are situated here in Iraq to be the end of the journey of our struggle, but it is part of another land (*ardh*) and wider objectives: that is, the homeland (*watan*) and objectives of the [larger] Arab struggle. . . . Similarly, we view our people, who number 12 million, to be part of a people which numbers 140 million; and we see the present situation of fragmentation (*tajziah*) to be unnatural.[11]

Yet by the time he had assumed the presidency in 1979, having pushed al-Bakr aside, Saddam had deviated considerably from party doctrine generally and pan-Arabism particularly. In a word, Saddam was better viewed as an "instrumental Ba'thist," a protean president who welcomed the equally protean contours of the philosophy Aflaq had delivered to him.[12] That is, Saddam emphasized different aspects of party orthodoxies as the occasion demanded and departed from them as the situation merited. It is precisely the malleability of Ba'thism that made it so useful. Aflaq, for instance, had written:

The nationalism to which we give a summons is love before anything else. . . . Young man . . . if love is that soil which nourishes your nationalism, then no domain persists for controversy over characterizing it and setting its borders.[13]

To read Aflaq is to find more passion than precision, less definition than political ardor. That malleability suited Saddam. He could, while maintaining rhetorical party purity, pursue other ends. Edward Luttwak's description is particularly apt:

The Ba'th [doctrine] is a fit ideology for Saddam Hussein . . . for it rationalizes oppression as justice (justice for the Arabs only being obtainable by a very "strong" government), tyranny as freedom (freedom for the Arabs only being obtainable by the unity of autocracy), and indeed death as the most valid expression of life—given that the highest purpose of life is to advance, by death if necessary, the cause of the Ba'th: the renaissance of a mighty Arab power.[14]

As Alexander the Great solved the mystery of untying the Gordian knot by slicing through it with a sword, Saddam cut through the conundrum that Faisal described—how to weld together "unimaginable masses of human beings, devoid of any patriotic idea"—by using force. Saddam had always been faithful to the Maoist doctrine that political power grows out of the barrel of a gun. He favored either straightforward purges, whether of private or public individuals, or purges-by-deportation, particularly of the Kurds (an estimated one million Kurds had been "resettled" by 1988, the year of the infamous gas attack on Halabja, part of the yet more infamous Anfal campaign) and Shi'a. Through the purges, Saddam emerged as one of the century's most able Machiavellians, choosing to be feared over being loved.[15]

The purges of 1969 and 1979 are instructive in that regard. The earlier purge, which Kanan Makiya has termed the "first spectacle" of the new Ba'thist regime, targeted the weak Jewish community in Iraq, accusing them of intelligence gathering and plotting subversion.[16] Apart from confirming the new government as brutal, the purge attacked Israel by proxy, an important political move after the debacle of the June 1967 war. The second serious purge followed Saddam's accession to power in 1979 by mere days. In this case, a "plot" was uncovered that involved over fifty senior members of the party and government leadership. Included among them were five members of the (then) twenty-one-member RCC. Saddam appointed a special commission to investigate, and within a month the circle of those killed for crimes against the state is said to have numbered over 500. Unlike the first purge, which targeted an enemy without that had somehow infiltrated the state, this one targeted the disloyal within. It underscored the omniscience of a regime from which no political sins could be hid. And it addressed the Shi'a in a particular way. Two of the five RCC members put to death were Shi'is. More importantly, the head of the special court that found them guilty, Deputy Premier Na'im Haddad, was himself a Shi'i. As Makiya observes, this has been a hallmark of the state: ensure others are complicit in the administration of violence against the wayward.

## FROM QAWMIYYA TO WATANIYYA

But Saddam did not rely on brute force alone. As he built power, he emphasized different aspects of doctrine and altered his tactics. The changing focus on pan-Arabism is an important dimension of this metamorphosis. At only one point is the observation of Edward Luttwak, above, amiss. When Luttwak wrote (1990), Saddam's focus was less on mighty Arab power and much more on his own and that of the nation. *Wataniyya* was eclipsing *qawmiyya*.[17] Saddam found continued rhetorical emphasis on pan-Arabism necessary, but his objective lay elsewhere: the building of his state.[18] For instance, as Chapter Two notes, Saddam declared in 1980:

The Iraqis are now of the opinion that Arab unity can only take place after a clear demarcation of borders between all countries. . . . The question of linking unity to the removal of boundaries is no longer acceptable to the present Arab mentality. . . . The Arab reality is the Arabs are now 22 states.[19]

And this marked change had been anticipated even in 1975 when Saddam had underscored for Iraq's national representatives their supranational orientation. Addressing Iraqi educators, Saddam (then vice president) admonished those engaged in rewriting textbooks to remember that

we must not submerge ourselves in the theoretical pan-Arab and neglect the direct, local patriotic (al-watani). . . . We must speak of the Iraqi who comes from Sulaymaniyya [i.e., a Kurd] and he who comes from Basra [i.e., a Shi'i], without pointing to his ethnic origins. . . . Let us delete the words Arabs and Kurds and replace them with the term the Iraqi people.[20]

In other words, Saddam's challenge was to forge something larger than the various ethnic divisions but smaller than qawmiyya.

Saddam moved on pan-Arabism because pan-Arabism could not move all the country. Something indigenous would have to serve. An exogenous doctrine could not provide the glue he needed for Iraq's disparate parts. Much of Ba'thist teaching would have been a hard sell in any event. The Kurds could not feel sanguine, as Kurds, about a pan-Arab doctrine. And many of the Shi'a would find no appeal in the secular character of the party's teachings.[21] In a perceptive passage written a year before Saddam pushed al-Bakr aside, Hanna Batatu asked whether the Ba'thist regime could

contribute, in a creative manner, to the process of nation-state building that the 1920 revolt had set afoot. This will involve, sooner or later, the necessity of binding peasants to the townsmen and the Shi'is to the Sunnis; and creating mutually advantageous relations between the Kurds and the Arabs; and, at the same time, raising qualitatively the standard of living and level of culture of the mass of Iraqis.[22]

To be sure, Saddam had not, at any time, abandoned pan-Arabism, at least in public discourse. But particularly after assuming the presidency, Saddam worked at creating and reinforcing a new sense of "Iraqiness" that was deeply situated in history and culture. Marvin Zonis has described organizing myths and their place in society, myths that "grow out of the structure of a society as a whole and cannot easily be implanted by [either] indigenous or foreign rulers or intellectuals." In his view, the "shattering of key organizing myths has constituted the principal historical dynamic of the Arab world in this century."[23] Saddam would refashion his country and advance his own power, but he recognized that he must work with the materials at hand to successfully offer a new organizing myth. For instance, elaborating in 1976 the doctrine he termed "specificity" (which holds that successful doctrine is itself necessarily culturally conditioned), the (then) vice president but de facto center of power wrote:

A man who is the philosopher of his people, then, *imposes his ideal* upon them. He must be one of them. He must start with the reality in which he finds them in order to change them. . . . He takes what is already there so that he may surpass it; he takes the people, the classes, the economic potentialities, the contradictions within the society in general, and in the light of these *he molds his ideology.*[24]

Or again, recognizing the unsuitability of western democracy, Saddam stated shortly after becoming president, "[O]ur own understanding of democracy should be based on the particular characteristics of the nation [here, Iraq], as well as of our party."[25]

But if this increasing focus on *wataniyya* required a shift in emphasis from the transnational to the national, it also necessitated a move from the temporal to the transtemporal. That is, if Iraqis were to stress their "Iraqi-ness" over their "Arab-ness" (although not neglecting the latter), they must also emphasize an identity that stretched over time.[26]

Writing in another context, Mircea Eliade, a scholar of comparative religions, observed:

For religious man, time . . . is neither homogenous nor continuous. . . . By its very nature sacred time is reversible in the sense that, properly speaking, it is a primordial mythical time made present. Every religious festival, any liturgical time, represents the reactualization of a sacred event that took place in a mythical past, 'in the beginning.' . . . In other words, the participants in the festival meet in it the first appearance of sacred time, as it appeared *ab origine, in illo tempore.*[27]

In political and social terms, Saddam sought to do something like that: to cause the past, with its enormous evocative powers, to be brought forward into the present. In the interests of nation building, the regime spent lavishly on attempts to recover its history. To paraphrase Clausewitz, history and archaeology became "the continuation of politics by other means." The regime generously funded the work of artists and poets, promoted new festivals with ancient motifs, established and expanded museums, supported the work of historians and archaeologists—anything that would pursue the "deep" history of Iraq, which stretched past the Abbasids and the early Islamic era, back over the millennia to embrace Babylonians, Assyrians, and Sumerians.[28]

The most important effort in this regard was the project to rebuild ancient Babylon, the most dramatic and unmistakable emblem of Mesopotamian identity. And because the site is located in the predominately Shi'a south, it could serve to illustrate the historical, transsectarian identity of all Iraqis.[29] As early as 1971, the Iraqi professional journal *Sumer* wrote of the Ba'thist plans: "Drawing upon the faith of the revolutionary government in the revival of the enormous civilizational heritage of our country, [the Administration of Antiquities] has adopted a mighty plan to build up the city of Babylon."

Work began in 1978, by which time Saddam was de facto leader, and proceeded for sixteen hours a day. Defined as one of Iraq's "principal national development projects," Saddam reportedly gave the work a "blank check," especially after 1980 and the onset of the war with Iran. The president believed Babylon rebuilt would serve as "an inspiration to his people [as they] engaged in the terrible conflict with Iran." The planners were selective about which periods would be rebuilt; certainly nothing from the Persian-Akhaemonian time would be of interest. Principal projects—often entirely new construction rather than faithful reconstruction—included the temple and gate of Ishtar, Marduk's gate, one of the fortresses of Nebuchadnezzar, the famous ziggurat, and much of the wall. One female archaeologist declared of the project, "It's a wonderful thing for a person to work on restoring his nation's civilizational heritage. Joy overwhelms when I find an archeological relic, for it is part of our civilization."

Eliade's observation that festivals "reactualize" the past in the present is pertinent in this regard. Babylon, as rebuilt under Saddam, has been host to a number of festivals. For instance, it was here, in September 1981, that Iraqis observed the first anniversary of the Iran-Iraq War. The theme of the festival was "Yesterday Nebuchadnezzar, today Saddam Hussein." The festival's speaker, Vice President Taha Ma'ruf, recalled (appropriately, in light of the war with Iran) how centuries earlier the "Persian Elamites" had attacked the "Iraqi internal patriotic unity." Similarly, seven years later at the Babylon Festival (themed "From Nebuchadnezzar to Saddam Hussein, Babylon arises anew"), the event stressed *wataniyya*. Folk dancers from Mosul, Baghdad, and Basra performed; and one of Iraq's most popular singers performed a new song about the homeland, a *watan* that stretched from the "mountains of the north [i.e., the Kurdish area] to the reed swamps of the south [i.e., the Shi'a area]."[30] In these instances, the festivals did double duty. Drawing on history to reinforce *wataniyya*, the festivals served *raisons d'état*. But they also reinforced reasons of self; the festivals specifically, and archaeology generally, advance the cause of Saddam, for it is his name and his image that occupy the center of almost all such activity.

## THE TURN TO ISLAM

But the protean president moved in another way to meet the needs of the state. Saddam found religion.[31] Indeed, Saddam *had* to find religion for two primary reasons discussed below, one internal and one external. And Saddam's discovery cannot be slighted. Any adequate history of political development in Ba'thist Iraq must take account of this—the successive movements from secularity, to Islam used defensively, to the state as standard-bearer of Islam.[32] Religion had never been absent, either as a part of Saddam's own cultural heritage or as a feature of Ba'thist ideology (Ba'thism, per se, is generally secular, but certainly not atheistic); but his instrumental employment of religion would become increasingly important. And it became important precisely because of its ability to appropriate powerful, indigenous cultural values and use them for political ends.

Clifford Geertz has defined religion as "a system of symbols which acts to establish powerful, pervasive, and long-lasting moods and motivations in men by formulating conceptions of a general order of existence and clothing these conceptions with such an aura of factuality that the moods and motivations seem uniquely realistic."[33] The true believer may assert that the "long-lasting moods and motivations" precede the symbols, and that the "general order of existence" is a given, the reality one discovers or is revealed through theistic volition. But that, for Saddam, was precisely the opening he needed. To manipulate those deeply grounded religious symbols and to do so as if he were a true believer could greatly help him realize his purposes. Yet the president did not arrive at that position immediately.

Initially, Saddam followed Michel Aflaq. Although an Orthodox Christian, Aflaq certainly understood the important place of Islam, regarding it as a critical part of the national culture of the Arabs, and Muhammad as embodying the "true spirit" of the nation. Aflaq's fundamental challenge was to square this heritage with his emphasis on *qawmiyya*, and much of *Fi Sabil* takes up that apologetic.

There is no fear that nationalism will clash with religion because, like it, [nationalism] flows from the heart and issues from the will of God. These two go forth cooperating and embracing, especially when religion represents the genius of nationalism and is harmonious with its nature. . . . The Ba'thist struggler (*munadil*) . . . understands both true religion and the true personal self which is positive, possessing faith, and intolerant of contestation (*inkaar*) and shirking. . . . Islam alone was able to awaken the latent depths of power in the Arab soul and was able to effect unity and solidarity and to kindle their souls and open their genius and, thus, to effect their renaissance (*nahdha*).[34]

Saddam readily espoused similar views. Shortly after Saddam took the presidency, his biographer, Amir Iskander, interviewed him on a range of issues.[35] Like Aflaq, Saddam spoke much of spirit (*ruh*), an exceptionally malleable term. By speaking of spirit when discussing religion, Saddam could evoke a panoply of powerful symbols, while avoiding rigid doctrine and remaining usefully vague. Thus, the president told his interviewer, the Ba'th must not return to the past, but draw forward the "spirit of the past." It should study the *rashidun*, not to imitate their external forms (*siyaagh*), but to understand the "spirit of the course" they followed.[36] Indeed, one could find in the behavior of Umar and Ali the "spirit and general values of Arab Muslim socialism." Further, the reality of the Arab nation (*umma*) is explicitly religious, and it could not now happen that there would be "no relation between earth and heaven."

But Saddam warned that the use of religion risked "taking the sword by its blade." Further—and here Saddam indirectly inveighed against the Iranians and the Saudis—the modern Arab state (*dawla*) must not be a "house of worship," a "mufti of worship," a "new mujtahid" (collection of jurists), or a "center for fatwa." Arguing as a strict separationist, Saddam warned that Islam cannot be a substitute for Arab nationalism. If the state did try to introduce religion into the affairs of life, it would either produce a hellfire (*jaheem*) that would kill people's creative abilities (*ibdaa'aat*) or empty religion of its "holiness, awe, and spirit."

Saddam had earlier followed the same approach in his 1978 *nathra fil din wal turath* (*A Look at Religion and Heritage*).

Our party is not neutral between atheism and faith. It is always on the side of faith, but it is not a religious party. . . . What we must do is to oppose the institutionalization of religion in the state and in society. . . . Let us return to the roots of our religion—but not bring it into politics. . . . Political entry into religious matters leads to a division of the people—not only into those who are religious and those who are not, but into the different adherents of different religions. . . . Let us tell everyone to practice his own religion and not interfere with it. But the condition for this is that no one should quarrel on religious grounds with policies of the Arab Ba'th Socialist Party.[37]

He repeated the same ideas a year later, as president, to Fuad Matar.

When we say that we are not neutral between apostasy and faith, we mean that Ba'athists are like all other believers, free to worship as they wish. . . . Yet although we may be inspired by religion and its laws, we do not deal with life by following a religious path. . . . We do not believe in dealing with life through religion because it would not serve the Arab nation. It would only serve to divide the nation into different religions and numerous sects and schools of thought.[38]

But Saddam changed, driven in part by realities within the Iraqi state and in part by those in Iran. Ofra Bengio, one of the leading scholars of contemporary Iraq and Ba'thism, has carefully described this increasing employment of Islam, and she merits quoting at some length.

The real test of strength of Ba'th doctrine occurred at times of crisis. . . . It was at such times that the doctrine was found wanting. Gradually the party had to drop the political discourse with which it had come to power and replace it with, or at least range alongside it, a different kind of public language. The latter drew on themes of historical, above all Islamic, provenance. In some measure, this process was intentional and guided from above; in part it was forced on the regime by specific circumstances; and in part it sprang spontaneously from deep layers of the Iraqi collective experience. . . . It is possible to discern several distinct phases in this process and to point to domestic and external developments that influenced it. From 1968 to 1977, the Ba'th regime was silent on the topic of religion; between 1977 and 1980, there were indications of an impending change; the war years, from 1980 and well into the first postwar year, 1989, constituted the phase of toeing the Islamic line; the last phase, from 1989 onward, was one of deliberate Islamic flag waving.[39]

Yet before we examine more closely what prompted such changes in a theretofore secular state, it is important to consider the potential genuineness of Saddam's religious declarations.

### EXCURSUS: SADDAM THE TRUE BELIEVER?

In our view, Saddam's embrace of Islam was instrumental only; but then, so was the employment of Ba'thism. Saddam's shifting attachments, allegiances, and espousals reflected both the needs of state and, more especially, his own interests, both *raisons d'état* and reasons of self. If the greater use of the language and symbols of faith aided these interests, then so be it; Saddam would pursue that course. Yet this conclusion raises a difficult question: was Saddam a true believer, or did he embrace Machiavelli, believing only the appearance of piety, and not piety itself, to be important? The evidence suggests the latter. To begin, the two sympathetic, regime-approved biographies (those of Iskander and Matar) make no mention of religious piety in Saddam's family or early life. Both were written around the time Saddam became president, yet neither mentions some crisis that prompted a turn to faith. Rather, as we indicate in this chapter, both biographers stress Saddam's caution about religion. In reviewing Saddam's early years, Iskander avers that Saddam learned "certain basic virtues" that stayed with him throughout life (patience, endurance, grim determination, affection for the poor, and so on), but not religion.

The biography by Said Aburish, which spends as much time refuting the anti-Saddam writers as correcting laudatory ones, focuses especially on the difficulty of Saddam's childhood; his role as *sanad* in the Iraqi Ba'th of the early 1950s (according to Aburish, sanad denotes a "backer-up in time of trouble, in particular someone who frightens others"); and his lifelong fascination with Stalinism.[40] What emerges in Aburish's portrait is a Saddam who is a capable but calculating and cruel survivor. Physically abused by his paternal uncle-*cum*-stepfather, Hajj Ibrahim Hassan, Saddam learned to live by his wits. (Significantly, the stepfather was known as "Hassan the Liar" because he falsely assumed the honorific *hajj*, one who has made the pilgrimage.) By the early 1950s Saddam participated in frequent antigovernment demonstrations and, because he carried a weapon, became known as *a bu massaddess*, "He of the Gun."[41] No display of Islamic piety is to be found—only the picture of a neighborhood tough.

After Saddam fled Iraq following the attempted assassination of Qassem in 1959, he headed to Syria, then to Cairo. There, Iskander tells us, Saddam avoided the city's "manifold pleasures," occupying himself instead, during those three years, with his studies and his "secret organization work" for the Ba'th. During that time he allowed himself few diversions: chess, at which he excelled, and perhaps two trips to the movies. Yet, there is no reference at all to attendance at Friday noon prayers or other evidence of religious activity in this, the city of al Azhar, the primary center of Sunni Islamic jurisprudence. The only reference to religion occurs when he wrote home to say he wished to marry his cousin Sajida. Hajj Ibrahim responded in typical cultural fashion: "God has put the idea in the boy's mind."[42] After returning to Iraq, Saddam spent time in prison when President Aref incarcerated Ba'thist leaders. Saddam recalls:

I didn't play cards, as prisoners do, nor did I smoke. Rather, I spent the time in contemplation [over the reasons for the November 1963 debacle] and in reading, till I hoped I wouldn't have a chance to escape before I completed my scheme [how to avoid repeating mistakes].[43]

As when he was in Cairo, Saddam seems to have given himself to study and to revolutionary activities, but not to Islam; prison did not foster "conversion" or prompt piety any more than did his (self-described) almost monkish life in Egypt. At the very least, one may say this: if any of his experiences up through his time in prison brought religious changes, Saddam failed to relate them to his biographers. Surely, since Saddam controlled the interviews, he would have ensured that such information, if he deemed it important, was included. This would be an odd omission, otherwise, in light of the elaborate detail he offers, for instance, of his escape from Iraq after the attempt on Qassem and the impact that event had on his life.

Evaluating Islamic religious leaders' assessments of Saddam is more difficult. It would be fair to say those outside the country were generally silent on the legitimacy of Saddam's Islamic credentials, at least until after the invasion of Kuwait (which will be discussed in Chapter Six). Within Iraq, one finds divided support, especially among the Shi'a. Many of the Iraqi Shi'a leaders supported Saddam during the war with Iran for several reasons: their sense of an Iraqi identity that took precedence over a connection to Iranian Shi'ism; their concomitant concerns about what the triumph of Khomeinism could mean; a quiescence after their brutalization by Saddam, when they were seen as a political threat; their effective co-optation by regime largesse from oil revenues.[44] In short, those who supported him had compelling practical reasons to do so, despite any inward reservations they may have had about the legitimacy of Saddam's religious claims; one would be hard pressed to read their support as untainted evidence of the president's sincerity.

But many other clerics were not convinced, and rejected his claims. Most significantly, Saddam failed to win over Muhammad Baqir al-Sadr, prominent Shi'i *marji'* (high-ranking jurist) and leader of al-da'wa, who repeatedly challenged Saddam's Islamic credentials and who is said to have consistently declared relations with the regime *haram*, religiously forbidden, because of its un-Islamic character.[45] Still others tried to distance themselves from political involvement altogether, chief among them the Ayatollah al-Khoi, whose role will be discussed in the next chapter.

None of this finally settles the matter. Despite no indication of marked religiosity in his family or his early life, the president's "faith" may be real. And maybe the question is misleading in any event; perhaps Eric Hoffer's "true believer" is a category better applied in the West, where it arose. Certainly Saddam was raised in a milieu in which Islam is interwoven with all areas of life. The faith would have been part of his inescapable cultural grounding, and one should not be surprised to find it informing his discourse. But even without finally deciding on the legitimacy of Saddam's belief or its intensity, we can at least make two essential points.

First, there is a discrepancy between his public declarations of belief and his practice. Witness the brutalities of the purges, the systematic use of torture, his patently false claim to be a descendant of the Shiʿa imams, his violent destruction of Shiʿa holy places in the 1991 intifada in the south—none of which could be considered to comport with the teachings of Islam. And on occasion his personal and candid remarks cast doubt on his profession of faith. Particularly telling is the observation of Khidhir Hamza, Iraq's leading nuclear scientist, who defected in 1994. He recalled a remark Saddam made in one of their meetings: "He once told me: 'If you are a believer in God, and you get killed following a certain path, then you are rewarded with heaven and you are a great man. But you are a greater man if you are not a believer. Because then you do it out of personal commitment. You know there is no reward on the other side.' "[46]

Second, it is ascertainably clear that in his public, political discourse, Saddam demonstrably increased the number of his references to Islam over the course of his career, moving away from a strict Baʿthist emphasis on a purely secular (but not atheist) state. There is a marked contrast between his statement to Iskander that the state should not be a center of fatwa and his forceful declaration of jihad barely a decade later when he invaded Kuwait. What would best account for such changes, in my view, are reasons of self and state. The embrace of Islam, in Machiavellian fashion, would secure Saddam's position and, simultaneously, serve *raisons d'état*. Aburish, who dealt extensively with Saddam on armament deals, is on point: "The first thing to remember is that Saddam Hussein spent twenty years creating a personality, an image for himself. . . . The real person has no ideology whatsoever. That is the most important thing to remember about Saddam Hussein. Saddam Hussein is into realpolitik."[47] Whether true believer or not, Machiavellian or not, Saddam found the invocation of faith "useful," much as Gibbon observed of the politicians of Rome.

## THE SHIʿA

We turn, then, to the two chief reasons, one internal and one external, for Saddam's increasing adoption of Islam. First, most Iraqis were (and are) Muslim, over sixty percent of them Shiʿis. Initially, as an instrumental Baʿthist, Saddam had sought to get around religious particularities via a nonreligious doctrine. In the first decade of Baʿthist rule, the regime accommodated religion but kept it at a distance; hence, Saddam's warnings about taking the sword by the blade. Yet over time, simple accommodation seemed insufficient for nation building, and as one of Saddam's key mentors had recognized some years before, Islam could serve as a tool for unity. After a trip to Mecca, Egypt's Gamal Abdul Nasser reflected, "The pilgrimage (hajj) should be a great political power. . . . [W]hen I visualize these millions united in one faith, I have a great consciousness of the tremendous potentialities that cooperation amongst them all can achieve."[48] His observation about the hajj and Arab nationalism would prove equally valid—employed in other ways—when applied to the Iraqi state.

Saddam's espousing of Islamic rhetoric made sense given the straightforward social realities of a country that is over ninety-five percent Muslim, and is dominated in the south by the Shi'a. The faith of the Shi'a is deeply and inextricably culturally embedded. In addition, the Shi'a had long been disenfranchised, at least since the establishment of the monarchy. During Faisal's reign, a saying current among Iraq's majority Shi'a community ran thus, "The taxes are on the Shi'i, death is on the Shi'i, and the posts are for the Sunnis."[49] From 1958 to 1968, the decade after the monarchy was overthrown, the disparity continued: of the top posts in government, Sunnis held eighty percent, the Shi'is sixteen percent, and other religious groups the remaining four percent. And in the first decade of the Ba'th (that is, 1968–1978), this imbalance continued. The Revolutionary Command Council (RCC) then numbered fifteen. Of those, fourteen were Sunni Arabs and one was a Kurd (dismissed in 1971).[50] By the time of the invasion of Kuwait, the RCC numbered seven. Two were Shi'is, but the most powerful three members were Sunni. Further, Saddam continued not only to monopolize power but also to place trusted family members and Tikritis over the all-pervasive security apparatus, most of whom were Sunnis.[51]

In part, this continued disenfranchisement simply reflected Saddam's promotion of people he already knew from Tikrit and from among earlier Ba'thist fellow strugglers, and they happened to be Sunni; thus, the advancement of Sunnis did not arise for doctrinal reasons, but from a primordial or clan predilection. Indeed, over time, Saddam not only "Ba'thized" the military ("who does not take our path, stays at home with his wife," said one party member) but, more importantly, "Tikritized" the power structure.[52]

Recognizing the power of primordialism, Saddam was concerned about Shi'ism as a rival source of identity. Sami Zubaida has written of religion as an "ethnic marker," and it is clearly of importance here: "Communalist sentiments do not presuppose any specific Islamic political ideas. . . . [but] they can be important mobilizing sentiments in favour of any movement calling for the restoration of Islamic superiority."[53] More specifically, Majid Khadduri writes of the religious *communitas* that had long straddled the Iran-Iraq border:

Shi'i teachers and students from both countries not unnaturally fraternized and developed an affinity for one another and a common identity before the era of nationalism, based on the principle of fealty (walaya) to the Imam, which in practice meant loyalty to the chief religious authority whether he was an Arab or a Persian, or whether he resided in Najaf or Qum.[54]

In short, Saddam saw the Shi'a generally as a potentially rival primordial group and, in its fundamentalist cadres, a possible source of subversive activity. In the event, he proved correct. He knew some, at least, among the Shi'a would reject the secular blandishments of the Ba'th; and to that extent, those Shi'is would, technically, be part of the state, but not of the nation. Kanan Makiya has observed:

No matter how completely Ba'thism succeeds in destroying all alternatives to itself in the public domain . . . it is much harder for it to be as thorough in the private and social domain of family, kinship relations, and religious group affiliation . . . [which provide a] . . . formidable obstacle to Ba'thist penetration.[55]

Bulloch and Morris are likely right in their assessment that the majority of the Iraqi Shi'a "preferred to separate religion and politics, to look to the state for the physical needs of society, and to the mosque for things spiritual."[56] Yet it certainly was not universally true, as they point out elsewhere. That 60 percent of Iraqis carried an ethnic marker other than his own worried Saddam. That numbers of the 60 percent might respond to fundamentalist calls from within the state or, especially in 1979 and after, from east of the Shatt, was a deeper concern, and it was not unfounded.

Disenchantment with secular Iraqi politics and anxiety about the drift of the Iraqi Shi'a from their roots had led to the formation of *hizb al-da'wa al-islamiyah*, the Islamic Call party, in 1957. Founded by the Ayatollah Muhammad Baqir al-Sadr and other Shi'i clerics, al-da'wa operated primarily in Najaf and Karbala, as well as in Baghdad, especially in the al-Thawra slum.[57] Prior to the Ba'th revolution in 1968, al-da'wa had operated fairly openly, and primarily as an educational effort.

It emphasized Islamic observance and generally steered clear of political activity. But the Ba'th would brook no potentially competing center of allegiance, and began to crack down on the religious educational institutions of al-da'wa. A special branch of the security service was devoted to countering subversive Shi'i activity, and the government took the added important measure of confiscating the Shi'a *waqf* (Islamic endowment fund) in 1978.[58]

The increasingly militant and now underground party clashed repeatedly with the government. The most violent of those clashes came in 1977 and 1979. The 1977 disturbances occurred when the government tried to prevent an annual Shi'a procession from Najaf to Karbala to mark the fortieth day of Imam Hussein's martyrdom. On this occasion some 2,000 were arrested, several executed, and—over the next couple of years—some 200,000 Shi'is were deported.[59] Then, in 1979–1980, activist mujtahids led demonstrations in the predominately Shi'i south, as well as in the al-Thawra slum of Baghdad.[60] Saddam had reason to view the development with concern. Crowds of marchers in Najaf and elsewhere chanted, "*Ash al Khomeini wil Sadr weddine lazim yantasser*" (Long live Khomeini and Sadr, and religion [i.e., Islam] must triumph) and "*kulana lak fada' Khomeini*" (All of us are yours to sacrifice, Khomeini).[61] Further, al-Sadr issued a fatwa in June 1979 that forbade Muslims to join the Ba'th and declared support for the Islamic revolution in Iran.

By that point, the government felt it had no recourse but to crush al-da'wa. The government made membership punishable by death and did, in fact, imprison and execute a number of the Shi'a. On 24 April 1980, following the assassination attempt on Tariq Aziz at Mustansiriya University, the government executed al-Sadr and his sister. Then, while visiting Najaf after the executions, Saddam made it clear, with an ironically bold statement, that he would brook no dissent: "I am the son of Ali," he told the Shi'a there, "and I kill with his sword."[62]

Yet the regime also extended the carrot. In a policy alliteratively termed *targhib wa tarhib* (reward and punishment), the government sought to improve its image and gain the loyalty of the sectarian community.[63] The government gave cash gifts to Shi'i communities and worked on infrastructure, especially in the holy cities of Najaf and Karbala, spending lavishly on shrines, mosques, and *husayniyahs*.[64] The government spent over 100 million dollars in Karbala alone in the eight-year period to 1982. Saddam frequently visited the shrines and made Ali's birthday a national holiday.

Pictures multiplied of the president reading the Quran or praying; public recitations of the Quran along with religious discussions in the media increased. The government distributed television sets (also useful, of course, for amplifying government propaganda), promoted literacy, and increased spending (albeit selectively) on improved health care. By a number of social measures, the Ba'th improved life in the south. And Saddam prominently ensured that more posts in the party and the administration were opened to Shi'is. By the time of the invasion of Kuwait in 1990, Shi'is held almost 50 percent of the regional Ba'th party posts, comprised 20 percent of the army's generals, and headed 50 percent of state-owned enterprises.[65]

These changes were cosmetic, of course. Saddam maintained clear control, and he continued to appoint his most trusted compatriots (usually Sunni) to the top positions in the ubiquitous security services. But as a community, the Sunnis often faced similar disabilities. The Shi'a, in fact, began to see greater parity. The implicit message in all this was that being a member of the Shi'a community was not automatically disenfranchising, provided one gave up any political activity independent of the Ba'th. The Shi'a could expect greater opportunities, although the Ba'th monitored them with the utmost attention.

More positively, Saddam seemed to take increasing care to speak favorably, even warmly, of the Shi'a as coreligionists. Especially after taking over the presidency, Saddam found myriad ways to cite Shi'a imams as exemplary Muslims. For instance, in a speech outside the presidential palace in August 1979, following the sweeping purge of party leaders, Saddam offered parallels from Islamic history to explain how traitors could have infiltrated the highest ranks of the Ba'th. Muhammad, too, he said, had faced the perfidious among his own followers, men who were in cahoots with the Quraysh. But Saddam extended the history lesson. "You all know the dispute that took place between Imam Ali, God bless him, and Mu'awiyah. Imam Ali was a man of honor representing all [the] meanings and spirit of the Islamic mission; Mu'awiyah was fighting for the sake of earthly temptations." The latter "won the earth on which he lived [but] lost the heavenly values." Ali, by contrast, "triumphed because he sought the heavenly values. Thus, he won those values forever and left his imprint on earth forever."[66]

This was a brilliant stroke. Saddam had just put to death two Shi'a members of the RCC, who had been condemned by a Shi'a he appointed as head of the special trial court. Then, Saddam reached out to the confessional community, lauding the first Shi'a Imam at the expense of the first Umayyad caliph. (It was a safe approach, since the Umayyad capital was Damascus.)

Similarly, in an October 1979 address in Najaf, the president declared, "Iraq will fight tyranny wherever it is, following in the path of Imam Ali, God rest his soul, and sayyed Hussein."[67] The government placed an official banner in front of the Imam Ali mosque in Najaf at the start of the war with Iran that read, "We take pride at the presence here of our great father Ali, because he is a leader of Islam, because he is the son-in-law of the Prophet, and because he is an Arab."[68] Two years after the start of the war, in an address calculated to ingratiate himself further with the Shi'a in one of their two most important cities, Saddam declared, "Al-Najaf is an Iraqi and an Arab town. Its soil is Arab and its great symbol is our grandfather Imam Ali ibn Abi Talib, who is definitely not the father of Khomeini."[69] He spoke, of course, in a way that emphasized the *Arab* character of the *watan*, but in a way that was clearly inclusive of Iraqi Shi'ism, a pattern he often followed.

But the most dramatic (not to say transparently manipulative) move was to identify his family with the Shi'a. At first the claim was oblique; Saddam referred to his "grandfather" Ali during his extended speech about the traitors of the RCC. "We have the right to say today—and we will not be fabricating history—that we are the grandsons of Imam Husayn [ibn Ali]." But that could be taken as metaphor, and the "we" is ambiguous. However, Saddam allowed the claim to be promulgated explicitly in the semiofficial biography by Amir Iskander, who pointed out that Saddam was of such character as not to advertise that his line goes back "to the noblest family of all, whose greatest scion was the Imam Ali bin Abi Talib." To do so, Iskander opined, would be inappropriate in "the presence of those who can make no such claim." The biography also includes a picture of the drawing of the family tree.[70] Three months after his mother died in 1983, Saddam claimed she had been Shi'i.[71]

And quite importantly, although not an aspect of turning Sunnis into Shi'is, the president directed another posthistorical "conversion," which fit the pattern of subordinating Ba'thism to religion. On 24 June 1989, the government announced, via Baghdad Radio, Michel Aflaq's death the day before. But the real surprise was the announcement that Ba'thism's founder had embraced Islam some time previously (the broadcast did not specify when). The broadcast added that neither Aflaq nor the party had wished to share the news any earlier, lest it be given a "political interpretation."[72]

The Saddam Hussein-Imam Hussein-Imam Ali link extended to the nation, as necessary. For instance, in 1979 the regime inaugurated a new celebration, the Festival of Ukhaydar, named for an early Abbasid fortress in Karbala, burial place of the martyred Hussein. In 1984, the festival took as its theme "The principles of the Imam al-Husayn are shining in Saddam's Qadisiyya." By this point, Iran and Iraq were four years into the war. Those celebrating in Karbala heard its opening speaker declare both the military virtues of Iraq's president and the glories of the "vast Abbasid state." He continued:

The sword that Saddam of the Arabs is unsheathing today in the face of the hateful enemies of the nation is the identical sword drawn by the Imam Ali. The banner which the Imam al-Husayn carried is the identical banner carried today by his heroic grandson, President Saddam Husayn, and by the heroes of glorious Iraq.[73]

The fusing of elements is important here. The festival was carefully orchestrated to draw on a pan-Arab dimension ("Saddam of the Arabs"), Sunni Islam (the "vast Abbasid state"), and—most importantly —Shi'ism, all in the service of continued mobilization of support for the war with Iran. In a speech the previous year Saddam had played similar chords to associate his listeners with a Shi'i past. He had encouraged his listeners in the war effort thus:

Oh brothers! Sons of Baghdad and Maysan and Dhi Qar and Nineveh [Iraqi provinces] . . . you are the sons of the Tigris and Euphrates, sons of the tree of knowledge and of Noah's Ark which cast anchor on your soil, sons of the Mesopotamian valley which cast their light upon humanity when humanity was in darkness, you [are] the sons of Ali and al-Husayn . . . and the grandsons of Salah al-Din . . . behold their swords are with you. . . . [W]ill the grandfathers abandon their grandsons when their grandsons are fighting for justice?[74]

Here one clearly sees Saddam's perennial concern over the Shi'a in southern Iraq falling under Khomeini's sway. That proved not the case, just as the Arab minority in Iran did not support Saddam.[75] What is important is the degree to which, in the employment of religion, Saddam sought to incorporate a Shiʻi Islamic dimension in his message of nation building, an approach far more accommodating than the pan-Arab message of secular Baʻthism.

## THE IRAN-IRAQ WAR

The need to work with indigenous cultural factors generally, and the Shiʻa specifically, prompted Saddam increasingly to blend religious elements with the party's pan-Arab message. But the January 1979 Iranian revolution and the war that followed twenty months later also prompted important changes.[76] The ductile borders of Baʻthist ideology could be shaped and reshaped to justify regime policies and, indeed, to obfuscate certain regime practices. What it could not do was keep men at their post in the Faw peninsula when under intense attack, and it would never propel Iraqi soldiers into human wave attacks shouting, "Unity! Freedom! Socialism!" One scholar has described Baʻthism as a "terrible combination of murky nineteenth-century European romantic nationalism with twentieth-century fascism."[77] Even if overstated, this does correctly point to the exogenous nature of Baʻthism's roots. In university settings or small cafes or diwans—wherever a radical intellectual elite might congregate—early Baʻthism could gain a hearing and assume plausibility, particularly as it promoted pan-Arabism. But not in war; not in the dark moments of stark fear the Iraqi *jundi* (soldier) would experience as Iranian artillery shells fell closer.

Early in the conflict, Fuad Matar, another of Saddam's biographers, could characterize the war as "the first in the region between a secular Arab national leadership and a religious leadership."[78] Indeed, in Matar's view, Khomeini wrongly believed "Iraq could not use nationalism to repel an assault in the name of religion." In this, Matar paralleled Saddam. Speaking in April 1980, the president declared,

When a clash is a patriotic and national duty, we shall wage it in all its forms. . . . Iraq is once again to assume its leading Arab role. Iraq is once again to serve the Arab nation and defend its honor, dignity, and sovereignty. Iraq is destined once again to face the concerted machinations of the forces of darkness.[79]

Saddam seemed to be of two minds.[80] He made appeals to religion, but he did so in the Aflaqian style. Aflaq had spoken of Islam as having once been a prime mover (*muharak asasi*) among Arabs; and in that spirit, Aflaq maintained, Arab nationalism had now become such a force. Echoing those words in 1980, Saddam addressed a military graduation ceremony:

Do not forget that you are soldiers with a message, and that you must be in the vanguard to carry the banner, like the Islamic armies when they reached China and Spain. *This new Arabism* is a new breath of Islam in all its aspects and a new breath from heaven. . . . Anyone who stands against the new Arabism stands against Islam.[81]

Saddam touched on the image of religion, but he preached the doctrine of the "new Arabism," as Aflaq had done. It was tentative, accommodative, not a full embrace of faith, rhetorical or otherwise. But war changes things; and in the clash of the maximalists, Khomeini had an important advantage.

Saddam recognized the strength of the competing ideology east of the Shatt al-Arab. Even more than Ba'thism, Khomeinism was an ideology both total and totalizing: the principles of the *vilayet e fiqh* addressed all society and government. Like Ba'thism, it addressed the world in categorical terms.[82] Unlike Ba'thism, Khomeinism was no European export. It drew its inspiration, as it were, not from the Sorbonne but from the *madrasa* in Qum, the city where the Iranian army surrendered to the Islamic militia in 1979. Khomeinism thus came as a completely indigenous ideology, one well rooted historically and culturally, and not—like Ba'thism—one that melded indigenous and exogenous elements. And while both Ba'thism and Khomeinism were categorical, the latter added a thorough and consistent metaphysic, one that could encourage its followers in the present with the promise of the hereafter, a notable deficiency in strict Ba'thism.

In the event, there was the usual logomachy before the physical clash of swords. Khadduri has characterized it well:

There is still another front [in the Iran-Iraq War] which may be called the war of words, stressing essentially its ideological aspect. This kind of warfare is fought not by armed forces, but by broadcasts over the media, confessional controversies, and, not infrequently, subversive forays. Unlike guns, which destroy physical targets, the war of words strives to influence the minds and attitudes of citizens by invoking stereotypes and distorting news to enhance one side's position and undermine the other's. The war of words may not have the immediate effect of a decisive battle, but it might have a permeating influence on the ultimate outcome of the war.[83]

Typical was Saddam's speech on 15 April 1980 (and such examples are easily multiplied), the guiding theme of which was the *shu'ubism* rampant in Iran.[84] The ayatollah was a "mummy," a "rotten man" who, with his clerical counterparts, had nothing to do with the true values of religion. Worse, though people thought the shah had gone, this was "the same shah but this time wearing a turban." Saddam also had words for the Iranian president. "Bani-Sadr bears rancor toward Arabism and Islam, because Islam's banners were carried by the Arabs . . . until [they] reached the furthest corners of the earth, including the land on which Bani-Sadr now stands." Additionally, Iraq sponsored a Persian-language broadcast that read letters purportedly from Iranians who ridiculed the ayatollah as "phony" and the "thirteenth Imam."[85] The Iranians responded in kind. Saddam was the "shah's heir," the "pharaoh of Iraq," and—in an interesting reference to Latin American dictatorial politics—the "Somoza of Iraq."[86] The Iranians also coupled unconventional warfare with this war of words that preceded the full commencement of hostilities in September 1980. They instigated the near-fatal attack on Tariq Aziz in April 1980 as he entered Mustansiriya University in Baghdad, as well as widespread unrest in Shi'a communities.[87]

After the invasion, Khomeini and other clerics consistently interpreted the war in Islamic-categorical terms. Addressing his own army shortly after Iraq invaded, the ayatollah spoke uncompromisingly:

You are fighting to protect Islam, and [Saddam] is fighting to destroy Islam. . . . There is absolutely no question of peace or compromise, and we shall never have any discussions with them, because they are corrupt and perpetrators of corruption. . . . It is not a question of a fight between one government and another; it is a question of an invasion by an Iraqi non-Muslim Ba'thist against an Islamic country; and this is a rebellion by blasphemy against Islam.[88]

The ayatollah was also clear from the start about the need for sacrifice. "We must fight for the sake of Islam. . . . We should show self sacrifice. We should sacrifice all our loved ones for the sake of Islam. . . . If we are killed we have performed our duty, and if we kill, again, we have acted according to our duty."[89] He turned his appeals west of the Shatt, as well.

I address this [Iraqi] army which is still collaborating with the dirty regime of Saddam to use this opportunity and join your brothers who are ready to help you throw this regime into hell. It is either the victory of Islam and the victory of justice or the defeat of Islam and a great shame for Muslim nations. Before it is too late, rise up.[90]

When, two years later, Iranian troops occupied Iraqi territory, the ayatollah addressed the wartime development as he spoke at the Haseyniyeh Jamaran in Tehran. The move was purely defensive, Khomeini said; Iran could not be a threat. Indeed, because "faith is our land," Iran really had no interest in occupying another Muslim country. On the other hand, those defending Saddam Hussein were traitors to Islam.[91]

Other clerics continued the assault. The Ayatollah Musavi-Ardabili, in a Friday sermon delivered in Persian and Arabic, described the battle as one between Islam and blasphemy. This was a battle in which the "Aflaqite Saddam," the self-styled hero of Qadisiyya, had violated international law, attacked the Islamic homeland, and killed the innocent. He appealed to the Iraqis to topple the "Ba'thist-Zionist regime" that had been imposed on them.[92] And a senior Iranian official, Sadeq Khalkhali, declared, "We have taken the path of true Islam, and our aim in defeating Saddam Hussein lies in the fact that we consider him the main obstacle to the advance of Islam in the region."[93]

Saddam was concerned. The Iranian attacks struck at the heart of his own rather shaky Islamic credentials since, after all, he had described himself as leading the vanguard of a secular ideology. He was also worried, as indicated above, that the challenge of Khomeini could draw Iraqi Shi'i support. In part, Saddam sought to match the Iranians, assault for assault, charging that they were categorically "other." Thus he attacked Khomeini and company as "Elamites" or as "Persians." In using the term "Persian," which he had done for six months before the invasion, Saddam sought to vilify his opponents as racially different and geographically expansive. Drawing on the historical memory of the Mongol invasion and the destruction of Baghdad in 1258 under Hulago, the regime used the connotatively charged "yellow," an obvious invective in that milieu, to describe the Iranians. Persia became the "yellow storm" and the "yellow wind," just as Qaddafi's teaching was a "yellow doctrine" and the Syrian Hafiz al-Assad, a "yellow snake." Particularly telling was the description of Khomeinism as the "yellow revolution."[94]

But the "Aflaqite Saddam" distinctly Islamized the attack. It is important to recall the expression, *fi sabil Allah*, in the path of God. Obviously, Aflaq's work, *Fi Sabil al-Ba'th*, drew consciously on the expression. Although Islam had not been eclipsed, in Aflaq's view, it had been transcended by the next "prime mover," pan-Arabism. But now, in a moment of political irony, exigencies of war compelled Saddam to return more pointedly to *sabil Allah*. Thus, Khomeini was not just another Hitler. He was a "fire-worshipping Persian" (a reference to Zoroastrianism) and a heretic, an infidel, a blasphemer. Using Quranic terms to castigate their foe, the Iraqis described Khomeini as *hubal* and *taghut*.[95] Both terms refer to idols, and the latter is used in the Quran explicitly of Satan (4:60, 67).[96] And Islam came first to the Arabs, in any event. "A Muslim who hates the Arabs cannot be a Muslim," declared Saddam, "because the Arabs are the leading force of Islam as they are of all heavenly religions."[97]

The government did more than castigate the Iranians in Islamic terms; its own self-descriptions and actions increasingly took on Islamic coloration. Early on, the RCC began using the *bismallah* to preface its communiqués, as did the military and other government publications.[98] In a January 1982 article in the party newspaper, *al-Thawra*, the regime specifically addressed the Iranians, saying:

> We tell you that Iraq is a true Islamic state, and the people of Iraq, as well as its leaders, believe in God and in the teachings of Islam as a religion and a heritage. Indeed President Husayn's regular visits to the holy shrines and his continuous efforts to provide for these shrines is a clear proof of his deep and unequivocal belief in the glorious message of Islam. Moreover, Iraq's recent donation for the purpose of building a new mosque in Yugoslavia is a living manifestation of Iraq's efforts to spread the values of Islam all over the world.[99]

Both Saddam and the media began referring to the war as jihad, and Saddam became known as *mujahid* (one who conducts jihad), a title he bestowed on other Iraqis in the war effort.[100] Quranic citations also regularly appeared in various media, practices that increased in 1986 and thereafter with the loss of al-Faw in February. To reinforce the point of these Islamic allusions, Saddam's visit to Saudi Arabia in December 1986 to bolster gulf Arab support at a dark time in the war included a rather public pilgrimage to Mecca.[101] The Iraqi regime named or redesignated standing regular and popular military units with Islamic titles or with the names of Mesopotamian figures.

For instance, the Special First Corps became the *quwwaat Allahu akbar* ("forces of God the most great"). Other unit names included "Hammurabi," "Nebuchadnezzar," and "Gilgamesh" to recall moments of Mesopotamian triumph. Detachments named "Caliph al-Ma'mun" and "Caliph Abu Ja'far al-Mansur" alluded to the Islamic caliphate under the Abbasids. The "Imam Husayn" unit was one of several intended to appeal to the Shi'a.[102] Additionally, specific operations were given Islamic names, just as the Iranians numbered their offensives sequentially, i.e., Karbala 1, Karbala 2, etc.[103] The Iraqis designated the campaign to retake al-Faw *Ramadan mubarak*, "[the] blessed [month] Ramadan."[104]

The brutal suppression of the Kurds in 1988 similarly took an Islamic name. The Anfal Operations were named for a chapter of the Quran (sura eight).[105] The chapter recounts the Battle of Badr in 624, a turning point in Islamic history when the badly outnumbered forces of Muhammad defeated the superior Meccans. The cynicism and contempt of the Ba'thist regime's rhetorical manipulation of Islamic symbols can be measured by looking at the specific verses the regime referred to. "[I]n the two armies / that met in combat / one was fighting in the cause / of God, the other / resisting God" (3:13). "It is not ye who / slew them; it was God" (8:17). The Quran also points out that a thousand angels came to the aid of Muhammad's beleaguered army (8:9). In keeping with the imagery, the Iraqis named the units that conducted the Anfal Operations *quwwaat Badr*, the forces of Badr.

Even weaponry took on Islamic names.[106] Developing its own variant of the Soviet's Scud-B missile, Iraq produced the 600 km-range al-Hussein. Named for the third Shi'a imam, this missile was ready for use in 1988, and was the primary Iraqi weapon in the "war of the cities" that year. It had the added bonus of using Saddam's patronym. More darkly, the regime was using a Shi'i-named missile to attack a Shi'i regime. In 1988 the Iraqis also developed the al-Abbas, named for the third imam's brother. Prior to its first use, the missile was renamed al-Hijara, meaning "the stones"; the name drew an explicit connection with the "children of the stones," the youth engaged in the Palestinian intifada.[107] The Iraqis used this missile and the al-Hussein in launches against Saudi Arabia and Israel in 1991.

Additionally, the Iraqis developed a satellite launch vehicle which they designated "Tammuz," an Akkadian god who symbolized death and rebirth. ("Tammuz" is also the also the Arabic name of the month in which the Ba'th revolution occurred in Iraq.) *Al-Thawra*, the party daily, editorialized, "Tammuz of the sacrifice and benevolence and revolution . . . from Ishtar's Tammuz to our glorious, contemporary Tammuz. . . . [This missile] is a new ray of light beaming, shining, from our leader's forehead . . . to the whole world."[108]

But of the steps the regime took, none could be more important than selecting "al-Qadisiyya" as its controlling metaphor for the conflict with Iran. It was more than simply a historical reference. Qadisiyya was the site, in 636, of one of the most important battles ever in the Middle East, that in which the Arab-Islamic army, although outnumbered six to one, defeated the Persian Sassanid army. Thus, "Qadisiyya" represented several things: the vindication of the prophet Muhammad's message, the triumph of the few over the many, the ineluctable spread of Islam, the victory of the Arabs over those who were culturally other. In this modern battle of the maximalists, a battle between Persians and Arabs in which *shu'ubism* was the most derogatory epithet, Saddam could hardly have improved on the selection. Iraq had used it prior to the war when the Iranians, following the revolution, rebuffed Saddam's initial offer of an olive branch. As relations deteriorated, the president returned to the trope. For instance, following the attack on Aziz at Mustansiriya University in April 1980, Saddam broadcast:

We [declare] by God, by God, by God and in the name of every particle of earth in Iraq, that the pure blood that was shed [here] will not go in vain. In your name, brothers, and on behalf of the Iraqis and Arabs everywhere, we tell those cowards and dwarfs who try to avenge al-Qadisiyya that the spirit of al-Qadisiyya as well as the blood and honor of the people of al-Qadisiyya who carried the message on their spearheads are greater than their attempts.[109]

During the war, the Iraqis renamed the (now daily) military newspaper as *al-Qadisiyya* to recall the battle, and the Baghdad daily *al-Jumhuriyya* began printing "Qadisiyyat Saddam" (Saddam's Qadisiyya) at the top of each page.[110] More importantly, the Iraqis were, at the same time, working on a movie by that name. Under the supervision of Izzat Ibrahim, the RCC's second in command, the film anticipated the Iraqi invasion that would come later that year. "We are most certainly moving toward decisive battles," Ibrahim promised. "Our present position forces upon us decisive battles against the enemies so as to open the road leading to the renewal of our glory and our civilization."[111] The words of the aging Khomeini in July 1988 are a fitting reflection on the clash between the maximalists at this second Qadisiyya and on his bitterly acceding to a cease-fire with the Ba'thist-*cum*-instrumental Islamic leader. "Happy are those who have departed through martyrdom. Happy are those who have lost their lives in this convoy of light. Unhappy am I that I still survive and have drunk the poisoned chalice."[112] And Saddam? There was an arch to be built, an "arch to victory and a symbol to this Qadisiyya [where] brave Iraqis have recorded the most legendary exploits in their defense of their land and holy beliefs against the Persian enemy."

## THE PROTEAN PRESIDENT AND REASONS OF SELF

It is important to see that the regime manipulated religious symbols for political ends. It is more important, however, to understand how one man manipulated a regime for his own ends. Although there is no attempt made here to outline a psychological profile of Saddam, his presidential praxis and discourse do, in the composite, offer some significant suggestions of his character.[113] Clifford Geertz has written of "cultural performances," those elaborate and public rituals where "a broad range of moods and motivations on the one hand and of metaphysical conceptions on the other are caught up [and thus] shape the spiritual consciousness of a people."[114] Especially since 1979, cultural performances—whether parades or literature or art or public executions—have abounded in Iraq, and the president has stood at the center of them. Indeed, it appears Saddam has, in a self-fulfilling way, taken on the challenge of one of his mentors, Gamal Abdul Nasser. In his apologia, Nasser (or his ghost writer Heikal) said in a rather histrionic way, "History is . . . charged with great heroic roles which do not find actors to play them on the stage. I do not know why I always imagine that *in this region in which we live there is a role wandering aimlessly about seeking an actor to play it.*"[115]

The idea of a "role" is one to which Saddam has recurred often, both for himself and for the people he leads. For instance, Saddam wrote that he "*plays the role* of leader" in his nation's journey.[116] Three months before invading Iran, Saddam addressed army officers,

The Iraqi people turned in the shadow of the July 17 revolution into one cell, one tree . . . stretching from Zakhu to al-Faw. . . . It is essential that we wrest the historical opportunity [to play] *the historical role performed by our grandfathers* in the service of the nation and humanity.[117]

And how carefully the role has been constructed. Makiya's observation is precisely on point:

To be such a Leader [as Saddam], the part must be well acted out. Authority is not in the form of "pure" Weberian charisma, rooted in personal attributes like extraordinary heroism or revelatory powers; it is rehearsed, staged, and elaborately organized. . . . The leader's image . . . must be visible, solid, and overpowering.[118]

This leader's image begins with a birth legend. Saddam's semiofficial biographer and virtual hagiographer, Amir Iskander, described the president's birth.[119] Coming when the Arab nation was at its nadir, "a new star appeared to herald a new time of travail. The moment of awakening had come. It was at that very moment in Arab history that Saddam Hussein was born." At this point, the echoes are not really Islamic, which would not have served, because Sunni Islam admits of no apotheosis. Rather, the tone is messianic. In quasi-Christological terms, Iskander continued: "His birth in 1937 was not a joyful occasion, and no roses or aromatic petals bedecked his cradle." Born into the home of a simple, poor woman (his father died before the son's birth), Saddam faced a difficult childhood. Yet despite being of peasant stock, the biographer writes (now emphasizing Islam), Saddam was descended from line running back "to the noblest family of all, whose greatest scion was the Imam Ali bin abi Talib." Similarly, Muhammad al-Hallab, an Iraqi poet wrote in 1986 of this natal scene:

> Since a thousand years or more
> Time expected the new birth
> Till April brought [Saddam's birthday]
> [And] the new dawn . . .
> Good tidings
> The baby is born
> The daring knight . . .
> And this is a day of festivity.[120]

As a child, Saddam (Iskander tells us) would readily sacrifice for friends. Without hesitation he would give his jacket to a playmate who had only a tattered one, for he "remember[ed], even at that early age, the words of Christ: 'Whosoever hath two, let him give one of them to him who hath none'."

A star. Noble lineage. Birth in poverty at a critical juncture in his people's history. Greatness to come. Deliverance of his fellows through generous self-sacrifice. All of this is to be found in Iskander, in Matar, and in numerous other Iraqi writers. Moreover, the stories and pictures that came later, following his accession to the presidency, whether in the biographies, magazines, newspapers, or—quite importantly—on billboards, presented a robust image of Saddam the everyman. He was variously presented in the garb of a military leader, a pious Muslim, a Kurd, and a peasant. He was shown as the leader of the Arab world and as the leader of the nonaligned. Saddam was all things to his people, and more. He fulfilled the boast of *l'état c'est moi* in a way Versailles had not anticipated.

Because his control of the public media was total, this picture of a protean president, one who can be all things to all his people, became ubiquitous and inescapable. In fact, in 1969 (within a year after the revolution) the government made the media *al-sultat al-rabia*, the "fourth power (or branch)" of government.[121] Using Orwellian propaganda, the government (and behind it, Saddam) was powerfully able to bestow meaning. As Ofra Bengio perceptively writes in the introduction to her work on Iraqi political discourse, "Saddam Husayn and his regime sought to manipulate language, tradition, and Islam in order to shape Iraqis' minds, mobilize them for his own political purposes, and portray a picture of virtual reality that was a far cry from the genuine one."[122] An approving translator of Saddam offers an unusual confirmation. Introducing a series of the (then) vice president's speeches, Khalid Kishtainy writes:

[T]he translator was soon struck by a new problem. Saddam Hussein does not lean heavily on the conventional style of Arabic political oratory. . . . [T]he translator was simply puzzled by a novel use of simple words delivered in a cool and detached tone. . . . As this translator puzzled over Saddam's new verbal coinage, a certain picture started to take shape before his eyes. Most of these words have something in common which conjures a world of dynamic movement; and this is the world of Saddam Hussein, with masira [march] as its emblem. . . . What Iraq needed most were the qualities of an ordered brain, a mathematical mind and a shrewd foresight. . . . Here is a mass leader who uses an elitist language to instill order, calculation and prudence into the volatile mind of the Iraqi masses.[123]

Saddam's lexicography became the order of the day. In 1988 the *Political Dictionary of Saddam Hussein* appeared, followed by *The Complete Writings of Saddam Hussein* a year later. The dictionary contains five hundred entries, select political expressions carefully explicated by the poet Muhammad Salih 'abd al-Rida; the writings fill eighteen volumes. The sayings of Saddam appeared on newspaper mastheads, and writers in various genres appropriated his words. In effect, this was discourse monopoly, a condition in which the regime controlled all levels of information and decided, as well, what that information signified.[124]

Saddam enjoyed placing himself in illustrious historical company. In an interview shortly after coming to power, he reflected on figures of Arab history from whom he drew special inspiration.

Nebuchadnezzar stirs in me everything relating to pre-Islamic ancient history. . . . [He] was, after all, an Arab from Iraq, albeit ancient Iraq. Nebuchadnezzar was the one who brought the bound Jewish slaves from Palestine. . . . Saladin [was] . . . of the same caliber, but with the spirit of Islam in him. He was a Muslim Iraqi. . . . He was able to make use of the nation's spirit; he breathed life into it, united it, and gave it one aim and purpose, and thus won a brilliant victory over the Crusaders.[125]

When asked which contemporary philosophers and statesmen most influenced him, Saddam named Lenin, de Gaulle, and Nasser; Lenin as a thinker, and the latter two as "personalities."[126]

But Saddam was more than his heroes. His totalizing inclinations demanded that he be seen as father of the country, and in a realm of discourse monopoly, the idea of Saddam as father takes on pernicious new meaning. For instance, in his 1979 publication *hawla kitabat al-tarikh* (*On the Writing of History*), Saddam wrote, "A leader is the son and the father of his people at the same time. He is the son of his society as it was originally constituted, and its father in its journey in which he plays the role of leader."[127] Speaking in 1981, Saddam pointed out in a speech that he had received numerous letters that addressed him as "our father and begetter." More popularly, the regime had seen the use of the expression *baba Saddam*, a diminutive form of *aba Saddam* and meaning "papa Saddam."[128] And like King Arthur traveling in disguise to gauge the attitudes of England's commoners, so the ubiquitous father Saddam visited the ordinary people of Iraq. A regular television program featured the president doing just that, going into simple homes, enjoying simple hospitality. The "unsuspecting hosts" would answer his indirect queries about himself and his policies with lavish praise. Only then would the bountiful father of his people reveal himself.[129]

Of course as father, Saddam would seek to bring forth a new people. Iraq, in the president's discourse, already occupied a special place, one that embraced the millennia. In an April 1980 speech, Saddam reflected:

If you read the history of the nation [here, Iraq], you will find that it was either a shining light leading the way, or that it was trampled under the feet of invading armies. Throughout its history, it has either been in the forefront of civilization, of leadership and history, and of the Arab nation, or it has been overwhelmed by tyranny. This is because Iraq's people have special characteristics; its people are the people of the mountains and the peaks, not of the plains and valleys.[130]

Now, as the new star that had appeared in a time of travail, Saddam would not only restore the peoples' fortunes in a new resurrection (hence, a "ba'th"), but also make them anew through the party. In 1974 on the twenty-seventh anniversary of the founding of the Ba'th, Saddam addressed Arab and foreign journalists on a range of issues (the recent cabinet reshuffle, the National Front, Kurdish autonomy, oil nationalization, etc.) Already advancing in power, he assured them with an air of omniscience,

Without any exaggeration, all that may be taking place or that you may be hearing about was included in our calculations years ago, and not just months ago. . . . We know and have learned a great deal. On this basis we have become accustomed to forecasting many developments, if not all, in advance. I can definitely confirm that nothing has taken us by surprise.

He then spoke of a part of the plan:

When our people realize that this government represents their present and strategic interests and that the men responsible for this administration (represented in the various organizations of which the most important is the Ba'th party) are the men who are trying hardest . . . to build up the new society which achieves the aspirations of all Iraqis, they cannot be deceived by what was said and heard in the past. *The man of Iraq is now a new man.* It may not be that everyone in Iraq is the "homo sapiens" of the future, but he is certainly a new man who has evolved from ancient man in every respect. This is our achievement.[131]

In 1980 he declared Ba'thism to be more than merely economic socialism. It also aims, he said, at "creating a new man, and satisfying [both] his spiritual and material needs."[132] That idea, "creating a new man," became paradigmatic. By purges and deportations, by recapitulations of the past, *abu-l-Iraq al-jaheed* (father of the new Iraq) would fashion his nation. That process, of course, would extend to children through Ba'thist youth organizations and the schools. Saddam wanted children who would carry on the revolution and whose first loyalty would be statist, not familial. For instance, as vice president, he declared in 1977:

To prevent the father and mother dominating the household with backwardness, we must make the [child] radiate internally to expel it. Some fathers have slipped away from us for various reasons, but the small boy is in our hands, and *we must transform him* into an interactive radiating center inside the family through all the hours that he spends with his parents to change their condition for the better. . . . You must place in every corner a son of the revolution, with a trustworthy eye and a firm mind that receives its instructions from the responsible center of the revolution.[133]

But Saddam did more. At times, it seems, he not only worked to constitute a country; he was, at least in his view, constitutive *of* that new country. Citing again the interview with Diane Sawyer noted in Chapter Two, the president stated, shortly before invading Kuwait,

As for Saddam Hussein, he is to be found *in every quantity of milk* provided to children and *in every clean new jacket* worn by an Iraqi. . . . Consequently the Iraqis put up [portraits of me]. . . . If we were to remove their portraits, we would hurt their feelings.[134]

Indeed, not wishing to hurt Iraqi feelings, Saddam graciously patronized the proliferation of all manner of literature and art that celebrated his centrality and, indeed, his "in-forming" of the people. For instance, writing in 1987, the poet Ghazay Dir' al-Ta'i offered these words in a song for children:

> We are Iraq and its name is Saddam
> We are love and its name is Saddam
> We are a people and its name is Saddam
> We are the Ba'th and its name is Saddam[135]

Since his ascendance in 1979, the visual arts have echoed the print media and literature in depicting the centrality of Saddam and making his image "visible, solid, and overpowering." Naturally, art in the 1980s often carried war themes celebrating Saddam as a glorious military leader.[136] He is shown integrated into specific battles (e.g., the first Qadisiyya) and as the leader of troops from ancient history: Babylonians and Sumerians alike follow him to the front.

Other pictures stressed his link with the past quite apart from war, and often as builder. In one painting, he is shown collaborating with King Nebuchadnezzar to complete a wall. A smiling Saddam lays the last brick in place, assisted by the ancient ruler. In the space of a gated arch in the wall (the king stands on the ground in the forefront; Saddam, atop the wall) appear the words, "From Nebuchadnezzar to Saddam Hussein, Babil rises anew." In other pictures he does not merely collaborate but is the sole figure. For instance, in one picture combining personalities, he is shown in traditional Arab dress, riding a white horse, reminiscent of Ali. But held aloft in his right hand is the flame of the Ba'th revolution rather than a sword. And before him, rising from the earth in a new spring, is a figure that represents Tammuz. Pre-Islamic and Islamic motifs are united with the true scion of Ba'thism; Saddam is all these.

Yet even more telling is a drawing by Mahmud Hamad that appeared in *al-Thawra* in April 1987. It features a map showing the countries of the Arab League, although without any borders demarcated. All save one are parched, the ground cracked. The one lush country, unsurprisingly, is Iraq, which is dense with date palms. A map of Iraq rises vertically as backdrop. On Iraq's eastern flank are guns pointing at Iran, as Iraq guards the Arab world's eastern gate. And in the center are two figures: Saddam and a little girl who arises, as it were, from the center of the Arab earth. Her hands are outstretched toward the maximum benefactor. Saddam's back is to the Iranian enemy, an indication of his confidence in the eventual outcome of the second Qadisiyya. The beaming president faces the little girl, and water pours from his hands for her to drink. Of all the images Iraq's artists used, this, perhaps, came closest to the president's vision of himself and summed up his reasons of self. Saddam was not merely a new leader for the sere Arab world—he was its life and hope.[137]

The reality of present-day Iraq, however, offered little life or hope. Ultimately, nothing stood between the Iraqi man Saddam was re-creating and Saddam himself, no multilayered civil society to cushion the blows of the Tikriti leviathan.[138] It was a state in which every crime could be construed as a *lèse majesté*; for if, ultimately, Saddam was the state, every crime was against his person. In this state, for both *raisons d'état* and reasons of self, Saddam was free to manipulate the full panoply of religious symbols to achieve ends he had designed. Any constraints Saddam felt about manipulating religion seem to have been practical only, not moral. That, perhaps, was the real message of the August 1989 parade to dedicate the victory arches of the new Qadisiyya. Saddam had unhesitatingly adopted any persona (and multiple personas simultaneously), appealed to any era in history, and made himself its embodiment, if doing so served to build the state and advance his power.

Religion fell within that purview. Islam, the president had found, especially during the exigencies of an eight-year war with Iran, could address the political and social infirmities of secular Ba'thism. When Saddam employed religious symbols in conjunction with his invasion of Kuwait, he simply continued a policy with which he had been experimenting for a decade. But in the summer of 1990, the use of religion was also elevated to a jihad for Palestine, for poorer Arab states, for the *dar al-Islam* ("house of peace"). The swords of the victory arch might point to Israel and Iran, but the parade route now seemed to lead toward Kuwait, and it would do so as a new *sabil Allah*.

*If oil is the most important thing for you, Jerusalem is the most important thing for us.*
SADDAM, DECEMBER 1990

*If [the Iraqis] talk of religion, our country is one of those who adheres most to this great . . . religion and we do not, as they do, don the garb of religion only in times of crisis.*
HOSNI MUBARAK, SEPTEMBER 1990

*We Warned You Frankenstein Would Torment His Own Creators*
TITLE OF AN IRANIAN NEWS AGENCY COMMENTARY,
AUGUST 1990[1]

# 5 | FI SABIL ALLAH
IRAQ AND THE EMPLOYMENT OF
ISLAM IN THE INVASION OF KUWAIT

At 2:11 P.M., gulf time, on the day after the Iraqi invasion, Kuwaiti radio made a brief, poignant appeal: "In the Name of God, the compassionate, the merciful. This is Kuwait. O Arabs, O brothers, O beloved brothers, O Muslims, your brothers in Kuwait are appealing to you. Hurry to their aid." With that, the transmission ceased, the last of thirty-one hours of desperate broadcasts. But the words were not only poignant; they carried a special irony. In its broadcasts, Kuwait made repeated pleas to all who might be listening to come to its aid against the "Tatars" who were "wreaking putridity" in their peaceful country, against an "invader who sings the praises of Arabism and then murders it." Declaring that there was "nothing save Arabism in our blood and Islam in our hearts," Kuwaitis appealed to Arab nationalism, an Arab sense of dignity and honor, Islam, humanitarianism—anything that might move the world community to help. This was an appeal Kuwait could make to other Arabs in particular because the country had "never abandoned its pan-Arab duties." Kuwait proclaimed: "[T]he Arab people of Kuwait will remain free and the master of its own land; our faith in God, Islam, Arabism, and our land is the motive that makes us protect our land and dignity. We will die and Kuwait will live. God is greater than the aggressor." And in the face of this onslaught, Kuwait appealed to its own people to "stand together against the Iraqi invasion. . . . The hour for jihad has come . . . we will make the aggressors drink from the glass of death."[2]

The irony is this: the Iraqis had used precisely the same words to justify what seemed unjustifiable. It had called the Iranians "Tatars" during their eight-year war, and it would use the same term to refer to the coalition forces that began to deploy to Saudi Arabia on 7 August. Iraq claimed that dignity and honor demanded Arabs not form alliances with non-Arabs against a fellow Arab state, and it described the Americans as invaders who defiled the land. Its "merger" with Kuwait, Iraq would claim, was its inescapable pan-Arab duty, necessary to reverse a geopolitical disfigurement imposed by the wealthy West. Most particularly, Iraq repeatedly appealed to Muslims to conduct jihad alongside her against the infidels. Not long before the coalition forces initiated the one hundred-hour ground war, and in an almost eerie bookend to the appeals made by the Kuwaitis six months before, Iraqi radio broadcast a statement of the usually secular Ba'th party:

In the name of God, the Merciful, the Compassionate. To the struggler Ba'thists everywhere; to all the faithful, pan-Arab and nationalist powers throughout the Arab world; to the struggling masses of our Arab nation and faithful Muslims wherever they are; to free, honorable, and benevolent men of the world. . . . [S]upport the people of Iraq; and provide it with volunteers, money, food, and medicine. . . . [L]et Arabs, Muslims, and all honorable people of the world declare that they will carry out jihad, sacrificing themselves and their resources, for Iraq . . . and [that they will] fight the . . . imperialist camp of the infidel.[3]

Such appeals to jihad, and to Islam more generally, permeated the public political discourse of the Iraqis. But it was not simply a manufactured language, even if Iraq used it instrumentally. Islam had become the rhetorical coin of the realm, one to which Kuwaitis and Iraqis and others would turn in their hours of need. "What was clear," John Voll writes, "was that Islam had become one of the most important bases of *normal* as well as revolutionary political discourse in the region" in the early 1990s.[4] So it had, and what invested the religious terminology with its potency was the gulf crisis itself. In that crisis, Saddam employed a shared language, one with profound regional and transregional resonance, and he sought to turn it to his advantage.

Eickelman and Piscatori address precisely this point. In writing of the "politics of language" in the Islamic world, they describe "the variable *usage* of language, [which suggests] that the utility of Islamic terminology to both rulers and opponents is enhanced in times of upheaval and stress. It also depicts an Islamic language that is more than simply a vocabulary. In addition to socially defined words, this language is made up of both symbols and mediators—those who modify and rework the symbols in specific circumstances." Thus, they write, "Words such as *jihad* do not automatically engender social and political action, but they acquire specific meanings in the context in which they are applied." As they point out, the arrival of "infidel" troops in the Arabian peninsula provided such a context.[5] In short, war gave a politicized Islam its effective setting. Saddam, the "mediator," took full advantage of that.

What emerges from an analysis of a vast array of examples, from both Iraqi public political discourse and specific symbolic actions during the gulf crisis, is the picture of a regime that quite consciously, very skillfully, interwove Islam into its wartime strategies. The past is prologue, and all the experience the Iraqis gained from appealing to religion in the Iran-Iraq War would be summoned during the invasion of Kuwait. On examination, Saddam's use of Islam proves considerably more nuanced and carefully coordinated than Western media have described. In fact, other regimes in the region recognized the alarming potency of Saddam's Islamic message, a recognition described in the following chapter. It was this use of Islam, and especially the fusion of Islam with pan-Arab themes, that constituted the substantive heart of what Chapter One termed Saddam's "Other Gulf War." This chapter will analyze how the Iraqis conducted that other war, leaving *sabil al-Ba'th* for *sabil Allah*.

## WAR BEFORE WAR

Well before the invasion on 2 August, Iraq had been engaged in its own Arab cold war, in Malcolm Kerr's memorable phrase. Authoritarian regimes cannot afford to be long without enemies if they are to justify repressive measures, and Iraq was no exception. In early 1990, however, Iraq set about changing the face of the enemy. The way in which it did so was an important indication (a rehearsal, really) of how Iraq would employ Islam later in the year and one possible sign that plans for invading Kuwait were already underway.[6] On 5 January 1990 (a Friday, in fact, the day of prayer) Iraq made a very public overture to the erstwhile "fire-worshipping Persians," the "Tatars of the East." Iraq appealed to Iran for their two countries to compose their differences as *Muslim* neighbors," a rapprochement that would include unimpeded access to each other's Shiʿa holy sites.[7] The Iranians were unimpressed. They found the proposals to be only a reiteration of old ones in new wrapping. In their view, Saddam was simply inhibiting the work of the UN Security Council, offering a smoke screen while avoiding the most critical demands of UN Security Council Resolution 598. And, quite understandably, they found Saddam's motives and Islamic coloration suspicious. This was, they said, a "gimmick," remarking that Saddam had become "pious overnight."[8] But they did not close the door altogether, and Saddam persisted in efforts at reconciliation.

In April, the Iraqi president began a letter-writing campaign with his Iranian counterpart, Ali-Akbar Rafsanjani.[9] Saddam carefully adopted explicitly religious terminology. In his initial letter (21 April), the president recast the world. The real enemy to both, he said, came from Zionism, the superpowers, and opportunists, not each other. Saddam proposed meeting in order to prepare for opposing the Zionist regime and liberating Palestine. The president suggested they meet the second day of *eid al fitr* in "revered Mecca, the *qibla* of Muslims and the ancient household which our lord Abraham (peace be upon him) constructed." Saddam signed himself, as he would elsewhere, as *abd-Allah*, the "worshipper" (or slave) of God. In a coordinated move, Arafat wrote Rafsanjani the next day, urging a constructive response to Saddam's proposals in light of the momentous conditions that faced both the Islamic umma and the Arab umma. Arafat was especially concerned about Jewish immigration that, he averred, was designed "solely to suppress the blessed Intifada of the *mujahid* Palestinian nation."[10]

Rafsanjani seemed unimpressed. Writing back on 2 May, the Iranian leader reminded Saddam that Iraq had imposed a war that squandered resources better used in the "struggle against blasphemy and atheism." He also gave little support to a meeting at the head-of-state level as Saddam wanted. Rafsanjani's next letter (18 June) also rebuffed Saddam. He challenged the idea that it was the "Arab umma," and not simply Saddam's personal cause, that had opposed Iran in the eight-year war. He further resisted the Iraqi's posturing as "custodian of Palestinian affairs."

Saddam was clearly distraught. He complained in his letter of 19 May that the Iranian had written a letter with double meanings and a severe ending. He was especially bothered by Rafsanjani's having given a religious affront. To Saddam's *as-salaamu aleykum* (peace be with you), Rafsanjani had failed to give the appropriate response, *wa aleykum as-salaam* (and with you the peace). Instead, he had replied, "and peace is on him who follows the guidance," a response one would give to a non-Muslim. But Saddam could not afford to seem offended. As the end of July approached and his troops were massing on the border of Kuwait, Saddam wrote again (30 July), obviously still needing to reduce his enemies by one.[11] Saddam wished to present a "new proposal," one that would quickly implement the substantive points of Security Council Resolution 598. He warned, at the same time, of outside "satanic forces who are searching in the dark," who might "ignite the fire of war" between the two countries. The day after the invasion, Saddam wrote once more, urging a speedy peace between Iraq and Iran and hoping the latter would not be drawn into conflict because of the "matter of Kuwait."[12]

The postinvasion results of the correspondence will be addressed later; what is noted here is the strategy involved. The Saddam-Rafsanjani exchange in the period between the gulf wars is illuminating because it shows the concern of the Iraqi regime with keeping its own country on a war footing, an orientation that served the double duty of averting attention from domestic problems while preparing for the next adventure.[13] As it happened, the Iraqis simply exchanged devils. Imperialists and Zionists, although not new enemies, took the place of those theretofore demonized, who in turn became the sought-after ally. More particularly, the letters indicate the increasing propensity of the Iraqis to employ Islam, as Michael Hudson puts it, in the continued "search for legitimacy." As the Ba'thist Iraqis had turned to religion in the war with Iran, so they did now in the war before the war, and would do so again when they invaded Kuwait in August. Iraq used religion to try to enlist new friends and excoriate others and to render the world in starkly categorical terms. More especially, religion would be fused with the mandates of pan-Arabism and the imperatives of Jerusalem, an effort implicit in the Saddam-Rafsanjani exchange and quite explicit in the crisis in Kuwait.

The regime pursued and reinforced these strategies in other ways during the spring of 1990. Particularly significant is that the frequency and stridency of verbal attacks on Israel markedly increased after a period of relative (but not total) quiescence. Ofra Bengio observes,

After a decade of relative aloofness from the Arab-Israeli conflict, Iraq made it the focus of its rhetoric, a change that was both quantitative and qualitative. President Husayn himself led the campaign, which surpassed all previous Ba'th campaigns in its intensity and militancy. There was a return to slogans that had long been subdued, such as liberating Palestine and destroying Israel.[14]

In February, Saddam had promised, "[T]he banners of justice shall fly over holy Jerusalem." Late the next month, Saddam assured his listeners in a speech that Jerusalem could be liberated if Arabs were determined and exercised faith in God. Iraq, he declared, which never tired of war, would lead in the effort.[15] In April, of course, Saddam delivered his famous fire speech, threatening Israel. The call was important, per se, but not unique; it simply took its place in the concatenation of threats that had begun in January and been taken up in the Rafsanjani correspondence.

This vigorous readoption of Zionism as an enemy also enabled Saddam and Arafat to make common cause with the strongly evocative symbol of Jerusalem. Both had something the other needed. The alliance with Saddam provided Arafat a boost in prestige at a time when the intifada was flagging and his effectiveness was being questioned. Now, Arafat had something tangible to offer his people in the seemingly unending struggle for recognition. Here was strength that gave some parity with Israel. For instance, in a speech on 11 April marking the beginning of the thirtieth month of the uprising, Arafat claimed, "The Abid missile was presented as a gift from Saddam Husayn, his army, and people to the struggling people of Palestine."[16] And for Saddam, reiteration of support for the Palestinians was a return to one of the chief perennial symbols of pan-Arab legitimation. For instance, speaking that April on the occasion of the forty-third anniversary of the founding of the Ba'th, Saddam declared,

From the beginning, there has been historical and theoretical unity between the struggle for unity and the principles of Arab nationalism on the one hand and the struggle for the liberation of Palestine on the other. The Ba'thists have been loyal to these principles and to this unity or association. They will continue on the same path and lead the Arabs with militant action.[17]

But the congruence of interests was especially fortunate because it coupled political aspirations and explicit Islamic goals at a time when appeals to religion were important to both leaders. Arafat's letter to Rafsanjani on 22 April supporting Saddam reflects that. In referring to the "*mujahid* Palestinian nation," Arafat was realigning himself politically and trying to outflank the Islamists in the territories, especially regarding directing the activities of the intifada.[18] That effort had been underway for some time. It cannot be coincidental that the PLO read its "declaration of independence" three months after Hamas announced its charter in August 1988. Hamas had staked out a strong position:

The Islamic Resistance Movement believes that the land of Palestine is an Islamic *waqf* consecrated for future Moslem generations until Judgment Day. It, or any part of it, should not be squandered: it, or any part of it, should not be given up. . . . *There is no solution for the Palestinian question except through jihad.* Initiatives, proposals, and international conferences are all a waste of time and vain endeavors.[19]

Three months later at the Palais de Nations in Algiers, Arafat read the PLO declaration.[20] Although it does not contain the density of religious references that the Hamas charter does, it does seek to offer something other than a purely secular document. Prefaced with the bismallah and concluding with a Quranic verse (3:26), the declaration speaks of "the land of heavenly messages to mankind," then "declares in the name of God and in the name of the Palestinian Arab people the birth of the state of Palestine on our Palestinian soil with Holy Jerusalem as its capital." Thus, writing to Rafsanjani about a "*mujahid* nation" in 1990 comported with Arafat's efforts over the previous year and a half.

In Saddam's case, the multivalent nature of "Jerusalem" allowed him to fuse a long-standing goal of pan-Arabism and secular Ba'thism (deliverance of the Arab Palestinians) with a goal of Islam, especially after the *nakba* (disaster) of 1967: reclaiming the first *qibla*, Islam's third-holiest site after Mecca and Medina.[21] Saddam's address to the "Arab Popular Conference for Solidarity with Iraq," which met in early May, is representative. The president warned darkly,

The holy City of Jerusalem is being subjected to a wide-ranging plot to annex the holy city, change its character, Judaise it, expel its original Arab inhabitants and replace them with alien immigrants and encroach on Islamic and Christian holy places, especially Al-Aqsa Mosque and the Church of the Holy Sepulchre, which is being done by the Zionist occupation authorities.[22]

The important Arab League meeting in late May in Baghdad underscored this pan-Arab attention to Jerusalem. Eickelman and Piscatori's observation that words gain specific meaning in context is pertinent here. Prime Minister Yitzhak Shamir's remarks in January about a big Israel (which the U.S. State Department termed "not helpful"); continuing Soviet Jewish immigration; the U.S. Congress's nonbinding resolution favoring Jerusalem as the capital of Israel (passed by the Senate on 22 March and the House on 24 April); and the shooting of Palestinian laborers by an Israeli soldier on 20 May all provided a particularly energizing context for the Arab League meeting. It should also be noted that Saddam used the meeting to expand his list of enemies. Whereas the Americans and the Israelis might constitute the enemy without, there were enemies within: the "deviants" who followed their own "whims and policies," especially in oil production policies.

Even more telling was the convening of the Popular Islamic Conference the next month in Baghdad.[23] When it opened on 16 June, Izzat Ibrahim, vice chairman of the RCC addressed seven hundred Islamic conferees from some seventy countries.[24] The aim of the conference was to "draw up a unified plan for confronting the challenges and conspiracies targeting Iraq in particular and the Arab nation and Muslims in general." Saddam addressed the three-day conference at its close.[25] In his presentation, the president drew together themes to which he had alluded all during the spring and from which he would not deviate during the course of the Gulf War. Opening with the bismallah, Saddam welcomed the "scholars of the nation of Islam" to "your country." Almost immediately he segued to "usurped Palestine" and "humiliated Jerusalem," combining political and Islamic dimensions. All Muslims are the "kinsfolk of Jerusalem," and in the face of continued Knesset declarations that Jerusalem is Israel's eternal capital, Arabs and Muslims would go to war over the issue. Of special importance here, Saddam laid out his views on the connection of Islam and Arabism and on the primacy of Arabs among Muslims generally. He merits quoting at length here because he would advance this connection throughout the coming war.

> The Arabs and Islam are an integral one; thus if the Arabs become weak, Islam will follow suit. Similarly, if the Arabs rise up—and this will not happen unless they heed the honorable concepts of Islam—Muslims in all parts of the earth will rise up and increase in dignity. . . . Arabism is at the service of man and Arabism is at the service of Muslims. The Arab nation is part of the Islamic nation. . . . Almighty God granted the Arabs a great honor when He revealed the Koran in Arabic and made Arabic the language of Paradise. . . . I believe that Arab Muslims will on doomsday be held to higher standards than non-Arab Muslims. . . . Since the Arabs were entrusted with the [Islamic] message, they have moral and social duties in addition to other practical sides. . . . When the Arabs neglect their duties, they will be defeated.

But Saddam did not restrict his "Arabism and Islam" message to religious conventions. Speaking in his capacity as his country's party leader eight days later, Saddam addressed a pan-Arab symposium on the thinking of Michel Aflaq.[26] At points, Saddam sounded like an unreconstructed Baʿthist, using the old "scientific" terminology of "correct thinking": "We must ask ourselves: How do we view the present; how can we link it organically with the future; and what steps must we take?" Or again, "Arab nationalism [must] take its proper, correct place and be balanced in its vision and, more importantly, in its policies, which emanate from its original thought." Or, "[I]f the right balance is achieved between established Arab regimes and their masses, and if the most is made of the capabilities of the masses and political organizations in the Arab world, the Arab world will make rapid progress."

But, in fact, Saddam had been significantly reconstructed. As he acknowledged in his address, eight years of war on "the eastern front" (significantly, he does not here specify the obvious, that it was with Iran) were sufficient to qualify one for a doctorate. Some of the lessons from his graduate program soon followed in the speech:

> We also know that, God willing, good times are ahead for the Arab nation, and this will come from within rather than from across the border. . . . I would underscore one point among many. Arabs spread Islamic religion around the Arab world and beyond. The Arabs were the swords

or spears of religion, and they were the agency that propagated it. . . .
*[W]e have nothing to fear from waging our struggle under the precept of
Islam* and its benevolent principles, except if these ideas are in conflict
with Arabism. *There is no clash whatsoever between struggling under the
banner of Islam anywhere in the world and Arabism* (emphasis added).

Of key significance in the lengthy speech is that the president repeatedly warned that no country may rightly withhold its resources
from the larger Arab nation. Rather, they must be shared in the interest of larger pan-Arab security and in support of the struggle to liberate
Jerusalem. When Saddam added, "[T]he national has merged with the
pan-Arab and the local merged with the general," he was not espousing
disembodied Ba'thist ideology; the reference, in context, is quite clear.
The "national" here indicates Kuwait, and he speaks as though its absorption were a *fait accompli.* Five weeks later, "under the banner of
Islam," he would make it so.

Only one thing remained to be done in the weeks before the invasion. Whereas Saddam had approached the topic of Arab enemies indirectly during the emergency meeting of the Arab League in May and
in his speech to the Ba'th in June, by July he no longer equivocated. Both
in the letters Saddam and Tariq Aziz wrote to Rafsanjani in mid-month
and in the peremptory meeting with Ambassador Glaspie on the 25th,
the two men made clear that Kuwait (and the emirates, secondarily)
was in view. In June the president had told his fellow party members,
"If country 'X' says God has relieved the believers of the evil of war, let
us live on our billions and leave things as they are, it will be wasting
the Arab nation's resources."[27] But in the July meeting with Glaspie,
Saddam identified country X. The Kuwaitis with their military patrols
had encroached on Iraqi borders. Kuwait (and the emirates) had, with
U.S. encouragement, disregarded Iraqi rights. Kuwait and the emirates
had led the movement to deprive Iraqis of a better standard of living.

Thus the president rounded out his list of belligerents. And Iraq, Saddam asserted, would "not accept death."[28] But in the midst of the bellicosity, the Iraqis included a final touch, ironic or cynical, depending
on one's point of view. Iraq made a pro forma gesture at reconciliation
on the last day of July, sending Izzat Ibrahim to conduct "talks" with
the Kuwaitis in Jeddah, Saudi Arabia. Ibrahim left Jeddah the next day
when talks collapsed. As Iraqi troops marshaled at the border, awaiting
word to advance into Kuwait, the vice chairman, the Saudi news service reported briefly, traveled to Medina "to visit the noble prophet's

mosque and to pray in it and salute the messenger of God."[29] Thus, with piety, were preparations completed.

## THE INVASION: ITS CRITICAL FIRST DAYS

When Iraq invaded Kuwait, the Revolutionary Command Council had the role of making the initial announcement, of legitimating the crushing of a sister Arab state. The announcement is brief enough, but it nicely confects symbols and strands of ideology the Iraqi regime had propounded, in some form, for months. Viewed in the context of the plethora of announcements the Iraqis had made since the beginning of the year and would make in the coming months, the RCC statement gives every sign of careful rhetorical planning and coordination. Indeed, as the weeks passed, the Iraqis further showed tactical finesse, adapting their strategic plan to changing events with considerable flexibility. But the gravamen of the RCC announcement at 7:10 A.M., gulf time, 2 August, over Baghdad Voice of the Masses radio should be seen as the unchanging core message of the Iraqis.[30]

The announcement begins with the bismallah and a Quranic verse: "Nay, we hurl the truth against falsehood and it knocks out its brain" (21:18). It then proceeds to connect Islam and Arabism, precisely what the regime had been doing for months. On the one hand, it makes its appeal to those who believe the Arab nation is one and must remain united and dignified; in traditional Ba'thist terms, it speaks of the voice and resolve of the whole people of Iraq and the "masses of the Arab nation and all Arab militants." Yet with the Quranic references, the repeated "Allahu Akbar," and the references to those who have unshakable belief in God, it adds a clearly Islamic dimension. Fusing the two elements, the announcement vilifies the al-Sabah for having betrayed both pan-Arab values and the values and principles of Islam that God intended to rule in the world. Notably, this initial announcement offered the canard, dropped after a few days, that it was "[Kuwaiti] liberals from among the honest ranks. . . . [men] who believed in their God" who overthrew the al-Sabah.

The first communiqué of the puppet government, the "Provisional Free Kuwait Government," followed a few hours later.[31] It is almost entirely an excursus on pan-Arabism, but the Islamic dimension is not lacking. The bismallah and Quranic verses bookend the text, and the message points out that "this glorious day," this "new era," had begun in the blessed month of Muharram, first month of the Islamic calendar.[32] It more fully explores the conspiracy motif that the al-Sabah were in cahoots with the colonialists and Zionists. It further adds that those inside Kuwait who had nobly toppled the corrupt government did so for "the Arab nation's glory and for restoring . . . usurped rights, particularly in beloved Palestine."

In marked contrast is the first statement of the Iraqi Ba'th on the "national uprising," delivered a day after the invasion.[33] It is thoroughly and exclusively pan-Arab, and it reiterates the canard of a national uprising. Like the new government's communiqué, it explicitly connects the uprising to the "Palestine question and its heroic intifadah." The statement forgoes the bismallah and Quranic verses, however. Instead, it praises the Kuwaiti uprising for being pan-Arab and leads up to a peroration to "leader Saddam Husayn . . . the shield of the nation and the safe haven for the aspirations of Arab masses." This posture of Ba'thist secularity was maintained for several months while the rest of the nation marched off to jihad. Communiqués the Ba'th jointly issued with the RCC throughout the fall contained Islamic references, but the messages from the Ba'th alone appeared to retain the older orthodoxy, where little of Islam appears.

Typical is the Ba'thist communiqué of 10 December, over four months after the invasion.[34] The message dispenses with the bismallah, omits any sort of Islamic close, and is devoid of Quranic references save one, a brief citation from 3:139: "So lose not heart, nor fall into despair, for ye must gain mastery if you are true in faith." There are two references to the Arab and Islamic nation and one to Jerusalem as the "first qibla." But the rest of the 2000-word message is given over to references to economic calculation, the Industrial Revolution, colonialist designs for obtaining raw materials, political orbits, popular revolutions, and this:

Masses of our militant Arab masses, the Arab Socialist Ba'th Party, which considers this pan-Arab confrontation the Arab nation's battle, calls on you to entrench *militant cohesion*. . . . *[and] to assert the reality of the dialectical relationship* between Iraq's steadfastness and the *inevitability of its victory* in the crucial battle on the one hand and the intifadah of the occupied territory and the liberation of Palestine . . . on the other. (emphasis added)

Yet it must be noted that there had been a "slow baptism" of the Ba'th going on for some time, which the approaching war had accelerated. For instance, the 1990 draft constitution made clear that only the Baʿth party could operate in the military or the security services, a facet of the regime's pervasive control.[35] And yet the constitution also stated, "The men of the Baʿth formed the vanguard of the jihad that ended with the victory of the [1968] revolution."[36] (The RCC, not incidentally, took the additional title of "the leading *mujahid* institution.") By late fall, several months into Desert Storm, Saddam had begun calling members of the Baʿth party *muʾminun*, believers. More importantly, he referred to the mission of the party as daʿwa. With respect to Islam, Saddam could hardly have taken a more dramatic step. The term, as Chapter Four indicates, means "call" or "summons." In a religious context, it connotes the call to embrace Islam, to give submission to Allah alone. But this was also the name of the Shiʿa group the government had outlawed in 1980, mandating the death penalty for any who joined it.

Adopting such a charged term to describe the Baʿth mission could not have been an oversight; it must be seen as part of the government's larger embrace and, indeed, co-optation of Islam. With the approach of the UN deadline for withdrawal, the publications by the party, it seems, slipped the confines of the older orthodoxy and became more explicitly Islamic. Thus, in late December, an article in *al-Thawra* titled "Hurry to Perform Jihad" asserted that the battle would be fought so that "religion shall be God's alone" and would be fought with the cry "Allahu Akbar."[37] A day after the UN-imposed deadline for withdrawal, and mere hours before the initiation of the air war, *al-Thawra* published a similar and quite explicit article, "Fahd Pays the Price." Holding the Saudi king chiefly responsible for the approaching conflict, *al-Thawra* promised, "[T]he blood of the Iraqis in the mother of battles will become volcanoes of immense anger," which only revenge and cleansing of the land of treason could assuage. It concluded, "When the battle starts, the Arabian desert will turn into a graveyard for the concentrations of the aggressive invaders because the struggling [*mujahidin*] believers and the shouts of 'Allahu akbar' will fill the entire Arabian Peninsula."[38] The first Baʿth announcement during Desert Storm (18 January) seemed almost to complete the baptism. Although it contained enough references to pan-Arabism and struggling masses that its good faith could not be impugned, it was also replete with references to Islam. Beginning with the bismallah and a Quranic reference, the Baʿth declared jihad in support of Iraq to be incumbent on all Muslims everywhere.[39]

From the outset, Saddam, the believing *mujahid* president, showed

no such indecision. Whereas the Ba'th had alternated between traditional expressions of secularity and more explicit Islamic discourse,
the president relied on religion from the beginning. His two significant announcements on 7 August underscored that. In addressing his
fellow Ba'thists that day, the president declared that the chief element
of the party's slogan, unity, would be fulfilled with the coming announcement of the merger with Kuwait.⁴⁰ But this was due not merely
to human effort, although the party and the masses were important; it
proceeded from their dependence on God and his assistance. In fact, it
was time to tell all "traitors" and "losers" that the only power greater
than Iraq's is God's. Indeed, *"the power of Iraq—dependent on the
power of God—will be much higher than it was in the past"* (emphasis
added). In this speech, Saddam opened with the bismallah and closed
with a declaration that, God willing, vice would be defeated.

The more significant speech of the day was one read by an announcer
on Saddam's behalf on the occasion of "The Great Victory Day," the
Iraqi "triumph" over Iran two years before.⁴¹ It neatly tied the developments in Kuwait to the previous war with Iran, boasting that the "second of August arrived to be the legitimate newborn son of the second
Qadisiyah and its people." It also linked Arabism and Islam in a specially forthright way: "[W]e cannot sleep without putting out the eyes
of those who encroach upon Iraqi and Arab and Islamic values. Death
is better than humiliation." More pointedly, Saddam averred, "The nation will return to its rightful position only through real struggle and
jihad to place the wealth of the nation in its noble objectives." This,
apparently, was the first reference to jihad after the invasion. But significantly, jihad was intended to serve pan-Arab objectives; it was not
described as meeting a specifically Islamic requirement, per se.⁴²

By far the most important announcement in the fall was that which,
for good or ill, has become known as the "jihad speech," Saddam's call
to arms on 10 August.⁴³ No speech seems to have galvanized the attention of Western media or various publics to the degree this one did, but
we must look past the sensationalism to consider what the speech says,
the audiences it addresses, and Saddam's reasons for giving it. To be
sure, the language is vivid, even when considered against a year's worth
of incendiary political discourse. Arguably, only Saddam's "fire speech"
on 2 April could match it. Speaking on the tenth, Saddam declared:

Arabs, Moslems, believers in God. . . . This is your day to rise and spread
quickly in order to defend Mecca, which is captive to the spears of the

Americans and the Zionists. . . . Burn the soil under their feet. Burn the soil under the feet of the aggressors and invaders who want harm for your families in Iraq. Until the voice of right rises up in the Arab world, hit their interests wherever they are and rescue holy Mecca and the grave of the Prophet Mohammed in Medina.

The speech comported with the regime's pattern and strategic plan, reflecting the sort of coordination that had been evident all year. As the Iraqis had done before and during the war with Iran, Saddam appealed to Islamic and Arab nationalist history to legitimate actions and orient his listeners. He began by addressing his fellow Arabs as the "grand-children of the men of the first Qadissiyah, Yarmuk, Hittin and Naha-vand,"[44] and reminded them they are a great nation chosen by God and called to a divine mission, and were at one time a "lofty banner, looked up to as an example in the east and west of the world." Saddam then re-counted that ideal time when foreigners respected the Arab and his na-tion, a time when the "chaste and decent" caliph faithfully, devoutly led the state, "distribut[ing] the riches of the nation to the people." But no longer. A time of apocalyptic darkness had come for Arabs and, indeed, all Muslims, one brought on by foreigners, Zionists, and traitors. Per-fidy has spread, dignity and honor are compromised, and the "oil emirs" humiliate Arab women. Saddam therefore called on others to follow Iraq, the "conscience of the Arab world," in order to defend Mecca and cleanse the land. If the faithful followed that lead, God would assist the Muslims as he did in the battles at the dawn of Islam against the Persians and Byzantium, giving "the best of all rewards—victory and the blessings of God and the nation." Then, Saddam promised, "the sun will rise on the Arabs and the Moslems and God will be happy after we purify our souls and land from the foreigners." Once again, the believers will live a life close to God and his laws.

Just as the Iraqis had done throughout the spring and summer, Sad-dam continually connected Islam and Arabism. "Arabs, Moslems, be-lievers in God wherever you are, this is your day to jump up and defend Mecca." The foreigners and traitors are "defying the Arab and Islamic *nations*" (emphasis added). "It is a battle of the entire Arab nation . . . [to secure] a life that is close to God and His laws." "The sun will rise on the Arabs and the Moslems." "God will be with you, and victory will be on the side of the faithful mujahedeen [and] on the side of the fight-ing pan-Arabists." Moreover, he also carefully adduced the Palestinian issue as he addressed Arabs and Muslims, telling them their battle will "contribute greatly to strengthening the ground on which the stone-throwing people are standing."

In sum, the speech was a remarkable conflation of all the themes the Iraqi regime had enunciated over the past seven months. Indeed, it echoed themes the government had posited since the mid-1970s, then modified. But most important here is the tactical change Saddam introduced. Saddam both refined his enemies list and made the call to jihad explicitly based on Islamic, not just pan-Arab, reasons, unlike what he had done three days previously. On first reading, it would appear Saddam altered the approach because of the deployment of U.S. troops to the region. And certainly he rather forcefully made the point that Mecca had come under the spears of foreigners: lands and littoral waters had been polluted by their presence. Even the choice of Quranic verses to close the speech supported that view: "Men said to them: 'A great army is gathering against you' and frightened them, but it only increased their faith; they said: 'For us, God suffices, and He is the best disposer of affairs'" (3:173).

But the presence of foreign troops must have been the secondary cause for the speech. The Iraqis, throughout the conflict, displayed an ability to respond immediately, if not always wisely, to national and international changes. Although the jihad speech railed against the West, it is our view that the West was neither the essential audience nor the primary target of its wrath. The chronology supports this. Four days before, on 6 August, Fahd had appealed to the United States to send troops, following the urging of his nephew Bandar and Secretary of Defense Cheney. On the same day, President Bush had ordered the initial deployment, and U.S. troops began arriving in the kingdom on the following day, the seventh. Saddam's jihad speech lagged behind these events by three days, a delay that cannot be accounted for if he delivered it simply in response to the deployment.[45] Bush upped the ante, as it were, on the eighth when he declared his aim to be Iraqi withdrawal from Kuwait. In response, it seems, Saddam made a counterannouncement—the eternal merger of root and branch, Iraq and Kuwait. But the Iraqi president still had not made a jihad speech.

What precipitated the fiery declaration must rather have been the events of 10 August. On that day the Arab League met again, this time at the head-of-state level (see Chapter Three). In passing Resolution 195, it rejected as null and void Iraq's annexation of Kuwait two days earlier and called instead for immediate withdrawal. More importantly, it reversed, although by a narrow margin, its earlier rejection of foreign intervention. Egypt, as well as Djibouti, Lebanon, Morocco, Somalia, and Syria, voted to send troops to Saudi Arabia. Mubarak and Saddam had vied for leadership in a cool, if not cold, Arab war. Now they were to be opponents in a hot war. It is worth noting as well that Saddam had not mentioned Mecca prior to his speech on 10 August. He became keenly interested in its desecration, but not when U.S. troops first landed in the kingdom. It was only when members of the Arab League met to deliberate an Arab response that Saddam employed this new gambit, and did so in late afternoon, shortly before the league voted. This is one of the clearest examples of Saddam's invoking religion for *political* delegitimation. When Fahd had taken the title *khadim al-haramayn*, "guardian of the two sacred sites," he had staked his political legitimacy on his Islamic bona fides. Now, Saddam was simply (and smartly) attacking Fahd at a point of vulnerability, as well as vying with Mubarak for Arab support.[46]

The jihad speech, then, resorted to religion in response to changing political dynamics; it represented "war by other means," a tactic at once Machiavellian and Clausewitzian. Approached in this way, Saddam's digression on the caliph (mentioned above and discussed further below) may be seen as a stratagem in the struggle for leadership, especially with Mubarak. The recourse to religion also accounted for the vigorous attacks on the Saudis, as Saddam modified his enemies list yet again. It further made sense of the frequent references to other Arabs as the "sons" and "grandsons" of various Islamic and nationalist leaders of the past (references that completely omitted the name of any living Arab head of state as praiseworthy). Saddam turned to jihad in the attempt to win a battle of legitimation and delegitimation in regional politics. This was, so to speak, a holy war for a secular mandate.

The regime had found its new theme.[47] Hereafter, it made repeated calls to jihad, and not exclusively to accomplish pan-Arab goals. Arabism remained, of course, but as a symbiotic partner of Islam. The adaptation was immediately evident. On the day of Saddam's speech, the Popular Islamic Conference issued a call for jihad, telling believers that Saudi Arabia had become "a staging point for the forces of blasphemy" and calling on them to assist Iraq.[48] Like Saddam's message, this also connected Islam, Arabism, and Jerusalem. The attack was against both Arabs and Muslims. Hence, the Arab and Muslim masses must take a united Islamic stand. But there should be confidence, even in this hour of perfidy. "There is a ray of hope for the revival of jihad from the land of jihad, Iraq, against criminal Zionists tampering with Muslim sanctities, above all, al-Aqsa mosque. It also coincides with the resolve of the Iraqi leadership to free the Arab and Islamic will from fear and hesitation." Also quite appropriately, the call for jihad included Quran 60:1: "Ye who believe! Take not my enemies and yours as friends."

The calls for jihad showed coordination by the regime. The next day (the eleventh) the National Assembly made a statement: prefaced with the bismallah and the Quran, it called on all Muslims and Arabs ("the Arab nation and the Islamic world") to confront the Tatar invasion that had desecrated the holiest of Muslim sanctities and to conduct jihad "to defend the values and dignity of Arabism and Islam." Especially noteworthy is that the assembly called for Muslims to conduct jihad "in defense of the message of Islam," an appeal that comports with the principle of daʿwa. Indeed, the assembly took a yet more dramatic, not to say Kharijite, turn by including jihad among the *ibadat:* "Jihad is our fate. Besides, jihad is a pillar of our true religion. Jihad is a duty to be performed by all Muslims."[49]

Then on the twelfth, Saddam reinforced the call to jihad in a special radio address to Iraqi women. Telling them that their ululations were Iraqi soldiers' "best motivation to forge ahead," Saddam asked them to take another leading role, that of "reorganiz[ing] the family's economic life."[50] Meal tables, he told them, should not be crowded with food. Rather, what they placed in cooking pots should meet only the essential needs of their families. This glorious role to which the president summoned them should not be thought of as merely technical, financial, or a matter of sustenance, however. This was a jihad. If they failed in it and the Iraqi will was bent, men would lose honor and the homeland would be humiliated. Naturally, if they prevailed, they would have had a part in liberating both Jerusalem and the *kaʿba.*[51]

## EXCURSUS: THE NEW IRAQI INTELLECTUAL UNIVERSE

At this point, it may be helpful to examine more critically the corpus of Iraqi "doctrine," this fusion of Arabism and Islam that the country presented to the world. The doctrine was certainly not new. Over the first ten days of the conflict, the regime refined it, but it was working with ideas it had put forward for months, the roots of which extended back to the war with Iran and even before. Themes the regime had experimented with and propounded in some form for fifteen years coalesced in these critical first days to inform what we may call a "discursive worldview." That is, a public language used to 1) elaborate a coherent set of beliefs and values, 2) contrast alternative or conflicting sets of beliefs and values, and 3) legitimate regime beliefs and values and actions while delegitimating those of others. The truth of these claims or the attachment of the user to any sort of metaphysic that might undergird them is not being evaluated. The aim here is simply to describe a system of public communication and to examine the political reasons for it.

The regime systematically disseminated a carefully constructed total message, a message categorical from beginning to end. Central to this public ideology were what could be called circles in opposition. In the center of one circle stood Iraq, vanguard of the Arab nation. The Arab nation, in turn, was at the center of the umma, the Islamic world, having been specially called and honored by God to be the first to receive the message of Islam and the initial responsibility for da'wa. And Islam stood at the center of all religions, a beacon to humankind.

Opposite this arrangement stood a triumvirate of evil. The primary malevolent power opposing Iraq was the West, presented under several cognomens: "colonialism," "imperialism," the "foreign powers," and sometimes simply "America" or the "United States," often acting in concert with the Atlantic alliance. Next came the primary agent of the West in the region: Zionism, often presented as parasitical on the West, its continuation in the Arab world owing solely to the West's desire for dominance in a region of staggering oil reserves. But the charges against Zionism hardly needed a special context, since for so long it had been the prime target of both secular Arabs and Islamists, especially in Iran after 1979. Here, as elsewhere, Israel was viewed as the creation and outpost of colonialism, a juggernaut in the Arab world.[52] Most immediately, Iraq accused Israel of organizing the coalition against it.

But during the Gulf War, the Iraqis necessarily expanded the list of agents.[53] Now the influence of the West was spread by *Arab* agents, the term of choice for the Kuwaitis, Emiratis, and Saudis. They also became, in this public lexicon, "traitors," "emirs of oil," "lackeys," and the like. A secondary tier of agents included the Egyptians and Syrians.

This opposition, of course, reflects the traditional Islamic dualism of *dar al-Islam* and *dar al-harb*, but it modifies the dichotomy. This structure had to account for faithless Muslims within what had traditionally been termed *dar al-Islam*. To do that, the regime accused its opponents of *ridda* (apostasy) or simply *kufr* (unbelief). In this context, the political crime of treason and the spiritual sin of apostasy became essentially synonymous. Now Iraq was fighting new ridda wars, just as the rashidun had done after Muhammad's death.

This approach to the older orthodox Islamic teaching on *dar al-harb* and *dar al-Islam* reflected the influence of Ba'thism, but in a special way. In the 1940s, Ba'thism had, in effect, absorbed Islam into pan-Arabism. It pictured the two, as Chapter Four indicates, as successive *muharakayn asasiayn*, two prime movers. But now the Ba'th of Iraq generated a new sort of symbiosis. This was not Islam followed by Ba'thism in some evolutionary fashion. Instead, the regime presented its ideology as Islam *and* Ba'thism simultaneously. In this new discursive worldview, the regime presented these oppositional circles as Islam *and* Arabism versus imperialism *and* unbelief, albeit with a number of variations.

We need look no further than the initial announcement of the RCC on the morning of 2 August to find this new approach at work.[54] Shaykh Jaber, in this proclamation, is guilty both of Islamic and pan-Arab failings. He is the "Qarun of Kuwait" (a religious epithet explained below) who, unlike those who deposed him, does not believe; he is one who has "betrayed and deceived pan-Arab values." Opposing him are those who are both faithful Muslims ("they hurl truth against falsehood") and good pan-Arabists (they believe "the Arab nation is one nation and that it must be a unified dignified nation"). Within a few days the Iraqis leveled this sort of double charge against Saudi Arabia. The Saudis, by inviting the West and joining the coalition forces, were simultaneously betraying the Arab nation and—by consorting with the unbelievers or *mushrikun* (polytheists)—acting like apostates.

Although this has not been elsewhere proposed, the arrangement further suggested an emulation, in this case the sincerest form of flattery, of Gamal Abdul Nasser. In his *Philosophy of the Revolution,* Nasser famously wrote of the circles that Egypt inhabits: "We cannot look stupidly at a map of the world not realizing our [i.e., Egypt's] place therein and the role determined to us by that place."[55] Nasser then described the Arab, African, and Islamic circles Egypt inhabited. Saddam appears to have adapted Nasser. Although Saddam did not call his structure "oppositional circles," as we do here, he offered a rough parallel. While the RCC announcement on 2 August suggested some imitation, Saddam's jihad speech on the tenth seemed more broadly indicative of borrowing from his mentor.[56]

Like Nasser, Saddam saw the Arabs as needing transformation.

Nasser's focus had been Egypt, but Nasser also described Egypt's shared condition with the Arabs: "[W]e have suffered the same hardships, lived the same crises, and when we fell prostrate under the spikes of horses of conquerors, they [i.e., the other Arab states] lay with us."[57] Similarly, Saddam declared, "Look at where the Arabs are today. The foreigner entered our homes, [and] western imperialism has divided us, setting up small states to facilitate the task of occupying Arab land."[58] Nasser asked what positive role Egypt, *and only Egypt*, could play in this troubled world, one in which she is located not by a joke of fate but by design. In his view, Egypt was the one to take the special role that (as in Luigi Pirandello's play) seeks one to play it.[59]

Saddam described Iraq similarly. Seeing a "disease" in the larger Arab body politic, Iraq responded to the call to "save" Kuwait. In this battle involving the entire nation, it was Iraq, "conscience of the Arab world," that led.[60] Saddam had anticipated something like this in a speech in 1980 (cited earlier in Chapter Four).

If you read the history of the nation [Iraq], you will find that it was either a shining light leading the way, or that it was trampled under the feet of invading armies. Throughout its history, it has either been in the forefront of civilization, of leadership and history, and of the Arab nation, or it has been overwhelmed by tyranny. This is because Iraq's people have special characteristics; its people are the people of the mountains and the peaks, not of the plains and valleys.[61]

Now the people of the mountains were again a shining light. Just as in Mahmud Hamad's artwork in *al-Thawra* in April 1987 (described in Chapter Four), Iraq, by its invasion of Kuwait, was offering the water of life to a sere Arab world, one that had been devastated by imperialists and oil emirs. In a joint statement by the RCC and the Ba'th in September, one oddly reminiscent of Henry V's speech before Agincourt (as imagined by Shakespeare), the Iraqis presented their own version of "only Iraq":

[T]he greater the number of evildoers, and the heavier their equipment, the more fitting for you [i.e., the Iraqis]—none but you can take them on. We do not think—indeed this is the hope of all—it will be fitting for the men of Qadisiyah army to rise against a gathering less or smaller than this opposing gathering. The greater the number and the heavier the equipment, the better and more fitting and the likelier that pan-Arab fervour and the fervour of the faith of the faithful will come to the fore. It will be more fitting that the men of Qadisiyah should rise to a battle of this type and meaning for people and history.[62]

Both Nasser and Saddam thought that the Arab circle was most important for their respective nations, but Saddam was not content to let the matter rest there; he extended his mentor's suggestive paradigm, adding more with respect to Islam and what lay beyond.[63] Iraq leads the Arab nation, which, in turn, holds primacy in the Islamic umma. "Your nation [here, speaking to all Arabs] is a great nation," Saddam declared in the August jihad speech. "God chose it to be the nation of the Koran. After choosing it and throughout the various stages of history [sic], he honored it with the task of upholding the principles of all the divine missions and being the preacher and keeper of [its] principles." Beyond that there is another realm not sharply demarcated or strictly defined. In the jihad speech, Saddam refers to it as constituting "believers in God wherever [they] are." Elsewhere, he refers simply to "humanity" or "humanitarians" or something similar. But the point is clear: Iraq leads the Arab nation, the Arabs lead the umma, and Muslims—who have the best religion—lead the world.

Saddam was also much more interested than Nasser in describing the foes ranged against him. As indicated above, these formed a triumvirate, so to speak, comprising the West (primarily the United States), Israel, and wealthy Arab governments in the gulf. In the jihad speech, an almost inexhaustible source of maximalist metaphors, the West was variously described as "colonialists, foreigners, and imperialists," terms the regime used repeatedly throughout the conflict. And the West had done more than simply split off Kuwait. Elsewhere, Saddam accused "malicious westerners" of having "fragment[ed] the Arab homeland . . . distanc[ing ] the majority of the population density and areas of cultural depth from riches and their sources, something new to the life of the Arabs."[64] The RCC concurred.[65] Western colonialism had "separated civilization with its high, strong sense of preparedness due to [its] rich culture and demographic density from the resources of the new wealth, petroleum and other minerals, where there is a small population, a lack of cultural depth, and a weak state of preparedness." Using the "spiteful pencil and scissors of imperialism," the West had drawn new maps of the Middle East to secure the oil wealth of the area for itself and to ensure the region's states would be incapable of a pan-Arab awakening.

This argument extended Iraq's views on its own civilizational depth; it had invoked a Mesopotamian identity to further its state-building aims over the years, as Chapter Four points out. But here the regime evaluated the cultural depth of a number of Arab states, and further adduced a charge of wealth disparity that had geopolitical merit, one to which poorer Arab states would certainly listen. In the year before the invasion, Egypt, a nation of undisputed population density and civilizational depth, had an estimated 51 million people, but its gross national product (GNP) per capita was $640 (U.S.). The oil emirates were a different case. Kuwait, with a population of 2 million and no civilizational depth to speak of, had a GNP per capita of $16,150; the emirates, with a population of 1.5 million, had a GNP per capita of $18,430. The next year, the figure for the emirates rose to $19,860. Egypt's fell to $600.[66] Clearly, the Iraqis declared repeatedly, this disparity could only be the work of the "spiteful pencil and scissors of imperialism."

But the imperialists had to work through various agents. The vituperation against the oil emirs was especially creative. Until the jihad speech, the Iraqis directed their attacks primarily at the al-Sabah, the "Croesuses" of Kuwait, seeking to exploit their vulnerability as wealthy rulers. "The oil people are . . . mean beyond belief," Saddam told Ambassador Glaspie in their July meeting. "It is painful to admit it, but some of them are disliked by Arabs because of their greed." Now, the Iraqis gladly played up what had earlier been painful to admit. But the regime also found an Islamic equivalent for the religiously neutral epithet of "Croesus." The emir became "the Qarun of Kuwait."[67] In so styling Shaykh Jaber, the Iraqis must have had an Islamic audience in mind, for the reference would not have been understood except by Muslims. And the allusion is particularly telling, for Qarun represents the unrighteous man, niggardly in his ways, foolish with his money, who—like his counterpart Korah in the Jewish scriptures—is swallowed by the earth with his family. Thus, what appeared to be an unwarranted invasion was instead the judgment of God visited upon Kuwait, and Iraq was his instrument. In subsequent communiqués, the al-Sabah were variously termed the "ruling tyrannical clique" in the employ of colonialists who aimed at the plunder of Kuwait and all Arabs, corrupt henchman, a malicious conspiracy, traitors who paid "lip service" to pan-Arabism on "ceremonial occasions," and so on.[68]

But the Arab League vote on 10 August led Iraq to alter the enemies list significantly, as described above. Up to that point, the Iraqis had focused on the Kuwaitis, particularly the al-Sabah family, as leading the conspiracy, the lackeys who served the interests of Zionism and the imperialists. Now it was the sons of Abdul Aziz ibn Saud who became the focus. The Iraqis accused Saudi Arabia, one of the "dwarf oil states," of having used sinister methods to control oil wealth. Hence, it too was a "statelet" mired in "financial and social corruption."[69] But the Saudis' real vulnerability lay with their quite public claim of Islamic credentials. At this point, Saddam could have borrowed his defamatory text from the late Ayatollah Khomeini. Several years before, the ayatollah had declared:

The ruling regime in Saudi Arabia wears Muslim clothing, but it actually represents a luxurious, frivolous, shameless way of life, robbing funds from the people and squandering them, and engaging in gambling, drinking parties and orgies. Would it be surprising if people follow the path of revolution, resort to violence and continue their struggle to regain their rights and resources?[70]

At the time of the Gulf War, such characterizations of the Saudis, however unfair, were regnant in the Muslim world. The next chapter will survey some of them, but we cite here one example to illuminate the character of the Iraqi attack. One Chinese Islamist observed, "We Muslims in China are twice as devout as the Saudi and Kuwaiti sheikhs who spend their money in the brothels of Southeast Asia and Bahrain."[71] In this milieu (recalling Eickelman and Piscatori's observation about words and context), the Iraqi president simply took materials ready at hand and made good use of them. That was especially true with regard to Fahd's appellation, *khadim al-haramayn,* guardian of the two holy sites. Because the monarchy readily described itself as the guardian in trust of Mecca and Medina, it bore the responsibility, as well as the prestige, of the title. Things could go dramatically wrong. For instance, in November 1979, Juhaiman ibn Sayf al-Oteibi led Sunni militants who seized the Grand Mosque in Mecca and held it for two weeks. By the time French commandos finally helped quash the riot, 102 militants and 127 Saudi troops had been killed. Muslims throughout the Islamic world charged that the Saudis had defiled the mosque. At the same time, but quite unconnected, riots broke out in the Eastern Province among the 250,000 Shi'a there. The two incidents made the royal family appear unable to maintain control, as well as being responsible for having defiled the mosque.[72]

Eleven years later, Saddam ensured that the monarchy would have to fend off the same charge, that its steps to protect the holy sites in the Gulf War were, in fact, leading to their desecration. After the deployment of U.S. troops, Saddam elaborated his conspiracy narrative, one that linked Saudi wealth, American military strength, and Zionist interests. He was certain there would be an audience, and he found one in the Maghreb. One chant used during demonstrations in Morocco went like this:

> Fahd, Fahd, ya himar
> Ba'ti-l-kaaba bil dular
>
> . . . . . . . .
>
> Fahd, Fahd, O donkey
> You sold the kaaba for a dollar[73]

The connection here to a donkey was hardly incidental. Quran 62:5 compares the Jews' handling of the Torah to the carrying of heavy tomes by a donkey on its back, with no understanding of what it bears. Because one of the slurs used against Fahd was that he was Jewish, the invective made sense. Moroccan crowds were charging Fahd, the supposed protector of Islamic sanctities, with being religiously ignorant and insensitive, no more than a pawn in the hands of the West.

Thus, it was to an audience prepared that Iraqi radio broadcast on 10 August, "The Saudi regime, when it invited in the foreigners, committed an unforgivable sin against the sentiments and sanctities, against Arab and Islamic histories;" or again on the twenty-third:

Criminal Fahd must be removed immediately from the custodianship throne. He no longer deserves to be called 'servant of the two holy places,' because custodianship does not permit him under any conditions to desecrate the land of Mecca and Medina with the boots of foreigners. *He assumes a big responsibility before Muslims and Arabs* for this hideous act.[74]

The Iraqis also continually appealed to Quranic texts to substantiate their claim that the formation of a coalition with non-Muslims was categorically forbidden. "O ye who believe! Take not my enemies and yours as friends—offering them (your) love" (60:1).[75] Thus, beginning immediately after the Arab League decision on 10 August, the Iraqis and their supporters were able to characterize the coalition as forbidden both in its very formation and in its deployment. In any event, the

Iraqis did little other than make the charges and refer to verses in the Quran—no sophisticated disquisitions were offered. For instance, on 24 August, Baghdad Radio aired a "special program" on the topic "Muslim Unity Needed." The host stated:

From the religious point of view a Muslim cannot ask for help from a non-Muslim under any circumstance but the infidel Saudi ruler asked for the protection of Israel and the U.S. which are both not only non-Muslims but also hold a grudge against Islam. It is the same old imperialist ways of intervention in an occupation of others' territories. The world cannot forget the American crimes in Hiroshima and Nagasaki nor can the world forget the lesson taught to the Americans in Saigon, Vietnam, and Korea where the Americans' poison gas and napalm proved to be of no effect.[76]

Once the regime leveled such charges, other individuals and groups throughout the Islamic world began to debate them, pursuing all possible theological niceties. That was certainly true for the term "jihad." It was other constituencies, not the Iraqis, who did the detailed Quranic exegeses and studies of both hadith literature and classical theologians. In a sense, broadcasting verses like 60:1 and using terms like "jihad" resembled nothing so much as the launch of Scud missiles after 17 January. The notoriously inaccurate Scuds had little *military* utility against the coalition or the IDF, the Israeli Defense Forces. But they had enormous symbolic value, and the Iraqis counted on widespread popular support in response to every launch, including unending discussion. Similarly with the verses either forbidding taking infidels as friends or the accusations that Mecca was under the spears of foreigners: the Iraqis "launched" the accusations, confident of repercussions throughout the Islamic world.[77]

The Iraqis took aim in another way at Fahd's legitimacy. Beginning on 15 August, the regime began publicly referring to his country as "the lands of Hijaz and Najd," implying that it should not be associated with the Saudi royal family.[78] The regime used the same terminology in an open letter to President Bush the following day.[79] Beginning with the bismallah, it informed the American leader that Saddam was aware of "heated comments [Bush made] before the staff of the American defense ministry," which revealed plans for a "policy of occupation that humiliates the sacred shrine and lands of the Arabs and Moslems in Hijaz and Najd." The Iraqis' reasons for referring to Saudi Arabia this way became clearer in a broadcast on 23 August.[80] There the announcer stated, "Saudi Arabia belongs to its people. It does not belong to the Saudi family. The name must be corrected by calling people 'Najdite' or 'Hijazite.' The people must be named after their place of origin, not by the Saudi family name. We do not want to go into details here. In brief, what we are saying is that Fahd is a traitor and a criminal and must be removed."

Saddam's reasons for referring thus to Saudi Arabia were made even clearer by an open letter he sent to President Mubarak that same day and read on Iraqi radio.[81] In the pertinent part, Saddam averred, "This speaker [i.e., Saddam], the slave of God, was the son of a peasant who died months before his mother gave birth to him. He is from an honorable family whose honor is basically derived from its labor and from being a descendant of the Muhammadan Qurayshi family, as his family's lineage goes back to our master and forefather, [Imam] Husayn." Mubarak could claim no such connection. "To the best of my knowledge, you, Mr. President, have come of an Egyptian family that has nothing to do with the princes and kings who ruled before the July 1952 revolution."

Apart from the repetition of biographical motifs (lowly birth, laboring family, but noble ancestry), the broadcast attacking Fahd and the letter slighting Mubarak's lineage reflected both a coordinated effort and a carefully crafted strategy. The Iraqis were declaring that only Saddam could lay claim to noble, and more especially, sharifan status. It was a way of bringing the claims of legitimacy of all three rulers to the table and saying Saddam's trumped those of Mubarak and Fahd. The claim was ironic, since Saddam's early predecessor King Faisal could truthfully have claimed sharifan status, whereas Saddam was simply making propaganda.

Fictions aside, what is noteworthy is that though the letter to Mubarak denigrated his standing, the broadcast about Fahd delegitimated the entire Saudi nation. It represented the country as being a wrongly manufactured fief of the Al-Saud clan. The unstated but broadly understood history here is that Abdul Aziz ibn Saud had displaced the one who might have had Islamic legitimacy, Sharif Hussein of Mecca, and had instead created a nation in his own name, for his own purposes. Saddam argued, in effect, that Fahd, the son of Abdul Aziz, could not then use religion to legitimate a political entity. Fahd was an interloper at best, and "Saudi Arabia" was artificial. Such an approach makes sense only when seen as an attack that combines Arab and Islamic histories.

Appropriately, in light of this letter, the Iraqi National Assembly claimed the day after the jihad speech that Saddam the Qurayshi (as he had claimed of himself repeatedly) was confronting the "Tatar invasion" to rescue "the tomb of the Qurashite Hashimite Arab Prophet Muhammad bin Abdullah from the filth of the invaders." In other words, the real khadim al-haramayn was none other than the Ba'thist president of Iraq, a lineal descendant of the prophet's own clan. It was he who had the family connection, not Fahd, the traitorous leader who had undermined his position by summoning unbelievers. Fahd was instead the "custodian of imperialism and Zionism," the "betrayer of the two holy mosques."[82]

The Iraqi ulama, acting in concert with the regime, was equally direct. In a statement on 14 September designed to coincide with a conference the Saudis had called in Mecca, the ulama announced, "The great catastrophe, corruption, and infidelity is that these unfaithful assemblies [the coalition forces] should come at the frank invitation of the rulers of Najd and Hijaz, who installed themselves, falsely and unjustly, [as] guardians over our religion and the Shari'ah of Muhammad, may the peace and blessings of God be upon him."[83] In short, the Other Gulf War found the Arab region's most explicitly Islamic state to be the most vulnerable religiously, just as it found Saddam, at one point the Arab world's leading exponent of a secular political doctrine, now leading an Islamic attack, especially after his jihad speech.

In counterpoise to the depiction of other rulers, especially the Al-Saud and the Al-Sabah, as illegitimate, the Iraqis presented Saddam as the ideal leader. Interestingly, the regime only rarely presented Saddam as the new Nebuchadnezzar, in contrast to its practice in previous years, especially in the early years of the Iran-Iraq War. One of those occasions came a day into the air war when a military communiqué from the general command stated that Nebuchadnezzar would "feel proud in his grave" in these auspicious times; Baghdad Radio averred five days later that the "sons of Nebuchadnezzar" had begun to play a role in the "rectification of the course of civilization."[84] But these were exceptions, and did not equate the president with the Babylonian leader.

The regime referred more frequently to Saladin, yet there was coyness in the approach, not unlike the ayatollah's temporizing about whether he might be the Mahdi.[85] Certainly Saddam never claimed to be Saladin, but one found the claim in the mouths of others, in a metaphorical sense, and apparently that was the way the regime preferred it. On occasion, the regime itself made the connection. For instance, a week before the ground war began, the commander of the surface-to-air missile force telegraphed the president, "It is the day of Salah al-Din al-Ayyubi [i.e., Saladin]; it is the day of Saddam Husayn. Let the strong men testify, as we do today, that you have carried out your duty. . . . May God reward you on behalf of the Muslims and Arabs."[86]

As the next chapter will detail, other Arabs were only too ready to take up the Saladin theme. To cite but one example here: Tayseer Barakat, a Palestinian refugee living in a camp near Ramallah, said in an interview shortly after the invasion, "We hope Saddam will be like Saladin; that he will liberate Palestine and Jerusalem."[87] But Saddam himself was demure. "All leaders in the world should serve for national liberation without fearing anyone but God," he said in interview with Japanese television. "I particularly respect Arab leaders. I think that Saladin, who repelled the crusaders . . . is one of them." Yet Saddam, although trying to learn, as he says, from Saladin, Nasser, and other leaders, does not put himself on their level. "I am Saddam Husayn, a worshipper of God. That is all. All I am is this person in front of you, Saddam Husayn, one of God's worshippers."[88]

The most telling image of Saddam, however, was as caliph. As with the Saladin references, this was an allusion the regime apparently felt it would be better for others, not Saddam, to make. And before the end of August, Palestinians and Jordanians obliged. For instance, an Islamic activist in the Gaza Strip, Dr. Mahmoud al-Zahar, said he would embrace a renewed caliphate. "Until now Saddam has not behaved in an Islamic way. But if he now frankly chooses Islam as the religion of state and his actions correspond with Islam, then we could consider him the Caliph. Islam can forgive what he did before."[89] Similarly, at a rally in Zarqa, Jordan, in late August, a Muslim Brother said, "Arabism is the raw material for Islam and the establishment of the Caliphate."[90]

But the regime itself sometimes found it useful to allude to particular caliphs, as it had done during the war with Iran. At the time, Saddam found in al-Mansur an exemplar for Iraq.[91] It was he who had founded Baghdad, and his works included suppressing the Shi'a, as well as expanding Abbasid territory. Saddam himself became, in the words of one writer, "Saddam Husayn al-Mansur," a leader who "will continue to be [our] moon." The Iraqi daily *al-Jumhuriyya* adopted the motif, calling the capital *Baghdad al-Mansurayn*. The expression means "Baghdad of the two Mansurs," and the paper pointed out that one Mansur had founded Baghdad and the other had rebuilt it. Significantly, *al-Jumhuriyya* continued, April was the month Baghdad was founded, the Ba'th formed, and Saddam born. Now, during the Gulf War, the regime made only a few oblique references to the caliph, generally letting others take up the theme. One of those few references came from the Armed Forces General Command. A day into the air war, following the triumphant counterlaunch of Scuds against Israel, its staff issued a communiqué that connected Saddam with one of the *rashidun*, the rightly guided caliphs.

[The caliph] Umar Bin al-Khattab blessed the gathering of the faithful after asking permission from his Almighty God and reminded the believers how God granted victory to the army of believers. And Umar Bin al-Khattab entered Palestine as a liberator. All our forefathers will feel proud when they learn that [Saddam] Husayn has arisen to rescue Palestine, the Dome of the Rock and Bayt al-Maqdis [Jerusalem]. The militant will of Husayn turns into missiles. These missiles poured out of the sky, making Tel Aviv and other targets a crematorium last night, the night of 18th–19th of January.[92]

But at one point Saddam took up the caliphal theme himself. On review, it was a masterpiece of subtle allusion, and it appeared in the jihad speech on 10 August. After recalling an ideal time in early Islamic history when Arabs from Morocco to Iraq were one nation, noble and proud, Saddam presented a sketch of their ideal leader. Saddam's portrait merits quoting at some length.

Their ruler was a wise man and one of the most courageous, leading the vanguard wherever the fighting was. . . . The ruler or leader was an honest man who never lied to his kinfolk in any matter. He was also chaste and decent. In all cases, moreover, the ruler or leader feared God, was loved and respected by his people. He was also capable of passing judgment on worldly and religious affairs, so that he could be a true leader of the state and the people. A real leader, he distributed the riches of the nation to the people. As for the affluent people who earned their money through their own endeavors and honest jobs, they used to cooperate and interact with the majority in the interest of the ethos of society and the public good. Thus, the ruler was at the time legitimate. Moreover, he acted in harmony with what pleased God and society. He didn't obey the foreigner. He was close to God and kept distance from evil.[93]

We will let pass any comment about what this may say of the psyche of the Iraqi leader and focus instead on its specific connection to the invasion. As Saddam and the regime had appealed to history over the years while trying to fashion a nation, he here appealed to it to critique the status quo. The idea that a real leader would distribute the riches of the nation precisely accorded with the stance he had taken months before the invasion. Such was the thrust of his argument to his fellow Ba'thists in June when he told them "local national resources [i.e., Kuwait's and the emirates'] should merge with the resources of the entire Arab nation and not remain isolated."[94]

Further, Saddam could not resist the jibe that the affluent in the golden age had earned their money "through their own endeavors and honest jobs"—unlike the oil emirs who simply pumped their wealth out of the ground.[95] But Saddam followed his picture of the chaste and decent caliph with a particularly telling line: "Look at where the Arabs are today." There followed the usual diatribe against the imperialists and the Zionists, but they were hardly the president's primary concern. His real *j'accuse* was reserved for Arab leaders who had become the corrupt "stooges" of the imperialists.

Several arguments were operating simultaneously here. He advanced the noncontroversial point that Arabs once enjoyed a glorious era in early Islam, whether among the *rashidun* or, say, the Abbasid caliphate. He advanced the also noncontroversial point that largesse should be shared. That, after all, was the point of *zakat*, the giving of alms to meet needs, which underscores the brotherhood of all Muslims. Only somewhat controversial was the issue of gulf oil wealth in particular. At least outside the region, many argued that the gulf leaders could have done far more to share their wealth. Also generating little controversy was the point that good leaders, devout and selfless leaders, were essential to the political health of Arab Muslim states.

The controversial point would have been calling for the resumption of the caliphate—but Saddam did not precisely call for it. He refrained from using the word altogether, although he defined "caliph," inter alia, when he spoke of one "capable of passing judgment on worldly and religious affairs," a rather standard description of what the caliph does. Thus, having described the caliph without using the term, he devoted the second half of his speech to giving a caliphal call to jihad. As indicated earlier, the jihad speech was not primarily intended for the West, although it attacked the West. In a sense, it was only partly defensive, for it was considerably more than an apologia for the invasion. Instead, from beginning to end it went on the offensive. It was primarily about a competition for leadership. In it, Saddam argued within an Arab-Islamic framework against the legitimacy of others and for his own, a tactic later paralleled by referring to Saudi Arabia as the lands of Najd and Hijaz. Saddam had long articulated a view of the ideal leader, sometimes subtly, sometimes not, with himself in that role. Now, on 10 August, as he gave the call to jihad to Arabs and Muslims against an array of foes, he presented himself before the watching world as caliph Saddam, the 'Umar of 1990—without ever using the title.

This heralded a new age. As Saddam's biographers Iskander and Matar had indicated a decade before, Saddam aimed at no less than the recrudescence of millennia of "Iraqi" glory and the creation of a new Iraqi man.[96] Now the aim was even larger. The age of abasement would soon be past; a new era was at hand for all Arabs and Muslims. But first, there must be a great, cataclysmic battle; apocalypse must precede eschatological glory. Never at a loss for categorical terms, the Iraqis on 20 September broadcast a joint statement by the RCC and the Ba'th that drew as bright a line as possible between the forces of good and evil. The distinction drawn was similar to those made during the Iran-Iraq War, but this one was even more expansive. Significant also (but not unusual) was the primacy accorded to Iraq, as well as the assertion that this titanic battle was being waged, in large part, on behalf of Palestine. And for the first time, the Iraqis used the most famous term to emerge for the battle.

With the passage of each day after the ranks of the unjust began to bare their teeth, especially after the forces of darkness occupied the holy lands, the boundaries of evil become clear. . . . Now that the confines of evil have been made clear and that the dimensions of the evil-doers have become clear, the magnitude of the well-meaning and faithful people who love God and people, fight the devil and whose gathering has redoubled and showed itself to be full of virtue and sacrifices, has shown itself. They are led by those whom God and history have chosen to play the role of the faithful vanguard, the great Iraqi people. . . . Everybody must realise that *this battle will be the mother of all battles*, and that God wanted us to wage the battle of liberating the nation and humanity, the battle of liberating Jerusalem and the holy shrines on the land of Iraq. In its victory will be realised and liberated all that is supposed to be achieved and liberated. What an honour for every Iraqi man and woman! What an honour for every zealous Arab and every honourable and faithful person! God is great, and may the lowly be accursed.[97]

Taha Ramadan, the first deputy prime minister, used equally categorical and specifically Islamic terms when he described the approach of war as "the embodiment of a grand confrontation and a battle known as the crucial battle in which we will strike at the entire camp of infidelity using the entire camp of faith."[98]

Yet in this titanic battle the faithful need not despair, for if God had called them to this, he would also supply the "weaponry." The theme of divine help against otherwise insuperable odds recurred throughout the conflict, and certainly was not unexpected; believers of any number of faith traditions have said the same. One need look no further than the "people of the book," Jews and Christians. The boy David told Goliath, "You have come against me with sword and spear and javelin, but I have come against you in the name of the Lord Almighty, the God of the armies of Israel." The apostle Paul assured the small band of Christians at Corinth, "The weapons we fight with are not the weapons of the world. On the contrary, they have divine power to demolish strongholds."[99]

But the Iraqis sometimes approached this matter of faith and weapons in ways that would strike many in the West as odd—odd, yet well situated within the cultural context of the region. Few things better illustrate their approach than the announcement of a new missile, one the Iraqis termed al-Hijara. The circumstances of the announcement of its readiness, the selection of its name, and the description of its capabilities all showed the Iraqis' continued ability to adapt to new political developments with considerable flexibility, speed, and intelligence. Moreover, the announcement of the missile really was paradigmatic, for it showed the regime's ability to connect deep history, traditional Baʿth doctrine, and a return to Islam, all in the service of the Palestinians and the Arab nation.

Riots provided the occasion for Saddam's announcement. On 8 October, two months after Iraq invaded Kuwait, Palestinians on the Temple Mount in Jerusalem heard that a conservative Jewish group had sought to take a cornerstone for a new Jewish temple up to *haram al-sharif*, the area around the Dome of the Rock. An Israeli judge blocked the request, but word of the injunction failed to reach the Palestinians. They began pelting Jewish worshippers at the Wailing Wall with rocks. In the ensuing melee, security forces killed 21 Palestinians and wounded over 150. Saddam wasted no time in turning the issue to his advantage. The next day, Baghdad radio read the president's response.[100] With a striking metaphor, Saddam described the situation. "Yesterday, in the very heart of Bayt al-Maqdis, the Zionist occupiers perpetrated a crime which is unlike other crimes, a crime which brought tears not only to the eyes but also to the very hearts of all zealous Arabs and all honourable men. The crime was perpetrated against our people, brothers, sisters, and sons, the sons of beloved Palestine." Only decisive action could "heal our wounded hearts." Saddam continued with a brief discussion of comparative technical abilities of the West and the Arabs. The Arabs were not to be despised. Recall, he directed his listeners, how the rod of Musa (Moses) swallowed the rods of the magicians in pharaoh's court, and how God instructed the prophet to throw dust in the air toward his enemies at the battle of Badr preliminary to the believers' victory.[101] Similarly, by a plan of God's devising, the Arabs would throw dust in the eyes of the Zionists and the Americans.

Then Saddam made his special announcement in a dramatic way. During a meeting of the Armed Forces General Command the day before, Saddam recalled,

[T]he Minister of Industry and Military Industrialisation whispered in my ear what he [had] already told me before, that the stones have become, God willing, capable of proceeding towards their targets hundreds of kilometres away from the place from where they are launched. It is the stones, the new missile, which the Iraqis have invented with the help of God, and which can reach the targets of evil when the day of reckoning comes from any place on Iraqi territory. There are plenty of stones in the land of Iraq. I have shouted and continue to shout Allahu Akbar. These are the stones baked with clay, God willing.[102]

The announcement was a masterstroke. "The stones" is the literal rendering of *al-hijara*, the name of the Iraqis' latest reconfiguration of the Scud missile. The missile's capability of striking "targets hundreds of kilometres away" indicated that weapons developers in Iraq had exchanged accuracy (of which there was little to begin with) for somewhat increased range.[103] While in development, the Iraqis had called the missile al-Abbas, the name of the brother of the third Shi'a Imam, Hussein ibn Ali. And the name made sense at the time; during the war with Iran, the Iraqis named several of their major weapons systems for the

Shi'a, for reasons Chapter Four explains. But at the moment, Saddam's first need was not to appeal to the Shi'a community. It was, rather, to connect in every way possible with something outside Iraq, most especially with the Palestinians.

Thus, the Iraqis renamed the missile and then announced its preparedness on the heels of rioting and death in Jerusalem. "Al-Hijara" could not have been a better choice. Those participating in the intifada had become known as the "children of the stones." When Saddam stated there were "plenty of stones in Iraq," he was thereby saying both that Iraq was fully armed (with "the stones" being missiles) and fully committed to the Palestinians; he would rearm them with more stones. The PLO wasted no time taking up the refrain. The Voice of Palestine radio broadcast (from Baghdad) the day after Saddam's announcement declared, "[W]e say that Palestinian blood is not cheap, and our people will know how to deal double retaliation. Before that, we tell all parties—enemies and friends—to understand and listen well to Saddam Husayn's shout 'God is great, God is great, these are the stones baked with clay'."[104]

Additionally, the announcement of the missile enabled Saddam to link his own role in delivering the Palestinians with those of other great historical figures. On the 12 October, *al-Qadisiyya*, the military newspaper, described the unfolding of a vast panorama, envisioning a scene in which Palestinian children greeted Saddam with jasmine flowers and asked him about earlier deliverers from Mesopotamia—Gilgamesh, Nebuchadnezzar, and Saladin. In response, "Saddam opens his generous hands and awards the children a missile called *hijara*."[105] And the day before the air war started, the government newspaper *al-Jumhuriyya* made a promise. If an attack should come, Iraqis would make the Zionists their very first retaliatory target. And they kept their promise to the children of Palestine. Hours after coalition aircraft struck Baghdad, Iraq launched eight Scuds at Israel.[106]

But the reference to stones worked at a much deeper level. The expression "stones baked with clay," which Voice of Palestine repeated was hardly accidental, and connected with an important aspect of regional history. As described in Chapter Four, the regime had chosen "Qadisiyya" as the chief name for the Iran-Iraq conflict because the war recapitulated history; "Saddam's Qadisiyya" was to be another defeat of the Persians. The eight-year war was the "book of Qadisiyya" and the cease-fire that followed, "the day of days."[107] Although the reference to "stones baked with clay" is considerably more oblique than Qadisiyya, it functioned in the same way. Indeed, it was part of a nexus of references the Iraqis had already begun to employ and would continue to use throughout the fall and into the months of Desert Storm.

On 5 September, Saddam issued his second major appeal for jihad. In it he connected the deployment of coalition forces to pre-Islamic history.

Muslims everywhere: Fahd, Husni, and their allies from among those who have evil and base records, have added to their injustice by repeating the role of Abu Rughal, who acted as the guide of the Abyssinian [A]brahah on the road to pre-Islam Mecca and was defeated by God with flights of birds and stones of baked clay. Indeed, the part played by Abu Rughal was less vicious than their [i.e., the Saudis or, possibly, the Arab League] role when they called in invading armies that have occupied and desecrated the land housing the sacred places of Muslims and Arabs.[108]

The Quran (105:1–5) alludes to the event Saddam had in mind. Sura al-Fil (the Elephant) reads:

> Seest thou not
> How thy Lord dealt
> With the companions of the elephant?
> Did he not make
> Their treacherous plan
> go astray?
> And he sent against them
> Flights of birds,
> Striking them with stones
> Of baked clay.
> Then did He make them
> Like an empty field
> Of stalks and straw,
> (Of which the corn)
> Has been eaten up.

"Stones of baked clay" (*hijara min sijjil*) is the same phrase Saddam used in his jihad speech and used again to announce the new missile, al-Hijara. But the Quranic reference gives no details about the "companions of the elephant" or when the attack occurred. For that, Saddam must have turned to a larger story embedded in Arab and Islamic culture, one with a historical core and traditional embellishment, and one to which the Quran only obliquely makes reference.[109] At its heart is the story of the historical Abraha, the (Christian) Abyssinian governor of Yemen in the mid-sixth century who was allied with Byzantium against the Sassanid Persians.[110] Abraha made an abortive attack on Mecca about 550, perhaps hoping to end its status as a place of (then) pagan pilgrimage rivaling Yemen and the magnificent cathedral he had built there. But Abraha's army, it seems, was felled by epidemic, perhaps smallpox.

Tradition renders the story more fully, and it is transmitted chiefly in the work of two important early Arab historians, ibn Hisham (d. 767/8) and al-Tabari (d. 923).[111] In their narration, the date of the attack on Mecca is moved to 570, the year Muhammad was born. The powerful Abraha determined to march on the city of Mecca, and he set out northward with his army and an elephant. (Because of the connection of this story and sura 105, "The Elephant," the year 570 is often referred to as "the year of the elephant.") Naturally, the Arabs were frightened. "News of this plunged the Arabs into alarm and anxiety and they decided it was incumbent on them to fight against him when they heard that he meant to destroy the ka'ba, God's holy house."[112] Along the way, Abraha enlisted the aid of a guide, one abu-Rughal of Ta'if, who showed him the way into Mecca. But then a miracle occurred.

God sent upon them birds from the sea like swallows and starlings; each bird carried three stones, like peas and lentils. . . . Everyone who was hit died but not all were hit. They withdrew in flight by the way they came. . . . As they withdrew they were continually falling by the wayside dying miserably by every waterhole. Abraha was smitten in his body, and as they took him away his fingers fell off one by one. Where the finger had been, there arose an evil sore. . . . They allege that as he died his heart burst from his body.[113]

From that time, Abraha became the picture of the arrogant transgressor who would march on God's sanctities. Abu-Rughal is noted as the perfidious traitor from within, having come from Ta'if, east of Mecca; stoning his grave in contempt is a tradition that persists to this day.

In Saddam's jihad speech on 5 September, the references to Fahd and Mubarak make sense against this background. They were like the perfidious within who have shown the "Abraha Americans" the way to the ka'ba; they are the abu-Rughals of the contemporary Arab world. The Ba'th followed the historical assault with one of its own the following day: "[W]e would like to tell them [i.e., the Saudis, who put their confidence in the army they led into the land] that God Almighty, who sent flights of birds against the army of Abraha to strike it with stones of baked clay until he made that army become like an empty field . . . can send other flights of birds to Bush's army to destroy its planes, tanks and vehicles, not to mention the snakes and scorpions which are attacking his soldiers, killing many of them."[114]

Having found the theme of Abraha, the Iraqis were quite prepared to use it in producing their best-known letter in the conflict. Like other documents of the war, this one may have appeared strange to many western readers, but it was quite intelligible and certainly warranted within the context so far described. On 8 September, Saddam wrote Presidents Bush and Gorbachev.[115] Opening with the bismallah, Saddam appealed to the two presidents before they began their summit meeting in Helsinki. They must consider, Saddam warned, that angels and devils would flank them, each arguing a case for what ought to be done. Saddam then followed with a history lesson on the unity of Kuwait and Iraq, telling them he prayed that God would "fill hardened hearts with the light of belief"—especially Bush's, he adds. Of interest here, "the believing slave of God," for so he signed himself, warned the two that "the house [the ka'ba] has a God who protects it." Saddam briefly related the story of Abraha the Abyssinian who, enticed by the devil and intoxicated with power, had marched on the holy city. God trounced him and smashed his armies. Obviously, Bush and Gorbachev would run the same danger as the hubristic Abyssinian did in the sixth century.

The references to Abraha and abu-Rughal continued through the fall and into the spring. Saddam's Christmas message made the connection, calling Bush a Judas who had betrayed the teachings of Jesus Christ and Fahd an abu-Rughal who had betrayed both the teachings of Islam and his sacred responsibility as *khadim al-haramayn*.[116] And the Iraqi press made what was an inevitable link: that between Abraha's elephant and the political party affiliation of the American president who had so lately made his own attack on Mecca. "The party of the elephant . . . and Bush, the new Abraha, have seized Najd and Hijaz." Bush would certainly suffer Abraha's fate.[117] Even in defeat, the Iraqis made the connection. In its commentary "Why We Are Victorious" on 3 March, Radio Baghdad offered several reasons for claiming triumph.

Iraq had withstood a thirty-nation onslaught without bowing its head. Iraq had resurrected Palestine as a critical issue in the hearts and minds of men. And Iraq could claim victory because "we stood fast against the treason of Abraha and because the flag of Allahu Akbar did not fall from our hands."[118]

In this light, announcing the readiness of a missile named al-Hijara did not seem so odd. It fit nicely with a carefully constructed, extended metaphor drawing on Islamic history and addressing a very current Palestinian need for empowerment. On the abu-Rughals of the lands of Najd and Hijaz and Egypt, who had shown the coalition Abrahas the way into Islam's holiest city, God would rain down his stones. He would do so on behalf of the Arab and Islamic nation, and he would do so through the vanguard nation Iraq and its leader president, the worshipper of God. What better hope could there be in this titanic conflict?

But what would follow battle? Iraqi radio declared one day into the air war, "This is the beginning of the end. It is the beginning of the age of the new Arab awakening and the end of the age of imperialist-Zionist corruption and economic hegemony over our continent and the world."[119] The regime had in view no less than a *novus ordo seclorum*. With an almost inexorable, Hegelian certainty, history was moving on its course, one that would eventuate in the triumph of Islam, the primacy of the Arabs among Muslims, and the clear establishment of Iraq at the vanguard. Saddam's Victory Day [i.e., over Iran in 1988] message on 8 August gives a glimpse of this new vision, one with the celestial hallmarks of a new millennial day.

At [the] time when the second of August arrived to be the legitimate newborn son of the second Qadisiyah [the battle with Iran] . . . its consequences shall be the beginning of a new, lofty, and rising stage in which virtue will spread throughout the Arab homeland in the coming days and profanity, treachery, betrayal, meanness, and subservience to the foreigner will retreat from it. Many of the goals of the Arabs will move closer after some believed they were moving away. . . . *New suns and moons will shine; stars will glitter; light will expel darkness; and lunar and solar eclipses will withdraw from the skies of Iraq and the Arab world.*[120]

The RCC agreed. In announcing its decision to approve the provisional government's request for merger, the RCC stated, "It is a decision for all Iraqis, from the land to the sea. At the same time, it is for all good Arabs from the [Atlantic] Ocean to the [Persian] Gulf. . . . The dawn will break and the sun will rise to brighten the paths of darkness and aberration."[121] Or to cite once again the jihad speech, this battle of the entire Arab nation would lead to a time when life would be "completely identical" with the law of God. This was no less than the implementation of shari'a, the long desired goal of the devout, and Saddam hereby offered to lead them to it.[122]

## CARRYING OUT THE MESSAGE

The task of promulgating this new vision, one that joined Arabism and Islam, was no easy business and became the task of everyone in Iraq. As the regime summoned men to jihad on the battlefield and women to jihad in the home, it waged a kind of jihad on itself: to use every avenue to convey the message. To begin, the regime propounded this worldview across the spectrum. It was not only total and totalizing, as Ba'thism and Khomeinism had been, but it was also inescapably presented. Until the Shi'a-Kurdish intifada the following March, the regime largely maintained a discourse monopoly. All participated in this massive exercise in coordination. As indicated above, the president's messages were quickly followed with similar announcements from elsewhere in the government and media.

That pattern held during all of Desert Shield and Desert Storm. The Ba'th, the RCC, and the National Assembly were quite obviously "in sync," both in timing and in content. (As noted above, the single exception is that Ba'th messages were notably more "secular" until the air campaign began, at which time the party adopted a notably more Islamic discourse. Apart from that, Ba'th messages were strikingly similar to the others in most particulars, and similar in all ways after 17 January.[123]) Thus, when Saddam gave a message on jihad, as he did on 10 August, the Popular Islamic Conference, the National Assembly, "Holy Mecca Radio" (a clandestine Iraqi broadcast aimed at Saudi troops), and Abdullah Fadil, the Iraqi minister of awqaf and religious affairs, immediately gave parallel and equally vigorous calls to a holy war.[124] This echoing of themes occurred constantly, whether the issue was the merger with Kuwait or descriptions of a new Arab-Islamic millennium or a revised enemies list. The news media carried the same message without deviation, writing editorials that squared exactly with what the regime had said and done.[125] Even military communiqués collaborated in presenting the message. Routinely prefaced with the bismallah, as were the announcements from Saddam and the government agencies, they reported on the marked success of the jihad, while giving unstinting adulation to the daring knight of the Arab nation. As with so many other announcements, these reports from the military fused Arabism and Islam. A typical example in February read, "[O]ur armed forces pray to God Almighty to preserve the homeland . . . and to bless [our] *jihad to defend the honor of the Arab nation and the dignity of Muslims*".[126]

## FURTHER PREPARATIONS FOR WAR

As it coordinated its messages, the regime also secured various loose ends. For instance, it moved vigorously to reach rapprochement with Iran. Saddam's letter of 30 July to Rafsanjani had indicated that the Iraqis were prepared to make substantive concessions on Security Council Resolution 598, excepting only the brief paragraph that called on the secretary-general to appoint an impartial body to inquire into responsibility for the Iran-Iraq War. Saddam, of course, was loath to see that done; the regime had portrayed Iran as responsible from the outset. Just the year before (1989), during the rebuilding of Basra, Iraq had placed ninety statues of war heroes along the corniche of the Shatt. Each points a recriminatory finger toward the east, a *j'accuse* in bronze.[127] But now Saddam, a week and a half into a new imbroglio of his making, was compelled to capitulate even on the issue of his responsibility, not to say culpability, for eight years of war. On 14 August, therefore, Saddam wrote to Rafsanjani offering an immediate withdrawal of forces and a prisoner-of-war exchange.[128] Saddam also acquiesced in not bracketing out Article 6 of Resolution 598, as Iran insisted. By so doing, Saddam hoped to "start a new life of co-operation under the canopy of Islam's principles" and, more importantly, "keep away those who are fishing in murky waters off our coasts." The gulf, the president hoped, would become a "lake of peace."

And the president was as good as his word. The withdrawal and POW exchanges began immediately, and in mid-October the countries restored diplomatic relations. The Iranians got what they wanted in the exchange; Saddam's gains, however, were mixed. On the one hand, he had reduced his list of enemies. He could now redeploy troops that had been tied down on the eastern border to new positions in the "nineteenth province." Iran reportedly allowed some humanitarian imports to pass through its borders. And Iran remained neutral. But Iran was among the first to condemn the invasion; the foreign ministry formally did so on 2 August. Although Iran also condemned the U.S. presence in the region, it continued to insist that Iraq withdraw from Kuwait. Perhaps the greatest blow was that the Iranians refused to countenance Saddam's characterization of the conflict as a holy war. Rather, the Iranians described it as *na-moqaddas*, "unholy." Under the circumstances, these mixed results were the best Saddam could gain.[129]

Mindful of the unstable mix that is the Iraqi body politic, in November the regime appointed a Kurd as its new chief of staff, General Husayn Rashid Muhammad. The next month, it appointed a Shi'i, Lieutenant General Sa'di al-Jabburi as minister of defense. To be sure, both men brought considerable experience to the positions, but the government also hoped they would appeal to their respective communities.[130] A far more important measure was to secure a fatwa from the Ayatollah Abu al-Qasim al-Khoi.[131] No other Islamic leader in Iraq commanded the respect Khoi did. Born in 1899, Khoi was scholarly, austere, and—most important—traditional; here was no firebrand trying to mix politics and religion. Indeed, Khoi opposed the vilayet e fiqh doctrine that the Ayatollah Khomeini had implemented in Iran, holding that the authority of the Islamic jurists does not lie in the political sphere. Khoi taught, *contra* Khomeini, that in the absence of the Imam, the authority the jurists exercise cannot be the prerogative of the few; it must be shared.

During the Iran-Iraq War the Iraqis had sought Khoi's endorsement of the war, but the ayatollah refused to take a political position. For its part, the government refused Khoi's request for an exit visa and kept him under virtual house arrest until his death in 1992. But the government had to recognize the esteem in which Iraqis, both Shi'a and Sunni, continued to hold Khoi—such was his reputation for scholarship and integrity. Thus the government turned to its virtual prisoner for a religious ruling in mid-August following the deployment of foreign forces. Khoi obliged, but only in part.[132] On the eighteenth the ayatollah ruled it was impermissible to "seek support from heretics against Muslims." His fatwa called further for a peaceful resolution to the crisis. But most significantly Khoi's fatwa did not call, as the regime had hoped, specifically for a jihad against the coalition. In a further ruling, the ayatollah forbade the Shi'a to purchase any goods brought back to Iraq from Kuwait, saying they had been stolen.[133]

Others were more compliant. In looking particularly at establishment Islam within Iraq, one quickly notes how its message exactly paralleled that of other agencies in the government. Here, obviously, was no independent voice. One example was Minister of Awqaf and Religious Affairs Abdullah Fadil. A long-term Ba'th party member, Fadil was a member of the RCC and had headed the Ba'th party office in the north of Iraq. When the regime uncovered a "plot" in July 1979 just after Saddam became president, Fadil joined six other RCC members on the special court designated to hear charges of treason levied against the perpetrators. In the early 1980s he was appointed minister of awqaf, replacing Nuri Faisal Shahir, who was transferred to the Youth Ministry. It is hardly surprising that Fadil was one of the early voices (12 August), following the Arab League meeting of the tenth, to condemn the Saudis who had "betrayed the trust of safeguarding the Muslim sanctities by bringing in forces of tyranny and atheism." Fadil also met many of the religious dignitaries who came to Baghdad during the fall, and opened a special conference in early December of Arab Christians who had declared solidarity with Iraq.[134]

Equally in step with the government was the commission of senior Iraqi ulama. The ulama, which offered no statement at all until six weeks after the invasion, had this to say in its first announcement:

As for seeking the protection of the infidel against the Muslim, even if this was done in accordance with an agreement with the infidels, it is categorically impermissible, because it contravenes definite Islamic rulings which say that the Muslim should not be under the tutelage of the infidel, and that whoever permits this is departing from definite rulings and violating the consensus of Muslim scholars. "And never will God grant to the unbelievers a way to triumph over the believers" (Quran 4:141). . . . Therefore, it is the duty of all Muslims, as mandated by the Shari'ah, to embrace holy jihad so as to deter these dangers that have desecrated homelands and holy places and begun to infringe upon honour. May God grant us success.[135]

No other public theological justification than this was offered in the body's initial appeal for jihad: the presence of U.S. troops in Saudi Arabia simply "contravenes definite Islamic rulings." But something significantly more illuminating, at least as far as showing how the regime had coached the ulama in how to render its pronouncements, is this from two weeks later. The passage is worth quoting at length.

Iraq, under its heroic mujahid leader Saddam Husayn, chose to defy the new world order as it came under the grip of U.S. brute force, and it has drawn the nation's attention to the dangers of unilateral control of the world by this brute force—dangers manifest in such acts as the gathering of the Soviet Jews in Palestine as a prelude to expelling its remaining Muslim Arab inhabitants and expanding over new areas in the Arab and Islamic homeland. Towards this end, the United States directed the treacherous swords of its conspiracy towards Iraq and its ascending power with a view to eliminating the hope radiating from the firm position of its brave leader and his bright Arab-Islamic policy. . . . It is time to have absolute belief in jihad; deep awareness of the gravity of the stage our nation is passing through. . . . It is time for all Muslims to stand in one line and one trench.[136]

Two items stand out in the declaration. First, although the ulama call for jihad over ten times in the full text and cite the Quran several times, the statement also has a distinctly political dimension: the new world order, a unipolar world, Soviet Jewish immigration. Elsewhere in the text, the ulama call on all Arabs and Muslims to oppose U.S. hegemony, U.S. colonialism, and the unilateral U.S. control of "both eastern and western worlds."

More particularly, these words the ulama chose reflected both the current wartime parlance of the government and traditional Baʿthist influence. "The stage our nation is passing through" was a way of describing the situation long favored by the Baʿth and Saddam rather than deriving from Islam. To pick one example among so many, here is part of the president's speech in 1974 on the "national front." "[D]espite this stage we have passed through along the road of the revolution . . . there are still some tools of reaction in Iraq. . . . We have started on the first stage of our forward march but the signs do not indicate that we are at the end of the march."[137] Similarly, the ulama's reference to "one line and one trench" reflects Saddam's own penchant. A book with such a title was published in 1977 (with Saddam indicated as author),[138] and the phrase appeared in a number of places, appropriate to a president who had kept his people on a perpetual wartime footing. Elsewhere in their statement the ulama declare, "Your brothers in Iraq have determined to engage in jihad, without any *hesitation, retreat or fear*, against the forces of the foreigners. . . . [A]s the President leader of the *struggling* nation said, 'Now that the nation of the infidel has stood in *one line*, let the nation of the faithful stand with Iraq on *the opposite line*'" (emphasis added). The words bear a remarkable resemblance to those of Saddam himself years before. "We cannot help being what we are because no noble *struggler* of any patriotic political movement or decent citizen of the people can accept *vacillation, bargaining, humiliation, or retreat. . . .* [T]he day to day experience of battle and *last-ditch trenches* purifies [Iraqis] of the residues of the past and strengthens their absolute faith in the programme of the [national] front" (emphasis added).[139] In short, while calling for jihad, the ulama appeared simply to have "Islamized" the speech of the party faithful.

Religious dignitaries in the provinces likewise supported the regime, and they did so in terms similar to those of the commission of senior Iraqi ulama and with similar adulations. In Diyala province, Iraqi media reported that religious leaders had "voiced their full support for leader President Saddam Husayn's call for jihad to expel the covetous invaders. . . . They reiterated the pledge to stand behind his excellency's courageous leadership to defend the nation's soil and holy places." Similarly in Dahuk, they declared "full support for leader President Saddam Husayn in the confrontation of the imperialist-Zionist conspiracy which seeks to harm Iraq and the Arab nation." Moreover, at the Dahuk gathering, "poems were recited praising the President leader's peace initiatives and readiness to defend great Iraq and the Arab nation and its sanctities."[140]

## BAGHDAD: VENUE OF ISLAMIC CONFERENCES AND NOTABLES

In this Other Gulf War, the battle claimed casualties before the fighting began. One was the Popular Islamic Conference (PIC) in Iraq. Formed in 1983 and headquartered in Iraq, the PIC had functioned to galvanize (Sunni) Islamic support for the Ba'thist regime in the Iran-Iraq War. But now, in this war of Sunni against Sunni and ulama against ulama, the PIC declared war on itself. As indicated above, in August the General Secretariat of the PIC appealed to "all Islamic organizations, societies, unions, centers, and intellectuals throughout the world" to conduct jihad alongside Iraq and against Saudi Arabia, and called on the "Islamic media" to mobilize others in the effort.[141] But the appeal was not simply to Muslims. Like the regime's announcements, this too appealed to Muslims and Arabs, casting the enemies in terms the Ba'th would appreciate. Indeed, the PIC hoped for an Arab-Muslim union that "will turn into a blazing fire to burn the feet of the aggressors and shake the ground under them."

In fact, the organization might well have extended the appeal for unity to itself, for the PIC effectively split at this point. A day after PIC members in Baghdad made their call for jihad, Muhammad al-Dawalibi, theretofore chairman of the organization, issued another sort of appeal, one carried by Saudi radio rather than Iraqi.[142] Directly (and respectfully) addressing the Iraqi president, Dawalibi told Saddam that he had conferred with a number of members who were in leadership in the PIC. Based on those conversations, Dawalibi wrote the president, seeking an "honorable solution . . . a noble Arab and Islamic solution" to those areas where they may "differ." Appealing "in the name of Allah . . . and Arab kinship," Dawalibi urged the president to "set a noble Islamic example in resolving conflicts by responding to your brothers' call in the ICO and Arab League Council, of which you are a member." That, of course, is precisely what Saddam intended not to do; after the Arab League decisions, Saddam had determined to take a contrary course.

From that point, rival branches of the PIC, now operating in Baghdad and Mecca, made counterappeals to Muslims. The commission of senior Iraqi ulama joined the Baghdad-loyal branch of the PIC in arguing against the legitimacy of meetings in Mecca, whether of the Mecca-loyal branch of the PIC or other Islamic bodies. For instance, in mid-September the Iraqi ulama admonished other Muslims to boycott the Islamic conference the Saudis were preparing to convene under the sponsorship of the Muslim World League.[143] They warned their brethren that those called to Mecca intended "to present a document which justifies [the Saudi rulers'] infidelity and wrongdoing and injustice to the nation and its sanctities and justifies to the infidels and polytheists the crime of occupying the land of the Arabian Peninsula and the Crusader aggression on Muslims."

The Baghdad PIC joined the Iraqi ulama in the attack on the Mecca conference.[144] The Islamic leaders in the holy city, they said, had simply wasted their time discussing ancillary issues. Indeed, in support of the coalition forces, they offered only "weak justifications which cannot deceive anyone who has the slightest knowledge of the Shariʿa." Indeed, the Baghdad PIC charged, even Jad al-Haqq (respected rector of al-Azhar), had capitulated, having legalized "the enlisting of the help of the Israeli entity against the Muslims in Iraq." The PIC asserted that the ulama in Najd and Hijaz were being harassed and imprisoned, and it encouraged them to stand fast against the depredations of the regime. Most significantly (and ironically) it asserted that the participants in the Mecca conference were *fuquha al sultat.* Meaning "(Islamic) legal authorities of the state," it was a way of accusing the Mecca conference participants of being mere hirelings, controlled by those in the government. "What a waste of education, religion and jurists" the attack concluded.

Of course, the regime could anticipate that others would not be particularly swayed by what Muslims inside Iraq had to say; the powerful and all-pervasive *mukhabarat* (the intelligence service responsible for internal security) could compel compliant statements. It was far more important to show that others outside Iraq sided with her in the hour of need and agreed with the regime's basic Islamic contentions. Undoubtedly, therefore, the PIC carried more weight than Iraqi ulama: it drew from the outside. But the PIC was, after all, headquartered in the country, and at the moment there were two PICs. It could only help to have additional Islamic visitors to Iraq. During the lead-up to the conflict, Iraq hosted any number of political delegations (e.g., those of Primakov and Javier Pérez de Cuéllar), nonpolitical figures (Jesse Jackson, Ramsey Clark, Muhammad Ali), unaffiliated peace organizations, and Christian groups. But more particularly, it hosted Islamists, both those involved in the PIC and others outside it.

Of the various non-PIC delegations, probably none was as important as the World Islamic Popular Gathering, an ad hoc organization that first convened in Amman, Jordan, in September, and styled itself as "an Islamic good-offices effort to resolve the Middle East conflict and the Gulf crisis within an Arab-Islamic context."[145] Promising to arbitrate in the crisis on the basis of the *shari'a,* the conference drew delegates from Jordan, Palestine, Egypt, Syria, Yemen, the Sudan, Tunisia, Algeria, Pakistan, Turkey, and Malaysia; notably none came from any of the GCC states. After concluding the inaugural meeting in Amman, the delegation traveled to Jeddah, Saudi Arabia, to meet with Fahd and various Kuwaitis, then to Iraq and Iran. Muhammad Khalifah, controller-general of the Muslim Brotherhood in Jordan, led the delegation, which included Hasan al-Turabi of the Sudanese National Islamic Front and Qazi Hussein Ahmad of the Jamaat-e-Islami in Pakistan.

The delegation proved helpful to the Iraqi cause. Although it tried to maintain a show of evenhandedness, saying it was looking for a solution that sought "tolerance, brotherhood, and adherence to Islamic principles" from the parties, the delegation also emphasized that the *shari'a* forbade seeking help from infidels. Moreover, the participants supported Saddam in a key facet of his apologia, stressing that "the wealth of the nation is the property of all Muslims." When the delegation reached Baghdad, it delivered an especially strong denunciation of the coalition. Khalifah termed the presence of the "invading American Zionist forces" in Saudi Arabia the "most serious sin against Islam." Necmettin Erbakan, leader of the Refah party in Turkey and later prime minister, appealed to Muslim states everywhere to unite against the invaders and protect the sacred lands from defilement.

After listening to several of the speeches, Saddam himself spoke, telling the audience that the current issue turned on two problems: Jerusalem, and American imperialism and oil. Jerusalem, the city to which those in Baghdad "always turned their eyes," must be liberated, he told the delegation (which, significantly, included Hamas). Of oil, Saddam observed that it had corrupted both the faith and morals of those who had hoarded the wealth it had brought. Saddam's purpose was to turn oil into the blessing God had intended and to share its bounty with the larger nation. And of Kuwait, the president promised that Iraq was prepared to fight for a thousand years to retain it, for not only had Kuwait been returned to the fold; it had "been returned to the faith after having been a place where infidelity was practiced."

After visiting Iran, the team members returned home, and Khalifa spoke with the media in Amman, Jordan.[146] The Muslim Brotherhood leader made some attempt at balance. He spoke respectfully of Fahd and remarked how cordial the delegation's visit with Iran had been. Khalifa even mentioned possible Iraqi withdrawal. But on balance, his statements favored Iraq, on which he avoided placing any blame.

We must intensify efforts to find an Arab-Islamic solution to the current crisis in order to remove the spectre of war, guarantee the foreign forces' departure and Iraq's withdrawal, consider *Iraq's legitimate demands* and Islamic arbitration, achieve the Kuwaiti people's legitimate aspirations in their homeland, and maintain security throughout the region in the future. If this solution is placed within an international framework, it should be linked to the Palestine question and Israeli aggression. (emphasis added)[147]

Most especially, Khalifa emphasized that the prime enemy of the Islamic world remained the United States. Because the United States had come to control Islamic sanctities in Mecca, Medina, and Jerusalem, jihad had become a duty for every Muslim man and woman. Finally, the delegation indicated it would develop its own peace plan to be presented at a conference in November. Neither the plan nor the meeting ever materialized, however.[148]

In December, Saddam had another opportunity to address a large Islamic group, the World Popular Islamic Leadership (WPIL) delegation, headquartered in Libya.[149] Like the delegation from the World Islamic Popular Gathering in September, the WPIL representatives had traveled through several countries on their way to Baghdad. Saddam spoke to them there, again tying the fortunes of Arabs and Muslims tightly together. "[M]y brothers, we believe . . . based on evidence and on clear texts in the holy Koran—that if Arabs are virtuous Islam will be in a good state, and if Arabs become corrupt Islam will be afflicted by many things." It was a very pointed and important return to theme. The previous June, Saddam had spoken to another large conference in Baghdad in quite similar words. Six weeks before invading Kuwait, the president had declared, "We are brought up on the belief that the Arabs and Islam are an integral one; thus, if the Arabs become weak, Islam will follow suit. Similarly, if the Arabs rise up—and this will not happen unless they heed the honorable concepts of Islam—Muslims in all parts of the earth will rise up and increase in dignity."[150] Not surprisingly, this had been an address to the Popular Islamic Conference in a plenum convened to deliberate how best to confront the "conspiracies targeting Iraq in particular and the Arab nation and Muslims in general." But by the December conference, matters of international law had come to the fore. Saddam spoke to the WPIL conferees on just that point by way of an extended literary apostrophe. Saddam imagined the imperialists and oil emirs ranked before him.

If oil is the most important thing for you, Jerusalem is the most important thing for us. . . . You consider our oil the most important thing for you. We consider, however, our sanctities the most important thing for us. . . . [W]hen we say that we respect international law, we put matters within the framework of the higher gains of the Arab nation and the Muslims. . . . [T]he only legitimacy in which we believe is the Islamic legitimacy; it is right and justice versus falsehood. [now to the conferees directly] Our guide in all this, brothers, is God's word in His holy Koran, and the action of the prophet Muhammad.

Others came.[151] In the months after the invasion, Baghdad hosted such Islamic notables as Shaykh As'ad Bayyud al-Tamimi, leader of the Islamic Jihad/Bayt al-Maqdis in Jordan;[152] Abbasi Madani, leader of the Algerian Islamic Salvation Front; and Rashid Ghannouchi, president of the Tunisian Renaissance Party. Others, not so well known, came as well. Qadir Khamush, secretary-general of the Hadith Ulama Society in Pakistan, led a delegation and promised that 50,000 Pakistani citizens had "volunteered for jihad to support Iraq in its just war against the forces of infidelity and tyranny."[153] The National Assembly received delegation leader Haytham Rahman, chairman of the Muslim Students' Federation in the Scandinavian countries and the imam of the Islamic League in Sweden. According to Iraqi media reporting, "Rahman described President Saddam Husayn's twelfth August peace initiative as a real peace policy designed to save the world from the grave consequences of tension in this vital area of the world. He also stressed the need for the departure of the invasion forces from the lands of Najd and Hejaz and for purging the ka'ba and the Tomb of the Prophet of the desecration of the aggressors."[154]

For all its emphasis on Islam, Iraq also appealed to Christians and even to Christian values for support after the invasion of Kuwait. The holy places in Jerusalem, after all, included Christian sites, so it was possible to include them as part of the justification for liberating al-Quds, the holy city. And as Saddam said to the WPIL delegation in mid-December, the Middle East was "the cradle of prophets and the land to which *all heavenly messages* descended".[155] Moreover, Isa (Jesus) was the penultimate prophet sent by God, excelled in importance only by Muhammad himself.

> Behold! The angels said:
> O Mary! Allah giveth thee
> Glad tidings of a Word
> From Him: his name
> Will be Christ Jesus,
> The son of Mary, held in honour
> In this world and the hereafter
> And of (the company of) those
> Nearest to Allah. (Quran 3:45)

It was quite natural, then, for the regime to appeal to Christians. The few Christians in Iraq (less than three percent of the population) had limited freedom of religion; and the quite peripatetic foreign minister, Tariq Aziz, was himself a Christian.[156] Thus, the regime welcomed

Christian gatherings, albeit much smaller than the Islamic ones it had hosted.

One such meeting was the Christian Peace Conference, which took, appropriately, the theme "blessed be the peacemakers."[157] Convened by churches in Iraq, the conference lasted for three days in early December 1990 and comprised Christians of orthodox and eastern rite churches (e.g., the Chaldean Catholic Church, the Syrian Catholic Church, the Greek Orthodox Church). Statements from the participants ranged from the conciliatory ("At this difficult time . . . we gather in Baghdad, the city of peace, to pray for peace") to the more polemical ("The Eastern Church is proud that it is taking part in the Arab struggle against foreign threats. Iraqi Muslims and Christians are united in their message, faith, and national dignity"). Saddam addressed this conference as he had others. Describing Baghdad as the "the city of Arabism, humanity and peace," the president called especially for justice, whether for the Palestinians or for the Iraqis who were suffering under an economic blockade. At the end of the conference, members presented a report, carried by Radio Baghdad, that praised the "wise initiative announced by leader President Saddam Husayn on [the] 12th of August [as] a sound and balanced foundation for resolving all regional problems peacefully."[158] Additionally, it called for foreign armies to "relinquish their hegemony over the holy places," and—agreeing with Saddam—it took special exception to the economic blockade as inhumane.

A week and a half later, Iraq hosted a special delegation, but this one garnered more attention in the American press than in the Iraqi. Presiding Episcopal Bishop Edmond Browning joined representatives of seventeen other churches in the United States on a "peace pilgrimage" to the Middle East. Leaving from Cyprus, the team split into three smaller groups that visited capitals throughout the region. Before going to the Iraqi capital, the Americans emphasized their hope to do all they could to avert war. One member, however, stressed that the team would urge Iraq to withdraw from Kuwait, promising, "We will be saying that in Baghdad." Apparently, Saddam found nothing particularly promising about meeting with the delegation. The Iraqi press noted only briefly that the minister of state for foreign affairs, Muhammad al-Sahhaf, met the delegation led by "Edmund Brown [sic], head of the American bishops." Al-Sahhaf underscored Iraq's commitment to serious dialogue, one that would follow Saddam's own peace initiative of 12 August. On the group's return, Bishop Browning met with President

Bush to share his conviction that "God does not desire this kind of destruction." President Bush, in turn, shared a copy of the Amnesty International report on atrocities in Kuwait.[159]

As necessary, the regime pointed to Christians who had failed their own religion's standard. Haj Muhammad Ali Clay (the term used by the Iraqi media) numbered among prominent Americans Saddam did receive. When he visited Iraq in late November, the Iraqi president told his guest, "[Y]ou see that the U.S. administration, instead of shouldering its humanitarian responsibility based on love and righteous action among all peoples on earth and on the good principles of religions, including the principles of Jesus Christ, is taking a hostile course against nations and peoples based only on the available brute force and the possibility of using it, forgetting that God the omnipotent is stronger than everybody and than all powers."[160] Saddam later likened Bush to Judas, who betrayed Jesus Christ and his teachings. He added that Fahd had done similarly, betraying the teachings of Islam and the principles of Arabism. And as he had charged in September, Saddam once again declared that Fahd was a modern abu-Rughal.[161]

Even in Islamic meetings, the Iraqis made a connection to Christianity. Addressing the Popular Islamic Conference a week before the UN mandated withdrawal from Kuwait, Taha Ramadan, the deputy prime minister, drew the attention of the Islamic delegates to Jerusalem. Reminding the delegates they were a part of the blessed "nation of heavenly messages. . . . a cradle of the heavenly faiths," Ramadan described the conspiracy against "Palestine and holy Jerusalem, the cradle of Jesus, son of Mary, may God's peace be upon him, and the destination of the nocturnal journey of the noble prophet Muhammad, may God's peace and mercy be upon him."[162]

But perhaps the most striking connection between the contributions of Jesus and Muhammad came in a special message from the Iraqi president. The Iraqi News Agency released a recorded message of Christmas and New Year's greetings the last day of 1990. In many ways, Saddam gave his standard stump speech, rendering the world in categorical terms, describing economic disparities, speaking of injustice in Palestine. Saudi Arabia is Najd and Hijaz, Saddam said, the faithful are engaged in struggle for the nation, and the nation occupies an especially prominent place in God's plan. But this message, which began with the bismallah, emphasized the birth of Jesus Christ, "prophet of God . . . and an Arab." This season, "fragrant with the aroma of Christmas and filled with joy" for all the world, invited special reflection on true and false happiness, the meaning of service, and security and peace. In this context Saddam described the titanic conflict as one in which the forces of Satan were confronting those "governed by lofty values dictated by God Almighty." After asking God to curse those leaders who had succumbed to Satan's temptations, Saddam prayed that his listeners would find deeper faith and that God would grant their aspirations for good, love, and peace.[163]

## PSYCHOLOGICAL WARFARE

As armies have done for millennia, Iraq's turned to unconventional warfare as a force multiplier, especially during Desert Shield.[164] Part of that effort was reflected in its use of radio broadcasts.[165] In fact, the government broadcast under a number of fictional station names, each with a particular audience in view. "Voice of the Jihad," broadcast in English, was designed for Pakistani and Indian audiences. "Voice of Egypt of Arabism" obviously targeted the "sons of Gamal Abdul Nasser." In an attempt to generate discontent with the coalition, the broadcast told Egyptian soldiers that the American GIs, on taking "R and R" in Egypt, shunned the justly famous Egyptian Museum and the pyramids for Pyramid Street, where many Cairo nightclubs are located. Over time, the radio warned, the soldiers would turn all of Cairo and Alexandria into one big Pyramid Street. The regime directed the English-language "Voice of Peace" to American GIs. Featuring both male and female announcers, the program asked if the soldiers were prepared to return home from the desert "psychologically broken." The program featured very old pop music, even some from the bandstand era. On Christmas, Baghdad Betty, as the female announcer became known among the GIs, asked the troops, "Did you get any presents? Of course not, because you're here." Sometimes, Iraq's cultural isolation was only too obvious. "Do you know who your wives and girlfriends are dating while you're here?" taunted Betty. "They're back home dating movie stars, men like Tom Cruise, Arnold Schwarzenegger, and Bart Simpson."[166]

The coalition fought back. By January, at least five anti-Saddam radio stations were broadcasting. "Cairo Voice of the Arabs" was one, a counterbroadcast that frequently overpowered the Iraqis'. Official Saudi radio denounced Saddam as "the Hitler of the Orient, the axman of Iraq, and the thief of Baghdad." Additionally, Voice of America (VOA) and the BBC increased their broadcasting directed at Iraq generally, providing an important alternative news source.

But not all Iraqi broadcasts were as feckless as those about Bart. Of far more significance in this war of the airwaves was Holy Mecca Radio (HMR), a program directed especially at the Saudis. HMR was a clandestine broadcast purporting to emanate from within Saudi Arabia and to be operated by the people of Najd and Hijaz themselves. The station first broadcast on 10 August, the day of the important Arab League decision to formally invite Western assistance and, of course, the day of Saddam's jihad speech. Again, the broadcast reflected regime coordination. An hour after Saddam delivered his call to arms, HMR carried a counterpart message. "The Saudi regime, when it invited in the foreigners, committed an unforgivable sin against the sentiments and sanctities, against the Arab and Islamic histories."[167]

From that time, HMR carried a consistent message. Foreign troops had desecrated the holy places. Fahd had betrayed his sacred responsibility to protect Mecca and Medina. The Saudi regime had a role in a massive imperialist-Zionist conspiracy. The Saudis had "opened the gates of the holy land . . . to be infiltrated by Rabbis, Mossad officers, intelligence agents, and Zionist pilots." HMR described Saudi harassment of faithful Muslims in Najd and Hijaz, the arrest of several, and the conversion of the Rub al-Khali (the vast desert in the southeast) into a "big prison." The deploying forces (routinely described as the Zionist and U.S. occupation forces) were "pork-eaters, sinners, and AIDS victims" who had made Dhahran a "brothel of atheism, immorality, and debauchery." Far worse, these infidels had made Mecca and Medina a place to party with seminude dancers. The HMR broadcast on 27 August powerfully connected both cultural and religious values.

Sons of Najd and Hijaz and the Arabian peninsula, may the peace and blessings of God be upon you. People of Arab zealousness and chivalry; you whose land was hallowed by the revelation of the Muhammadan message; you whose land embraces Holy Mecca and the tombs of the prophet and the caliphs Abu Bakr, Umar, and Uthman. What has befallen you? Why has this American build-up desecrated your land with the boots of its soldiers? What is the Muslim saying as he faces Mecca five times a day in prayer? No doubt, when he prays, meditates, or bows, the Muslim can imagine the American, British, French, Italian, Zionist, and other soldiers, as well as the Arab forces, which have come to stay and make money. What a psychological blow the criminal Fahd has caused to Muslims![168]

The picture is extraordinarily striking. Devout Muslims, turning toward Mecca and the ka'ba to pray, would be focusing, instead, on *al-kafirun, ahl al-shark, al-yahud,* the unbelievers, the polytheists, the Jews. It was a quite intelligent connection by the Iraqis of powerful and multivalent cultural and religious values. Furthermore, the Iraqis' assertion that American forces would remain in the region as part of a long-term security structure was a masterstroke—and it proved true, more evidence that the regime was closely monitoring international politics.[169] The oft-repeated claim that American troops had gone to Mecca was patently false, but neither was the Saudi government's claim that they were "at least 1,500 kilometers away" true.[170] As with so many other announcements and communiqués of the regime, these of HMR appealed over the heads of state and sought to reach the masses directly; hence the use of phrases like "sons of Najd and Hijaz." As detailed in the next chapter, such broadcasts may have failed to fracture the coalition, but they were not without effect.

## ALLAHU AKBAR

Over the months, much had been done to ready the nation for this, the mother of all battles. Yet, as the UN-mandated deadline of 15 January approached, there was still some hope war could be averted. Even after Foreign Minister Aziz and Secretary of State Baker failed to reach an agreement on 9 January, there was yet some slight hope. On the day of the deadline, 15 January, the Speaker of the Iraqi National Assembly stated Iraq's "sincere desire for a comprehensive peace" in the region, one that would implement President Saddam's 12 August peace initiative.[171] But that proposal was doomed to failure, perhaps intentionally so; conditioning any movement on Kuwait on the prior resolution of the Arab-Israeli dispute was, in the parlance of the times, a nonstarter. A week before Saddam's peace proposal, the government daily *al-Jumhuriyya* had stated, "[O]ur calls for peace come as a shining sword that cuts the necks of anyone who encroaches on Iraq's security and people and the Arab nation's security and future."[172]

A call for peace that cuts necks: the phrase is a glaring non sequitur—yet apt. For the Iraqi regime, the perpetual road to peace would be cut with the sword. And the regime had made clear it was prepared to use it. But surely, many in the West mused, Saddam would capitulate in the face of overwhelming force? In fact, there was no chance of that, and Saddam had already answered the question. Speaking the previous July in commemoration of Revolution Day, the president had declared, "[T]he lofty Iraqis [have] proudly announced that fear no longer exists, that we prefer death to humiliation and that confronting danger is better than turning our backs to it."[173] On 7 August, in his Victory Day message, Saddam reiterated the same: "Death is better than humiliation and subordination to the foreigner."[174] A day later, in approving Kuwait's "request" for merger, the RCC announced, "while the vicious men do not mind leading lives of humiliation and dependence, the men who will heed His commands want nothing more than to die when the only option open to them is to die in the cause of God."[175]

Now, as 15 January approached, Saddam simply could not back down; he could not suffer the indignity, the shame, of "having his face blackened." The cultural onus Saddam bore could be dealt with only by proceeding to battle. And politically he had no other choice: he could not drag his people to the brink of war, compel their sacrifices for war preparation, then simply abandon Kuwait. To do that would compromise everything on which he had staked his legitimacy and would invite domestic disaster; Saddam would be faced with the ruination of an inglorious retreat. And so on the fifteenth, the same day the National Assembly spoke of its earnest desire for peace, his party's paper, *al-Thawra*, made clear the position he must take: "There will be no retreat concerning the nineteenth Iraqi governate—the land of dignity and pride and the arena of honour, belief and the big confrontation—and . . . there is no retreat on the liberation of Palestine or the Islamic sanctities in Najd and Hijaz."[176]

Determined for war if war must come, Iraq turned once again to Islam in the few days before the UN deadline. In one last gathering of eagles, Iraq summoned the faithful to Baghdad.[177] And the faithful came, some 350 delegates from at least 17 countries assembled in the capital for the final meeting of the Popular Islamic Conference before war started. Notable attendees included Rashid Ghannouchi, leader of al-Nahda in Tunisia; Abdelamin Zebda, vice president of Algeria's Islamic Salvation Front; Shaykh Abd al-Hamid al-Sayih, mufti of the PLO and president of the Palestine National Council; and Shaykh Saʿd al-Din al-Alami, mufti of Jerusalem. The first order of business was to declare null and void the countersummons of Maʿruf Dawalibi (theretofore secretary general of the PIC and now the "advisor to the betrayer of the two holy mosques") for the PIC to convene.

Taha Ramadan, member of the RCC and deputy prime minister, addressed the conference opening. As Iraq had done many times over the months, Ramadan combined the themes of Arabism and Islam. Opening with the bismallah and the Quran ("A great army is gathering against you" 3:173), he made clear that the country was fully prepared for one of two glorious outcomes: victory or martyrdom. Led by its faithful and *mujahid* son Saddam, whom many saw as Saladin, Iraq would lead the fight in this clash between the entire camp of faith and the entire camp of infidelity. Committed to the heavenly message as a "creed to be observed in daily life and as a code of ethics that will remain eternal and capable of application in all ages," Iraq would fight for the liberation of Jerusalem and the spread of the nation's wealth to its entire people.

As was his wont, the president addressed the conference at its conclusion, on the eleventh. Like Ramadan, Saddam fused Arabism and Islam in his appeal. Thanking the Islamists there for their strong support, Saddam declared, "We thank God that he set us on the path from which there is no return, the path of belief and jihad, not for the sake of Iraq and the Arabs only, but for the sake of all Muslims—nay, even for the sake of humanity wherever it has been tortured, oppressed, and unjustly treated." Although the coalition forces would "play Rambo in the air," Iraq had made some surprise preparations. And Saddam could not resist a cultural jibe. Fahd the treacherous had brought in American women wearing shorts to defend his regime: to defend it, in fact, against the Saudi people, the people of Najd and Hijaz. Reminding his brothers that "the basic thing is faith," the president assured the conferees, to their applause, that Iraq would certainly "defeat the aggressive armies because the slogan of 'Allahu Akbar' is the lofty banner our fighters are guided by and believe in."

The conference closed with an expression of thanks to the leader struggler President Saddam Hussein, praising his initiative of 12 August as a "reliable key for radical, just and permanent solutions to all problems in the region." Conferees spoke of the new revival that had come to the Arab nation and of a day of vengeance against insults and indignities that agent rulers had committed. Most particularly, the conference obliged Saddam with its fatwa. It declared, "Holy Islamic jihad is a must for every sane Muslim of age at a moment when Iraq or any other Muslim country comes under attack from the infidels, hypocrites and their agents, foremost of which is the United States."

But one other matter remained, the most critical of all preparations —indeed, the single most important indicator of the willingness of Saddam Hussein and his Ba'thist regime to use Islam to baptize political decisions. As Chapter Four indicated, Saddam had told a biographer in 1980 that the use of religion risked "taking the sword by its blade." The modern Arab state (*dawla*) must not be a "house of worship," a "mufti of worship," a "new mujtahid," or a "center for fatwa."[178] Now he reached for the sword. On 13 January, two days before the UN deadline, the leader-struggler-president chaired a meeting of the Armed Forces General Command. Perhaps the order he was about to give had been contemplated for some time. Perhaps it came as an inspiration just in those moments. Certainly what he was about to order had already been done metaphorically for months. But now it would be done in reality: Saddam ordered that the Iraqi flag be changed. Latif al-Jasim, the minister of information, relates the moment. When "his Excellency grasped the flag of Iraq, his eyes were sparkling . . . and he showed with his noble hand that the words *Allah akbar* were to be embroidered on the flag of Iraq." "Carrying the flag of *Allahu Akbar* into battle" would be literary trope no more. Henceforth, the president said, this would literally be "the banner of jihad and monotheism."[179]

The flag of Saudi Arabia features Arabic script over a sword on a field of green. Green is the color traditionally associated with the prophet of Islam. The Arabic script is the *shahada*, the creed, which says "There is no god but God (and) Muhammad is the messenger of God." Five times a day the believer turns toward Mecca for *salat*, prayer, to make precisely that confession: There is no god but God. The flag is unequivocal: Saudi Arabia is a state founded on belief in the one true God. But now, just across the border, there would be another such flag. Between the stars would be the words *Allahu Akbar*, God is most great. When the *mu'ezzin* climbs the minaret and gives the call to salat to the believers, he begins this all-important call with two words, then repeats them: *Allahu Akbar, Allahu Akbar*. Henceforth, these two words, so important in Islam, would be part of the national political symbol of the sovereign state of the Republic of Iraq. And Saddam's armies would carry them into war.

*The Believers are but / A single Brotherhood; / So make peace and / Reconciliation between your / Two (contending) brothers; / And fear Allah, that ye / May receive Mercy.*
QURAN 49:10

 | **ISLAM AND THE REGION AT WAR**

Saddam kept his promise. Shortly after the coalition forces initiated the air war on 17 January, Iraq launched Scud missiles at Tel Aviv. A day later, in one of the most dramatic pro-Saddam demonstrations of the entire conflict, an estimated 400,000 Algerians marched in their capital in response.[1] Many of the marchers chanted slogans or carried banners calling for peace, and virtually every political party took part; but the Islamic Salvation Front (FIS) was especially prominent. Its members had slogans of a different sort: "Tremble, Jews, the army of Muhammad has returned." Saddam had not always enjoyed such popularity with Algeria's foremost Islamic party. Indeed, Shaykh Abbasi Madani, one of the leaders of FIS, had immediately denounced the invasion in August, using the technical Quranic term *baghi* (an injustice, an outrage) to inveigh against it.[2] Earlier Shaykh Ali Belhadj, another of its leaders, had punningly referred to the Iraqi president's name as *haddam* (destroyed) and *khaddam* (servant), while offering his condemnations of the wealthy Kuwaitis. And shortly before the war, the FIS leadership cautioned its followers against venerating Saddam. But the Hijara missiles, the "stones" he threw against the Zionists on behalf of "the children of the stones,", proved Saddam a man of his word. Now he was *fahl*, a term indicating the male of any species of large animal; hence, a man of exceptional virility and power. Saddam had kept his promise.

A little over a week later, FIS called for a demonstration just of its own supporters. An estimated 60,000 to 100,000 turned out. "Victory to Islam and the Muslims," they chanted during the march. But the demonstration had another aspect. In a speech to the National Assembly on 23 January, President Chadli had denounced the "blackmail and demagogy" of the FIS, which was contesting power in Algeria. The Islamists, in response, called for this subsequent march, not just to support Saddam, but also to defy the National Liberation Front (FLN), Algeria's ruling party, and to demonstrate its own power. In the march, FIS protestors called on the government to set a date for national elections. After some delays the date was set for December 1991.

Saddam's call for jihad against the neo-imperialists proved enormously powerful, and Muslims from Morocco to Malaysia responded, as seen in the demonstrations in Algeria. But the numbers can be misleading: they give the impression of a monolithic response, a uniform, almost unthinking uprising of the Muslim street on behalf of Baghdad. Most of those who marched did so to support Saddam, but also for an array of domestic, regional, and international factors. Certainly, there was no single cause for which 400,000 marched through Algiers, and Algeria was facing its own *descensus ad infernum*.[3] Saddam happened to invade Kuwait at a time when Algerians were debating national identity, electoral politics, the role of the military, and economic issues; they likely would have marched (although not in such large numbers) even if the border of Kuwait had remained inviolate. Thus, the FIS-only march on 31 January reflected both support for Saddam and a statement about domestic power sharing. And Algeria was not unique.

In every country in the Middle East, support or opposition to Saddam was affected by a range of factors. The response was massive, but never monolithic, whether looked at regionally or state by state or within a given state. Such, for instance, was the case in Egypt, where the position of the Islamists changed over time and reflected considerable contestation within.[4] In the Middle East and across the world, Islam supplied, once again, the language of legitimation and delegitimation, the language of social analysis and social protest, the language of political aspirations and religious denunciation.[5]

This chapter surveys some of the region's responses to the Iraqi's carefully orchestrated appeal to jihad. Studies by other writers have shown that Muslims responded in large numbers, and this chapter is not as detailed as those specialized essays.[6] Instead, this chapter furnishes background to the closely connected questions examined in Chapter Seven. First, why did many Muslims respond to the appeal, while others rejected it? Stated another way, why did Muslims respond to appeals from a noted secularist who had so brutally repressed religionists at home and whose instrumental adoption of Islam seemed transparent to so many? Second, how effective were Saddam's appeals, both during the war and in its aftermath?

## OTHER CALLS TO JIHAD

Saddam, of course, was not the first to call for jihad in the modern Middle East. Various nationalist movements, as well as government and religious elites and other Islamists, had done so. For instance, the charismatic Shaykh Muhammad Ahmad ibn abd Allah (1843–1885) announced himself the Mahdi and led a revolt in the Sudan. The followers in his religious movement gave this *bay'a* (oath of loyalty) to him: "We pledge allegiance to Allah and to his prophet. . . . We pledge allegiance to thee [i.e., the Mahdi] in renouncing and abandoning this world and contenting ourselves with what is with Allah. . . . We pledge allegiance to thee in that we will not flee from the jihad."[7] The nationalist Palestine Revolt, 1936–1939, prominently featured a call for jihad against the Zionist "colonizers" and the British mandatory power, and one proclamation during the revolt reads in part, "The fighters [*mujahidun*, those who carry out jihad, the same word Saddam later appropriated to himself] have sold themselves to Allah. . . . They try to get ahead of one another [in hurrying] to the battlefield of jihad and martyrdom. . . . We call upon any Moslem and Arab to set out for jihad in the way of Allah and to help the fighters in defending the holy land."[8]

In World War I, the Ottoman government turned to religion to secure supporters for the Central Powers. In November 1914, the Shaykh al-Islam, the highest religious figure in the Ottoman government, issued this fatwa: "When it occurs that enemies attack the Islamic world . . . it [has] become an individual duty for all Muslims in all parts of the world . . . to partake in the jihad."[9] Interestingly, the fatwa stipulated that those Muslims living under British rule outside the Ottoman Empire were also commanded to obey the summons to jihad. Sharif Hussein of Mecca, great-grandfather of King Hussein of Jordan, issued a countercall to jihad; and the ulama in Egypt and India were prevailed upon to issue fatwas charging the people to obey the British.

More recently, Anwar Sadat couched the 1973 war against Israel in terms of jihad, naming the operation to cross into the Sinai "Operation Badr" after the early victory of the Muslims in 623. And in 1981 Sadat himself fell victim to an extremist group whose creed is embodied in a small book written by the group's leader, Muhammad abd al-Salam Faraj. Titled *al-faridah al-ghaibah (The Absent Duty)*, this manifesto calls for offensive jihad against the corrupt Egyptian regime and vigorously rebuts the "false view" of jihad as defensive only.[10] In the years following the Iranian Revolution in 1979, several different groups took the name (or some similar form) of "Islamic Jihad," most prominently the Islamic Jihad Organization in Lebanon, which held Americans and others hostage. And, of course, the Iran-Iraq War abounded with calls to jihad from both sides. Such examples are easily multiplied, but what set apart Saddam's appeal for a holy war is that so many responded, and not just in the Middle East. The Algerians did not march alone. Cities from Rabat, Morocco, to Lahore, Pakistan, and well beyond witnessed demonstrations. The next section summarizes the kind and extent of that response, looking first at the coalition forces, particularly in Saudi Arabia, that bore the brunt of Iraq's Islamic attack.

## ISLAM AND THE COALITION FORCES

King Fahd knew that turning to the West would lead to problems. It was, as Chapter Three argues, the second-worst decision he could have made. But not to invite the West (the worst decision) was to risk the integrity and security of the kingdom, and Fahd simply could not afford to do that. Thus, Fahd summoned U.S. (and other) forces that were culturally alien. The step was dramatic, more so than many in the West may realize. An observation made years earlier by Fahd's father, Abdul Aziz ibn Saud, the founder of the desert kingdom, underscores the difficulty: "I am the friend of the English and am their ally. But I will walk with them only as far as my religion and my honor permit."[11] That nervousness regarding outsiders remained. For instance, Saudi Arabia never issued tourist visas in the West. Americans and Europeans who lived there had come to work, not visit, and they lived in walled compounds. Emblematic of the caution of the Saudis is that for many years, until shortly before the war, Western embassies were located in Jeddah on the coast of the Red Sea rather than in Riyadh, the capital. But now, in pointed need, the Saudis turned to non-Arabs for help, a quite difficult step for Fahd to take in light of traditional Arab cultural sensibilities.

Not everyone was happy. As mentioned in Chapter Three, one Saudi critic complained, "The fact that this once fierce warrior society was suddenly reduced to a bunch of women who needed to summon a man to defend us is definitely offensive."[12]

Even worse, Fahd had turned to non-Muslims, and that provided the bigger challenge, a vulnerability that Saddam quickly exploited. Inviting non-Arabs was primarily an issue for the kingdom, something the Saudis alone would have to face. Inviting non-Muslims was an issue for the umma.[13] The royal family had to exercise special care in the way they spoke of Mecca and Medina, for Muslims saw it as the patrimony of all Islam, not the proprietary right of the house of Saud. Thus, Fahd, who had staked the legitimacy of his rule on his Islamic authenticity and who was but *khadim* (servant) of the two holy places, had to offer an Islamic rejoinder when Saddam charged Mecca and Medina were "under the spears of foreigners."

In a radio address on 13 August, three days after Saddam's jihad speech, Fahd offered a cautious apologia for foreign forces in Islamic Saudi Arabia. His preeminent concern, Fahd assured Saudis, was the safety of the kingdom. In pursuing it, Fahd promised,

I would like to reassure the sons of the Kingdom of Saudi Arabia that I could never allow anyone or myself to intervene in the public or private affairs of the citizens, including their freedom, to which Islam has entitled them. Also, we do not intervene in the affairs of the people, rather we work towards protecting them and do everything possible for that and for the existence of the Islamic faith.[14]

Then, having finished most of a rather lengthy speech, Fahd hailed "the response the Kingdom of Saudi Arabia has received from the Arab brothers and from friends to involve a multi-national force to assist the Saudi armed forces." Significantly, this oblique reference to U.S. and British forces came precisely one week after Fahd had invited them; the king, apparently, was not anxious to broach the subject.

The Saudis, of course, had sought Arab legitimation for this major step through lobbying for passage of Arab League Resolution 195 on 10 August, which approved measures taken by the Saudis and the other gulf states in "implementation of the right of legitimate defense"—i.e., bringing in foreign troops. But the Saudis wanted explicitly Islamic legitimation for this bold step, and Saddam's flinging down of the Islamic gauntlet at the time of the Arab League meeting made it imperative. The Saudis turned, then, to the Muslim World League (MWL).[15] In a formal statement a day after Saddam's jihad speech, the League addressed "all Arabs and Muslims" specifically to rebut his false charges.[16] Speaking from the "the proximity of the noble Kaba," the League declared that the "two pure noble sanctuaries and all the cities of the Kingdom are not under American or any other occupation, and that the two noble sanctuaries are clear of this, and that they are only touched by the foreheads of worshippers when they kneel in prayers." For the benefit of "brother Muslims who do not understand geographical matters," the League promised that the conflict was some 1,500 kilometers away, and, therefore, the charge of an American-Zionist occupation was a "blatant deception which is not supported by reality." The statement then appealed directly to Saddam to fear God, remove his troops, and agree to have Islamic forces under the supervision of the Islamic Conference Organization oversee that withdrawal. That, the League said, would help prove before a watching world that Muslims are a single umma.

More important than the imprimatur of the MWL, however, was an explicit statement regarding non-Muslim troops that was issued on 13 August by the Saudis' own Supreme Religious Council (SRC), a seventeen-member body of senior ulama. Having met in special session, the council addressed the people on "the need to defend the nation and its constituents by *all possible means*, and the duty of those in charge of its affairs to embark on taking *every means* that repels the danger, halts the advance of evil and secures for people the safety of their religion, money, honour and blood, and preserves for them the security and stability they enjoy" (emphasis added).[17]

This necessary step, the council stated, comported with the Quran and sunna, both of which "have indicated the need to be ready and take precautions before it is too late." All seventeen members of the council signed the statement, including Abd al-Aziz bin Baz, the most prominent cleric in the kingdom and one who had in the past shown antipathy to the presence of non-Muslims in the kingdom. Concerned about the "moral pollution" brought by foreigners to Saudi Arabia, bin Baz had earlier ruled that foreigners in the kingdom should fast during Ramadan. He had also discouraged Saudis from traveling to non-Muslim countries. In his view, "There could not be two religions in the Peninsula, but only one."[18] But the invasion of Kuwait, which bin Baz termed *thulm* (oppression), changed his outlook dramatically, and he joined the other members of the SRC in the fatwa. A week later, bin Baz gave further sanction to the coalition forces. "Even atheists, Christians, and women deserve appreciation and will be rewarded for coming to the defense of the kingdom and its holy places."[19]

The next month (September), the MWL convened a larger conference, drawing over two hundred ulama from sixty-seven countries.[20] Chaired by Burhan al-Din Rabbani, minister of justice in Afghanistan's mujahidin-led government, the conference included such notables as Shaykh al-Azhar Jad al-Haqq; the mufti of Egypt, Muhammad Sayyid Tantawi; Nur Misuari, leader of the Moro Liberation Front in the Philippines; and even Warith al-Din Muhammad, leader of the American Nation of Islam. Both Shaykh Jaber, the emir of Kuwait, and King Fahd sent messages read on their behalves to the conferees.[21] The king addressed what must have been uppermost on their minds, the presence of foreign troops. Having ascertained that the Iraqis had massed troops at the Saudi border in preparation for an attack, "[W]e assumed our religious, security and historical responsibilities and asked for Arab, Islamic and friendly forces to come to our support. This is a right given to us by the teachings of the Islamic religion, and international conventions and traditions, as corroborated by Muslim ulema everywhere."

After meeting for three days, the conference released a statement that condemned the Iraqi aggression and called for the withdrawal of Iraqi troops and the restoration of the Kuwaiti government.[22] Moreover, the conference called for the establishment of a permanent Islamic force that could resolve such conflicts in the future. And the conference addressed the single most contested point, the presence of non-Islamic troops. Based on a review of studies by religious scholars, the conference declared the presence of such forces legitimate, according with the shari'a. The conference gave assurance that as soon as the threat was over, the troops would leave the region. In the meantime, the conference stated its "regret" that delegations from Iraq, Jordan, Libya, Palestine, Sudan, Tunisia, and Yemen had not attended, for there was concern the nonattendees "may have been misled and don't know the truth."

During the fall, the MWL continued to support the Saudi position, sending representatives throughout the Islamic world to present the position of the Saudi government, issuing further statements, and organizing more conferences.[23] Additionally, Saudi television featured a popular Egyptian preacher, Shaykh Muhammad Mutawalli al-Sha'rawi, who explained the Saudi rationale for inviting non-Muslim troops.[24] Noted for his "brilliant, seamless interpretations of Quranic verses,"

Sha'rawi cited the life of the prophet to show that he, too, had turned to non-Muslims for help in his battles with those who were a threat to the early Islamic community.[25] Also important, both for the Saudis and the coalition generally, were the individual fatwas published by respected muftis like Jad al-Haqq, Tantawi, Yusuf al-Qaradawi (rector of the University of Qatar), and Ahmad Kaftaro (mufti of Syria). Kaftaro ruled that "the Syrian position concerning the Gulf crisis is sound and in accord with the *shari'a* and the judgments of Islam."[26]

As the UN-imposed deadline of 15 January approached, the Saudis turned yet again to a conference, this time the Popular Islamic Conference. At the close of its three-day meeting, 9–11 January, the conference issued a vigorous statement condemning Iraq's "cunning exploitation of Islam" and expressing its astonishment that some who claimed to have knowledge of Islam should have aligned with Saddam, especially after it became clear he used religion "only as a tool."[27] The Mecca conference reminded those who still supported the Iraqi president of his brutal repression of the Sunni Kurds, as well as the Shi'a who were members of al-da'wa. And while fellow ulama still languished in Iraqi prisons, the government continued to rule on the basis of its "secular socialist constitution." The conference also issued a "sincere and loyal call to the Iraqi army," urging it to disobey its commanders. They should not be swayed by false promises of paradise, for anyone killed in the war (defending Saddam) would be "a loser awaiting [hell] fire." The conference also accused the Iraqis of being the "direct cause of the coming of foreign forces," maintaining that the kingdom, under the circumstances, had every right to invite them. Such was the example of the prophet himself, who had turned to neighboring Jewish tribes against Arab adversaries, a precedent the caliph Umar had followed. The statement closed with thanks to "all the states, organizations and peoples" who had "sided with right in the face of wrong," preventing "Saddam Husayn [from] continuing his aggression and tyranny." Shaykh Abd al-Aziz bin Baz followed the conference statement a short time later with his own fatwa, calling for jihad and defending the use of foreign troops.[28]

Egypt sent the largest contingent of Arab forces (40,000) for the physical defense of Saudi Arabia, and so was also the most prominent in its Islamic defense. As detailed in Chapter Three, virtually every segment of Egyptian society initially opposed Saddam's invasion. Even the Muslim Brotherhood condemned it. Ma'mun al-Hudaybi, speaker of the National Assembly and a Brother, averred, "We strongly oppose the

Iraqi invasion of Kuwait and call upon Iraq to withdraw."[29] Although the majority of Egyptians continued to offer at least a modicum of support for the government's participation in the coalition,[30] significant opposition developed after U.S. troops began to deploy, most especially after the onset of the war itself. But establishment Islam stood firm in supporting Mubarak and the efforts of the coalition to turn back the Iraqi invasion.

Of particular importance was the fatwa Muhammad Sayyid Tantawi, mufti of Egypt, published in January 1991. In the fifty-page opinion, which was also translated into English and made available through the Egyptian embassy in the United States, Tantawi offered an extended defense of Fahd's decision to seek help from non-Muslims, a decision taken after consultation with capable jurists. In an obvious comparison of coalition leaders with the Iraqi president, Tantawi wrote, "Wise leaders always seek the advice of others and consult with them, especially regarding decisive matters, while foolish and arrogant rulers say, 'I am the state.'"[31] Although acknowledging that seeking assistance from non-Muslims "involves certain dangers," the mufti placed the blame squarely on the one who made it necessary. Furthermore, Tantawi wrote, the coalition decision was supported by the shariʿa and warranted by the biography of the prophet (al-sira). Interestingly, Tantawi pointed out that Saddam's invasion was not only proscribed by Islam but by international law as well.[32] Further, Saddam could have sought redress of grievance through legal channels rather than resorting to treachery. At the same time, Tantawi made clear that his fatwa was made necessary, in large measure, because it was incumbent on the Egyptian *dar al-ifta'* (fatwa office) to "confront arbitrary fatwas steeped in falsehood that were issued through ignorance by unqualified persons," a striking example of contestation within Islam itself. Similarly, Shaykh al-Azhar Jad al-Haqq issued fatwas in defense of Mubarak's decision to support the coalition. Coming from the leader of the chief school of Sunni jurisprudence, al-Haqq's statements carried considerable prestige. Al-Haqq accused Saddam of "wearing the robe of Islam and reciting verses from the holy Koran, while killing, stealing and raping." And his seizure of Kuwait the shaykh termed an act of "religious rebellion" that must be contained.[33]

Egypt also had independent Islamists who spoke with measured pragmatism and insight. One such was Fahmy Huwaidy, who led a distinguished panel of Islamists in the preparation of "A Statement to the Nation," a manifesto designed to offer Egyptians and others "another

Islamic view."[34] The panel made clear that, while "preoccupied with the issues of Islam," its members were not part of any "organization, group, or agency working under the name of Islam," thus distancing itself both from establishment Islam and groups like the Brotherhood. The group was wary of Western hegemony. It also clearly favored an Arab-Islamic solution to the crisis. Additionally, it stated that if it were necessary to go outside the region for assistance, it must be under the auspices of the UN, not "the flag of any Eastern or Western country." Yet Huwaidy, speaking for the panel, warned those who rallied to Saddam's cause that they were "putting themselves in the same camp as the criminal," and he dismissed Saddam's appeal to Islam as clearly calculated. Even the prominent Ma'mun Hudaybi of the Brotherhood commented on this transparency. Although Hudaybi was categorical on the impermissibility of a coalition comprising non-Muslims ("Islamic law does not permit any enlisting of assistance from polytheists"), he had no deep respect for Saddam. "We were not fooled by him or by his Islamic call or his talk of holy war."[35]

In sum, the coalition's Islamic posture turned on several points:

- The Quran and the sunna of the prophet forbade an attack on a fellow practicing Muslim. In so doing, Saddam had put himself outside the shari'a.
- Saddam's attack also contravened the principles of the Organization of the Islamic Conference (OIC) and the Arab League, as well as international law.
- Seeking non-Islamic assistance comported with examples from the sira and accorded with international law.

What was most evidently at issue in all the deliberations of the Saudi's Supreme Religious Council, the Muslim World League, the Saudi-aligned half of the Popular Islamic Conference, and the fatwas of the ulama of the Islamic countries in the coalition was the delicate nature of inviting non-Muslims to aid in the effort to reverse the aggression against Kuwait. What was most evidently lacking was direct Quranic warrant for doing that. For the expertly trained ulama were certainly aware of verses like the following:

> O ye who believe!
> Take not My enemies
> And yours as friends

(Or protectors),—offering them
(Your) love, even though
They have rejected the Truth
That has come to you. (60:1)

Those outside the coalition, however, knew the verse and others like it, and they were quick to exploit this weakness in the coalition position. We examine their position next.

## ISLAM AND THOSE OUTSIDE THE COALITION

Outside the coalition, groups ranging from Arabs and Muslims in the street to Islamists to rulers in the palaces generally came around to supporting Saddam, although they did not do so at first. Even inside the coalition, Saddam often gained support from the street and Islamists. Generalizations here are difficult, and exceptions arise at once. What is apparent, however, is that Saddam's fusion of Islam and pan-Arab themes proved a potent mixture. Eight years before Saddam invaded Kuwait, Albert Hourani had observed:

For most regimes and in most countries . . . Islam does not provide the exclusive language of politics. To be effective, it needs to be combined with two other languages: that of nationalism, with its appeal to unity, strength, and honour of the nation, however defined; and that of social justice, and specifically an equitable distribution of wealth. All kinds of combinations of these three languages are possible, and all that can be said in general terms is that any government which wishes to claim legitimate authority, and any movement which wants to mobilize support in order to obtain power, will try to produce a convincing blend of all three.[36]

That Saddam, who had systematically suppressed Muslims as the harsh leader of a secular country, could invade an Arab-Islamic country with which he was not at war; that he could do so in such a brutal way after giving assurances to Arab leaders that he would pursue negotiations; and that his actions could then prompt marches of support from hundreds of thousands proves that he found a "convincing blend." Whether or not Saddam could "claim legitimate authority," he was certainly able to "mobilize support." But the support did not come immediately.[37]

Initially, the Arab world almost universally repudiated Saddam's seizure of Kuwait, even those who would later come to support him. For instance, in Egypt the first party to condemn the invasion was the Muslim Brotherhood.[38] The general guide of the Brotherhood, Muhammad Hamid al-Nasr, termed the invasion "terrifying" and called on other Muslim leaders to convince Iraq to withdraw before others intervened.[39] And Ma'mun al-Hudaybi, the Muslim Brother and speaker of the National Assembly mentioned earlier, declared, "We strongly oppose the Iraqi invasion of Kuwait and call upon Iraq to withdraw."[40] The (largely Islamic) Labor party stressed its "total rejection of the use of armed force to solve differences" and called for the "restoration of the pre-invasion situation in that fraternal country."[41]

In Algeria, which would see such massive demonstrations the following January, the foreign ministry immediately called the invasion a "tragic development . . . [and] an exceptionally dangerous precedent," adding that the situation "requires an immediate withdrawal of Iraqi forces and respect for the sovereignty and independence of Kuwait."[42] The Algerian Renewal Party issued a statement that "vehemently condemn[ed] the Iraqi intervention in the Kuwaiti territory."[43] In Morocco, where an estimated 300,000 would march in protest next January, King Hassan chaired an emergency meeting that "strongly condemned" the invasion. Two weeks later, in an interview in *Le Monde*, the king observed that "all the Arab countries—and they are unanimous on that—condemned the invasion of Kuwait."[44]

In the Persian Gulf, Iran immediately spoke out: "In the Name of God, the Compassionate, the Merciful. With regards to Iraq's military invasion of Kuwait, the Ministry of Foreign Affairs of the Islamic Republic of Iran rejects any form of resort to force as a solution to regional problems. It considers Iraq's military action against Kuwait contrary to stability and security in the sensitive Persian Gulf region, and condemns it."[45] Later, President Rafsanjani would strike the pose of a true pragmatist. On the issue of whether Iran would join Iraq in its declared jihad against its common enemy the United States, Rafsanjani said to do so would be "suicidal." He added, "Why should we shed our blood? So Iraq may stay in Kuwait?"[46] And of course Iraqi opposition groups condemned the invasion. Ayatollah Muhammad Baqr al-Hakim, chairman of the Supreme Assembly for the Islamic Revolution in Iraq (SAIRI), said the invasion came as no surprise and that his group had warned the UN secretary-general that the Iraqi regime could survive only by creating "hotbeds of tension." Such "artificial crises" were part of Saddam's strategic plan to divert attention from internal problems. The Iraqi president's Islamic pose was simply an attempt to "play with the sentiments of the Muslims."[47] Al-Daʿwa and Amal ("Organization of Islamic Action") joined SAIRI in condemning Iraq, agreeing the invasion violated the shariʿa and Islamic principles.[48]

Even Hamas, the chief Islamic group in the Occupied Territories, spoke out against the invasion. Although Saddam claimed he had gone into Kuwait to liberate the Palestinians and al-Quds (Jerusalem), in late August Hamas called for unconditional Iraqi withdrawal and declared, "Our Palestinian people will not forget the noble and favorable stands adopted by the brotherly Kuwaiti people during [our] own trials and disasters. . . . We appeal to Islamic nations to assist the Kuwaiti people."[49] In short, the Arab and Islamic worlds to which Saddam would make his jihad appeal on 10 August—whether government leaders, official ulama, Islamists, or the elusive Arab "street"—joined in repudiating the forcible seizure of Kuwait. And although the leaders of countries like Yemen, Jordan, and Sudan did not approve Arab League Resolution 3036 on 3 August, which condemned the invasion, they registered "reservations." Further, they seemed to be concerned that formal collective denunciation would hamper Arab mediation efforts. No one applauded Saddam's reducing the number of Arab League members by one.[50]

Yet the mood quickly changed. The key event, of course, was the introduction of foreign (primarily U.S.) forces into Saudi Arabia. Many in the region had anticipated precisely that development and warned against it. Thus, immediately after the invasion, Jordan's leading press took up the theme of "interference" and urged against it, almost brushing off the invasion itself. For instance, *Al-Raʾy* called the invasion simply "the Iraq-Kuwait affair," and warned of international forces whose "real interest [is] in stripping Arab oil of its pan-Arab function," exactly mirroring the arguments Saddam had advanced at the Baghdad summit in May and all through the summer. *Al-Dustur* stated, "[W]e regret and feel pained at the course of events between Iraq and Kuwait," but it did not censure Iraq in any way, and it cautioned that "foreign fleets and warships are approaching the region." Then it offered this apologia: "If some are inclined to blame Iraq, we remind those of the train of events that preceded those which took place at dawn yesterday. We also urge them not to ignore a long series of moves . . . that compelled Iraqi decisionmakers to make this move and . . . defend Iraq's interests and natural rights."[51]

What Jordan's press and many others had predicted happened a week later. When the Arab League meeting in Cairo approved Resolution 195 on 10 August, it thereby authorized the introduction of foreign troops, although obliquely: the league stated it supported measures taken by "Saudi Arabia and the other Gulf states . . . in implementation of the right of legitimate defense."[52] At the same time, Saddam gave his jihad appeal, for reasons Chapter 5 notes. But the league was taking a rearguard action; U.S. paratroopers had begun arriving in Saudi Arabia three days before.

Their arrival did not go unnoticed. That same day (7 August) Jordan's Muslim Brotherhood issued a statement that pointed to U.S. intervention in the region, denouncing it as a "crusade."[53] Two days later some fifty protestors marched through the streets of Amman to the Iraqi embassy, shouting "Allahu Akbar" and demanding the right to join in the defense of Iraq.[54] The next day, more than five thousand members of the Brotherhood gathered at Amman's University Mosque, where they burned U.S., Israeli, and British flags and demanded Jordan declare jihad against Israel and the United States. Because the Brotherhood made its appeal after Friday noon prayers, its call for jihad preceded Saddam's, which came later in the day.[55]

Jordan was certainly not alone. With the deployment of foreign troops to the gulf, many who had earlier denounced Iraq or simply temporized began to speak out more forcefully for Saddam and against the West. In their view, the character of the conflict had significantly (and for some, completely) metamorphosed because of the egregious act of introducing Western troops. In Egypt, which had initially enjoyed a remarkable unanimity, various opposition parties spoke out against the coalition. While the major parties on the right (Wafd, al-Ahrar) continued to side with the regime and establishment Islam, those on the left moved into a tactical alliance with the Islamists.[56] The largely Islamic Labor party made clear its changed views. Its paper, *al-Sha'b*, editorialized,

[T]he issue has changed from an Iraqi-Kuwaiti confrontation into an Arab-American one. . . . *Now the question of who started it and whether he was right is meaningless. Arab and Islamic peoples* are concerned now that armies of all the arrogant [powers] are flocking to hit an *Arab-Islamic country.* . . . How can disgrace and concession go as far as bringing enemies to protect the territory of Islam and its sacred places?[57] (emphasis added)

The Labor statement was of enormous import, appearing as it did on 14 August. It shows that Saddam had been able to successfully change (or at least exploit) the frame of political and moral reference in only a few days. Now the debate was about matters of faith. Where many Islamists, including the Jordanian Brotherhood, had, over the years, dismissed Saddam's regime as secular Ba'thist, now Iraq was described as an "Arab-Islamic country" in need of support. The sin of inviting non-Muslims into Saudi Arabia eclipsed the "Iraq-Kuwait affair." More importantly, the aggressor had become the aggrieved; not Kuwait but Iraq was under attack. And time worked for Saddam. Many Muslims and Arabs might slowly forget the *status quo ante bellum* and acclimate to the idea that Iraq comprised nineteen provinces; but they could never become inured to the dominating presence of American imperialists. Yemen's permanent representative to the UN, Ambassador Abdalla Saleh al-Ashtal, described the change:

At the beginning our people were strongly sympathetic to Kuwait, which enjoyed much good will in our country, especially because of its sponsorship of many projects relating to the University of Sanaa. . . . Public opinion began to change when the foreign troops started arriving en masse, and Iraq was seen as the target of these forces. But even then the feeling was not pro-Iraq but against the intervention. What really changed everything was the outbreak of war on 16 [sic] January, when Iraq suddenly looked like the underdog in a terribly unequal confrontation. People had viewed Kuwait as the victim after 2 August, but now Iraq became the victim in their eyes, especially because of the excessively massive firepower being used not only in Kuwait but in the whole of Iraq. So the public sympathy has shifted completely.[58]

And so throughout much of the Arab world and beyond. Kuwait seemed to disappear for a second time: first in the invasion, now in the new discourse. On the same day the first U.S. troops arrived (7 August), an editorial titled "What We Feared Is Happening" ran in the Jordanian daily, *Sawt al-Sha'b:* "If we insist that we are Arabs, living in an Arab homeland that extends from the Arabian Gulf to the Atlantic Ocean, we must make sure that this homeland remains free of foreign intervention and must protect its Arabism. . . . O Arabs: This Iraq, which is under attack, is Arab—pulsating with Arabism and assuming a mission to awaken Arabs. Hence, Iraq is being singled out for attacks."[59]

Not once in the rather lengthy editorial does the word "Kuwait" appear. But the editorial was also important for another reason: Islam does not appear. Its language is that of Arab nationalism. And here, precisely, was the power of Saddam's appeal: it reached both Arab nationalists and Islamists and offered an enemy common to both. And with the jihad speech on 10 August, the languages increasingly merged, as detailed later.

In the meantime, a variety of voices took up the rallying cry, almost always returning to this point: the presence of non-Muslim forces changed the nature of the crisis. From that point on, ulama outside the coalition, independent Islamists, and great numbers of ordinary Muslims pointed to Quran 60:1 ("O ye who believe . . .") and verses like it, arguing that such texts categorically enjoined on believers to shun the very sort of alliance that the coalition forces represented. Significantly, 60:1 goes on to say that if one goes out to strive (*jahada*) in God's way while maintaining friendship (*mawadda*) with His enemies, then one has strayed from the straight path (*sawa' al-sabil*). This idea of the "straight path" is critical to understanding Islam, and is perhaps the most important trope of the Quran to describe the religion Allah has revealed. To leave that path is to leave the faith. To strive in it is to fulfill the commandment of God.

"And they set up (idols) / as equal to God, to mislead / (men) from the Path (*sabilihi*)! Say: 'Enjoy (your brief power)! / But verily ye are making / straightway for Hell!' " (14:30)

"Those who would hinder (men) / from the path of God (*sabil Allah*) . . . They are the ones who / have lost their own souls. . . . Without a doubt these / are the very ones who / will lose most in the Hereafter!" (11:19, 21, 22)

"Those who reject God / and hinder (men) from the Path / of God (*sabil Allah*)—for them / will We add Penalty / to Penalty." (16:88)

"And those who strive (*jahadu*) / in Our (cause),—We will / certainly guide them / to our Paths (*subulana*): / For verily God / is with those / who do right." (29:69)

From the point of view of Muslims who opposed the coalition, Fahd had embraced the enemies of God. Moreover, he had done so to fight another Islamic country; and in the process, he had put Mecca Mukarrama, venerable Mecca, "under the spears of the foreigners."

Indeed, the stronger religious argument seemed to rest here. Those who opposed the coalition had explicit Quranic warrant for doing so. Even if Saddam should be punished (and many so argued), it should not be at the hands of the forces of unbelief. The coalition ulama, on the other hand, could, as Tantawi did, turn to the Quran to argue that peace is the rule or that justice should govern all relationships.[60] But they could not point to specific Quranic texts to justify employing non-Muslim troops; hence their appeal to the biography of the prophet instead, looking for examples of his necessary resort to non-Muslims for aid in crisis.

Islamists outside the coalition were not persuaded. One wrote "[T]hese forces are the forces of unbelief (*kufr*)—their enmity to us and our enmity to them is established until the Hour," i.e., the day of judgment.[61] Similarly, Maʾmun Hudaybi of the Egyptian Brotherhood: while opposing the Iraqi invasion, he added, "Islamic law does not permit any enlisting of assistance from polytheists (*mushrikun*). In fact, what is happening now is not assistance-seeking but surrender."[62] In Jordan, the Brotherhood declared that "any regime that accepts foreign protection places itself in the ranks of those who oppose the Islamic nation, and [it] loses justification for its existence."[63] Outside the region, other Islamists took up the same position. For instance, in a direct response to ulama who supported the coalition, the Islamic Council of Europe stated, "[T]hose who provide a fatwa that [legitimizes the] seeking of aid from non-Muslims under current circumstances have not an iota of support in either the Quran or the Sunna."[64] From all this (to abbreviate noncoalition arguments) it followed that the coalition must be opposed and, indeed, the Islamic country of Iraq protected, Islamists declared.

This line of argument resonated with many other Muslims. Some, like President Zine Ben Ali of Tunisia, were relatively moderate, although certainly clear. "As an Arab and Moslem nation, Tunisia refuses to confer an imaginary legitimacy on the foreign intervention in the affairs of the Arab world," he said on 11 August.[65] But opposition elsewhere was far more direct and increased in intensity as the UN deadline approached. What the Islamists argued in their exegeses and propounded in articles, many shouted in the streets, galvanized by Saddam's call for jihad. The following is a sample from the region and elsewhere.

Immediately after Saddam's summons to jihad on 10 August, demonstrators in Lebanon burned effigies of Bush, Thatcher, and King Fahd, chanting, "The Arab soil will be a furnace for the invading crusaders."[66] And as the mother of battles approached, some fifteen thousand marched in southern Lebanon. Once again burning flags and effigies, marchers chanted, "Saddam, Saddam, wipe out Israel. . . . Oh Saddam, use gas! Oh Saddam, use chemicals. . . . It's jihad time." At the same time, some twenty thousand demonstrators marched in Mauritania, chanting "Death to America" and "Muslims have to defend Iraq."[67] Sudanese leaders issued a call for "holy war and solidarity among Arabs and Moslems wherever they are to protect the Arab and Islamic holy places."[68]

Probably the country in the region most unified in its response was Jordan. Unlike divided Egypt, the Hashemite kingdom overwhelmingly rallied to Saddam's cause, the king's protestations of neutrality notwithstanding. One specialist on Jordanian politics remarked on the paradox that took place: "Ironically, the August 1990 invasion of Kuwait temporarily interrupted the polarization that [had been] surfacing in Jordanian society as a result of . . . liberalization."[69] The complex brew of Jordanian politics, where over half of the population is Palestinian, caused the king to move as adroitly as possible. Following the bread riots in the spring of 1989, the king promised an opening of the political system, calling for a new national charter. In the parliamentary elections that followed in November, the Brotherhood and other Islamists took thirty-four of the eighty seats. And in January 1991, while his international standing plummeted, the king moved to shore up domestic legitimacy, appointing seven Islamists to his cabinet. His popularity at home reached a new high.

Thus, the invasion and—more importantly—the subsequent internal political maneuverings forged, for a time, a national unity that supported Saddam.[70] As the editorials in Jordanian papers cited earlier in the chapter indicated, Jordanians were among the earliest to speak out against possible foreign interference. Two days after the invasion of Kuwait, the speaker of the Jordanian House of Representatives sounded the same warning: "We all hope that God will hold back the western and other countries—I mean foreign countries—from interfering in this region. All of us—the entire House of Representatives—call for a *purely Arab solution* through the Arab League and its countries. We do not want the foreigners to poke their noses in because we know what their goals and objectives are" (emphasis added).[71] Like the editorials, this statement reflects nothing of Islam, except for the ceremonial deism ("We all hope that God . . .").

But as Saddam Islamized the conflict, the nature of protest in Jordan changed. Where Islamists had refrained from comment after Friday prayers on the third, on 10 August, three days after the Americans had begun arriving, they responded. At a large rally outside the University Mosque in the capital, protestors stretched banners across the palm trees that read "Down with Americans, the new crusaders" and "Train your guns against the Zionists and the Americans." Shaykh Khalifa of the Brotherhood (the same who led a deputation to several capitals the following month calling for an Islamic solution) warned the protestors about imperialists and Zionists who were threatening the Arab nation. Two days later some twenty thousand marched in Mafraq, fifty miles north of Amman. And at the end of the month, the Brotherhood led fifty thousand supporters in a march in Amman.[72] The following January, the demonstrations again showed marked intensity. On a single day, Amman University went on strike, the country's largest youth union marched in support of Iraq, and a group of Jordanian women demonstrated under the slogan "Let's go for jihad." At the same time a Brotherhood spokesman declared, "Now we are at war, everything is legal," an indirect reference to the Brotherhood's training of its followers in small arms.[73]

Outside the Middle East, many took up the call for U.S. forces to withdraw. The World Islamic Council, an India-based organization of Sunni ulama, demanded the "anti-Islamic U.S. troops" be withdrawn immediately, declaring the Saudi rulers had committed a "black treason" against Islam for inviting them. Were the holy places in Iraq to be damaged (e.g., the shrines in Najaf and Karbala), Muslims around the world would retaliate, turning the "palaces of the pro-Zionist rulers of the [Gulf] region and the White House into a graveyard."[74]

Muslims in Pakistan argued similarly. Among Islamic, non-Arab nations, Pakistan sent more troops to join coalition forces than any other, but that was hardly a decision the nation took with equanimity. Qazi Hussein Ahmad, leader of Pakistan's Jamaat-e-Islami, the nation's most important Islamist group, characterized the American-European alliance as comprising "anti-Islamic forces" that had joined hands to "destroy the fighting power of the Islamic world." General Mirza Aslam Beg, head of the Pakistani armed forces, denounced the allied bombing of Iraq, comparing it to the battle at Karbala.[75] Additionally, Islamists were able to organize massive demonstrations, and hundreds made their way to centers in Pakistan to volunteer for jihad against the coalition.[76]

Such demonstrations spread to Malaysia, Indonesia, and to the Muslim community in South Africa. Malaysia's protestors graphically captured the sense that things had gone badly awry in the holy cities. Posters depicting the ka'ba under "guard" by American soldiers proliferated across the country. *Aliran,* an independent Malaysian publication, published an article entitled "Exposing U.S. Motives: A Third World View," which condemned the U.S. invasion and cited an extensive record of hypocritical double standards the United States had followed with respect to Islamic countries.[77]

In Morocco, a key U.S. ally in the Maghreb, King Hassan had long been involved, in a quiet way, with mediation efforts in the region on matters of interest to the United States. That Rabat sent two thousand men (an infantry battalion) to support the coalition effort was an important gesture both to his fellow Muslims and to the United States. But the decision was not popular at home. All eight opposition parties demanded the withdrawal of Moroccan troops from the Persian Gulf, one conservative party warning that the coalition was there "not to defend Arabs, but to carry out a Zionist plan."[78] Newspapers roundly supported Iraq, praising the regime when it launched missiles against Tel Aviv. The king had already acknowledged the unpopularity of the coalition in his interview with *Le Monde* in mid-August. After affirming that the Arab countries were unanimous in condemning Saddam's invasion, Hassan also pointed out the issue on which there was not unanimity: "Riyadh's appeal to some foreign troops in the Arab world." He added that the Arab-Israeli dispute, if unresolved, would be "the powder keg in this part of the world."[79]

The king, therefore, was compelled to give some room for expression of popular discontent. Thus, on 28 January the government sanctioned a general strike by the country's trade unions, a strike through which its organizers intended to show solidarity with the Iraqi people.[80] Six days later Moroccans from across the spectrum, including a large number of fundamentalists, took part in a massive demonstration in the capital, the first the government had permitted since the beginning of the air war.[81] An estimated three hundred thousand marched through the streets of Rabat; opposition leaders claimed a half million. Demonstrators burned American, British, French, and Israeli flags while waving those of Iraq and Palestine and chanting, "Assassin Bush, Mitterrand his dog, Fahd his donkey. . . . Palestine is Arab, Kuwait is Iraqi." And as they marched, protestors did something that certainly would have pleased the Iraqi president. They displayed his picture and that of Arafat. More importantly, they held aloft copies of the Quran and carried pictures of Scud missiles. Thus, both the call for jihad and the announcement of al-Hijara, the "stones" missile, had reached the Maghreb. Saddam had kept his promise, and Morocco marched with jubilation.

*This is indeed the blackest day in the history of the Arabs, which has
made them regress to the pre-Islamic days of barbarism, when the sword
was the master and bloodshed was the means of resolving problems.*
AL-AHRAM, CAIRO DAILY NEWSPAPER

*There is not one Arab country where the political system is not under
attack. Change is necessary but I fear it won't be a natural birth but
a Caesarean operation marked with blood and trauma.*
FAHMY HUWAIDY, EGYPTIAN ISLAMIST

*Forget the Palestinians. I don't care if the Palestinians end up in
Israel, or in the sea, or in hell. . . . Saddam sent a Scud on my
children and Arafat applauded.*
SAUDI NEWSPAPER EDITOR[1]

# 7 | REFLECTIONS ON JIHAD AND THE OTHER GULF WAR

One day before the cease-fire on 28 February that ended the Persian
Gulf War, the Baghdad-based Popular Islamic Conference issued a statement. It was the final plea, the last call for Muslims to come to the
aid of Iraq, cradle of jurisprudence, religion, and civilization, before it
was too late. There is almost a poignancy about it, for—despite the tens
of thousands across the Middle East and throughout the Islamic world
who had sworn blood and life for Saddam—Iraq stood by itself at that
last hour when the United State Army's First Infantry Division rolled
through the southern desert. But it is a poignancy marked by defiance.

O zealous and honourable Muslims, Iraq has confronted the entire gathering of infidelity alone. Its audacious and mujahid army has waged the
mother of battles on behalf of the whole nation. . . . Iraq has contributed
its share. It has kept its promise and has waged a jihad in the cause of
God in the best possible manner. It has paved the nation's way to eternal salvation from humiliation, subjugation and lowliness at present and
in the future. Its people have chosen not to be supporters of the infidels
and apostates and lackeys to the traitors. They are now, as they have
always been, defending the nation and its sanctities, vindicating Islam

and its creed and fending off the disgrace brought about by the traitors and apostates.[2]

It would be easy to term this simply the jihad that failed. Certainly the volunteers failed to show themselves on Iraq's Crispin's Day; it was the hapless Iraqi *jundi,* and he only, who died before the air-land battle onslaught. Similarly, it would be easy to pronounce March 1991 the month pan-Arabism and pan-Islam died. But the situation proved rather more complex. This chapter offers some reasons for the vast appeal of Saddam's call to jihad and an assessment of the results. We maintain that the call to jihad was not without effect, and that the visions of pan-Arabism and pan-Islam have persisted, operating alongside the Arab interstate order.

## A TIMELY CALL

Saddam received the response he did because he made the right appeal at the right time, not because his Islamic credentials were above reproach. Indeed, Muslims throughout the region had long found his claims of piety to be suspect, believing him to be an instrumental Muslim. Not to multiply examples, here is one from a perceptive Egyptian Islamist, Fahmy Huwaidy, which captures this instrumentality. Writing in February 1991 in *al-Ahram,* Egypt's largest daily newspaper, Huwaidy recalled: "In his last visit to Kuwait, Saddam was keen to perform the [required] prayers on the seashore. When the visit was broadcast by British television, I and others noticed that Saddam was not praying in the right direction. . . . And since the correct direction was certainly known to everybody accompanying him, it is most likely that the prayers were simply a display for television."[3] But during the crisis, Muslims responded nonetheless when Saddam made his appeal. In a telling comment, Rashid Ghannouchi, leader of the Tunisian Islamist group al-Nahda, stated: "We are not worshipping personalities, but anyone who confronts the enemies of Islam is my friend, and anyone who puts himself in the service of the enemies of Islam is my enemy."[4]

But what "enemies of Islam" might be in view? To answer that is to begin to uncover the appeal of Saddam. We suggest that, for the majority of those who marched in Algiers and Rabat and Amman and Lahore, the answer is not strictly doctrinal—"enemy" here does not simply denote a strictly Islamic jurisprudential concept. Rather, "enemy" conveys a much broader idea, an entire order from which Saddam seemed to offer hope of deliverance. Walid Khalidi, a Palestinian who has been a senior research fellow at Harvard University, holds that Arab support for Saddam was

an index of the abysmal depth of disillusionment with the Arab status quo—political, social, and economic—as well as with the regional policies of the United States. If this support spans, as it were, a spectrum, the poles of which are cerebral-analytical and despairing-nihilistic, the least common denominator between these poles is the yearning for change, even if the process is initiated by the brutality of Saddam's assault upon this status quo.[5]

Or, less eloquently but more forcefully from Hanna Siniora, a Palestinian journalist: "When a drowning man sees land disappear slowly in front of him, and suddenly a man throws him a rope, he will not ask who that man is."[6]

When Saddam threw the rope, there were plenty of signs that the region was going under: the Palestinian intifada, the contestation for power in Algeria between the ruling FLN and the Islamists, labor unrest in Morocco, bread riots and parliamentary wrangling in Jordan, and so on. In large part, these issues represented the larger deliberation on, and struggle for, political enfranchisement throughout the Middle East.[7] There were also stark economic disparities. While those countries of civilizational depth (as Saddam termed them) struggled with enormous debt and sought restructuring terms from the IMF, the nouveaux riches next door enjoyed a rather different standard of living. "These were bad people," said Mansour Murad, leader of the Jordanian Youth Union, about the Kuwaitis. "They were greedy, they drank whiskey, and slept with European women while tens of millions of their Arab brothers live in poverty."[8] In one pronounced contrast at the time of the invasion, the GNP per capita in the Emirates (with 1.5 million people) was 33 times that of Egypt (with 51 million). In some ways, therefore, the Gulf War and its opposing sides represented an "Arab *thawra* (revolution) against Arab *tharwa* (wealth)."[9]

But a larger, more international issue lent support to Saddam. It was an outlook on the West involving colonialism. When the London-based Islamic Council issued its statement in September 1990 opposing western involvement in the coalition arrayed against Iraq, it warned of a new era of semicolonialism.[10] In support of its contention, it cited the case of the Egyptian Khedive Tawfiq. The reference would not have been lost on anyone in the region. It was the khedive who had asked the British to put down the nationalist revolt of Urabi Pasha in 1881. The council's point was that an Arab Muslim leader had appealed to a non-Muslim, non-Arab power for help with an internal issue—and had brought about a colonialist occupation.

In fact, although many during the gulf crisis often warned of "new crusaders," the even more frequent reference was to imperialism. And imperialism was of a piece with several issues. Arabs had not forgotten what had happened in 1915–1917, the promises betrayed, secret colonialist plans carefully laid, and Zionism supported by the West. For in those years, the British promised to support Sharif Hussein of Mecca in his aspirations for an Arab kingdom in return for Arab support against the Turks (Hussein-McMahon correspondence, 1915); promised the Jews a national home in part of the same lands promised to the Arabs (Balfour Declaration, 1917); and elaborated a secret deal with the French that would protect their respective interests in the Middle East (Sykes-Picot, 1916). In this telling, the European powers had divided the Middle East to suit their own interests (a charge not wide of the mark) and had done so with little regard for local Arab sensibilities.

A case in point, of course, was the "artificiality" of Iraq, which, as Chapter Two notes, comprised a Sunni Kurdish north, a Sunni Arab middle, and a Shi'a Arab south. When the Iraqi Revolution Command Council later claimed, "One of the most egregious criminal acts of colonialism was its partition of the homeland, which was a single homeland in the days that Baghdad was the capital of all the Arabs," the allusion to Baghdad as capital was so much national posturing, but the rest of the statement had merit. "Following the independence which Arab countries won, imperialism started intensifying its malicious actions. Thus it partitioned many countries in line with the calculations of its aims and objectives."[11]

The further history of the modern Middle East is, in large measure, the story of a U.S. presence replacing a British one. The zenith of U.S.-Arab relations in the region came in 1956 when Eisenhower intervened in the Suez crisis. But since then, Arabs have complained inveterately of a U.S. policy calibrated to interests other than their own. Hermann Eilts, former ambassador to Saudi Arabia and an astute Middle East commentator, testified before the House Subcommittee on Europe and the Middle East several years *before* the Gulf War: "Regrettably, the U.S. is no longer seen by most Middle Easterners, Muslims included, as the symbol of decolonization, self-determination, human rights, freedom. . . . Rather it is seen as the legatee of British and French imperialism, and as an interventionist element in local politics."[12] Thus, when the United States rapidly intervened in the gulf crisis, many in the region saw the talk of upholding a moral order and international legal standards as only so much rhetoric. After the United States had supported Iraq in its war with Iran, Arabs treated the Americans' sudden "discovery," in 1990, of Iraq's human rights record, coupled with their statements about protecting the moral high ground in Kuwait, as evidence of "an almost indecently narrow self interest."[13]

But self-interest was clearly not the only issue that concerned many Arabs. They were troubled as well by U.S. support of Israel that seemed almost absurdly one-sided. For example, Arabs have pointed to consistent U.S. vetoes of UN Security Council censures of Israel. Irrespective of the validity of the claims, and they certainly have merit, is the view that Israel operates in the region as the "Zionist agent." That is, the United States extends its reach through the Middle East by employing a surrogate. Many Arabs have felt that the United States cannot pursue a balanced policy vis-à-vis the Palestinians because it would, ipso facto, work to the detriment of its plans for the Zionists. Moreover, as Chapter Five notes, in the months preceding the crisis, the gulf states also took on "agent" status in Saddam's rhetorical political lexicon. Through them, the West operated to control the oil resources of the region.

And the charge seemed to catch on. To cite Khalidi again: "[I]f the incongruence between the geographic distribution of wealth and demography could be said to be God-made and hence immune to critical assault, no such reprieve could be won for the man-made western orientation of the investment strategies of the oil-rich countries. . . . [There is a] lack of proportionality between the investments *inside* and those *outside* the Arab world and [a] perpetuation, at least partly by this lack, of the continued underdevelopment of the non-oil-rich Arab countries" (emphasis in original).[14] Hence, many Arabs concluded that gulf regimes profit from serving U.S. interests, thus becoming "agents" in the Saddamite lexicon. In doing so, they therefore neglect their Arab and Islamic duties to poorer countries in the area.

Using agents is simply colonialism by other means: rather than physically occupy territory, the new approach is to manipulate governments. Thus, in the triumvirate of evil mentioned in Chapter Five, there were imperialists, Zionists, and lackeys—here, the various GCC states. It is important to note that "imperialism" renders the Arabic *isti'amar*, which comes from a root meaning "to colonize." Whether by direct physical occupation or indirect economic and political manipulation, the West has been seen as a colonizing force.[15] Those familiar with Arab political cartoons know well the traditional caricatures used: the United States presented as Uncle Sam; the Israeli wearing a large hat with a Star of David on it; the Arab, hoping for peace but tricked or humiliated by the Zionist or the American.[16] Such cartoons appear in a multitude of venues, and not just in the popular Arab dailies like Cairo's *Al-Ahram*. They appear also in mainstream, sophisticated magazines like *Al-Majalla*. The common theme is that the United States pursues its interests, often through an agent, at the expense of Arab governments—in a word, neocolonialism, however implemented.

The view that the West has some kind of conspiracy in place is not restricted to mass publics. It is also held by many educated elites. In an important study of elite attitudes during and after the war, researchers Tareq Ismael and Jacqueline S. Ismael looked at the views of academic and professional people from across the Middle East on three broad topics: the nature of Arab society, the causes and effects of the gulf crisis, and prescriptions for change.[17] Prior to the start of the air war, 86 percent of respondents cited Saddam's invasion of Kuwait as the primary cause of the crisis, a view held irrespective of ideological orientation. In assigning secondary responsibility, ideology was significant. Marxists and Arab nationalists pointed to the role of "imperialism." Islamists pointed to the Saudis and the Egyptians for allowing the West to interfere.[18] After the war, however, views changed. In May 1991, 64 percent of respondents, regardless of ideological orientation, saw the crisis as primarily an externally hatched conspiracy. And by September 1991, this figure had risen to 76 percent. The Ismaels concluded, "This is not a radical or fringe opinion, let us emphasize, but the dominant perspective."[19]

## THE BILINGUAL PRESIDENT

When Saddam invoked issues of imperialism, insidious Zionism, or economic disparities, he had no need to invent themes. These had long been causes of concern in the Arab nation, and these issues could be argued and advanced in the language of nationalism. But of critical importance was that the various publics Saddam addressed spoke "languages" besides nationalism; most significantly, the Iraqi president could turn to Islam. Especially after the *nakba* (disaster) of the 1967 war and the 1979 Iranian Revolution, Islam had increasingly been looked to for the language of protest, of legitimation, of delegitimation, of analysis. And to Islamic discourse many turned, both to articulate political aspirations and to call for redress of social inequalities. To cite John Voll again, "Islam had become one of the most important bases of *normal* as well as revolutionary political discourse in the region" in the early 1990s.[20]

Further, Islam had become the civil society of many.[21] Left without other effective means of social identification and participation, particularly without the opportunity to participate in a robust democracy, people turned to mosque and family. And in the city, especially at times of demographic dislocation, the mosque took on increasing importance; it became a surrogate family as well as a place of instruction and worship. This tendency had gone even further in countries like Egypt. Although Egypt features a lively press and a comparatively robust civil society, Islamic groups have been especially important, and groups like the Brotherhood have provided social services the Egyptian bureaucracy could not, especially during times of crisis.[22]

All of this argues that in the two decades prior to the gulf crisis Islam took on added importance as a public discourse, as a resource for social identity, and as vehicle for significant protest. Saddam's appeal for jihad came in the midst of the concerns described above and at a time when it was only natural to employ religious categories to address them. Islam, therefore, provided a resource from which the Iraqi president could draw when shaping justifications for the invasion and making his appeal for aid. Eickelman and Piscatori remark, "As the second Gulf War suggests, Muslim politics becomes incomprehensible if the symbolism and shared assumptions of Muslims are disregarded. There is an implicit consciousness of common notions—an underlying framework of language, ideas, and values which, while not always self evident or explicitly expressed, becomes apparent when the shared assumptions are violated or attacked."[23] Saddam was effective in mobilizing mass sentiment because he addressed issues of key concern in a language that resonated with many.

But Saddam's use of language took one extra step, perhaps the most important of all. He masterfully fused *two* languages, Arabism and Islam. Although Saddam lacked the charisma of Nasser, he seemed to have captured something of his mentor's ability to appeal to pan-Arab values. One would be hard-pressed to think of any Arab leader since

1970, when Nasser died, who has done as well. To be sure, Saddam was more feared than loved. Yet his manipulation of national symbols, his public recollection of national heritage, his call for restoring national pride—especially when fused with Islamic discourse—were powerfully evocative.

The locus classicus of Saddam's confection, of course, is the jihad speech on 10 August. Before then, he had espoused pan-Arab values and embroidered the edges of his discourse with Islam, but the jihad speech deeply connected the two. "*Arabs, Moslems,* believers in God wherever you are, this is your day to jump up and defend Mecca." The foreigners and traitors are "defying the *Arab and Islamic nations.*" "It is a battle of the entire *Arab nation* . . . [to secure] a *life that is close to God* and His laws" (emphasis added). That Saddam could employ both languages simultaneously reflects a coincidence of what we would call "alternative global narrations."[24]

Both Arab nationalism and Islam share important similarities of description. For both, there is a *glorious past.* The Arab nationalist Sami Shawkat, an Iraqi intellectual and educator, wrote, "We have up to now neglected a most vital aspect of our glorious history. . . . [T]he history of our illustrious Arab nation extends over thousands of years, and goes back to the time when the peoples of Europe lived in forests and over marshes."[25] Similarly, Muslims regard the time of the prophet and the *rashidun* (the "rightly guided ones," i.e., the first four caliphs) as such an era, a template of moral rectitude by which following times may be measured.[26] Both languages also tell of present decline and an array of enemies. Nationalists may speak of the inroad of imperialism or Zionism and the fracturing of Arab unity. Muslims can point to a new *jahiliyya* (period of ignorance) or *kufr* (unbelief). For goals, nationalists point to the restoration of the one nation *min al-khaleej ila al-muheet* (from the [Arabian] Gulf to the [Atlantic] Ocean). Muslims look for the unity of the umma or the worldwide spread of *dar al-Islam* (the abode of peace, that area where Islam holds sway) or the implementation of the shari'a. To be sure, most Muslims have come to accept the validity of the nation-state system, but the notion of umma yet resides alongside that acceptance, a powerful "organizing myth."[27]

The importance of this for the Gulf War was that people in the region had two ways of rendering the same events. Saddam's invasion of Kuwait could be narrated as either a fracturing of Arab unity or a blow to the umma. The arrival of Western forces could be narrated as the arrival of either the imperialists or the *kafirun* (unbelievers). Fahd's invitation could be described as coming from an agent in league with colonialists or from one consorting with the *mushrikun* (polytheists). The nationalists could charge Fahd with treason; the Islamists could employ *takfir* (to charge with unbelief). Moreover, one notes as well the capacity for nationalists and Islamists alike during the conflict to order the world in large and rather categorical terms.

When Samuel Huntington's famous essay appeared in *Foreign Affairs* in the summer of 1993, it engendered something of a cottage industry of rebuttals.[28] To be sure, Huntington's "clash" leaves little room for fine-grained analysis; to use only his approach forces one to call "monolithic" what is really massive but varied. It leaves much to be desired. Yet the essay merits revisiting when one considers the attitudes expressed in the Middle East during the war. Just as in Iraq, where categorical terms had long been the order of the day, many nationalists consistently used such large terms: this was the clash of the Arab nation and imperialism. Islamists used equivalent terms. Azzam Tamimi, director of the Jordanian Brotherhood's parliamentary office, stated, "The Muslim community extends from the Atlantic Ocean to the Pacific Ocean. If the Muslim community was given the freedom to choose, it would choose to be re-united." As he described it to a journalist from *Time,* the crisis was nothing less than a struggle between Islam and Western civilization, a sentiment that was often expressed in the region.[29]

This cross-dynamic of languages abounded. So, for instance, the first statement of the Palestinians after the invasion reflected nationalist discourse. The speaker of the Palestine National Council told *Sawt al-Sha'b* (*Voice of the People,* an Amman daily) that "Israel does not want the good of the Arab nation, and when it saw Iraq as a strong and powerful country, it trembled with fear." He continued by stressing that what happened was "purely an internal Arab affair" and that the Arab solution would "take into account the wishes and interests of the Kuwaiti people and the interests of the entire Arab nation from the Gulf to the ocean."[30] Warning of U.S. interference, the Popular Front for the Liberation of Palestine (PFLP), headed by George Habash, declared that resolution of the conflict "must remain within the Arab household." Otherwise, "internationalizing the differences" would "allow the imperialist forces, especially the United States, to exploit these differences and employ them in service of their aims and interests in the region."[31] Yet looking at that same interference, an Islamist could narrate it differently, as did Abbasi Madani of FIS in mid-August. "What is taking place in the Gulf is a new form of Crusades. In addition, it is a violation of Islamic sovereignty and an aggression against the sanctity of the two holy mosques. . . . It is God's land, the land of Islam, the land of all Muslims. The Islamic nation cannot endure such regimes [here, the Saudis] anymore. . . . Therefore, the FIS is calling upon the [umma] . . . to topple such regimes."[32]

In fact, people often employed both languages rather than only one. Islamists might readily speak of the events in nationalist terms even as, most prominently, the maximum Ba'thist of Iraq took up Islamic ones. Thus, Ahmad al-Azaidah, a Jordanian Muslim Brother in the parliament, stated, "In the past we did not support the regime of Saddam Hussein but, when we are faced with western aggression aimed at the destruction of Iraq's power, a prelude to the shredding of Arab power and culture, this becomes insignificant."[33] More significantly, al-Azaidah added, "We are not judging Saddam Hussein as a person, but what he is doing is right. *He is using Islam* to rally all Arabs to the cause of unity of the *Arab nation,* which was artificially divided" (emphasis added). Similarly, the Islamic-oriented *al-Sha'b,* the paper of the Egyptian Labor party, ran an editorial in mid-August that stated, "Now the question of who started it and whether he was right is meaningless. *Arab and Islamic peoples* are concerned now that the armies of all the arrogant [powers] are flocking to hit an *Arab-Islamic country*" (emphasis added).[34] Maha Azzam also noted this phenomenon, writing of "the depth of nationalist sentiment among the Islamists coupled with a weak respect for most existing national boundaries. In a sense this represented a pull between a worldview based on territorial states as they currently exist in the Middle East and the ideal of a return to a greater unity, which the Islamists share with the pan-Arab secular nationalists."[35]

And if imitation remains the sincerest form of flattery, Mubarak showed it. The Egyptian president declared, "The position adopted by Egypt is the correct Islamic position, and the exact Arab position, and the fundamental, lawful and ethical-cultural position—which relates to Muslim Arab, basic, ethical and cultural Egypt."[36] In a word, Saddam drew such numbers to the streets and to the press because he was bilingual. Of equal importance, the bilingual president had a missile called "the stones," the military capability to transform rhetoric into action.

And yet, as indicated above, when the war closed, the many who had volunteered for service in Saddam's jihad simply never materialized.[37] Neither were there revolutions following the demonstrations: when the masses left the streets at the end of the march, they headed off neither to topple governments nor to the Kuwaiti Theater of Operations. How to account for the apparent failure of jihad? One assessment appeared in the Jordanian daily *al-Ra'y* a week after the air war began. "All these calls for Jihad have, at best, continued to be shouts in the air, ink on paper, or hopes welling up in breasts. Of course, the reason is clear: namely, that every committee, thinker, or leader was content with issuing a statement calling for Jihad. This means that the call for Jihad has continued to lack a mechanism to implement it. Enthusiastic individuals do not know how to translate their enthusiasm into action."[38] An even more astringent assessment appeared in March 1991 as an article entitled *harb al-fatawa wa fatawa al-harb* ("The War of Fatwas and Fatwas of War").

Thus, the Muslim world [not only] disintegrated into contending and warring factions, but Islam itself disintegrated into contending and contradictory texts, jurisprudence, theories, concepts, and fatwas. The Muslim world was fighting itself by referring to Islamic texts that were meant to unite it. When the various governments and political entities differed and fought for their own narrow transient interests, the 'ulama', the religious leaders, the jurists, and the Islamic organizations appeared as mere instruments and tools for the respective authorities and leaders who used them to implement their designs and interests.[39]

Several issues are apparent here. First, these assessments underscore the absence of an Islamic organization, some Islamic center, that can effectively arbitrate differences of doctrine or political issues among all the Islamic nations. The OIC certainly was not such an authoritative body, and it did little more than issue statements during the conflict. Other organizations, although enjoying the respect of many Muslims, were nonetheless seen as enmeshed in the policies of their sponsoring governments. That was the case with groups like the Muslim World League (Mecca), the Popular Islamic Conference (Baghdad, and during the crisis, Baghdad and Mecca), or al-Azhar University (Cairo). And certainly the nonestablishment Islamic groups (e.g., the Egyptian or Jordanian Brotherhoods, Hamas, Palestine Islamic Jihad, FIS) could not assume such an arbitrative role, irrespective of their prestige in the streets.

In a word, there was no "official Islam" to which all subscribed or a single body to which all looked for the definitive Islamic answer in crisis situations. Neither was there one court to which all Muslims might turn for a final ruling on whether, say, Saddam (or Assad or Fahd or Mubarak or Hamas) was simply "politicizing religion." And the crisis raised a set of related questions. In the absence of such a body, who may issue authoritative fatwas? Who decides among conflicting fatwas? Moreover, in the absence of a caliph, who may call for jihad? Who decides the issue of responsibility, whether collective or individual, for conducting the jihad? What relation does jihad have, say, to international law or to a just-war doctrine? Or, to state the most obvious, in the case of aggression by one Muslim state against another, what outside assistance may be sought? In fact, none of these absences necessarily implies weakness: to have a single, completely authoritative body is to risk what invariably happens with the aggregation of power; one recalls Lord Acton's warning. Yet this is to say, with Yvonne Haddad, "[T]he Gulf crisis left the Islamists with profoundly troubling questions as to who will provide the independent judgment for the future of the Muslim nation."[40]

But the authors cited here raise a more immediate issue, the matter of complexity in the Gulf War. As Islam itself is not monolithic, neither the opposition to nor the support for Saddam was monolithic. There was not a clear dichotomy, a bright line separating the anti-Saddam coalition from the Saddam supporters. Saddam's rhetoric said there was such a line. For instance, as Chapter Three notes, Taha Ramadan, the Iraqi vice president, speaking for the regime just days before war began, promised that this would be "the crucial battle in which we will strike at the *entire camp of infidelity* using the entire *camp of faith*" (emphasis added).[41] But the situation proved considerably more complex. Rather than see the confrontation as between two opposed sides solidly behind their leaders, it is better to see a continuum of attitudes and a great deal of doubt on both sides about certain issues.

Those who seemed to support Saddam after his putsch often were also contesting power in their homeland. For instance, putative Saddam supporters like the FIS in Algeria and the Brotherhood in Jordan were, at the same time, vying with the ruling FLN and King Hussein, respectively, and venting dissatisfaction with local conditions and those in the larger Arab world. On the other hand, some who opposed the invasion did so expecting a quid pro quo after the war. For example, some of the Saudi ulama who stood with Fahd (or at least remained quiescent) wished to further Islamize the regime at the conclusion of the conflict, as indicated below. Especially protean was Hamas, which sought simultaneously to oppose coalition forces, contest Islamic legitimacy with Arafat, and maintain financial support from the Saudis. Indeed, for all parties the battle lines in the war were complex, shifting over time, and quite often blurred.

A more fruitful approach than simply drawing the (misleading) bright line between those who supported Saddam and those who did not is to see, instead, Islamists and government elites throughout the region as generally sharing a constellation of values, values that they weighted differently throughout the crisis. None of the Arab coalition members felt sanguine about having to turn to outsiders for help. This was simply a matter of survival, in their view, of keeping thrones and heads. Conversely, few of the anticoalition elites and Islamists genuinely saw Saddam as the "daring knight of the Arab nation," as he liked to be styled; rather, they were deeply distraught over the possibility of a new colonialism. And we should also grant the sincerity of many who argued that the presence of non-Muslim troops would defile the holy places. Although both sides politicized Islam (including the Islamists themselves) for reasons other than mere piety, one still finds a profound genuineness in their concerns. One finds as well a deep uncertainty, for no choice was easy or straightforward; and none had the luxury of time to be Hamlet, deliberating, deliberating. Unity and clarity, where apparent, were something of a façade, as the following illustrations show.

On the coalition side, none of the leaders gladly embraced the presence of a half million non-Arab, non-Muslim troops. As chapter three points out, Fahd had to be persuaded that his kingdom was in mortal danger before he would give consent for them to come. Then, once they had arrived, he repeatedly said (and, I am convinced, not disingenuously) that they would leave when the conflict had passed, a position he voiced in the Arab League meeting on 10 August and from which he did not waver.[42] Fahd had deep Islamic misgivings about non-Muslim troops, but he gave greater weight to *raisons d'état*. Yet even here, as Fahd and others argued, *raisons d'état* constituted his Islamic duty. As an Islamic ruler, he had to preserve the safety of his people. Although the senior ulama in the kingdom issued a fatwa authorizing the invitation to foreign forces as a critical necessity, others disagreed, challenging Fahd's calculations and giving greater weight to Islamic misgivings about the defiling presence of the troops in sacred lands. Safar al-Hawali, a respected theologian and dean of Islamic studies at Umm al Qura University in Mecca, warned Saudis that in looking to the West, "America has become your God."[43] An Islamic scholar at Muhammad bin Saʿud University warned the royal family that Islamic nations necessarily decline when they maintain themselves through corruption and fail to consult with the ulama. An imam in Riyadh, with the Arab fondness for pungent analogy, asked, "If a dog has come onto your land, would you invite a lion to get rid of it?"[44]

Even more striking was a petition that over one hundred leading Saudi religious scholars and academics presented to Fahd in May 1991. The ten-point petition, which called for, among other things, the Islamization of all social, economic, administrative, and educational systems, had two key points that dealt indirectly with coalition forces. The third point called for the creation of "modern, strong, and independent Islamic armed forces" that would be structured on "the pattern of the Prophet Muhammad's armies" and for the "diversification of modern arms procurement sources," indicating that the United States and Britain should no longer be primary suppliers. More importantly, the ninth point called for the preservation of the interests, purity, and unity of the umma by "keeping it out of non-Islamic pacts and treaties."[45] This expressed strong Saudi disquiet with the coalition, as well as for any future security arrangement that involved keeping large numbers of foreign troops in kingdom.

Similarly, Mubarak was extraordinarily reluctant to build a coalition that would involve foreign forces. Days after the invasion, the Egyptian president emphasized to Secretary of Defense Cheney his "absolute rejection" of foreign intervention in the crisis. And from the start of the crisis until the end of the war the next February, Mubarak sent no fewer than thirty appeals to Saddam, attempting first to avert war, then to achieve an early withdrawal. Mubarak warned in his New Year's message that if war came, there would be "a merciless hell . . . in which heads will turn white, minarets will bend, and the mutilated bodies of victims will be scattered in seas of blood."[46] Although the prediction was exaggerated, Mubarak—as former commander of the Egyptian Air Force—knew the horror of war, and most certainly wanted to avert another one. More tellingly, both Syria's Assad and Mubarak assured their people that their nations' contingents were to be used defensively and kept separate from outside forces. As Chapter Three indicates, Assad added that Syrian forces would be used to protect the holy places and were, in fact, to gradually replace foreign troops.

In sum, no Arab leader in the coalition saw the invitation to foreign troops as other than a necessity, something forced on them by Saddam. All of them, as the Arab League deliberations made clear, much preferred an Arab-Islamic solution to the crisis. All of them feared what large-scale outside intervention could mean.

Alternatively, those who did not participate in the coalition were not thereby approving of Saddam's invasion. As Walid Khalidi observed, none "of the dissenting countries at the government level condone[d] the invasion of Kuwait or the violation of the moral and legal principles it entailed. All of them denounced the invasion in face-to-face meetings with Saddam and in repeated unilateral public statements. What they balked at was formal, collective denunciation."[47] In fact, several of those who did not join the condemnation of Iraq at the Arab League apparently placed their hopes for mediation in a minisummit, although the effort proved abortive.[48] Leaders outside the coalition were wise enough to know that giving their imprimatur to Saddam's forcible seizure was tantamount to undermining the moral authority of their own rule. But public pressure and their own opposition to another Western intervention prompted them either to abstain or to oppose the majority during the Arab League meetings. Additionally, they pointed to the West's double standard: moving rapidly to reverse the acquisition of territory by force in Kuwait, yet countenancing the acquisition of territory by force in the West Bank and Gaza.

Similarly, in this constellation of shared values, Islamists believed that averting the defiling presence of non-Muslim troops in the holy places carried greater weight than supporting the coalition, just as Arab nationalists feared that the troops were an imperialist intrusion rather than a force for restoring order. But by and large, neither the Islamists nor the nationalists who supported Saddam initially approved of the invasion, as indicated above.[49] And after the crisis, their distaste for Saddam became even clearer. For instance, following the war, the Egyptian Brotherhood issued a statement on Iraq's suppression of the Sunni Kurds in which they condemned "the barbaric measures" the regime took under its "Baʿthist ruler." It went on to call for replacing the present Baʿthist regime with an Islamic government. Separately, Maʾmun al-Hudaybi, spokesman for the group, declared, "Our position is that his regime will never change. Our principle is that acceptance of the Baʿth regime is impossible, because the Baʿth creed clearly opposes

Islam." Elsewhere, Hudaybi pointed out, "If you screen our statements you will not find a single sign of identification with the person of Saddam Husayn. . . . Saddam Husayn is a Ba'thist and I am a Muslim Brother, and he still murders Muslim Brothers."[50]

Like his Egyptian counterpart, a spokesman for the Jordanian Brotherhood pointed out that the Brothers were "banned and persecuted in Iraq," and he urged that "Islamic parties be given freedom to operate" there. The Brotherhood did mount rallies in Jordan, but—as Martin Kramer points out—they did nothing to put themselves at risk.[51]

The Palestinian position was especially interesting, for it was largely on their behalf, after all, that Saddam claimed he was waging his jihad. But the Palestinians were not solidly united behind Saddam. The majority supported Saddam, hoping for deliverance after what they repeatedly described as a military occupation by Israeli forces in the West Bank and Gaza. And, as the press broadly noted, Palestinians did cheer Scud missiles. But not all cheered. One Palestinian who repudiated Saddam's invasion and Palestinian support for it was Edward Said. "What sort of muddled and anachronistic idea of Bismarckian 'integration' is this that wipes out an entire country and smashes its society with 'Arab unity' as its goal? The most disheartening thing is that so many people, many of them victims of exactly the same brutal logic, appear to have identified with Iraq and not Kuwait."[52] Another was Walid Khalidi: "[T]he Iraqi invasion of Kuwait, in concept and execution, constitutes a violation of the central humane values of the Islamic heritage and of the accepted norms of international behavior." Of the PLO, Khalidi maintains that its "failure to come out publicly, repeatedly, and forcefully against the invasion" did the organization grave harm.[53] Within the territories Professor Hanan Ashrawi was unequivocal: "We do not condemn occupation in one area and condone it in another. We do not condone the acquisition of land by force. We do not have . . . double standards."[54]

Despite what many might have anticipated of the fundamentalist Hamas, its leadership steered a pragmatic course. Although it described the coalition as "nazi forces" and new crusaders, it also demanded Iraq withdraw from Kuwait before the coalition forces withdrew from the peninsula. And it commiserated: "We here in Palestine are aware of what it means to lose a homeland and we understand the agony of the Kuwaiti people. We appeal to Islamic nations to assist the Kuwaiti people."[55] Hamas's statements, in fact, brought it praise in the Saudi press but clashes with the PLO. And other Palestinian Muslims had misgivings about Saddam. By the second week of the conflict, the *Jeru-salem Post* could report that two different imams were ejected from their mosques by their assemblies for having criticized Saddam.[56]

Such examples abound, but these suffice to point to the larger reality. There was widespread but not unanimous support for Saddam, and across the region varying levels and kinds of support frequently re-flected domestic considerations and the pursuit of *raisons d'état*. In Jor-dan there was an important contestation, in Islamic terms, over the distribution of power. The king sincerely seemed to wish for a regional solution to a regional problem and just as sincerely seemed to reject the acquisition of territory by force. But the king was vulnerable to the Islamists; and as the parliamentary elections represented his conces-sion on domestic economic issues, the inclusion of seven Islamists in his cabinet in January 1991 must be seen as a concession to social and religious pressures. His removal of the seven the following summer, when the gulf crisis was passed, seemed to underscore that.[57]

Similarly, in the Occupied Territories, the PLO and Hamas had vied for popular support, as indicated in Chapter Five, and the gulf crisis saw a pronounced jockeying for support. The routinization of the inti-fada was bad news for Arafat, since the United National Leadership of the Intifada was primarily the voice of the PLO, and Arafat's authority was thus tied to the fortunes of the uprising. Saddam's announcement of a rough military parity in his fire speech in April offered a break in the impasse; tactical alliance with Iraq could benefit Arafat and the uprising. When Saddam offered his much (self-) touted peace plan on 12 August, the one that linked resolving the Kuwait "situation" to first having Israel withdraw from the territories, Arafat and most Palestini-ans were elated. Roger Heacock observes:

[W]ith Saddam Hussein's [12 August] proposal, there suddenly shone be-fore the Palestinian street the mirage of a diplomatic trade off, rendered potent by the threat of destructive war, which would result in an end to their twenty-three-year-old occupation. Saddam Hussein became the paladin who would bring them what almost three years of their own vari-ous forms of struggle in the form of the intifada had failed in bringing, namely national independence.[58]

Arafat's support for Saddam was a gamble, and it seemed to work in the short term. But what if Saddam were humiliated in the matter of Kuwait? Hamas, as indicated just above, considered the odds and elected to take a more pragmatic course, believing that Saddam had little chance against the coalition. In quite literal terms, it would not pay to support the wrong side in the war, for much of Hamas's financial support was extraterritorial. Ironically, the secular PLO responded more positively to the call for jihad. On the other hand, the Islamists—who state in their charter, "There is no solution for the Palestinian question except through jihad. Initiatives, proposals and international conferences are all a waste of time and vain endeavors"—took a shrewdly mediating position.[59]

And for the Iranians, the Gulf War was a godsend. Under duress, Saddam made concessions to them he would never have made otherwise, including rerecognizing the 1975 Algiers Accord, which he had torn up so ostentatiously on Iraqi television in 1980. And in an ironic twist, the war afforded the Iranians the pleasure of seeing the United States caught in precisely the difficulty they themselves had faced during the eight-year war. The United States had been, as a matter of calculated policy, pleased to watch Iraq and Iran battle each other, supplying weaponry and intelligence to the one and F-14 fighter parts to the other. Now, the Iranians could more easily propound their credentials as the true patrons-in-chief of the Palestinian cause (Saddam being otherwise engaged), wish both the coalition and the Iraqi leadership all the worst, and do so in Islamic terms.[60]

Several Iranian leaders condemned the United States and the coalition (Khameini, Mohtashimi, Khalkhali), but none praised Saddam. Khameini, in fact, said the invasion proved Baghdad was unfaithful to Islam; and Ahmad Khomeini, son of the late ayatollah, declared Saddam would never be a "human being." What became apparent is that the policy course Iran followed during the Gulf War was primarily pragmatic, not radical. Iran dealt out fiery statements of condemnation to both sides and stayed neutral. One clear reflection of that pragmatism was the Iranian response after the war when their coreligionists in the south of Iraq rose up against Saddam. The Iranians provided some small support, but it was limited; and the government kept the Supreme Assembly for the Islamic Revolution in Iraq (SAIRI) on rather a "tight leash." President Rafsanjani, with others, essentially wished the Iraqi Shi'a all the best but little more. The president said, "We do not hesitate to prove our moral and political solidarity with the Iraqi people. Yet we will not intervene through the use of arms." And so, another anomaly in this Other Gulf War. Iran, for a season the epitome of Islamic radicalism, proved a skillful and pragmatic player in the regional political situation, shrewdly positioning itself throughout the conflict for maximum benefit and minimum exposure to risk.[61]

Still, apart from Islamists and elites, were the majority of those who marched, the most numerous but the least empowered. For them, "Islam" was a language for articulating political hopes and calling for the redress of social inequalities. But lacking power, they could do little except protest; they could not expect to enter into a dialogue as political equals, despite their Islamic equality. Rosemary Hollis has rightly observed that the "'Arab masses' were essentially powerless to alter the course of the war: a reflection of the very circumstances that gave rise to their general sense of frustration with the status quo, and which predisposed them to support the stand of Saddam Hussein against the western powers and allied Arab governments."[62]

Hollis is right: the majority of people had little chance of directly changing the course of the war. And the Jordanian editorialist quoted above is at least partly right: "the call for Jihad has continued to lack a mechanism to implement it." But he may be on less sure ground, I argue, when he holds, "enthusiastic individuals do not know how to translate their enthusiasm into action." Just as "Islam" is a language, a march of 300,000 can be remarkably articulate. During the crisis, no Arab leader could simply write off the voice of the street, at least not during the seven months of Other Gulf War.

## OF LANGUAGES AND NATION STATES

Saddam's capitulation on 28 February did not end his battles. Within two days the Shi'a launched their own intifada, and the Kurds followed soon thereafter.[63] The insurgents assumed that Saddam's military power had been smashed and that the United States would either give some support or at least prevent Saddam from using attack helicopters. They were wrong on both counts, and in the vicious fighting during the next month, thousands died before Saddam had managed to quell the rebellions. The fiercest fighting took place in the holy cities of Karbala and Najaf where, most unfortunately, the Shi'a shrines sustained heavy damage in Saddam's attempt to restore control.[64]

Yet in Karbala the rebels graphically repudiated Saddam and his claim to Islamic authority. Some years before, the regime had placed "Saddam Hussein's Family Tree," which purported to show the Iraqi president's descent from the family of the prophet of Islam, in the

Imam Abbas mosque. Of the hundreds of names on the tree, three were effaced in the uprising: those of Saddam and his sons, Uday and Qusay.[65] One other extraordinary picture of repudiation emerged from the uprising: an Iraqi tank commander, whose unit had fled the coalition advance, rolled into Sa'ad Square in the southern city of Basra. After positioning his tank in front of a gigantic mural of Saddam in military uniform, the commander stood on the chassis of the vehicle to address the huge likeness. "What has befallen us of defeat, shame, and humiliation, Saddam, is the result of your follies, your miscalculations, and your irresponsible actions." The commander then climbed back inside and began firing away. The crowd standing by began cheering, "Saddam is finished. All the army is dead." Kanan Makiya, who relates the story, has been unable to verify its details. The story spread quite rapidly through the south, however, and became a metaphor, Makiya writes, for all those who joined in the fighting.[66]

But during the same month, there were those laying the groundwork for peace, hoping to prevent a third gulf war. On 6 March 1991, the Arab states of the coalition met in Damascus to issue a declaration, the victors' view of what the region ought to look like in the wake of the crisis.[67] Altered somewhat in subsequent meetings, the text was issued in final form in August, five months later. The Damascus Declaration spoke of building a "new Arab order," but what it really did was to affirm the old. No state boundaries were erased and no new organizations created. The initial draft proposed that Egypt and Syria would form the nucleus of an Arab peace force to protect the gulf region. But the members retreated even from that. According to the final text, "any GCC country has the right to employ the services of Egyptian and Syrian forces on its territory if it so wishes." The Arab League and the Organization of the Islamic Conference (OIC) had been unable to broker a solution to the Gulf crisis, and both did little after the first week of the conflict other than issue statements. Perhaps now those who issued the Damascus Declaration saw little point in creating a new defense force.

Two further points stand out. One is the final wording of the fifth, and last, principle. It states simply the signatories' joint pledge "to uphold the sovereignty of every Arab country and its control of its natural and economic resources." In other words, the declaration precisely repudiates Saddam's rationale for invading Kuwait. The other important point concerns what was not stated in the declaration. Apart from the opening bismallah and two passing references to Islamic norms and organizations, there is no other mention of Islam. After months of saturation with Islamic discourse, the omission was only too obvious. These eight signatories—the GCC states, Syria, Egypt—simply reaffirmed all the borders of the Arab *status quo ante bellum,* with little worry about their much maligned "artificiality." Islam seemed to be more comfortable living in a world of nation-states than in conducting jihad under the banner of a Ba'thist caliph.

The war, it seems, did nothing except reaffirm existing conditions. Islam had briefly provided a powerfully mobilizing language, one to which hundreds of thousands on both sides responded. Yet there were no revolutions, and the umma was not established. Similarly, no mighty Arab nation was formed, stretching *min al-khaleej ila al-muheet.* But despite predictions, pan-Arabism and pan-Islam have not disappeared. Rather, they have persisted alongside the practice of interstate politics. There is a sense of kinship, based on religion, language, and history, that cannot be easily removed. Four years before Saddam launched his invasion of Kuwait, James Piscatori wrote of this coexistence of the pan-ideologies and the reality of particular state boundaries. In the conclusion to *Islam in a World of Nation States,* Piscatori observes,

[T]he yearning for some larger political identity—pan-Islam or Arab nationalism—may coexist along the particular nationalist sentiments. . . . [I]t remains the case that many Muslims dream of something greater while at the same time identifying with their particular homeland out of habit, pragmatism, or desire, or a mixture of all three. . . . Several views of the Muslim world . . . assume that the nation state is either impossible in theory, or so inherently contradictory to Islamic values that it will be very troubled in practice. But the fact of the matter is that, in Islam, the nation-state is no less possible, or no more fraught with problems, than it is in the non-Muslim world.[68]

To Piscatori we add this: the "yearning for some larger political identity," whether through a return to pan-Islam or Arab nationalism or both, seems to intensify with crisis. That was true in the Iran-Iraq War, in the intifada, in the Gulf War. The next war, we believe, will show that to be true again.

## THE UNCONCLUDED OTHER GULF WAR

On 27 February 1991, President Bush declared, "Kuwait is liberated," and the next day Iraq announced it would agree to cease-fire terms. And yet battles go on. Sometimes breaking out openly, always agitating more subtly, the battles go on. All the elements that provoked the first war remain, although of different strengths. There are still the oil-rich and the oil-less poor. The ability of governments in those poor countries to deliver basic goods and services has not really improved. In most of the countries of the region, populations are increasing rapidly. None of the countries can boast a robust democratic government, although some have taken tentative steps. The Palestinians still do not have a state, Jerusalem is yet contested, and the innocent (among both Israelis and Palestinians) and the not so innocent have died in the confrontations. And Saddam. Saddam has less power, but he is not powerless; and the region will not persist long without someone having real power. International concern about his weapons program persists, even as Arabs decry the impact upon ordinary Iraqis of an arms-control regime intended to curb those weapons. Moreover, to enforce the controversial sanctions, Americans remain in Saudi Arabia and in other countries around the region.

It is this last point that is especially troublesome, that culturally alien forces would remain in the gulf long after the war, Fahd's promises notwithstanding. In 1992, a year after the cease-fire, the superb Egyptian writer Mohamed Heikal reflected:

The causes of the tension [in the Middle East] are many and complex, but many Arabs feel that an important element is the American military presence . . . and Washington's influence over a number of Arab governments. The continuation of a high U.S. profile in Middle East affairs in the months after the Gulf War was the opposite of what the region needed. . . . A profound sorrow over the destruction of Iraq was felt, in countries which participated in the coalition no less than in those which did not, and a sense of humiliation which was caused by the American management of the crisis overwhelmed all other aspects of the war. Americans assumed that Arabs were glad of protection against Iraq's ambitions to dominate the region . . . without realizing that the whole affair was wounding to Arab self-respect. . . . Washington wanted Arabs to feel that the U.S. was defending them against an aggressor: the reality was that the U.S. defended its own interests, and used methods of divide and rule to achieve its aims after the invasion of Kuwait.[69]

And Heikal's view is hardly atypical. The work of the Ismaels, cited above, underscores it: six months after the cease-fire, fully three-fourths of Arab elites polled believed that the gulf crisis was an externally hatched conspiracy.

And the view is not simply academic. What Heikal expressed in reasoned speech, others have taken up with fury. In February 1998, an organization calling itself the "International Islamic Front for Jihad against the Jews and the Crusaders" (*al-jabhah al-islamiyah al-alamiyah li-jihad al-yahud wa-al-salibiyin*) issued a fatwa. In it, this heretofore unknown organization stated, "The Arabian Peninsula has never—since God made it flat, created its desert, and encircled it with sea—been stormed by any forces like the crusader armies spreading in it like locusts." The fatwa continued, "[F]or over seven years the United States has been occupying the lands of Islam in the holiest of places, the Arabian Peninsula." It concluded,

[W]e issue the following fatwa to all Muslims: the ruling to kill the Americans and their allies—*civilians and military*—is an individual duty for every Muslim who can do it *in any country* in which it is possible to do it, in order to liberate the al-Aqsa Mosque [of Jerusalem] and the holy mosque [in Mecca] from their grip and in order for their armies to move out of all the lands of Islam. . . . We—with God's help—call on every Muslim who believes in God and wishes to be rewarded to comply with God's order to kill the Americans and plunder their money *wherever* and whenever they find it.[70] (emphasis added)

The lead signature is "Shaykh Usamah bin Muhammad bin Ladin," implicated in the bombing of the U.S. embassies in Kenya and Tanzania in August 1998 and suspected in the attacks on the U.S. military compound in Dhahran, Saudi Arabia, in June 1996, and on the USS *Cole* in September 2000. Forty-eight Americans died in those several attacks, as well as 289 Kenyans and Tanzanians. Most tragically, of course, the Saudi-born radical carried his fury to the United States. In September 2001, bin Ladin, in effect, answered Saddam Hussein's summons to jihad:

Arabs, Moslems, believers in God. . . . This is your day to rise and spread quickly in order to defend Mecca, which is captive to the spears of the

Americans and the Zionists. . . . Burn the soil under their feet. Burn the soil under the feet of the aggressors and invaders who want harm for your families in Iraq. Until the voice of right rises up in the Arab world, *hit their interests wherever they are* and rescue holy Mecca and the grave of the Prophet Mohammed in Medina. (emphasis added)

The text, of course, is the Iraqi president's call for jihad from 10 August 1990. There is a striking similarity between it and the fatwa signed by bin Ladin. And what the secularist had called for as a Machiavellian Muslim, Osama achieved, at the cost of 3,000 innocent lives.

So the battles go on. Americans, Europeans, and Arabs may once again see sons and daughters boarding ships and C-141s for uncertain duty in a war of moral and logistic complexity. But now, that tragic battle has been carried to shores well beyond the Persian Gulf. The cease-fire in the Other Gulf War, it seems, has yet to be declared, and the scope of battle has significantly increased.

*Postscript, June 2003*

Several months after the manuscript for *Saddam's War of Words* was completed, a coalition force comprising (predominantly) American and British troops did indeed return to the gulf for a war that toppled Saddam Hussein and his Ba'thist regime. Coalition forces prevailed easily in March 2003; attaining peace has proved more elusive. The complex demography of Iraq—welded together with brute force by Saddam—has not been simplified by this most recent war, and it will make the task of democratization, which the United States has undertaken, daunting. But more than Iraqi demographics makes the task daunting. The elements of instability cited above remain unsettled, most especially the Israel-Palestinian conflict. Coalition action removed a brutal dictator, but it did not ameliorate the wider political pathologies of the region. Moreover, the pronounced and quite visible presence of the western troops in Iraq may well precipitate a very negative and unintended result.

In March 2003, exactly one week before coalition forces attacked a bunker suspected of hiding Saddam and his top aides, I visited with several Egyptian academics in Cairo. After several cups of coffee, one of them, an urbane and quite articulate computer scientist, remarked, "You know, Arab intellectuals are beginning to use the dirty word again."

"And what is that word?"

"Isti'amar," he quietly replied.

*Isti'amar.* The word may be rendered "colonialism" or "imperialism." It is the word Arab writers used to describe the British presence in the Middle East, especially before 1948, when Great Britain relinquished mandate responsibilities in Palestine. It is a word to which Saddam often recurred when describing the U.S. presence in the Arabian peninsula during and after the war in 1990–1991, calling, for instance, the no-fly zones imposed on Iraq after 1991, an "imperialism in the sky."[71] It is a word that should give U.S. policymakers pause, for if Arab intellectuals who eschew violence use it to describe the western presence, how much more will radicals, whether secular or religious?

Saddam Hussein, as a political rhetorician, may have been silenced. His rhetoric has not been. The violent few will likely turn again to Saddam's categorical language to trouble the lives of the peaceful many. And if so, no one is exempt from the potential repercussions of yet another gulf war.

# 8 | CLOSING REFLECTION
## THE VIEW FROM THE MOUNTAINS

The most spectacular view in Saudi Arabia is one from atop the sheer escarpment just outside Taif, the summer capital. The sun-baked rocks fall away from the cliff's edge to a floor 2,500 feet below. The view to the west shows little except rocks wrenched up from the earth in some early geologic catastrophe and now strewn about in a plain that stretches for fifty miles to the Red Sea. The few mountains that remain in this march to the sea are the jagged western edge of the Hijaz range, and set among them is a city, the holiest spot on earth for the followers of the seventh-century prophet Muhammad. The modern highway that carefully crawls down the face of the escarpment and wends its way to Mecca broadens to six lanes when it reaches the valley floor. But approaching the city, one sees signs directing that non-Muslims exit and take the bypass. Guards are posted just beyond the bypass to see that the injunction is enforced. For in this country, the non-Muslim may neither enter, nor even see, Mecca mukarrama, venerable Mecca, the city of Allah's last prophet.

Yet from this austere place, this bleak and remote place, the armies of Islam went forth twelve-and-a-half centuries ago, changing history's trajectory in the Middle East, then Africa and Asia, and ultimately the world. As they went, they carried no volumes of theology. It was enough that they knew the shahada: There is no god but God, and Muhammad is the messenger of God. To this God, they declared, one owes absolute Islam, submission. Perhaps one does not think of Mecca and the religion revealed there in just this way, but we of the West will never understand the Other Gulf War without doing so. We must see the appropriateness of the image of a sacred city, remote and terrible with holiness, and know that one billion of the world's people today are Muslims, who hold it in such awe that they turn toward it in prayer five times daily.

Shaykh Ahmad Zaki al-Yamani, former Saudi oil minister, once observed, "If I have to say one thing that this kingdom stands for, above all others, it is not oil. It is Islam. One day even we will run out of oil. But we will never run out of Mecca and Medina."[1] The problems, the aspirations, the political issues that preceded the Gulf War of 1990–1991 persist, but so do Mecca and Medina. As long as they all continue, Islam will, no doubt, sometimes be the resort of the unprincipled. But for the faithful—the multitudes who turn in obedience toward Mecca mukarrama when they hear the mu'ezzin's call, "Come to prayer! Come to peace!"—Islam will always be an invitation to the best of paths, *sabil Allah*.

> Say: "O ye
> My servants who believe!
> Fear your Lord.
> Good is (the reward)
> For those who do good
> In this world.
> Spacious is Allah's earth!
> Those who patiently persevere
> Will truly receive
> A reward without measure!"
> (Quran 39:10)

# NOTES

1. Cited in Kenneth Walsh, "Very Clearly, Good vs. Evil," *U.S. News and World Report*, 31 December 1990, 24.

2. Cited in the *Washington Post*, 29 January 1991, A1.

3. Malcolm Kerr, *The Arab Cold War: Gamal 'Abd al-Nasir and His Rivals, 1958–1970*, 3rd ed. (New York: Oxford Univ. Press, 1999).

4. While the present study does not make Arab nationalism and religion, per se, its focus, it does recognize the importance of Islam as a component of nationalism in the theoretical writings of a number of Arab writers, most pertinently in the work of the Ba'thist ideologue Michel Aflaq (see especially Chapter Four of this book). A vast scholarly literature treats both the relation between nationalism and religion and the Arab writers who reflect on it. For a general discussion of legitimating ideologies, see "States, Beliefs, and Ideologies," in James A. Bill and Robert Springborg, *Politics in the Middle East* (New York: HarperCollins, 1994). Useful summaries of the work of Aflaq are in Majid Khadduri, *Political Trends in the Arab World: The Role of Ideas and Ideals in Politics* (Baltimore: Johns Hopkins Univ. Press, 1970) and Albert Hourani, *A History of the Arab Peoples* (Cambridge, Mass.: Harvard Univ. Press, 1991). For an overview from a social scientist who surveys contending theoretical approaches for understanding Arab nationalism, see Baghat Korany, "Arab Nationalism," in John L. Esposito, ed., *The Oxford Encyclopedia of the Modern Islamic World*, 4 vols. (New York: Oxford Univ. Press, 1995). For a useful recent monograph, see Youssef M. Choueiri, *Arab Nationalism: A History* (Oxford: Blackwell Publishers, 2000). I take as my starting point the premise set forth by Saad Eddin Ibrahim shortly before the Gulf War: "There is neither a basic contradiction nor an inconsistency between the Islamic religion and Arab nationalism. Any attempt to create artificial preferences between the religious and secular identity would lead to a vicious circle" ("Concerns and Challenges," in *Pan-Arabism and Arab Nationalism*, ed. Tawfic Farah [Boulder, Colo.: Westview Press, 1987], 63). In any event, the focus here is on the vast extent to which regional actors, and Saddam in particular, appealed to Islam to legitimate courses of action in what otherwise appeared to be a strictly secular conflict.

5. President Bush's address to the National Religious Broadcasters convention is the most obvious example. Speaking a week and a half after the air war began, Bush disavowed a religious dimension to the war, then quickly segued to the language of civil religion. Bush observed, "Saddam tried to cast this conflict as a religious war. But it has nothing to do with religion per se. It has on the other hand everything to do with what religion embodies—good vs. evil, right vs. wrong, human dignity vs. tyranny and oppression. The war in the Gulf is not a Christian war, a Jewish war or a Muslim war—it is a just war.... We will

prevail because of the support of the American people, armed with a trust in God and in the principles that make men free. . . . I salute . . . your Operation Desert Prayer and worship services for our troops held by, among others . . . the Rev. Billy Graham. America has always been a religious nation—perhaps never more than now. Just look at the last several weeks. . . . [W]ith the support and prayers of so many there can be no question in the minds of our soldiers or in the minds of our enemy about what Americans think. . . . I have been honored to serve as president of this great nation for two years now and believe more than ever that one cannot be America's president without trust in God. . . . Thank you for this occasion. And may God bless our great country." The full text is in James Johnson and George Weigel, *Just War and the Gulf War* (Washington, D.C.: Ethics and Public Policy Center, 1991), 137–140.

6. Speaking to the National Association of Evangelicals in 1983, the president acknowledged the importance of military strength but declared, "The real crisis we face today is a spiritual one. . . . There is sin and evil in the world, and we are enjoined by Scripture and the Lord Jesus to oppose it with all our might." He went on to make clear that the "focus of evil in the modern world" is the totalitarian state. Quoted in John Diggins, *The Lost Soul of American Politics* (New York: Basic Books, 1984), 344.

7. Generally, the approach of the texts is to examine Bush's appeal to the just war tradition, as in the address cited in note 2, supra. Among those texts are Thomas C. Fox, *Iraq: Military Victory, Moral Defeat* (Kansas City, Mo.: Sheed and Ward, 1991); Alan Geyer and Barbara Green, *Lines in the Sand: Justice and the Gulf War* (Louisville, Ky.: Westminster/John Knox Press, 1992); Kenneth L. Vaux, *Ethics and the Gulf War: Religion, Rhetoric, and Righteousness* (Boulder, Colo.: Westview Press, 1992); David Campbell, *Politics without Principle* (Boulder, Colo.: Lynne Rienner, 1993); and Johnson and Weigel, *Just War*. Most of the texts are critical of the president's handling of the just-war doctrine or his decision to prosecute the war rather than rely on sanctions alone, or both. One dissertation that examines what its author terms the "discursive structuration of the Persian Gulf Crisis" is Heidi Tarver, "Words of War: The Persian Gulf Crisis and American Public Discourse" (Ph.D. diss., University of California, Berkeley, 1997). It examines the moral dimension, particularly as set out in presidential speeches, of the war.

8. *Islamic Fundamentalisms and the Gulf Crisis* (Chicago: The Fundamentalism Project, dist. Univ. of Chicago Press, 1991), ed. James Piscatori, does a good job of surveying religion and the war; but as the title indicates, its focus is on nongovernmental Islamic groups, not on the state's employment of Islam. John Kelsay's *Islam and War: A Study in Comparative Ethics* (Louisville, Ky.: Westminster/John Knox Press, 1993) was prompted by the Gulf War and is useful as a study of both the Islamic doctrine of jihad and the comparison of jihad to the just-war tradition. A cross-cultural examination of ethics and warfare, it does note Saddam's appeal to Islam, but does not offer a sustained treatment of it. A dissertation that examines classical and contemporary Islamic thinking on war and international relations is Sohail Hashmi, "The Islamic

Ethics of War and Peace" (Ph.D. diss., Harvard University, 1996). The focus in the present work, however, is on praxis, not doctrine, and on governmental elites, not Islamic theorists. Ofra Bengio's *Saddam's Word: Political Discourse in Iraq* (New York: Oxford Univ. Press, 1998) is especially helpful in its analysis of political discourse in Ba'thist Iraq. The Gulf War and religion, although treated, is not its central focus, however.

9. One article of exceptional merit is Yvonne Haddad, "Operation Desert Storm and the War of the Fatwas," in *Islamic Legal Interpretations: Muftis and Their Fatwas*, ed. Muhammad Khalid Masud et al. (Cambridge, Mass.: Harvard Univ. Press, 1996). Haddad notes the proliferation of formal religious opinions and their conflicting content. She does not, however, take up the acts of governmental elites directly; rather, the focus is on NGOs or governmentally sponsored groups (e.g., al-Azhar).

10. Cited in Thomas Friedman, "A Dreamlike Landscape, a Dreamlike Reality," *New York Times*, 28 October 1990.

### CHAPTER TWO

1. Cited in Peter Mansfield, *The Arabs* (New York: Viking Penguin, 1985), 37.

2. A number of good sources may be cited for this background. Glenn Frankel gives a concise account in "Lines in the Sand" in Micah Sifry and Christopher Cerf, eds., *The Gulf War Reader* (New York: Random House, 1991), 16–20; see p. 18 for the Parsons quote. The Lawrence quote is in Mansfield, *The Arabs*, 185. A summary of the six borders is in Simon Henderson, *Instant Empire: Saddam Hussein's Ambition for Iraq* (San Francisco: Mercury House, 1991), 12–24; Ibrahim Ibrahim, ed., *The Gulf Crisis: Background and Consequences* (Washington, D.C.: Georgetown Univ. Press, 1992), 4ff; and Alasdair Drysdale and Gerald H. Blake, *The Middle East and North Africa: A Political Geography* (New York: Oxford Univ. Press, 1985), 63–66. The British concern about the Germans and the Russians is covered in George Lenczowski, *The Middle East in World Affairs* (Ithaca, N.Y.: Cornell Univ. Press, 1980), 76–79; 654–657.

3. David Fromkin, *A Peace to End All Peace* (New York: Holt, 1989), 191–192, gives a superb review, focusing especially on Churchill. For an account of the "orchestration" of Feisal's "popular" selection and reception, see Fromkin, 506–508.

4. Cited in Pierre Salinger, with Eric Laurent, *Secret Dossier: The Hidden Agenda behind the Gulf War*, trans. Howard Curtis (New York: Penguin, 1991), 13. Speaker not identified.

5. The number is given in Judith Miller and Laurie Mylroie, "The Rise of Saddam Hussein," in *Gulf War Reader*, ed. Sifry and Cerf, 66–78.

6. Robert Kaplan, writing in *The New Republic*, 8 October 1990, 15, captured this nicely: "Iraq at peace is an unstable element. One reason Hussein has remained in power so long is because he has kept the country at war. His invasion of Kuwait could almost be seen as the ultimate, albeit perverse, result of Iraq's own legitimacy crisis."

7. Other analytic distinctions have been made. Walid Khalidi follows A. J. P. Taylor's distinction of profound and particular causes in examining the roots of the war. See his "Iraq vs. Kuwait: Claims and Counterclaims" in *Gulf War Reader*, ed. Sifry and Cerf, 57–65. Musallam Ali Musallam, *The Iraqi Invasion of Kuwait: Saddam Hussein, His State, and International Power Politics* (London: Tauris, 1996) uses a Waltzian approach, distinguishing a "nexus of causes": man, the state, and war. Majid Khadduri and Edmund Ghareeb distinguish *sabab* from *illa*, "deep causes" from "immediate factors." See their *War in the Gulf, 1990–91: The Iraq-Kuwait Conflict and Its Implications* (New York: Oxford Univ. Press, 1997). None of these approaches needs be taken to exclude the others.

8. For instance, the disastrous economic picture in Iraq constituted a *raison d'état* that could at the same time, and with some merit, be presented as a media reason. On the other hand, the need to keep a million-man army away from the throne and occupied elsewhere could hardly be presented as a credible media reason. Such divergence between what one tells the press and what really prompts an action is often the case in international politics, and it was certainly true of the United States during the Gulf War. U.S. involvement had less to do with magnanimous, disinterested opposition to aggression (media reasons) than with Gulf stability and access to oil (*raisons d'état*). One pundit's remark that we would not have intervened if the national cash crop of Kuwait had been broccoli instead of oil is cynically on point.

9. Phebe Marr, "Iraq's Uncertain Future," *Current History* 90 (Jan. 1991): 3.

10. Ibid., 3. Others present different figures. For instance, the CIA *World Factbook 1999* (Internet version) indicates 36 miles; Drysdale and Blake, *The Middle East and North Africa*, 111, cite 12 miles. The figure for Kuwait is in Drysdale and Blake, 111.

11. If a cease-fire with Iraq in 1988 was Khomeini's "poisoned chalice," the 1975 accord was Saddam's, marking a low point in his developing political career, for it represented a reversal of a 1937 treaty that set the border as the low-water mark on the Iranian side. The shah dealt with Saddam from a position of strength in 1975, compelling the humiliating reversal. Launching the war in 1980 was, in large part, an attempt to reverse the reversal.

12. See the discussion in Marr, "Uncertain Future," 1–3; and Marion Farouk-Sluglett and Peter Sluglett, "Iraq since 1986: The Strengthening of Saddam," *Middle East Report* (Nov.–Dec. 1990): 23–24. The islands have been in dispute since the formation of Iraq. Although of real strategic importance to Iraq, their value to Kuwait is largely symbolic. As an indication of their control, the Kuwaitis built a bridge to Bubiyan in the early 1980s. At the formal inauguration of the bridge, the French engineer responsible for its construction said, "If the Kuwaitis now let me tarmac over the whole of the island, there will be some point in having the bridge" (Henderson, *Instant Empire*, 23).

13. Ofra Bengio holds that gaining maritime access to compensate for loss of the Shatt al Arab was the primary reason for the invasion on 2 August, secondary reasons being economic needs and a bid for pan-Arab leadership. See

her discussion, as well has her unfolding of Saddam's "grand strategy," in "Iraq," *Middle East Contemporary Survey* (hereafter, *MECS*), 1990, 379–381.

14. The discussion that follows is taken from Efraim Karsh and Inari Rautsi, *Saddam Hussein: A Political Biography* (New York, Macmillan, 1991), 201–202; Efraim Karsh, "Survival at All Costs: Saddam Hussein as Crisis Manager," in *The Gulf Crisis and Its Global Aftermath*, ed. Gad Barzilai et al. (New York: Routledge, 1993), 51–66; *The Middle East and North Africa: 1991* (London: Europa Publications), s.v. "Iraq"; CIA *Factbook*, s.v. "Iraq;" and Marr, "Iraq's Uncertain Future," 1–3.

15. Farouk-Sluglett and Sluglett argue for a figure of almost twice as much, $450 billion ("Iraq since 1986," 20).

16. A number of writers treat this. For good brief accounts, see Faleh abd al-Jabar, "The Roots of an Adventure," in *The Gulf between Us: The Gulf War and Beyond*, ed. Victoria Brittain (London: Virago, 1991), 33–35; and Marr, "Iraq's Uncertain Future," 1–3. See also *The Middle East Military Balance, 1988–89,* (Tel Aviv: Tel Aviv University, Jaffee Center for Strategic Studies, 1989), s.v. "Iraq."

17. One of the most thorough accounts of various Iraqi purges is Kanan Makiya, *Republic of Fear: The Politics of Modern Iraq* (Berkeley, Calif.: Univ. of California Press, 1998). For more on purges during and after the Iran-Iraq War, see Karsh and Rautsi, *Political Biography*, 183–193.

18. The discussion here follows Efraim Karsh and Inauri Rautsi, "Why Saddam Hussein Invaded Kuwait," *Survival* 33 (Jan.–Feb. 1991), 18ff. Karsh's comment that invading Kuwait had "less to do with a pre-meditated grand design than with [Saddam's] perennial sense of insecurity," is an observation which underscores the concern of beleaguerment. But the contention here is that both operated together, as the chapters on Iraq will point out. The phrase *diabolus ex machina*, used here in the plural, is that of L. Carl Brown, "Patterns Forged in Time: Middle Eastern Mindsets and the Gulf War," in *Political Psychology of the Gulf War*, ed. Stanley Renshon (Pittsburgh: Univ. of Pittsburgh Press, 1993), 12, and it describes a mechanism to deal with acute psychic distress. Saddam's distress was also rather existential and political.

19. One other point of beleaguerment: there was no progress in peace talks with Iran, which became especially important early in 1990. Saddam courted his former enemy, perhaps anticipating his need for all to be quiet on the eastern front when he made a move for Kuwait later that summer. His proposal in May to Iran that, together, they form a joint Arab-Islamic army to battle western hostility must be read as part of that strategy. See the discussion on attempted rapprochement with Iran in Bengio, *MECS* 1990, 396ff.

20. Previous border "challenges" occurred in 1961 and 1973. In 1961 Qassem laid claim to newly independent Kuwait, saying it was but a district (*qadha'*) of the old Basra vilayet. British troops and naval units returned immediately (July). It was not until September that a pan-Arab force arrived. Significantly it included the soon to be defunct U.A.R., as well as the Saudis. See the discussion in Lenczowski, *Middle East in World Affairs,* 667. In 1973 Iraq attacked two Kuwaiti border posts. The Saudis mobilized, the Arab League interceded,

and the Kuwaitis reportedly paid $85 million to mollify the Iraqis. A number of texts discuss both events. In addition to Lenczowski, see also Mary Morris, *Regional Dynamics of the Gulf Crisis*, RAND Papers P-7700 (Santa Monica, Calif.: RAND Corp., February 1991).

21. Cited in Amir Iskander, *Saddam Hussein: The Fighter, the Thinker, and the Man*, trans. Hassan Selim (Paris: Hachette, 1980), 319.

22. The text is in Fuad Matar, *Saddam Hussein: The Man, the Cause, and the Future* (London: Third World Centre, 1981): 89–91.

23. Cited in Musallam, *Iraqi Invasion*, 74.

24. Rubin, "The Gulf Crisis: Origins and Causes of Events," *MECS* 1990, 78.

25. See the *BBC Summary of World Broadcasts* (The Middle East, Africa, and Latin America) and the *Jerusalem Post*, both of 23 July 1990. Hereafter, the *BBC Summary* will be abbreviated *SWB*.

26. The untranslated 1992 publication is discussed in Musallam, *Iraqi Invasion*, 57–58, 87. In a postwar conversation with Taha Yasin Ramadan, Bazzaz posed the question whether "means other than war" might have been employed. Ramadan ambiguously responded, "I refuse to say that we could have avoided what had already been [predetermined] for us to do." He had just said that history is made both by the will of God and the will of man; see Khadduri and Ghareeb, *War in the Gulf*, 255–256.

27. Abd al-Jabar, "Roots of an Adventure," 37.

28. Comments made in summer 1989 to Dr. Phebe Marr. See her "Iraq's Uncertain Future," 4.

29. Formed 16 February 1989, the ACC comprised Egypt, Iraq, Jordan, and Yemen, and was intended to promote economic cooperation among members with a regional common market. The Arab Maghreb Union (AMU) was formed a day later, comprising Algeria, Libya, Mauritania, Morocco, and Tunisia. The GCC (comprising Saudi Arabia, Kuwait, Bahrain, Qatar, the UAE, and Oman), which had furnished something of a template, was formed in May 1981, eight months after the start of the Iran-Iraq War. Thus, of the major members of the Arab League, only Syria had not entered into a regional alliance.

30. See the discussion in Barzilai and Rekhess, "Israel," *MECS* 1990, 439.

31. A good, brief discussion of the ACC meeting, as well as the Arab summit in May, is available in Bruce Maddy-Weitzman, "Continuity and Change in the Inter-Arab System," in *Gulf Crisis*, ed. Barzilai et al., 36ff. A longer account by the same author is "Inter-Arab Relations," *MECS* 1990, 131–175.

32. Iraq's opposition to Egypt's rapprochement with Israel was most pointedly evident in the November 1978 "Baghdad Summit." Saddam remarked in an interview with Fuad Matar that the summit had "defeated Sadat and American imperialism with all its might" (*Saddam Hussein*, 88). But the antipathy abated during the Iran-Iraq War, and Egypt became, at least, an instrumental friend: a million Egyptian workers took the places of Iraqis who went to the front. Additionally, Egypt and Iraq, in concert with Argentina, had inaugurated the Condor 2 project, a program to develop a long-range missile; see Ali Dessouki,

"Egypt's Response to the Persian Gulf Crisis," *Current History* 91 (Jan. 1992): 34–36. Now, the political paths of the two were once again markedly diverging.

33. The speech is reported in the *Foreign Broadcast Information Service — Near East, South Asia* edition, 27 February 1990, 1–5; hereafter, *FBIS*. Peter Rodman, "Middle East Diplomacy after the Gulf War," *Foreign Affairs* 70 (Spring 1991): 1–18, explores Saddam's view that the end of the Cold War was a potential disaster for the Arabs and the strategies he had adopted.

34. "Satan" is not precisely identified, but the context demands that it include the U.S. It is likely also to include a range of "oil emirs" as well as the Zionists. During the Iranian Revolution parades in Teheran, President Carter's face appeared on huge posters as one of a triumvirate of satans, joined by Begin of Israel and Sadat of Egypt. "Satanizing" was *not* initiated by Saddam.

35. Cited in Karsh and Rautsi, "Why Saddam Invaded Kuwait," 21. The amount required was $30 billion.

36. This observation in February paralleled statements he made ten years earlier. Fuad Matar, a semiofficial biographer, made this observation based on his interview with the president: "President Saddam remains unconvinced that the United States can defend any country, particularly as this has become a dangerous gamble that American will not now undertake for anyone's sake" (*Saddam Hussein*, 95).

37. Bazoft had investigated the September 1989 explosion at a secret chemical weapons facility south of Baghdad. He was accused and convicted of spying for Israel, then hanged. On the Bazoft affair, see Rubin, *MECS* 1990, 81–82. See also the *Daily Telegraph*, 27 March 1990.

38. For information about U.S. military and dual-use technology sales to Iraq as late as 1990, see Joe Conanson, "The Iraq Lobby: Kissinger, the Business Forum, and Co.," and Murray Waas, "What Washington Gave Saddam for Christmas." Both are in Sifry and Cerf, *Gulf War Reader*, 79–95.

39. Rubin, *MECS* 1990, 81.

40. Saddam's impressive insight anticipated much of the debate in the United States throughout the fall of 1990. But Lebanon had neither oil nor anything else for which Americans had developed a national appetite. Kuwait was very different, and Saddam had underestimated an American president and his government's commitment to ensuring access to foreign oil. Thirty-two years before, during another U.S. intervention in the region (Lebanon, 1958), Secretary of State Dulles had made clear what America would protect. The U.S. must "regard Arab nationalism as a flood which is running strongly. We cannot successfully oppose it, but we could put sand bags around positions we must protect . . . Israel and Lebanon and the . . . oil positions around the Persian Gulf." Israel and oil remained on the must-protect list in 1990. Quoted in Sheldon Richman, "Washington's Interventionist Record in the Middle East," in *America Entangled: The Persian Gulf Crisis*, ed. Ted Carpenter (Washington, D.C.: Cato Institute, 1991), 68.

41. Amatzia Baram points out that the boast reflects a colloquial Iraqi ex-

pression, *ukhruk nus beitak* ("I shall burn half your house"). To Baram, that indicates that Saddam's comment was intended for a domestic audience; see "The Iraqi Invasion of Kuwait: Decision Making in Baghdad," in *Iraq's Road to War*, ed. Baram and Barry Rubin (New York: St. Martin's Press, 1993), 12. A weapon of this sort represented the culmination of long-term planning. Eight months after assuming the presidency, Saddam stated in a speech, "Israel does not fear the present Arab armies which are three million strong. But it would fear an Arab army of half a million which was backed by a strong economy and an integrated community which was scientifically and technologically advanced" (Matar, *Saddam Hussein*, 98).

42. Cited in Karsh and Rautsi, *Political Biography*, 210. Karsh and Rautsi have informed much of the present discussion on beleaguerment and bellicosity. See especially their chapter, "The Road to Kuwait," 194–216.

43. See coverage in the *Jerusalem Post*, beginning with its 21 May 1990 issue.

44. Government principals met in Taif, Saudi Arabia, to broker a national reconciliation for Lebanon after the civil war. They restructured power-sharing to more accurately reflect religious groups in the country.

45. The texts of Saddam's speeches that are summarized here may be found in *FBIS*, 29 and 30 May 1990. Shibley Telhami observes that the level of anti-Americanism was commensurate with that of anti-British sentiment in the region in the 1950s. A number of factors could account for this, including the course of the intifada and deepening concerns about Soviet immigration. The Americans were seen as financially supporting the immigration, as well as failing to pressure the Israeli government to end its "breaking of bones" policy (Rabin's term) toward the intifada; see his "Arab Public Opinion and the Gulf War," in *Political Psychology*, ed. Renshon, 187. Bengio comments on Iraq's increasingly strident attacks on Israel and the U.S. in *MECS* 1990, 393–395.

46. Despite the public bluster, Saddam was having misgivings about his fire speech. In a private meeting with Prince Bandar and others in Baghdad, Saddam worried that his speech could precipitate an attack by the West. He appealed to the Saudis for their intercession to obviate that possibility. (Recalled by Bandar in an informal presentation this writer attended at Baylor University, 11 March 2000.) The sort of attack feared was not specified, but could well have been something similar to Israel's preemptive attack on the Osirak reactor in 1981.

47. Ann Mosely Lesch, "Contrasting Reactions to the Persian Gulf Crisis," *Middle East Journal* 45 (Winter 1991): 32.

48. The choice of names for the Iran-Iraq War is instructive. Qadisiyya was the place of Muslim victory in 637 when Islamic forces routed the Sassanid Persians, thus consolidating gains in Iraq and beyond. Examples of the use of history to explain, vindicate, or give encouragement in the present could be multiplied.

49. Apart from loans (which Saddam regarded as rightful wartime support), the gulf states had given Iraq the proceeds from the sale of oil from the (then) Kuwait-Saudi "neutral zone," about $3 billion a year in revenues from 300,000

b/d sold on Iraq's behalf. After the Iran-Iraq War, the two countries integrated the production into their respective quotas. See Henderson, *Instant Empire*, 19, and *The Middle East and North Africa: 1991* (Europa), s.v. "Iraq."

50. Quoted in John Kifner, "Confrontation in the Gulf," *NYT*, 12 August 1990.

51. The description is Bengio's in *MECS* 1990, 394. Arafat is reported to have ordered 2,500 PLO members to Baghdad at the time to help defend Iraq in case of Israeli attack.

52. The text is in *FBIS*, 27 June 1990, 22–25. With its mixture of rambling pomposity and tortured logic, the address is somewhat of a trial to read, but it is rewarding nonetheless for its extended disquisition on pan-Arabism and Saddam's none too subtle desire to lead in it. Along the way, he informed his hearers that the lessons of the eight-year war with Iran would "qualify one for a doctorate degree."

53. *The Economist* summarizes key indicators of hostile intent in "Kuwait: How the West Blundered," 29 September 1990, 19–22.

54. The complete text, broadcast on Baghdad Radio, is available in the *SWB* for 19 July 1990.

55. See the Associated Press (hereafter AP), Business News wire, 17 July 1990; and the *Jerusalem Post*, 19 July 1990.

56. The Kuwaiti response is cited in Karsh and Rautsi, "Why Saddam Hussein Invaded Kuwait," 26.

57. In fact, the two countries did respond to Saddam's charges and saber rattling. On 26 July, exactly a week prior to the invasion, they had agreed at the Geneva OPEC meeting to new, lower production ceilings, which would raise the price of oil by about $3 a barrel, to about $21 (although Saddam and Aziz had publicly pressed for $25.) They also agreed to limit production to 1.5 million barrels per day. It suited Saddam's purposes to simply ignore that. Yet the Kuwaiti (and Emirati) overproduction had been widely recognized in OPEC, and the Kuwaitis must have also felt pressure from the Saudis to reduce, and not simply from Iraqi bluster. Earlier in July a senior Arab oil official said that further quota infractions by Kuwait would "not be tolerated" and that if Kuwait persisted, Saudi Arabia would not protect Kuwait from Iraqi anger (*NYT*, 18 July 1990, D1).

58. The State Department continued to reiterate its old policy rather than put forward a new one supporting freedom of navigation and movement of oil in the gulf. See Rubin, *MECS* 1990, 82. The Glaspie text is in Sifry and Cerf, *Gulf War Reader*, 122–133.

59. Quoted in *The Economist*, 29 September 1990, 22.

60. Text reported in *FBIS*, 2 July 1990.

61. See the discussion in Maddy-Weitzman, *MECS* 1990, 147–148, for this and the intense effort at negotiations in the latter part of July.

62. On the Egyptian role, see Dessouki, "Egypt's Response," 34–36.

63. As recalled by King Fahd from a conversation with Shaykh Jaber. Fahd mentioned it in a speech on Islamic values given in March 1991. The text of the

speech is in *FBIS*, 6 March 1991. It is also referenced, in a slightly different form, in Nasser Rashid and Esber Shaheen, *Saudi Arabia and the Gulf War* (Joplin, Mo.: International Institute of Technology, 1992), 159.

64. Several articles in the western press had raised a warning, most prominently a series of them in successive issues of *The Economist* through the spring and summer. But others include "The World's Most Dangerous Man," *U.S. News and World Report*, 4 June 1991, 38–44; "Sword of the Arabs," *Time*, 11 June 1990, 32–33; and Morton Kondrake and Seth Carus, "Neighborhood Bully," *The New Republic*, 20 August 1990, 12–15. This last article had been completed prior to the invasion.

### CHAPTER THREE

1. Quoted in Michael Hudson, *Arab Politics: The Search for Legitimacy* (New Haven, Conn.: Yale Univ. Press, 1977), 277.

2. See *NYT*, 12 August 1990, and *The Economist*, 18 August 1990, 36. Danielle Pletka surveys the early and broadly divergent reactions in "Invasion Drives a Wedge into the Arab Nation," *Insight on the News*, 20 August 1990, 11–13.

3. Quoted in *NYT*, 5 August 1990. The use of the word "black" must be noted. For the West, a "black day" could indicate cataclysmic destruction, or infamy, perhaps. But for the Arabs, it has a distinctly nuanced meaning. In Arabic, the expression "blacken the face" means to suffer an egregious loss of honor. *Al-Ahram*'s expression was therefore connoting not simply calamity, but a great loss of honor for the Arab *umma* (community).

4. Quoted in *NYT*, 9 August 1990. All quotes from Mubarak in this paragraph are from the text of his speech printed there. In an interview shortly thereafter with *Time*, Mubarak said, "I didn't have the slightest thought that one Arab country would swallow another. I [had] thought President Saddam was very reasonable" (10 September 1990, 36–37).

5. In fact, the UN Security Council passed its first resolution the day of the invasion. From its initial resolution condemning the invasion until the one on 29 November setting a 15 January deadline and authorizing "all necessary means," the Security Council passed nineteen resolutions; twelve of them dealt with the Persian Gulf crisis. Five passed unanimously; Yemen, the only Arab country on the Security Council at the time, objected or abstained seven times. The complete text of the resolutions may be found in *Gulf War Reader*, ed. Sifry and Cerf, 137–156. Mubarak may well have been recalling the dilatory Arab League response in 1961 when Qassem laid claim to Kuwait.

6. See, for instance, Fahd's own recounting of the steps he took in Rashid and Shaheen, *Saudi Arabia*, 150ff. Prince Bandar, Fahd's nephew and the Saudi ambassador to the U.S., observed that Saddam succeeded in achieving "strategic surprise" because the invasion, in Bandar's words, was "thoroughly stupid" and "against his [Saddam's] own interests" (author's notes, informal presentation by Bandar at Baylor University, March 11, 2000). Saudi Prince Abdullah bin Faisal was also surprised: "We never thought Saddam would do what he is doing to us.

We are still in shock. We wake up every morning and say, 'Maybe I was in a bad dream.' " *Washington Post*, 6 September 1990.

7. *NYT*, 1 March 1992.

8. Quoted in James Akins, "The New Arabia," in *Foreign Affairs* 70 (Summer 1991): 39. In fact, the secretary felt that many of the poorer Arabs were guilty of the same sort of extortion.

9. The text of the council's declaration is found in *FBIS*, 6 August 1990, 1. A helpful summary may be found in Barbara Ebert, "The Gulf War and Its Aftermath: An Assessment of Evolving Arab Responses," *Middle East Policy* 1, no. 4 (1992): 77–95.

10. The text of the IOC declaration is given in *FBIS*, 6 August 1990, 12.

11. The full text of Mubarak's speech is in *FBIS*, 13 August 1990, 2–4.

12. The full text of the king's speech is in *FBIS*, 14 August 1990, 1–2.

13. Some Palestinians at the meeting claimed that the PLO had not voted against the resolution, but had abstained along with Algeria and Yemen, holding that the vote had been taken in an atmosphere of "indescribable disorder." Other diplomats dismissed this as temporizing, but the disorder is certainly credible. See *NYT*, 14 August 1990.

14. See the reporting, with Maksoud's statement, in *NYT*, 12 September 1990.

15. A good account of Iraqi temporizing is in Bengio, *MECS* 1990, 403–405. There are also several good chronologies. One of the best, and that used here, is the BBC *Gulf Crisis Chronology*, compiled by BBC World Service (distributed in the U.S. by Gale Research, 1991).

16. *Nida'* also means "summons, appeal." The implication is that the Kuwaitis had made an urgent appeal, one over the heads of the al-Sabah, to come to their aid.

17. "Merger" is a translation of *indimaj*, which is more than simple confederation. The verbal noun may be rendered, according to Wehr, "annexation," "incorporation," or "absorption."

18. Fouad Ajami, "The Summer of Arab Discontent," *Foreign Affairs* 69 (Winter 1990/91): 2–3.

19. John L. Esposito, *Islam and Politics* (Syracuse, N.Y.: Syracuse Univ. Press, 1984), 4.

20. Quran 2:143.

21. Bernard Lewis, *The Political Language of Islam* (Chicago: Chicago Univ. Press, 1988), 32.

22. Michael Hudson explains several Arabic terms that denote a community (*Arab Politics*, 34ff). Umma he describes as "the broadest, most inclusive, least elaborated category of affective, primordial affiliation" (ibid., 37). See also Bassam Tibi, *The Challenge of Fundamentalism: Political Islam and the New World Order* (Berkeley, Calif.: Univ. of California Press, 1998), 53, 94–95, 97, for a discussion of the appropriation of the term by Arab nationalists.

23. Quoted in *NYT*, 9 August 1990.

24. Cited in Ajami, "Arab Discontent," 16. The *thawra-tharwa* pun is at-

tributed to Muhammad Sid-Ahmed by Barbara Ebert, in "Gulf War and Aftermath," 83.

25. This was the first major U.S. intervention in the region, excepting Lebanon in 1958 and 1982, and the first-ever commitment of U.S. ground troops to fight an Arab country. See Halliday's instructive comments in "The Gulf War and Its Aftermath: First Reflections," *International Affairs* 62, no. 2 (1991): 223ff.

26. The text appears in *NYT*, 9 August 1990.

27. Although the Israeli dimension lies outside the scope of this analysis, it should be noted that Israel's restraint was one of the marvels of the conflict. A superb article describing the "gruesome associations" Israelis made with the Holocaust and the "humiliation of passive resistance" is "Israel after the War" by Ze'ev Schiff, defense editor of the Tel Aviv daily *Ha'aretz* (*Foreign Affairs* 70 [Spring 1991]: 19–33). Schiff describes how Israel would be compelled to "reassess" its strategic posture and military relationship with the U.S.

28. Full text in *NYT*, 11 August 1990; quotes in this paragraph and the next are from this source. Saddam sent an "open letter," obviously intended for consumption both domestically and in the Arab region, to President Bush on 16 August continuing these themes. "I have seen your infuriated statements and comments to officials at the American Defense Department," he told Bush, "in which you affirmed your determination to continue following a policy of harming Iraq and occupying and defiling Arab and Muslim holy shrines." Saddam had imagined that Bush had some sensitivity to "the Arab mentality" and "popular feelings." Now, however, Saddam "could see how shallow" the American president was (*NYT*, 17 August 1990).

29. See the *Gulf War Chronology* (BBC), 7 August 1990.

30. As reported in the 16 August edition of *The Jerusalem Post* and carried by *FBIS*, 17 August 1990. In fact, Palestinians in the U.S. called the Kuwaiti embassy to offer financial assistance. The *Post* article offers an interesting dichotomy also made by gulf states between Palestinians, whom they had been willing to support, and Arafat, whom they were not. See also Ian Alexander, "Can Saddam Climb Down?" *National Review*, 1 October 1990, 19–20.

31. Both Ashrawi and the fund spokesman are quoted in Lesch, "Contrasting Reactions," 47.

32. Quoted in *The Economist*, 18 August 1990, 35. Of course, the syllogism also applied in the other direction. The West seemed to be selective in its outrages. Voice Of Palestine Radio in late August expressed anger that the U.S. immediately went to the aid of Kuwait but never asked "about the fate of an entire nation which Israel has been holding hostage" for years (Lesch, "Contrasting Reactions," 46).

33. The intifadan legacy is well documented in Dick Doughty, *Gaza: Legacy of Occupation* (West Hartford, Conn.: Kumarian Press, 1995). Written in conjunction with Mohammed al-Aydi, a Palestinian friend, the book presents wrenching text and photographs of the Gaza Strip's poorest refugee camp, "Canada Camp."

34. It is implausible to assume that Arafat had control over Abu Abbas and the PLF. The PLF had split from the Popular Front for the Liberation of Palestine-General Command (PFLP-GC), which itself had split from the PFLP, which itself was a rival faction to Arafat's Fatah within the PLO. The PLF's primary supporter at the time of the attack was the new Saladin, Saddam himself. Abu Abbas remained in Baghdad during the Gulf War along with other terrorist group leaders, such as the infamous Abu Nidal and others who headed to the Iraqi capital and pledged their fealty. Bill Quandt holds that the abortive PLF attack on the Israeli coast on 30 May must have had Iraq's backing. It was in Saddam's interest, Quandt argues, for the Baker peace plan talks in Cairo to be scuttled. That would force the Palestinians to look to him as a sponsor in light of renewed Israeli intransigence (William Quandt, "The Middle East in 1990," *Foreign Affairs* 70 ["America and the World" issue, 1990/91]: 55–56).

35. See *The Economist*'s assessment of this lack of Arab support in its issue of 26 May 1990, 13–14.

36. Youssef Ibrahim, in a special to *NYT*, 14 August 1990, gives an account of just how divided the PLO was.

37. From interviews conducted and printed in *NYT*, 12 August 1990.

38. Ibid.

39. Quoted in *NYT*, 14 August 1990. A number of articles afford good summaries of the king's dilemma. One of the best is in Stanley Reed, "Jordan and the Gulf Crisis," *Foreign Affairs* 69 (Winter 1990/91): 21–35; see also Lesch, "Contrasting Reactions," 44ff.

40. Quoted in *NYT*, 5 August 1990. Several days later, in an interview with Dan Rather, the king warned that "other tigers have been loose in the area for a long period of time. . . . Such a tiger exists in our neighbor Israel in its continued occupation of the Syrian Golan and Jerusalem" (quoted in Lesch, "Contrasting Reactions," 45).

41. One Jordanian business executive commented that he would personally defy the UN embargo, packing his car with food and driving to Iraq. "We are the same people. We have the same language, the same origins. Why should I let these people suffer? You won't find a Jordanian who will not send food to Iraq" (*NYT*, 17 August 1990). The comment is especially instructive because it reflects the sort of Arab solidarity that many felt when non-Arabs prevailed against an Arab state.

42. Economic figures here are taken from "Jordan" in *The Middle East and North Africa 1991* (Europa). Some have placed the Iraqi purchase of Jordanian exports at a much higher figure. Cf. "Interview: King Hussein," *Time*, 5 November 1990, 41–42. The Europa figures derive from IMF data and seem more credible.

43. Lesch, "Contrasting Reactions," 45.

44. Quoted in *NYT*, 14 August 1990.

45. *The Economist*, 1 September 1990, 35–36.

46. See, for instance, Ajami, "Arab Discontent," 8; Lesch, "Contrasting Reactions," 39; Danielle Pletka, "Riding the Anti-Saddam Tide to the Top of the

Pyramid," *Insight on the News*, 10 December 1990, 26–27; and Stanley Reed, "Jordan: Bitter Refugees," *Business Week*, 3 September 1990, 29. The Jordanians also fell victim to Iraqi robbery on the way out.

47. *U.S. News and World Report*, 10 December 1990, 28–30, summarizes benefits that accrued to the Syrians and the Egyptians.

48. I am particularly indebted here to Ebert's wide discussion of the issue in "Gulf War and Aftermath"; see 85ff for all quotes cited in this paragraph.

49. Augustus R. Norton, "Breaking through the Wall of Fear in the Arab World," *Current History* 91 (January 1992): 38.

50. Ebert, "Gulf War and Aftermath," 81.

51. See the discussions in Lesch, "Contrasting Reactions," 43; Maha Azzam, "The Gulf Crisis: Perceptions in the Muslim World," *International Affairs* 67, no. 3 (July 1991): 478; and Eberhard Kienle, "Syria, the Kuwait War, and the New World Order," in *The Gulf War and the New World Order: International Relations of the Middle East*, ed. Tareq Ismael and Jacqueline Ismael (Gainesville, Fla.: Univ. of Florida Press, 1994), 386. One Syrian rug merchant captured the sentiment of some: "Saddam is a hero in Syria because he is breaking the head of the U.S. He is sticking his finger up its nose. He has made America crazy" (*Time*, 15 October 1990, 55).

52. See the discussion in Lesch, "Contrasting Reactions," 41–42, on these four points.

53. A fascinating account of Fahd's decision is in Bob Woodward, *The Commanders* (New York: Simon and Schuster, 1991), 240ff.

54. Cited in Ebert, "Gulf War and Aftermath," 84. Yemen's ambassador to the UN made clear that his countrymen were sympathetic to Kuwait, but that public opinion had changed with the arrival of foreign troops. He stressed that even then the feeling was not "pro-Iraq but against foreign intervention" (ibid., 85).

55. *Vital Speeches of the Day* 56 (1 September 1990), 675–676, carries the full text.

56. The complete text is in *FBIS*, 24 August 1990.

57. As reported in *FBIS*, 13 August 1990.

58. The 27 November speech is in Rashid and Shaheen, *Saudi Arabia*, 150ff. As reported, it seems rather contrived. Ostensibly the speech was an answer to a question from a 'citizen' attending a dinner party at the Salaam Palace in Jeddah, but it is given as a very detailed narrative. It hardly looks impromptu. The king, under tremendous scrutiny for his decision, must have had this speech prepared as an *apologia pro vita sua*.

59. Nadav Safran, "Strike Supporters," *The New Republic*, 24 September 1990, 26. See also his authoritative *Saudi Arabia: The Ceaseless Quest for Security* (Ithaca, N.Y.: Cornell Univ. Press, 1988).

60. Based on author interviews with the U.S. Military Training Mission (USMTM) in Riyadh, Saudi Arabia, in 1989 and 1991.

61. Cited in *NYT*, 13 January 1991.

62. For instance, one such book features a map showing the "Saudi and Arab Forces" as commanding the frontline against the Iraqis, with "American and

Allied Forces" arrayed behind. My personal acquaintance with the disposition of forces would have led to the drawing of a different map.

63. Hans Wehr's *Dictionary* defines this as "the ideal of manhood, comprising all knightly virtues, esp. manliness, valor, chivalry, generosity, sense of honor."

## CHAPTER FOUR

1. Amir Iskander, *Saddam Hussein*, 326.

2. Saddam to Saudi Prince Bandar in 1979 on what to do when the Grand Mosque in Mecca was taken over by militants; cited in Elaine Sciolino, *The Outlaw State: Saddam Hussein's Quest for Power and the Gulf Crisis* (New York: Wiley, 1991), 77.

3. Kanan Makiya, *The Monument: Art, Vulgarity, and Responsibility in Iraq* (Berkeley, Calif.: Univ. of California Press, 1991), 3.

4. Details are taken from Makiya, *The Monument;* and Sciolino, *Outlaw State*, 184. The orientation of the swords is mentioned in Bengio, *Saddam's Word*, 138.

5. See Fromkin, *A Peace to End All Peace*, 506–508, for a description of the British connivance at the imposition of Faisal and the carefully orchestrated "reception" they arranged for him. Among other measures, the British essentially kidnapped an opposition candidate for the kingship and carted him off to Ceylon. Faisal's words cited in Hanna Batatu, *The Old Social Classes and the Revolutionary Movements of Iraq* (Princeton, N.J.: Princeton Univ. Press, 1978), 25.

6. "Millet" is the Turkish form of the Arabic "millah," a religious community. Under the Ottomans, millets were semiautonomous, non-Islamic communities that ran their own internal affairs but recognized Ottoman sovereignty.

7. For background on the Baʻth, Kamel Abu Jaber's *Arab Baʻth Socialist Party: History, Ideology, and Organization* (Syracuse, N.Y.: Syracuse Univ. Press, 1966) is older but still serviceable. Treating Syrian Baʻthism are Raymond Hinnebusch, *Authoritarian Power and State Formation in Baʻthist Syria* (Boulder, Colo.: Westview Press, 1990) and Itamar Rabinovitch, *Syria under the Baʻth, 1963–66: The Army-Party Symbiosis* (Jerusalem: Israel Universities Press, 1972). Khadduri offers a helpful summary in *Political Trends*, 150–175. Unfortunately, there is no complete edition of Aflaq's *Fi Sabil al-Baʻth* currently in print in English. However, an introduction to Aflaq and a selection of his writings is available in Kemal Karpat, ed., *Political and Social Thought in the Contemporary Middle East* (New York: Praeger, 1982), 138–157. Regarding Arab socialism more generally, but also containing primary materials from Aflaq, is Sami Hanna and George Gardner, *Arab Socialism: A Documentary Survey* (Leiden, Netherlands: Brill, 1969); see also Sylvia Haim, ed., *Arab Nationalism: An Anthology* (Berkeley, Calif.: Univ. of California Press, 1962). For the Arabic text of *Fi Sabil* (revised a number of times), I have used the 1975 edition published in Beirut by dar al-taleʼah wa al-nashr. Most of the text is also available in

Arabic on-line (as of this writing) at http://www.multimania.com/iaflak/Baath-home.htm. For understanding Baʿthism and Iraq, Amatzia Baram's *Culture, History, and Ideology in the Formation of Baʿthist Iraq, 1968–89* (New York: St. Martin's, 1991) is indispensable. Helpful studies of Baʿthism in Iraq include Phoebe Marr, "Iraq: Its Revolutionary Experience under the Baʿth," in Peter Chelkowski and Robert Pranger, eds., *Ideology and Power in the Middle East: Studies in Honor of George Lenczowski* (Durham, N.C.: Duke Univ. Press, 1988), 185–209; and Makiya, *Republic of Fear*, 183–228.

8. Nasser reflected on the task of molding a people. A typical family in the capital comprised a father who was a "turbaned fellah," a mother of Turkish stock, a son in British schools, and a daughter in French. In time a society would crystallize from the different elements, but the leaders would have to "strain [their] nerves during the period of transition" (*Philosophy of the Revolution* [Buffalo, N.Y.: Smith, Keynes, and Marshall, 1959], 53).

9. Abbas Kelidar, "The Wars of Saddam Hussein," *Middle Eastern Studies* 28 (October 1992): 782. Kelidar writes perceptively of Saddam's use of primordial ties to gain totalitarian control; see especially 782–784. On the resort to primordial affiliation in response to Iraqi totalitarianism, see Peter Sluglett and Marion Farouk-Sluglett, "Sunnis and Shiʿis Revisited," in *Iraq: Power and Society*, ed. Derek Hopwood et al. (Reading, U.K.: Ithaca Press, 1993), especially 90.

10. Aflaq, *Fi Sabil*, 111–112 (my translation). Here as elsewhere, I have tried to compare my translations with others, such as those in Karpat, Hanna, and Haim (note 6, above). I have also worked with both the English and Arabic texts of Iskander's *Saddam Hussein*. The superb translation of Iskander by Hassan Selim is especially noteworthy, and has been a key aid in my own work.

11. Saddam Hussein, "Al-qadarat al-wataniyya wal-siyasah al-duwaliyya" ("National Capabilities and International Politics"), in *nidaluna wa al-siyasah al-duwaliyya* (*Our Struggle and International Politics*) (Baghdad: dar al-hurriyah lil-tabaʾah, 1980), 11 (my translation).

12. No attempt is made here to evaluate the sincerity of Saddam's initial attachment to Baʿthism, which is likely impossible to ascertain in any event. But what is clear is that the president's praxis began to diverge markedly from party orthodoxies, even as he continued to declaim his adherence to them. Helpful in seeing this change is Amatzia Baram's "Qawmiyya and Wataniyya in Baʿthi Iraq: The Search for a New Balance," *Middle Eastern Studies* 19, no. 2 (1983): 188–200. Karsh and Rautsi take an even stronger position on Saddam's instrumentality. Saddam Hussein "carries no ideological baggage whatsoever. Quite the reverse. From his point of view, ideology is purely a means for the promotion of the one and only goal which has guided him . . . [that of] reaching the country's top position and staying there" (*Political Biography*, 268). Among issues Saddam appears to have used instrumentally are the Palestinian cause and the rights of women, both of which Karsh and Rautsi discuss extensively. More especially, at many points Saddam subverted the core tenets of Baʿthism (unity, socialism, freedom). It is instructive to compare the two constitutions the country has had

since the ascendance of Ba'thism: the 1970 constitution, under which it continues to operate, and the draft 1990 constitution, which was discussed, then eclipsed, in the month before the invasion of Kuwait. For example, the draft constitution described the regime as "presidential republican" rather than as a "popular democratic republic," and it gave secondary importance to socialism. The full text of the draft is carried in *FBIS*, 31 July 1990.

13. Aflaq, *Fi Sabil*, 111–112 (my translation).

14. Edward Luttwak, "Agencies of Disorder," in *Gulf War Reader*, ed. Sifry and Cerf, 294.

15. The *locus classicus* of the use of fear in Iraq as a political tool is Makiya's *Republic of Fear*, republished in 1998. Makiya describes how a "new Kafkaesque world came into being, one ruled and held together by fear. . . . Fear . . . was not incidental or episodic, as in more 'normal states'; it had become constitutive of the Iraqi body politic" (p. xi). Purges and deportations of the Shi'a and the Kurds are well documented in much of Ofra Bengio's work; see especially *Saddam's Word*. See also Bengio's entry on "Iraq" in *MECS* 1990: 521–525. The Center for Middle Eastern Studies at Harvard University maintains a special on-line database, the Iraq Research and Documentation Project (located at http://fas-www.harvard.edu/~irdp/). Note especially its documentation of the Anfal campaigns, the military operation against the Kurds in 1988. In *Political Biography*, Karsh and Rautsi also provide a helpful survey of purges, assassinations, and deportations.

16. See Makiya's discussion in *Republic of Fear*, 46–72. See also Karsh and Rautsi, *Political Biography*, 42–45, 113–118, for additional background on these two purges.

17. Others have charted this changing direction. See, for instance Baram, "Qawmiyya and Wataniyya," 188–200, for an important study of these two concepts. Ofra Bengio, "Ba'thi Iraq in Search of Identity: Between Ideology and Praxis," *Orient* 28, no. 4 (1987): 511–518, also describes the distinction between the two and the increasing emphasis on *wataniyya*. It should be pointed out, however, that although *qawmiyya* and *wataniyya* are often used in contradistinction, there is not always a bright line separating them. Sometimes, for instance, the latter term is used of the larger Arab homeland, and is then roughly analogous to umma. As always, context must be the guide for the translator and the political observer.

18. This is not to argue that pan-Arabism lost all importance for Saddam, nor to suggest he had forsworn a bid for Nasser's mantle as *primus inter pares* in the Arab world. It is to say that, in practice, *raisons d'état* trumped attachment to the umma.

19. Musallam, *Iraqi Invasion of Kuwait*, 74.

20. Baram, *Culture, History, and Ideology*, 20, 35. Explanatory glosses for "Shi'i" and "Kurd" added.

21. The *da'wa* party (Islamic Call), although not necessarily representing mainstream Iraqi Shi'a views, did reflect the general disenchantment with the secular Ba'th teachings. It was formed even before the Ba'th revolution in

1968, largely to counteract the increasingly secular tendencies among the Shi'a. *Da'wa* is discussed further below.

22. Batatu, *The Old Social Classes*, 1133.

23. Marvin Zonis, "Leaders and Publics in the Middle East: Shattering the Key Organizing Myths of Arab Society," in *Political Psychology*, ed. Renshon, 270.

24. Iskander, *Saddam Hussein*, 183 (emphasis added). The text reflects the Marxist dimension of Ba'thist doctrine. More especially it shows Saddam reworking Ba'thist teaching for his own needs.

25. Matar, *Saddam Hussein*, 271.

26. The most important work dealing with this is Baram's *Culture, History, and Ideology*. Baram notes that the Iraqis' 1975 accord with the shah effectively excluded the Kurds from a Mesopotamian identity, 21–22. Later, they would be at least partially reincorporated, as indicated below.

27. Mircea Eliade, *The Sacred and the Profane: The Nature of Religion*, trans. Willard Trask (New York: Harper and Row, 1961), 68–70.

28. One seemingly insignificant but quite important way in which Saddam did that is by giving his sons Uday and Qusay pre-Islamic names. This is noted in Henderson, *Instant Empire*, 4.

29. See Baram, *Culture, History, and Ideology*, 45–48. My discussion largely follows Baram's work.

30. Baram, *Culture, History, and Ideology*, discusses a number of festivals at length. This is drawn from 45, 49, 50, and 110.

31. The Ayatollah Khomeini cynically remarked on this transformation that Saddam had apparently "just been converted to Islam" (quoted in Bruce Maddy-Weitzman, "Islam and Arabism," *The Washington Quarterly* 5 [Autumn 1982]: 188).

32. Bengio's *Saddam's Word* is an example of an account written to survey such changes; see 15 and 176 for a summary of the changes.

33. Clifford Geertz, *The Interpretation of Cultures* (New York: Basic Books, 1973), 90–91. Halim Barakat is an Arab sociologist who has written on the social embeddedness of religion; see his *The Arab World: Society, Culture, and State* (Berkeley, Calif.: Univ. of California Press, 1993), 119ff. While I disagree with several of his conclusions about religion as a social force, he surely is correct in his emphasis on a praxis study rather than an ancient-text focus to understand the religious realities of the Middle East.

34. Aflaq, *Fi Sabil*, 112–113, 216, 308 (my translation).

35. Amir Iskander, s*addam hussein: munadilan, wa-mufakirran, wa-insanan* (Paris: Hachette, 1980), 318–324 passim (my translation), for quotes in this paragraph and the next. In those instances where I note my translation of Iskander, I am, of course, referring to the Arabic version. If it is not so annotated, then I am using the English translation by Hassan Selim.

36. *Rashidun* (literally, "rightly guided ones") designates the first four caliphs in Islam. This period in early Islam is considered exemplary, a time of pristine faith.

37. Iskander, *Saddam Hussein*, 173, 175, 176, 178.

38. Matar, *Saddam Hussein*, 278.

39. Bengio, *Saddam's Word*, 159, 176. At one point, my research must offer a small corrective to Bengio's observation. The early years, as indicated in citations above, are better characterized as a time of caution, not silence.

40. Said Aburish, *Saddam Hussein: The Politics of Revenge* (New York: Bloomsbury, 2000). Phebe Marr writes similarly: "Underground, conspiratorial activities were most influential in shaping Husayn's outlook and mentality. His secretiveness, his cautiousness, and his distrust of outsiders sprang from years of being hunted, and from his own considerable talents in organizing conspiracy. At the same time, courage and fearlessness contributed to his image as a *shaqawah*, a local term denoting a kind of tough guy or bully—a man to be feared. These experiences also inclined him to the Stalinist model of political control" (*The Modern History of Iraq* [Boulder, Colo.: Westview Press, 1985], 220).

41. The reference to "Hassan the liar" is in Aburish, *Politics of Revenge*, 14; "he of the gun" is cited on 34.

42. Iskander, *Saddam Hussein*, 74–80, 393–395.

43. Quoted in Amatzia Baram, "Saddam Hussein: A Political Profile," *Jerusalem Quarterly* 17 (Fall 1980): 117. Interpolations are Baram's, slightly emended.

44. For instance, the Shi'i cleric Kashif al-Ghita' praised Saddam shortly after the onset of the war for his leadership and development of the Arab and Islamic nation as he fought the "enemies of Islam." Significantly, he also praised the financial support Saddam had extended to Najaf and its shrines (Baghdad Radio, as reported in *FBIS*, 6 October 1980). It is worth noting that the praise from al-Ghita' followed the arrest, execution, and deportation of large numbers of Shi'a, as well as the bestowing of oil largesse. Then, in 1982 al-Ghita' gave Saddam the honorific *mujahid*, one who conducts jihad, but the more militant among Shi'a leaders considered him and others like him to be part of *al-ulama al-hafiz*, the "service ulama." (The phrase is similar to the derisive term "placemen" in eighteenth-century British politics.) On Ghita' and his calling Saddam *mujahid*, see Bengio, *Saddam's Word*, 186.

45. "Da'wa" (Arabic, "call") in a religious context means "the summons [to Islam]." In Iraq, al-da'wa (short for the Islamic Call Party) designates a Shi'a organization in Najaf in the late 1950s that was often repressed by the government. See the helpful discussion in Hanna Batatu, "Iraq's Underground Shi'a Movements," *Middle East Journal* 35 (Autumn 1981): 591–594. See also Makiya, *Republic of Fear*, 106–109, on Ba'thism and the Shi'a. Similarly, see Sluglett and Farouk-Sluglett, "Sunnis and Shi'is Revisited," 87–90.

46. From an interview with Jonathan Broder, "Saddam's Bomb," *New York Times Magazine*, 1 October 2000, 43. There is an echo of the same distinction in Matar's biography. Saddam declared, "We rejoice and feel deeply with any young man who believes in the Islamic call and is ready to die for it in his struggle against corruption. . . . However, the Baathists fight for the same causes and are ready to die for them" (*Saddam Hussein*, 280).

47. Aburish, in PBS Frontline interview, Internet version, www.pbs.org/wgbh/pages/frontline/shows/saddam/interviews/aburish.html, 15 September 2000.

48. Nasser, *Philosophy of the Revolution*, 77–78.

49. Batatu, *Old Social Classes*, 26.

50. Ibid., 1086–1092, has relevant tables profiling the RCC composition. See also Karsh and Rautsi, *Political Biography*, 140ff.

51. See Bengio, *MECS* 1990, 416; *The Economist*, 29 September 1990, 43–44; Marr, "Iraq's Uncertain Future," 40. In 1998, Amatzia Baram wrote, "[U]nder Saddam's influence, a few Shi'is were promoted to prominent positions in party and government. Yet the problem of underrepresentation was solved only very partially. Numerically, there have always been more Sunnis in the highest echelon; they also have nearly monopolized the positions of real power. Shi'is today comprise the majority of lower-rank party membership, but their climb up the party ladder has been perceptibly slower. . . . [T]he situation still falls short of true equal opportunity" ("United States Institute of Peace Special Report—Between Impediment and Advantage: Saddam's Iraq," http://www.usip.org/oc/sr/baram/baram.html). In the shadowy history of Iraq's application of terror as a means of population control, a Shi'i, Nadhim Kzar, figured prominently as the first head of Internal State Security. Kzar was put to death in 1973. See Makiya, *Republic of Fear*, 6–7.

52. The terms are suggested in Batatu. See his still-relevant discussion in *Old Social Classes*, 1086–1095. The quote about party membership is cited on 1095. This primacy of family over party is also discussed in a number of places. See, for instance, Kelidar, "Wars of Saddam," 782–784. Particularly instructive is the superb work of Charles Tripp, "The Iran-Iraq War and the Iraqi State," in *Iraq: Power and Society*, ed. Hopwood et al., 91–115. Tripp writes of *al-intisab*, the informal system of power derived from familial affiliation, and its place in Iraq: "[I]t is the informal, clan-based hierarchy which is the true repository of power and authority" (96). He describes Iraq as a country in which there are "European *forms* of state organization," but where "locally derived perceptions of how power can and should be organized" are the reality (114). Similarly, Aburish observes, "Family and tribal connections are supreme. They come ahead of ideology. They come ahead of the nation state. They come ahead of all commitments . . . [Saddam] weakened the party and strengthened the family" (PBS Frontline interview). See also Aburish, *Politics of Revenge*, 160–162.

53. Sami Zubaida, *Islam, the People, and the State: Political Ideas and Movements in the Middle East* (New York: Tauris, 1993), 152–153; the larger discussion is on 152–162. For a related discussion, see Roger Owen, *State, Power, and Politics in the Making of the Modern Middle East* (New York: Routledge, 1992), especially his chapter "The Politics of Religion," 166–196 (Owen's work pointed me to Zubaida).

54. Majid Khadduri, *The Gulf War: The Origins and Implications of the Iraq-Iran Conflict* (New York: Oxford Univ. Press, 1988), 111.

55. Makiya, *Republic of Fear*, 105. At times the word "Shi'a" itself was sub-

jected to a news blackout. "al-Ja'fariyya" was used instead (the reference is to the sixth Shi'a Imam). See Bengio, "Iraq's Shi'a and Kurdish Communities: From Resentment to Revolt," in *Iraq's Road to War,* ed. Baram and Rubin, 52, and Bengio, *Saddam's Word,* 98–100.

56. John Bulloch and Harvey Morris, *The Gulf War: Its Origins, History, and Consequences* (London: Methuen, 1989), 76.

57. For a brief but helpful background of the party, see Amatzia Baram's article in the *Oxford Encyclopedia of the Modern Islamic World,* s.v. *hizb al-da'wah al-islamiyah,* 2:121–124, from which this discussion partly derives. For a brief discussion of Iraqi Shi'a ideology and its role in the 1977 and 1979 disturbances, see Yitzhak Nakash, *The Shi'is of Iraq* (Princeton, N.J.: Princeton Univ. Press, 1994), 136–138. Nakash points out the Shi'a were concerned about the "Sunnization" of the Iraqi leadership and the challenge to their own standing as Iraqis, who, nonetheless, had little regard for Khomeini's *wilayat al-faqih.*

58. Karsh and Rautsi, *Political Biography,* 142.

59. The figures are from Makiya, *Republic of Fear,* 316.

60. See the related discussion in Bulloch and Morris, *Gulf War,* 26–29.

61. Aburish, *Politics of Revenge,* 184. I have altered his translation.

62. Ibid., 186.

63. See the discussion in Batatu, "Iraq's Underground Shi'a Movements," 591–593; see also Adeed Dawisha, "Invoking the Spirit of Arabism: Islam in the Foreign Policy of Saddam's Iraq," in *Islam in Foreign Policy,* ed. Adeed Dawisha (New York: Cambridge Univ. Press, 1983), 124–126.

64. "Husayniyahs" are sites where ceremonies are held to commemorate the life of Shi'a Imam Hussein (Husayn) and his martyrdom in 680.

65. Sciolino, *Outlaw State,* 99.

66. *FBIS,* 9 August 1979.

67. Matar, *Saddam Hussein,* 109.

68. Dawisha, "Invoking the Spirit of Arabism," 122.

69. Bengio, "Ba'thi Iraq," 515. Note the similarly warm words for Ali in the extended interview with Saddam (cited above) that appears in Iskander's biography.

70. For the indirect claim, see *FBIS* 9 August 1979. Iskander's claim is in *Saddam Hussein,* 20, and the family tree is reproduced on 24. The issue is also covered in Makiya, *Republic of Fear,* but on one point we must diverge from Makiya's authoritative study. He writes that the link to Ali "was not made in weakness, or as an attempt by Saddam to ingratiate himself with the Shi'is at a time of their regional activism. On the contrary, it signified total contempt for the populace" (115). That Saddam had contempt is certain, but contempt is not an adequate explanation for the employment of this genealogical exercise. Saddam clearly recognized the enormous potential for instability in the country held by Shi'i sectarianism. Saddam drew himself into the family tree of Ali because he felt he must, even as he contemptuously drew it.

71. Sciolino, *Outlaw State,* 64.

72. *FBIS,* 26 June 1989.

73. Baram, *Culture, History, and Ideology,* 57.

74. Ibid., 63.

75. The Slugletts' comment is pertinent: in the war, "most Iraqi Shi'is proved to be Iraqis, Arabs, and Shi'is, in that order" ("Sunnis and Shi'is Revisited," 88). The president and the ayatollah did work at mutual destabilization in each other's countries. The Iraqis, for instance, encouraged discontent in Khuzestan and oil-field sabotage, and also supported autonomy for that region (whence derived most of Iran's oil rents); see Bulloch and Morris, *Gulf War,* 23–24. The Iranians' support for radical Shi'i activity in southern Iraq and for the Kurds, and the problem of Iraqi-Kurdish relations more generally, has been extensively surveyed in standard works on the war, as well as in political histories of modern Iraq. See, for instance, Karsh and Rautsi, *Political Biography;* Marr, *Modern History of Iraq;* Marion Farouk-Sluglett and Peter Sluglett, *Iraq since 1958: From Revolution to Dictatorship* (New York: Routledge, 1988); and Makiya, *Republic of Fear.*

76. A number of writers survey the religious dimension of the conflict. Maddy-Weitzman, "Islam and Arabism," depicts a defensive president increasingly having to incorporate religion as a part of his Arab nationalist posture. Baram, *Culture, History, and Ideology,* also treats that aspect, although more emphasis is given to the incorporation of historical (and often pre-Islamic) motifs, as indicated above. Karsh and Rautsi, *Political Biography,* survey some aspects of the change. Makiya, *Republic of Fear,* underscores the depth of Saddam's cynical manipulation of religious symbols. Khadduri, *Gulf War,* is especially good for its analysis of the Shi'a. Most important is the work of Ofra Bengio, especially *Saddam's Word,* the last third of which offers an extensive critical analysis of Saddam's use of Islamic discourse.

77. L. Carl Brown, "Patterns Forged in Time," 15.

78. Matar, *Saddam Hussein,* 18. In "Invoking the Spirit of Arabism," Dawisha maintains that nationalist, not Islamic considerations, primarily directed foreign policy in Ba'thist Iraq, even in the Iran-Iraq War, a point with which I strongly agree, despite Saddam's increasingly religious rhetoric.

79. Sciolino, *Outlaw State,* 103.

80. Saddam faced a difficult balancing act. At least initially, stressing Arab nationalism could allay gulf concerns about the fundamentalists next door, as well as mollifying U.S. fears. The new Islamic government in Iran was, after all, holding U.S. citizens hostage. But Saddam could not discount religious appeals altogether.

81. Quoted in Matar, *Saddam Hussein,* 152, 161 (emphasis added). As indicated supra, "spirit" terminology was often repeated at the time. In his interview with Matar shortly after he assumed the presidency in July 1979, Saddam described the Arab revolution as one that "derive[d] its spirit from heaven." He promised to welcome any revolution that "takes place with the spirit and goals of Islam" (Ibid., 263, 264).

82. "Vilayet e fiqh" is an expression of Khomeini's that means, roughly, "government by [Islamic] jurisprudence." On one level, Saddam's eventual transi-

tion to more explicit use of Islamic terminology is not as violent a change as might first appear. Traditional Islamic terminology that rendered the world as *dar al-Islam* and *dar al-harb* could be "re-vocabularized," as it were, made secular under the Ba'th. Ba'thist writings are replete with such changes, and Saddam's works constantly feature the titanic struggle between pan-Arabism and hostile, "reactionary" states. But he was not alone. For instance, Tariq Aziz, in a 1971 editorial, declared, "The Zionist invaders . . . [c]ame with a long-term colonialist-Zionist plan to build an aggressive and discriminating doctrinal base for expansion whose target is to prevent the Arab Nation from achieving liberty, unity, and the construction of a strong progressive society" (*The Revolution of the New Way* [Milan: Grafis S.p.A, 1977?], 74). Again in the same work: " 'Israel' does not stand alone; it is the product of world imperialism and its tool in the area. The [oil] companies are not just trading companies; they are the outpost of imperialism" (60). Many of the essays in Aziz's collection read very much like that, like Saddam's earlier writings. As odd as it first seems, the work of Sayyid Qutb, for instance, and the Ba'thists converge at this point of rendering the world in starkly categorical terms. Perhaps if Marxism is a secular reworking of Christianity, something similar may be said of Ba'thism and Islam.

83. Khadduri, *Gulf War*, 104.

84. The full text is given in *FBIS*, 17 April 1980. The doctrine of *shu'ubism* is critically important in Iraqi Ba'thism. It has no precise equivalent in translation, but is an invective conveying treasonous, anti-Arab, racist attitudes, deriving from the time of the Abbasid caliphate. Makiya writes that it is "the idea of the enemy from within, the insidious, ubiquitous agent of a hostile outside whose presence is needed to reassure believers of what it is they are supposed to have faith in" (*Republic of Fear*, 219); for a larger discussion, see 218–220, as well as 153–154. See also Hanna and Gardner, *Arab Socialism*, 80–97, and *The Encyclopaedia of Islam*, new ed., ed. H. A. R. Gibb (Leiden, Netherlands: Brill, 1960–), s.v. *shu'ubiyya*. The epithet could be applied to any number of groups, including the Kurds and Shi'a, although the term could also be applied to outsiders. During the Iran-Iraq War it was often applied to Iran to further underscore their categorical "otherness" and the threat they posed to Iraqis and to Arabs more generally.

85. Maddy-Weitzman, "Islam and Arabism," 186. The reference to the thirteenth Imam reflects the Shi'ism of the Iranians, who believe in a succession of twelve Imams, the last of whom was "occulted" and will one day return. This insult, then, was tantamount to calling Khomeini a false messiah, a religious leader outside the recognized Imams.

86. Ibid., 186.

87. See Karsh and Rautsi, *Political Biography*, 138–139. In the same month Aziz was attacked, some twenty other Iraqi officials died in bomb attacks.

88. Shahram Chubin and Charles Tripp, *Iran and Iraq at War* (Boulder, Colo.: Westview Press, 1988), 38.

89. Ibid., 40.

90. Sciolino, *Outlaw State*, 103.

91. *FBIS*, 26 July 1982.

92. Ibid.

93. Karsh and Rautsi, *Political Biography*, 138.

94. See the larger discussion in Bengio, *Saddam's Word*, 139–145, from which this draws.

95. The discussion that follows is particularly informed by the extensive research presented in Bengio, *Saddam's Word*, 176–202.

96. For background on these idols, see Philip Hitti, *History of the Arabs from the Earliest Times to the Present* (New York: St. Martin's Press, 1970), 100, and *The Encyclopaedia of Islam*, s.v. *hubal* and *taghut*.

97. Bengio, *Saddam's Word*, 144.

98. "Bismallah" means "in the name of God" and abbreviates "In the name of God, the merciful, the compassionate." The longer expression heads each chapter of the Koran and is often employed in speeches, formal pronouncements, official papers, and the like. Bengio indicates the *bismallah* had not been used by the RCC prior to the war (*Saddam's Word*, 188). Although its use certainly increased during the war, the expression was employed in Ba'thist Iraq before then. Significantly, the National Charter, which Saddam ostentatiously presented in February 1980, opened with the *bismallah*. According to Matar, *Saddam Hussein*, 92, the charter was coordinated with the RCC. Yet the *bismallah* was rather perfunctory. As Dawisha points out, the charter makes no further mention at all of Islam, nor was a parallel charter for the Islamic world advanced ("Invoking the Spirit of Arabism," 119).

99. Dawisha, "Invoking the Spirit of Arabism," 125.

100. The use of "jihad" is important because another, and secular, term is quite serviceable to describe what the West usually calls war: *harb*. For a good general discussion of jihad pertinent to the modern Middle East, one should consult Rudolph Peters, *Islam and Colonialism: The Doctrine of Jihad in Modern History* (New York: Mouton, 1979), as well as his collection of primary materials, *Jihad in Classical and Modern Islam: A Reader* (Princeton, N.J.: Marcus Wiener, 1996). The latter contains the fatwa issued by the Ottomans in World War I calling for jihad, an earlier twentieth-century attempt to use Islam to rally forces and destabilize the opposition. On *mujahid* and the Iran-Iraq War, see Bengio, *Saddam's Word*, 186–187. The next Gulf War would make more consistent use of the term.

101. Saddam made the *'umra*, a minor *hajj* (pilgrimage). *'umra* is undertaken at a time other than *dhul-hajj*, the last month of the Islamic calendar, when the major (and mandatory) *hajj* is performed with quite specific rituals. Baghdad Radio, which noted the pilgrimage, also relayed the text of Saddam's thank-you letter to Fahd. It exemplifies the sort of self-conscious Islamic coloration the Iraqi regime frequently used during the war. "In the name of God, the merciful, the compassionate. [To] my brother King Fahd ibn Abd al-Aziz, the custodian of the two holy harams. Greetings. As we leave the territory of the fraternal kingdom, the territory of love and peace, prophets and glory, we are pleased to affirm that relations between Iraq and Saudi Arabia will be further strengthened. . . .

Please accept my good wishes for yourself, your brothers, and the Arab and Muslim people of the Kingdom. Your brother, Saddam Hussein." *FBIS*, 29 December 1986, includes the text.

102. Baram, *Culture, History, and Ideology*, 66, gives these and other examples.

103. "Karbala" was intended to invoke memories of noble martyrdom at the hands of the powerful but misguided. It would play on cultural dichotomies as well. In the event, Iraqi Shi'a observed the festival of Ashura commemorating Karbala, as did their coreligionists in Iran. Khomeini hoped these Iraqi Shi'a would make common cause with their Iranian brethren. For the most part, they did not.

104. Ramadan, a month of fasting in the Islamic calendar, is the month in which the Quran was first revealed (Quran 2:185) and the month in which the Meccans submitted to Muhammad in 630. The Iraqis launched their campaign in this special month, so the designation had manifold significance.

105. See the Iraq Research and Documentation Project of Harvard University for details. *http://fas-www.harvard.edu/~irdp/*

106. This discussion derives from *Conduct of the Persian Gulf War: Final Report to Congress* (Washington, D.C.: Department of Defense, 1992), 13–14; Anthony Cordesman, *After the Storm: The Changing Military Balance in the Middle East* (Boulder, Colo.: Westview Press, 1993), 484–489; and Baram, *Culture, History, and Ideology*, 66, 98. Also, I owe a special thanks to Major Richard A. Krakoff, U.S. Air Force, for supporting research.

107. Chapter Five will further explore the rhetorical importance of so designating this missile.

108. *Baram, Culture, History, and Ideology*, 109.

109. The full text of the speech is in *FBIS*, 3 April 1980.

110. Bengio, *Saddam's Word*, 244, n. 41.

111. Ibid., 172.

112. Bulloch and Morris, *Gulf War*, 1.

113. The most important attempt to profile Saddam is the work of Dr. Jerrold Post, a psychiatrist on the faculty of the American University, who has done significant profiling of world leaders for the CIA. In his view, Saddam is a "rational political calculator" who has "a flawed perception of reality." The Iraqi president "epitomizes Lasswell's *homo politicus* or power seeker who displaces a private need onto a public object and rationalizes it as being in the public good." Post describes Saddam's personality disorder as "malignant narcissism"; see his "The Defining Moment of Saddam's Life" in *Political Psychology*, ed. Renshon, 49–50. Karsh concurs. In the president he finds a man who has a "permanently beleaguered mind . . . where personal interests are nationalized and national affairs personalized" ("Why Saddam Invaded," 24).

114. Geertz, *Interpretation of Cultures*, 113.

115. Nasser, *Philosophy of the Revolution*, 61 (emphasis added). See also Tripp, "The Iran-Iraq War," 98, on the development of "a personality cult of truly impressive proportions."

116. Iskander, *Saddam Hussein*, 153 (emphasis added).

117. Baram, *Culture, History, and Ideology*, 108 (emphasis added).

118. Makiya, *Republic of Fear*, 113–114.

119. See the discussion in Iskander, *Saddam Hussein*, 18–22. It is important to emphasize that Dr. Iskander, an Egyptian academic and writer, produced his laudatory biography with Saddam's approval, one drawn from interviews with the president and from a review of works purportedly authored by Saddam. If the image that emerges in Iskander's work is inaccurate, it is the inaccurate image the president wished presented.

120. Baram, *Culture, History, and Ideology*, 94

121. Bengio, *Saddam's Word*, 8.

122. Ibid., viii. According to Geertz, "social discourse" conveys "the imaginative universe within which . . . acts are signs" (*Interpretation of Cultures*, 13, 18). Saddam sought to control both literal discourse and the larger social discourse to reconstruct an "imaginative universe."

123. Khalid Kishtainy, "Translators Preface" to *Saddam Hussein on Current Events in Iraq* (London: Longman, 1977), vii, ix.

124. Bengio observes, with respect to Islam, "[U]nlike in Iran, Iraqi politicians and functionaries continued to be barred from participation in religious discourse. Only Husayn had the right to make statements on religious issues and to take action on them. As a rule, other officials or party figures kept silent on the issue of Islam except in Husayn's presence or with his prior permission. Husayn had two reasons to insist on his monopoly: he wanted to stop party members from being carried away by the Islamic wave, a development likely to have utterly unpredictable consequences; and he wanted to be seen in the tradition of Arab-Muslim rulers who combined religious authority, political power, and military command in a single person" (*Saddam's Word*, 182). The facts about the *Dictionary* and the *Writings* are on 78.

125. Matar, *Saddam Hussein*, 235.

126. Iskander, *Saddam Hussein*, 397–398. In an interview with Majid Khadduri in the 1970s, Saddam was asked which books he most preferred, and he indicated history in general and political thought and ideology in particular. He singled out, as especially inspiring, the memoirs of Colonel Salah al-Din al-Sabbagh as exemplary of an Arab nationalist leader (*Socialist Iraq: A Study in Iraqi Politics since 1968* [Washington, D.C.: Middle East Institute, 1978], 73). Sabbagh was one of four army colonels who, in 1941, were part of the Rashid Ali affair.

127. Iskander, *Saddam Hussein*, 153.

128. See the discussion on this general area in Bengio, *Saddam's Word*, 77–79.

129. Karsh and Rautsi, *Political Biography*, 122.

130. Matar, *Saddam Hussein*, 176.

131. *Saddam on Current Events*, 47, 48, 51 (emphasis added).

132. Iskander, *Saddam Hussein*, 368.

133. From Saddam's book, *Al-Dimuqratiyya Masdar Quwwah li al-Fard wa al-Mujtama'* (*Democracy: Source of Power for the Individual and Society*). For

the extended quote from which this is taken and a relevant discussion, see Makiya, *Republic of Fear*, 77–78 (emphasis added).

134. Text reported in *FBIS*, 2 July 1990 (emphasis added).

135. Bengio, *Saddam's Word*, 78.

136. Much of my discussion on art and Saddam is informed by Baram, *Culture, History, and Ideology*; see especially 78–82. The pictures to which I refer are included in the center of the book, numbered but not paginated; see plates 15–22, 29.

137. To be sure, the Ba'th under Saddam had brought improvements. From 1968 until the middle of the war with Iran, when earlier largesse had to be cut back, the party had expanded health services and improved infant-mortality rates. Per capita food consumption increased. Educational opportunities expanded, especially for women, and adult literacy improved significantly. Additionally, unions and other associations expanded. See, for instance, the discussion in Marr, "Iraq: Its Revolutionary Experience," 200–202. But all this came at a price. The Ba'th placed trusted members in the unions, and its multitiered and overlapping security service permeated society. Iraq became, as Makiya reminds us repeatedly, a "society of informers," one in which the president was "the only genuinely free man." Makiya, *Republic of Fear*, 272; on the intelligence services, see 12ff.

138. This is recognized in a document adopted by dissident Iraqi intellectuals and titled simply "Charter 91." It maintains, "Civil society in Iraq has been continuously violated by the state in the name of ideology. As a consequence the networks through which civility is produced and reproduced have been destroyed. A collapse of values in Iraq has therefore coincided with the destruction of the public realm for uncoerced human association" (Makiya, *Republic of Fear*, xxx). See also Kanan Makiya, *Cruelty and Silence: War, Tyranny, Uprising, and the Arab World* (New York: Norton, 1993) 204–206.

## CHAPTER FIVE

1. Saddam's remark was made during an address to the World Popular Islamic Leadership group meeting in Baghdad. The text of the address is in *FBIS*, 17 December 1990. Mubarak's remark came in a speech to Egyptian troops about to deploy from Egypt for Saudi Arabia. The text is reported in *SWB*, 19 September 1990. The Iranian News Agency item is from *SWB*, 8 August 1990.

2. The broadcasts may be found in *FBIS*, 2, 3 August 1990. The reference to jihad is in Lee Stokes, "Iraq Warns against Foreign Interference in Kuwait," UPI international edition, 2 August 1990.

3. The complete text is in *SWB*, 18 February 1991. I have changed the translation somewhat at the end to render the Arabic *jihad al nafs wa al mal.* The phrase is Quranic; see, for instance, 9:20, 81.

4. John Voll, *Islam: Continuity and Change in the Modern World* (Syracuse, N.Y.: Syracuse Univ. Press, 1994), 317 (emphasis added).

5. Dale Eickelman and James Piscatori, *Muslim Politics* (Princeton, N.J.:

Princeton Univ. Press, 1996), 12–13 (emphasis in original). See the larger, helpful discussion 11–16.

6. The geopolitical reasons for the invasion were already in place and have been described in Chapters Two and Three: the long-standing need for access to the gulf, domestic unrest, instability in the oil market, and so on. What appears to be the case in early 1990 is that the regime began to manufacture media reasons to justify its *raisons d'état*. The thesis of Saad al Bazzaz in *harb taled okhra* (*War Begets Another*) that a "strategic punch" had been planned for months seems entirely plausible; see note 25 to Chapter Two above.

7. Emphasis added to quote. The peace proposal was widely reported. For coverage, see, for instance, Lee Stokes, "Iraq Announces New Peace Initiative," UPI international edition, 5 January 1990, and Mona Ziade, "Iran Dismisses Saddam's Peace Proposal," AP international edition, 6 January 1990.

8. Noted in Bengio, *MECS* 1990, 396. Regarding Saddam's "fire speech" later in April, the Iranians were not about to be misled. They "knew" that Saddam's bluster was part of a Western-orchestrated conspiracy and that the new weaponry was intended primarily for them, not the Israelis. The Tehran paper *Kayhan International* editorialized, "When Iraq's Saddam Husayn pledged to wipe out half of Israel with chemical weapons, he was hitting two birds with one stone. The despot was actually telling the Islamic Republic of Iran to mend its ways. . . . Iran, and not Israel, was in Saddam's mind when he spoke of attacking with nuclear and chemical arms." *FBIS*, 4 May 1990, carries the editorial, which appeared in English.

9. The correspondence is available as *The Texts of Letters Exchanged between the Presidents of the Islamic Republic of Iran and the Republic of Iraq, 1990*, trans. Maryam Daftari (Tehran: Institute for Political and International Studies, 1995). I cite here by date rather than page number in this dual-language text.

10. Arafat was rightly concerned after Prime Minister Shamir's remarks in January describing the "big immigration" of Soviet Jews as requiring "Israel to be big as well" (*Jerusalem Post*, 15 January 1990). At that point, some estimates indicated 300,000 might arrive over the next three years, an influx that could be housed only by building in the territories.

11. The two nations did meet in Geneva on 3 July 1990 for their first direct talks since the cease-fire. Although mediators expressed optimism about the future, they announced no substantive progress in the talks. Real progress would come only after the invasion, when national exigencies made Saddam considerably more pliable.

12. Saddam's expression here and elsewhere in these letters, *qadiyya al-Kuwait*, could not be more oblique. *Qadiyya* can mean "lawsuit" or more simply "matter," "affair," "issue." Here the phrase would mean something like "the Kuwait matter." The quite neutral term is a way of ignoring the violence and eschewing responsibility. It was a device he favored. For instance, in his "peace proposal" of 12 August that outlined various withdrawals, Saddam

first referenced the crimes of the United States, then spoke of the situation in Kuwait. The text is in *FBIS*, 13 August 1990.

13. One piece of evidence for the "war footing" is that Saddam had directed the formation of a new Ministry of Industry and Military Industrialization at the end of the Iran-Iraq War. It was initially headed by his son-in-law, Hussein Kamil Majid. This followed changes that became known as the *thawra idariyya*, "the revolution of the bureaucracy." The new ministry brought together the petroleum industry and military research and development. Since petrochemicals constituted the largest revenue source for the country, the ministry joined weaponeering with the most important sector of the economy—and put it under family control. See the brief but helpful discussion in Farouk-Sluglett and Sluglett, "Iraq since 1986," 21–22. Kishtainy notes with approval the propensity of Saddam to favor military terminology in his expressions: "[T]here is more military matter in his vision and understanding than we find in many generals" (*Saddam on Current Events*, preface). Kishtainy lists "battle," "trenches," "bastions," "mobilization," "strategy," and others as among favorites; see ix. Note that this book appeared two years before Saddam became president. He waited only a year after taking the office before launching a major war. Even in peace Saddam spoke of war and rendered the world in terms not only categorical but also militaristic.

14. Ofra Bengio, ed., *Saddam Speaks on the Gulf Crisis: A Collection of Documents* (Tel Aviv: Moshe Dayan Center for Middle Eastern and African Studies, 1992), 18.

15. Ibid., 19. See also her related discussion in *MECS* 1990, 393–395. It was during this time, Bengio writes, that Saddam called for a jihad against Israel.

16. *SWB*, 13 April 1990. The *al-'abid* (also sometimes designated Tammuz II) had been unveiled the previous fall and was designed for satellite launches. The name denotes "worshipper (of God)," and Saddam is reported to have so named it as an act of thanks for the success Allah had given Iraq and the Arab nation. For a related discussion see Ofra Bengio, *Saddam's Word*, 189, 198. See also the related discussion in Chapter Four.

17. The text of the speech is in *SWB*, 9 April 1990.

18. The *mujahid* expression, not incidentally, appeared repeatedly in the communiqués of the Unified National Leadership of the Intifada. It is obvious Arafat was worried about his Islamic authenticity, since the Islamists sometimes promulgated countercommuniqués. Islamists often exploited Arafat's perceived vulnerability on this point during the uprising. Like Saddam, Arafat appears to have been compelled to increase his Islamic references. A helpful discussion on this, vis-à-vis the intifada, is Ziad Abu-Amr, *Islamic Fundamentalism in the West Bank and Gaza* (Bloomington, Ind.: Indiana Univ. Press, 1994); see esp. 68–72.

19. The entire charter, as well as other pertinent documents on Palestine and Israel, is available on-line at MidEast Web, http://www.mideastweb.org/history .htm. The quotes used here were accessed 23 February 2001 (emphasis added).

20. See the reporting, as well as the text of the declaration, in *SWB*, 16 November 1988.

21. *Qibla* indicates direction (of turning in prayer). Initially, the early Islamic community faced Jerusalem; hence, "the first *qibla*." After the prophet Muhammad migrated to Medina in 622, Mecca was fixed as the new *qibla*. *Nakba* indicates "disaster, calamity" and is used most often in reference to the 1948 founding of Israel, but sometimes with reference to 1967 Six-Day War, also seen as a great setback.

22. *SWB*, 12 May 1990. The reference to Christianity was not unique. Saddam would return to theme several times in the coming months, especially in hosting Christian "peace envoys." More will be said later in the chapter.

23. Formed in 1983 by Egypt, Saudi Arabia, and Iraq, and headquartered in Baghdad, the PIC was intended to galvanize Islamic support for the Iraqis during the war with Iran. It had, in effect, lost its mission with the cease-fire in 1988. It now began once more to take an active role. It became a deeply politicized, not to say conflicted, institution after the invasion of Kuwait, as will be detailed later.

24. The reporting was carried in *SWB*, 19, 20 June 1990.

25. *SWB*, 20 June 1990, reports the text.

26. All quotes in this paragraph and the next two are from the text in *FBIS*, 27 June 1990.

27. Ibid.

28. The complete transcript of the meeting is in *Gulf War Reader*, ed. Sifry and Cerf, 122–133.

29. *FBIS*, 2 August 1990.

30. The complete text is in *FBIS*, 2 August 1990.

31. The full text of the communiqué is in *FBIS*, 2 August 1990.

32. In the Islamic calendar, this was the eleventh day of Muharram. Perhaps the Iraqis emphasized the month because of the importance of *'ashura*, especially to the Shi'a, which fell the day before. But apart from calling this the "blessed" month, the announcement itself does not otherwise indicate the reason for the emphasis.

33. The full text is in *FBIS*, 3 August 1990.

34. Carried in *SWB*, 12 December 1990.

35. See the draft text in *FBIS*, 31 July 1990.

36. This appears in the version carried by the party newspaper, *Al-Thawra*. On this point and for part of what follows regarding the Ba'th I am indebted to Bengio, *Saddam's Word*, 183–184, 187, 188.

37. Ibid., 188.

38. *SWB*, 18 January 1991.

39. *SWB*, 22 January 1991.

40. *SWB*, 10 August 1990, carries the address. This address and the next, both on 7 August, are the first formal announcements of the merger attributed to Saddam that this research uncovered. Earlier notices in the media mentioned Saddam's meeting with the RCC and the Ba'th, dispatching envoys, and the

like, but gave no formal transcripts. The party's slogan was "Unity, Freedom, Socialism."

41. The full text is in *FBIS*, 8 August 1990.

42. The next day the RCC made an announcement "approving" the merger with Kuwait after the Provisional Free Kuwait Government requested it. The pan-Arab–jihad connection is even more explicit. "Woe be to us from God's torture if we are late in performing our duties toward him. Some of our duties to him and His land are struggle and *jihad for the sake of a deep pan-Arab awakening*" (emphasis added). The merger statement is in *FBIS*, 8 August 1990. The wording, as well as the timing of the message, does appear to reflect precise coordination of regime elements.

43. The text was carried by AP, international news, 10 August 1990, and by *SWB*, 13 August 1990. Saddam gave a second such forceful speech on 5 September that is reported in *SWB*, 7 September 1990.

44. These were significant Muslim victories. The Arabs, under the second caliph 'Umar, defeated the Persians at Qadisiyya and the Byzantines at Yarmuk, both in 637, five years after the death of Muhammad. The Arab Muslims defeated the Persians again in 642 at Nahavand. Saladin defeated the Franks at Hittin in July 1187, preparatory to taking Jerusalem a short time later.

45. To be sure, Saddam did mention jihad on the seventh, as indicated above, but he did so without citing the deployment. Further, he called it a jihad to aid the "nation" in returning to its "rightful position," a description very much like the one he had given when addressing fellow Ba'thists in June (and in much cooler moments). The much more vigorous call to jihad, in fact, was that made by al-Tamimi of the Islamic Jihad/Bayt al-Maqdis on 9 August, which will be discussed later.

46. The meeting on 10 August had been scheduled to begin the day before, but was postponed when an unexpected Iraqi delegation showed up, ostensibly to block Arab participation in a multinational force. During the meeting the next day, the Kuwaiti minister collapsed as the conferees argued. Tariq Aziz strongly opposed a draft being circulated that condemned Iraq's invasion and called for restoration of the Kuwaiti government. This, Aziz said, was "an American solution being given on Arab cover." Late that afternoon (6:00 P.M., Baghdad time), Saddam issued his jihad speech, and shortly after that the league voted to endorse Resolution 195. Two days later, Aziz described the meeting as a "farce," a conspiracy orchestrated by the United States and carried out by Mubarak. Against this backdrop, Saddam's speech shows an inter-Arab, not primarily international, focus. What he could not do in Cairo, Saddam sought to do via a television broadcast. For related reporting see *NYT*, 10, 11 August 1990; AP, "Saddam Calls for Holy War," 10 August 1990; AP, "Ministers Propose Protecting Saudi Arabia," 10 August 1990; *SWB*, 13, 14 August 1990.

47. For an examination of how others before Saddam "found the theme" of jihad, Majid Khadduri, *War and Peace in the Law of Islam* (Baltimore: Johns Hopkins Univ. Press, 1955), has long been a standard. For a more recent study, the reader is especially referred to works of Rudolph Peters: *Islam and Colo-*

*nialism* and *Jihad in Classical and Modern Islam. Islam and Colonialism* demonstrates particularly how regimes turned to jihad to oppose the British presence in the region. See especially his treatment of the Mahdist movement in the Sudan and the opposition to the British and Zionism in Palestine. *Jihad in Classical and Modern Islam,* a broadly historical reader, includes the Ottoman summons to jihad (largely ignored) during World War I. Both books include helpful bibliographies, and that in *Islam and Colonialism* is especially extensive. More will be said in the following chapter about how Islamists evaluated Saddam's summons to jihad.

48. *SWB,* 13 August 1990.

49. Ibid. The "ibadat" are the "pillars" of Islamic practice, ordinarily comprising five: reciting the creed, praying, giving alms, fasting, and making the pilgrimage. A few Muslims add "waging jihad" as a sixth.

50. *SWB,* 14 August 1990.

51. The *ka'ba* is the large cube-like structure in the center of the Grand Mosque in Mecca. It existed in pre-Islamic times, and was held to have been founded by Adam and rebuilt by Abraham. Muhammad cleansed the ka'ba of idols shortly before his death. Those who make the pilgrimage today circle the ka'ba seven times, then perform additional rituals.

52. Reflecting on his experiences in Palestine in 1948 during the war and after seeing destitute refugee children, Nasser took up the cause against imperialism and its assistance to the Zionists. Nasser summarized part of Chaim Weizmann's autobiography (the first president of the new state of Israel), quoting him at several points, to include this: "It was essential that a big power should assist us." Then Nasser generalized, "Imperialism is the great force that throws around the whole region a fatal siege" (*Philosophy of the Revolution,* 70). Saddam had the same view, changing only his emphasis in the Gulf War from the British to the Americans.

53. This is not to say the Iraqis had not previously cited other Arab governments as agents; the list was malleable, and was changed according to political needs.

54. *FBIS,* 2 August 1990.

55. Nasser, *Philosophy of the Revolution,* 59.

56. All references to the jihad speech, here and elsewhere, draw from the text in *SWB,* 13 August 1990.

57. Nasser, *Philosophy of the Revolution,* 62.

58. "Text of Saddam Speech," AP International News, 10 August 1990.

59. Nasser, *Philosophy of the Revolution,* 59, 61, 78. Nasser's recollection of the play is a little muddled. He remembers it as *Six Personalities in Search of Actors.* It is, rather, *Six Characters in Search of an Author.*

60. Chapter Four describes at more length the national role Iraq felt called to take.

61. Matar, *Saddam Hussein,* 176.

62. Statement of 20 September 1990. The text is in *SWB,* 22 September 1990.

63. See Nasser, *Philosophy of the Revolution,* 62: "There is no doubt that

the Arab circle is most important and the most closely connected with us. Its history merges with ours."

64. *FBIS*, 8 August 1990.

65. *FBIS*, 9 August 1990.

66. These figures are from *MECS* 1990 and 1991. The corresponding figure for Kuwait in 1990, unsurprisingly, is unavailable.

67. See, for instance, the RCC announcement of the invasion, where the "Qarun" reference first occurs (*FBIS*, 2 August 1990). Quranic passages about Qarun are 28:76–82 and 29:39–40.

68. See the provisional government's initial statement in *FBIS*, 2 August 1990, and Saddam's Victory Day message, *FBIS*, 8 August 1990.

69. *SWB*, 10 August 1990.

70. Quoted in John Esposito, *The Islamic Threat: Myth or Reality?* (New York: Oxford Univ. Press, 1992), 21.

71. Quoted in Piscatori, *Islamic Fundamentalisms*, 12.

72. An insightful discussion of the precariousness of the Saudi guardianship is provided by Hermann Eilts in "Saudi Arabia: Traditionalism versus Modernism—A Royal Dilemma?" in *Ideology and Power*, ed. Chelkowski and Pranger, 58–88. Eilts served as U.S. ambassador to Saudi Arabia and Egypt in the 1960s and 1970s, and in other senior State Department positions.

73. Cited in Eickelman and Piscatori, *Muslim Politics*, 15.

74. *SWB*, 13 and 25 August 1990. The emphasis has been added to underscore the Iraqis' continued and unvarying connection between Islam and Arabism. Emphasis added.

75. The choice of verses is significant. *Auliyaa'*, "friends," may also be translated as "protectors" or "benefactors." This verse, first used by the Popular Islamic Conference in its companion call to jihad on 10 August, was repeated *ad infinitum*, as were similar verses (e.g., 3:28, 4:144, and 60:13).

76. *SWB*, 24 August 1990.

77. The point here is the Iraqi regime needed only *level* the charges; other Islamic constituencies would keep them very much alive in their public discourse, vigorously debating the religious issues the deployment raised. The next chapter will look at how others took up the issues that the Iraqis raised. Very good surveys of the response of the Islamists include John Esposito, "The Persian Gulf War, Islamic Movements, and the New World Order," *Iranian Journal of International Affairs* 5, no. 2 (1993): 340–364; and Haddad, "War of Fatwas."

78. See the initial reporting in *SWB*, 15 August 1990. "Hijaz" refers to the western part of Saudi Arabia bordering the Red Sea, and is the area where both Mecca and Medina are located. "Najd" is central Saudi Arabia, the location of Riyadh, and the area from which the al-Saud came.

79. AP, international news, 16 August 1990, carries the text.

80. *SWB*, 25 August 1990.

81. Ibid.

82. Such descriptions proliferated throughout the fall. These happen to be from the messages of the National Assembly on 11 August (*FBIS*, 13 August

1990) and the Popular Islamic Conference meeting on 8 January 1991 (*SWB*, 10 January 1991).

83. *SWB*, 18 September 1990.

84. See the reporting in *SWB*, 22, 23 January 1991.

85. The regime also used the term "crusade" to depict the deployment, but not with the frequency one would expect. In a Lexis-Nexis survey of all BBC reports from August 1990 through the following January, the Iraqis are reported as having used the term or a derivative only seven times. The Iraqi media did carry reports of others' using it. The Iraqis broadcast the supporting comments of Shaykh As'ad Bayyud al-Tamimi a week after the invasion: "The crusaders, led by the United States, have brought in their armies and fleets to prevent unity between two parts of the nation." On 12 August the Iraqi minister of awqaf called for jihad to oppose the crusader army led by the U.S. and the British. At the end of August, "Holy Mecca Radio" described the "anti-Arab policies pursued by traitor Fahd, the servant of the crusaders, and his conspiracies against fraternal Iraq." And the commission of senior Iraqi ulama warned in September, "The Crusaders are coming, wave after wave, seeking to decimate your Muslim brothers." See the reporting in *SWB*, 11, 14, 30 August and 18 September 1990. The Saladin-crusader connection would have been a natural one to make. It is unclear why the regime did not exploit it more than it did, a point that merits further research.

86. The telegram was read on Baghdad Radio the next day, and is carried in *SWB*, 19 February 1991.

87. *Daily Telegraph* (Britain), 11 August 1990.

88. The story is carried in *SWB*, 24 October 1990. "Worshipper" renders *'abd*, a word that can also be translated as "servant" or even "slave." "Abdullah," servant of God, is a common enough name.

89. See the very helpful reporting of Ben Lynfield, "Saddam as an Islamic Leader," *Jerusalem Post*, 22 August 1990.

90. Cited in *The Independent* (London), 28 August 1990.

91. The discussion about the Caliph al-Mansur summarizes Bengio, *Saddam's Word*, 81.

92. Communiqué No 7, reported in *SWB*, 22 January 1991. As with other references from history, this allusion to 'Umar is quite purposeful. The second caliph after Muhammad, 'Umar is a rightly admired figure in early Islam. He was at once an extraordinary battlefield commander and a zealously devout Muslim, responsible for changing the Islamic calendar to date from the time of the hijrah. He conquered Jerusalem in 637; and the Dome of the Rock, built some fifty years after his death, is sometimes called the Mosque of 'Umar in his honor. He is often referred to as *amr al-mu'minin*, "commander of the faithful (or the believers)."

93. *SWB*, 13 August 1990.

94. *FBIS*, 27 June 1990.

95. In a remark to an Islamic delegation in September, Saddam averred, "The

individual who owns property without work cannot be anything but a terrorist" (*SWB*, 26 September 1990).

96. The National Assembly invoked the idea of deep history when it made a public-relations appeal to the American people in late August, saying President Bush had misrepresented Iraq. "We are an ancient people of successive human civilizations, the most ancient of which dates back to about 6,000 years. We are the nation of Mesopotamia, the inheritors of Sumer, Akkad, Babylon and Ashor. Our people were the first to invent writing and the first to promulgate laws and specify rights 4,500 years ago. . . . Baghdad [was] the capital of peace when Europe itself was still plunged in the darkness of the Middle Ages" (*SWB*, 27 August 1990). A week and a half later Saddam used these same words almost verbatim in writing to Presidents Bush and Gorbachev before the Helsinki Summit; see the text of the letter in *FBIS*, 10 September 1990.

97. The text of the communiqué is in *SWB*, 22 September 1990 (emphasis added).

98. This was in an address to Islamic leaders; see *SWB*, 11 January 1991.

99. 1 Samuel 17:45; 2 Corinthians 10:4 (New International Version).

100. *SWB*, 11 October 1990, for quotes in this paragraph and the next.

101. Quran 20:69; 28:31–32; 8:17.

102. The minister was Hussein Kamil, Saddam's son-in-law.

103. The Hussein variant, named for the third Shiʿa Imam, had a range of 650 km and was the primary missile used in the "war of the cities" with Iran in early 1988. Its CEP (circular error probable, a measure of accuracy) was poor: about 3,000 meters, which qualified it more as an instrument of terror than a capable military weapon. This new variant, al-Hijara, was estimated to have a range of 750 km, which indicated an even greater (i.e., worse) CEP. For an overview, see *Conduct of the Persian Gulf War*, 13–15. See also the discussion in Chapter Four above.

104. *SWB*, 12 October 1990.

105. Cited in Bengio, *Saddam's Word*, 199–200.

106. Few things so captured the essence of Iraq's larger political strategy than this, making its first target the noncoalition member Israel rather than something like a troop concentration or an air base in Saudi Arabia. The attack on Israel clearly showed Saddam's good faith as ally of the Palestinians and further corroborated his claim that his invasion of Kuwait was really to liberate Jerusalem and serve the interests of the Arab nation. The *al-Jumhuriyya* article is carried in *SWB*, 17 January 1991.

107. See the text of the Victory Day message that contains these allusions in *FBIS*, 8 August 1990.

108. *SWB*, 7 September 1990.

109. Traditional commentaries on the Quran also make this connection. See, for instance, that of Yusuf Ali, a widely used edition, on this sura.

110. For this historical background, see Hitti, *History of the Arabs*, 54, 62, 64; and Bengio, *Saddam's Word*, 195.

111. The principal works of ibn Hisham and al-Tabari are, respectively, *sirat rasul Allah*, translated by Alfred Guillaume as *The Life of Muhammad* (New York: Oxford Univ. Press, 1955); and *tarikh al-rusul wa al-muluk, History of Messengers and Kings*. The State University of New York Series of Near Eastern Studies has produced a 39-volume translation of the latter as *The History of Prophets and Kings*. The pertinent part of the story of Abraha is related in ibn Hisham, *Life*, 20–30, and in al-Tabari in vol. 5 of the series, *The Sassanids, the Byzantines, the Lakmids, and Yemen*, trans. C. E. Bosworth (Albany, N.Y.: State Univ. of New York Press, 1999), 212–235.

112. Ibn Hisham, *Life*, 23. It is important to bear in mind that the pre-Islamic period came to be called the time of *jahiliyya*, "ignorance," and according to Islamic teaching, the ka'ba was then filled with idols. Mecca did not become the *qibla*, the direction of prayer, until after the prophet's migration to Medina in 622, and the ka'ba was not cleansed until Muhammad returned in triumph in 630. What gave the ka'ba its importance is that, tradition holds, it was built (or reconstructed) by Abraham and his son Ishmael.

113. Ibn Hisham, *Life*, 26–27.

114. Published in *al-Thawra*; carried in *SWB*, 8 September 1990.

115. *FBIS*, 10 September 1990 carries the letter.

116. *SWB*, 1 January 1991.

117. Bengio, *Saddam's Word*, 198–199, offers several examples of this sort.

118. *SWB*, 5 March 1991.

119. The broadcast is reported in *SWB*, 22 January 1991.

120. *FBIS*, 8 August 1990 (emphasis added).

121. *FBIS*, 9 August 1990.

122. This promise of implementation of shari'a explains, in part, the appeal of the message, if not the messenger, to so many Islamists. The next chapter will say more about the teachings of modern Islamists who call for a state guided by God's law.

123. I again emphasize more secular but not entirely secular. Even if the allusions were the equivalent of "ceremonial deism," every organ of government referred to Islam to some degree. And in the founding of the Ba'th, Aflaq had always given proper recognition to Islam, believing it to inform the national culture of the Arabs. It is true that some inconstancy persisted during the Gulf War. The Ba'th increasingly employed religious expressions, but it also retained the hallmarks of "correct thinking." Bengio notes that when other media changed logos, the party kept the old masthead of "Unity, Freedom, Socialism" on *al-Thawra*, the party paper (*Saddam's Word*, 191). The "slow baptism" was sometimes also an uncertain one, like the Christian emperor who marched his troops by a river for "baptism," where priests dipped branches in the water and sprinkled them.

124. Saddam's call for jihad came on the tenth. The Popular Islamic Conference made its call the same day a few hours later. The National Assembly gave its call the following day, and both "Holy Mecca Radio" and the Minister of

Awqaf gave theirs on the twelfth. See their respective texts in *SWB*, 10 August 1990; *SWB*, 13 August 1990; *FBIS*, 13 August 1990; *SWB*, 14 August 1990.

125. One interesting illustration of the degree of media coordination is an article that *al-Qadisiyya*, the military newspaper, ran twelve days after the invasion (carried in *FBIS*, 28 August 1990). Apparently sensing the need, during the multiple calls to jihad, to present the leader president as a man with an earnest, uncomplicated faith and lifestyle, the paper ran an article by Saddam's son Uday entitled, "The Other Face of Saddam Husayn." The piece describes a simple leader devoted in an exemplary way to widows, orphans, and all in need. Here, Uday writes, is a man who resorted to selling some of his sheep to build tombs for his mother and for Michel Aflaq, the Ba'th party founder. Indeed, fishing and sheep raising are his primary hobbies, for they provide "ample time for meditation." And what does this knight of the Arabs most fear? God Almighty, whom he must face on the day of judgment, and the people, whom he must face in this life.

126. Military Communiqué #41 issued by the Armed Forces General Command, 8 February 1991 (*SWB*, 11 February 1991, emphasis added).

127. See "The Rise of the Iraqi Phoenix," *The Economist* (2 December 1989): 45.

128. The text is in *SWB*, 16 August 1990.

129. See the helpful summary by David Menashri, "Iran," *MECS* 1990, 370–375.

130. See the discussion in Bengio, *MECS* 1990, 415–416. The uprisings in the Shi'a and Kurdish communities that followed the war are discussed in the next chapter.

131. A good biographical sketch is by Joyce Wiley, s.v. "Khoi," in *The Oxford Encyclopedia of the Modern Islamic World*, ed. John Esposito. The discussion here summarizes her work, as well as drawing on Bengio, *MECS* 1990, 412.

132. See the discussion in Bengio, *MECS*, 1990, 412.

133. Wiley, "Khoi."

134. See reporting in *SWB*, 14 August and 5 December 1990.

135. *FBIS*, 14 September 1990.

136. *SWB*, 3 October 1990.

137. *Saddam on Current Events*, 80, 81.

138. *Khandaq wahid am khandaqayn fi qadhayya al-jabha al-wataniyya* (*One Trench or Two Trenches in the Issue of the National Front*) (Milan: Grafis, 1977).

139. *Saddam on Current Events*, 80, 84. Note also Kishtainy's preface where the translator approvingly cites Saddam's strong predilection for military terminology, a predilection that seems to have carried over in large measure to the regime ulama and other religious figures; see n. 13 above. Without belaboring the point, the pronouncements of the ulama within Iraq consistently demonstrated their having been co-opted. The Iraqi media carried no opposition voices, certainly. After years of brutal repression of *any* sort of dissent, religious

or otherwise, there was little opposition inside the country that could or would speak up. The draft constitution of 1990 did allow formation of various parties, religious and political; but then it quickly stipulated the regime was prohibiting any parties, clubs, or societies "which are based on mingling religion with politics, or on atheism, sectarianism (ta'ifiyya), racism, regionalism (iqlimiyya) or anti-Arabism (shu'ubiyya)"; see the helpful discussion of these terms in the context of the constitution in Bengio, *MECS* 1990, 382–384. The regime had made only too clear through its purges over the years that it would brook neither rival authority nor independent thinking. If religion *were* to be mixed with politics, Saddam would do it, along with those whom he so directed. In short, the thinking of the ulama was hardly independent, and unlikely to blaze new lines of Islamic enquiry.

140. These demonstrations of support are described in *SWB*, 8 September 1990.

141. See reporting in *SWB*, 13 August 1990.

142. Dawalibi's letter is in *FBIS*, 13 August 1990.

143. See reporting in *SWB*, 18 September 1990. The Saudi-sponsored Muslim World League will be looked at in more detail in the next chapter.

144. *SWB*, 17 September 1990.

145. See reporting in *SWB*, 18, 26, 28, 29 September 1990; *FBIS*, 27 September 1990

146. In Tehran, the team stressed the importance of Iran's potential contribution to resolving the conflict, and Khalifah diplomatically called Iran "the land of the ulama." Rafsanjani, who met the delegation, thanked it for its efforts, then added, "We consider ourselves to be the standard-bearers of the anti-arrogance and anti-US struggles, and we have proved this through all periods." He added Khameini had already issued a call for jihad to oppose American plans for the region. The Iranian president's remarks reflected Iran's view not only that it, not Iraq, led in the struggle against imperialism, but also that it possessed the legitimacy to call for jihad.

147. *FBIS*, 2 October 1990, carries Khalifa's comments both to *al-Dustur* newspaper and on Jordanian television.

148. This last point is cited in Martin Kramer, "The Invasion of Islam," *MECS* 1990, 203; he helpfully summarizes the delegation's work on 202–203.

149. See reporting in *SWB*, 15, 17 December 1990; *FBIS*, 17 December 1990.

150. *SWB*, 20 June 1990, for this quote and the next two.

151. The Iraqi News Agency carried extensive reporting of the great number of Muslims visitors and Islamic delegations. This brief representation draws from *SWB*, 1 September, 29 October, 17 December 1990; *SWB*, 15 January 1991.

152. The next chapter will say more about Tamimi. It is important to note that he issued a fatwa of support, calling for jihad, a day *before* Saddam's jihad speech on the 10 August. See reporting in *FBIS*, 10 August 1990, which carries the text of the fatwa.

153. *SWB*, 17 December 1990.

154. *SWB*, 29 October 1990.

155. *SWB*, 18 December 1990 (emphasis added).

156. As indicated earlier, at the end of July 1990 the Iraqis announced the draft of a new constitution. It designated Islam the "official" religion of the state (where the old had said simply it was the state's religion), but it also guaranteed "freedom of religious rituals" as long as they did not infringe state security. The draft also prohibited any party that mixed politics and religion. The invasion shelved plans for this new constitution. The text is reported in *FBIS*, 31 July 1990.

157. See the reporting in *FBIS*, 5, 6 December 1990; *SWB*, 7 December 1990.

158. The initiative called for withdrawals, beginning with the oldest occupation, that of Palestine, Syria, and Lebanon by Israel. The proposal did not call the Iraqi invasion an occupation, but described it as "the situation in Kuwait." *FBIS*, 13 August 1990, has the text.

159. The brief Iraqi notice is in *FBIS*, 20 December 1990. For other reporting, see Inter Press Service, 17 December 1990, and AP, 20 December 1990.

160. *SWB*, 29 November 1990. Saddam had told Diane Sawyer the same thing in an interview the previous June: forgetting that God is more powerful than any force on earth is the greatest sin one could commit (*FBIS*, 2 July 1990).

161. *FBIS*, 3 January 1991.

162. The full text of Ramadan's speech is in *SWB*, 11 January 1991.

163. *FBIS*, 3 January 1991.

164. Iraqi psychological warfare included the use of Scuds, staged events carried by Western media in Iraq, and radio broadcasts. For a good discussion, see Frank Goldstein and Daniel Jacobowitz, "PSYOP in Desert Shield/Desert Storm", in *Psychological Operations: Principles and Case Studies*, ed. Frank Goldstein and Benjamin Findley, (Maxwell Air Force Base [Montgomery, Ala.]: Air University Press, 1996), 341–356. According to Goldstein (a colonel in the U.S. Air Force, former commandant of the U.S. Air Force Special Operations School, and clinical psychologist), the operations had four primary goals: 1) rationalize the invasion, 2) gain the support of the masses, 3) discourage participation in the UN embargo, and 4) discourage or hinder attacks on Iraq.

165. The discussion here draws primarily on transcripts of Iraqi broadcasts carried by *SWB*, 13, 25, 28, 29, 30 August; 26, 29 September; 23 October; 7 November; and 6 December 1990; and *FBIS*, 14, 24, 28 August 1990. Additionally, it uses Dilip Hiro, *Desert Shield to Desert Storm: The Second Gulf War* (London: HarperCollins, 1992), 155; Donna Abu-Nasr, "Mideast Radio Stations Intensify Propaganda War," AP, 12 January 1991; Peter Feuilherade, "Voices in the Wilderness," *Guardian* (London), 17 December 1990; Daniel Pipes, "Sex, Lies, and Holy Mecca Radio," *Jerusalem Post*, 14 January 1991; Neil MacFarquhar, "Baghdad Radio Begins Propaganda," AP international, 17 August 1990; and my debriefings of U.S. military personnel immediately following the war. The earliest text to deal with psychological warfare is Sun Tzu, *The Art of War*.

166. Noted in Goldstein and Jacobowitz, "PSYOP in Desert Shield/Desert Storm", 346. One broadcast claimed the coalition forces were bringing in pig units. The Saudis, on hearing it, joked that they cleared customs by being

declared "sheep wearing gas masks" (Ghazi al-Ghosaibi, *The Gulf Crisis: An Attempt to Understand* [London: Kegan Paul, 1993], 74). More seriously, al-Ghosaibi notes that the Iraqis referred to gulf Arabs as Bedouins in these programs, another salvo in the cultural war (69). It was similar to the charge the Iraqis made elsewhere that the oil emirs had the wealth of the region but no cultural depth. As used here, "bedouin" would be equivalent to "country hayseed" in the U.S.

167. *SWB*, 13 August 1990.

168. *SWB*, 29 August 1990.

169. See, for instance, *SWB*, 7 November 1990.

170. I visited classified U.S. air bases that were considerably closer.

171. *SWB*, 17 January 1991.

172. Article of 5 September 1990, reported in *SWB* 7 September 1990.

173. *SWB*, 19 July 1990.

174. *SWB*, 9 August 1990.

175. *SWB*, 10 August 1990.

176. Carried in *SWB*, 16 January 1991.

177. See reporting in *SWB*, 10, 11, 12, 14, 15 January 1991, and Nissim Rejwan, "Saddam Moslems vs. Fahd Moslems," *Jerusalem Post*, 18 January 1991.

178. Amir Iskander, *saddam hussein*, 321, 322, 324 (my translation).

179. See reporting in *SWB*, 15 January 1991, and Bengio, *Saddam's Word*, 191.

**CHAPTER SIX**

1. See reporting in *The Economist*, "The Maghreb Boils Over," 26 January 1991, 21. For an examination of both the FIS and fundamentalism generally in Algeria during the Gulf War, see Hugh Roberts, "A Trial of Strength: Algerian Islamism," in *Islamic Fundamentalisms*, ed. Piscatori, 131–154. The discussion here draws on Roberts, 140–143.

2. Noted in Walid Khalidi, "Why Some Arabs Support Saddam," in *Gulf War Reader*, ed. Sifry and Cerf, 164.

3. After the FIS successfully contested round one of national elections in December 1991, the government canceled the next round set for January. In the ensuing violence over the next several years, tens of thousands died.

4. On the division among Egyptian Islamists, see, for instance, Raymond Baker, "Islam, Democracy, and the Arab Future," in *The Gulf War and the New World Order*, ed. Ismael and Ismael.

5. My thinking in this chapter on both the language of politics and the nonmonolithic nature of Islam has been informed by several authors, including Mohammed Arkoun, *Rethinking Islam: Common Questions, Uncommon Answers*, trans. Robert D. Lee (Boulder, Colo.: Westview Press, 1994); Akbar Ahmed and Hastings Donnan, eds., *Islam, Globalization, and Postmodernity* (New York: Routledge, 1994); John Esposito and John Voll, *Islam and Democracy: Religion, Identity, and Conflict Resolution in the Muslim World* (New York: Oxford Univ. Press, 1996); John Voll, *Islam: Continuity and Change;* a

number of monographs by John Esposito, but especially *Islam and Politics*; Tibi, *Challenge of Fundamentalism*. Especially helpful, as in earlier chapters, has been Eickelman and Piscatori, *Muslim Politics*. See also Piscatori, "Religion and Realpolitik: Islamic Responses to the Gulf War," in *Islamic Fundamentalisms*, 1–27.

6. Helpful articles which look at Muslim responses across the region include Esposito, "The Persian Gulf War"; and Azzam, "Gulf Crisis." *Islamic Fundamentalisms*, ed. Piscatori, cited above, offers country-by-country assessments. Surveying the responses of Arabs more generally are Ebert, "Gulf War and Aftermath," and Lesch, "Contrasting Reactions." *MECS* 1990 and *MECS* 1991 also offer good country-by-country surveys.

7. See the discussion in Rudolph Peters, *Islam and Colonialism*, 63–74. For the text of the *bay'a*, see 65–66.

8. Ibid., 94–104. For the text of the communiqué, see 99; the first interpolated note is mine. See also Nels Johnson, *Islam and the Politics of Meaning in Palestinian Nationalism* (Boston: Kegan Paul, 1982). Johnson looks particularly at Izz al-Din al-Qassam, an Islamist and pivotal figure who was killed in 1935 and who largely inspired the 1936–1939 revolt. Palestinian Islamist groups today draw inspiration from him.

9. Peters, *Jihad in Classical and Modern Islam*, 55–57, carries the text and a brief discussion. The Ottoman fatwa was stated as a series of yes-no questions; I have put it here in the affirmative for simplicity of quotation.

10. Translated by Johannes J. G. Jansen as *The Neglected Duty: The Creed of Sadat's Assassins and Islamic Resurgence in the Middle East* (New York: Macmillan, 1986). On the "jihad of the sword," see esp. 193–198.

11. Quoted in Ajami, "Arab Discontent," 13.

12. Cited in *NYT*, 13 January 1991. This violated the concept of *maru'a*, or manliness, which Chapter Three mentions.

13. The Saudis' anxiety showed when they initially levied special restrictions on religious practices: no Bibles were to be brought into the kingdom, and no services were to be held for Jews. The restrictions prompted General Colin Powell, chairman of the joint chiefs, to remark to Ambassador Bandar: "They can die defending your country but can't pray in it?" A compromise was struck that permitted for the direct airlift of Bibles to military installations and for Jewish services to be held onboard ship. Cited in Steve Yetiv, *The Persian Gulf Crisis* (Westport, Conn.: Greenwood Press, 1997), 15.

14. *SWB*, 15 August 1990.

15. The league had been formed in 1962 at the height of the Egyptian-Saudi Arabian crisis regarding Yemen. Headquartered in Mecca, the league is a supranational body. Although largely financed by the Saudis, it does not always favor it in its decisions. It is headed by a constituent council that numbered some sixty members at the time of the invasion. For a succinct discussion of the body, see Reinhard Schulze, s.v. "Muslim World League," *Oxford Encyclopedia of the Modern Islamic World*, ed. Esposito.

16. The text of the league address is in *SWB*, 13 August 1990.

17. *SWB*, 15 August 1990.

18. Ajami, "Arab Discontent," 15. In November 1990, bin Baz joined in issuing a fatwa that ruled women should not drive cars because it would "degrade" their dignity. This followed the "women's demonstration" in Riyadh in which a number of women did just that. See Muhammad Muslih and Augustus R. Norton, *Political Tides in the Arab World* (Ithaca, N.Y.: Foreign Policy Association, 1991), 35.

19. Cited in Jacob Goldberg, "Saudi Arabia," *MECS* 1990, 607.

20. See the description in Kramer, *MECS* 1990, 201–202, from which the present discussion draws.

21. Excerpts from both are in *SWB*, 13 September 1990.

22. *SWB*, 14 September 1990, carries the statement.

23. Martin Kramer, "Islam in the New World Order," *MECS* 1991, 179.

24. See Kramer, *MECS* 1990, 197; and Goldberg, *MECS* 1990, 607.

25. Kramer, *MECS* 1990, 197.

26. Cited in Haddad, "War of Fatwas," 301.

27. *SWB*, 14 January 1991, has the statement. Recall that there were effectively two "PICs" at the time, one in Mecca and the other in Baghdad, the leadership having split over the invasion. See also Nissim Rejwan, "Saddam Moslems vs. Fahd Moslems, *Jerusalem Post*, 18 January 1991.

28. See reporting by Paul Basken, "Top Saudi Religious Official Calls for Jihad," UPI international news, 31 January 1991; and "Anti-Iraq Fighting Amounts to Holy War," AP international news, 31 January 1991.

29. Kramer, *MECS* 1990, 197.

30. See, for instance, Yoram Meital, "Egypt in the Gulf Crisis," in *Iraq's Road to War*, ed. Baram and Rubin, 195; Ami Ayalon, "Egypt," *MECS* 1990, 332, 333; and Uri M. Kupferschmidt, "Egypt," *MECS* 1991, 341. The most significant demonstrations in Egypt occurred in late February on university campuses. One such took place on the University of Cairo campus, where an estimated 10,000 students demonstrated "in solidarity with their Iraq brothers." When the rally grew more heated, security forces closed in, killing one student and injuring dozens more. By the beginning of March, however, the student unrest had died down; see Kupferschmidt, *MECS* 1991, 343.

31. Haddad, "War of Fatwas," quotes significant portions of the fatwa, offering a helpful commentary. The discussion here draws from 297–299.

32. This was a continuing feature of the war, in which both sides appealed to international law as well as to the *shari'a*, Arabism, and culture. For an insightful discussion of this point, as well as the connection of the just-war doctrine to Islamic jurisprudence on jihad, see Ann Elizabeth Mayer, "War and Peace in the Islamic Tradition and International Law," in *Just War and Jihad: Historical and Theoretical Perspectives on War and Peace in Western and Islamic Traditions*, ed. John Kelsay and James T. Johnson (New York: Greenwood Press, 1991), 195–226.

33. See the reporting in Ben Lynfield, "Egypt Blasts Saddam," *Jerusalem Post*, 7 September 1990. See also "Al-Azhar Condemns Saddam, Justifies Western

Intervention," AP international news, 21 August 1990; and *SWB*, 23 August 1990.

34. The discussion here follows Baker, "Islam, Democracy, and the Arab Future," 490–491, 497.

35. The comment on polytheists is cited in Kramer, *MECS* 1990, 197. The comment on not being fooled is in Baker, "Islam, Democracy, and the Arab Future," 497.

36. Albert Hourani, "Conclusion," in *Islam in the Political Process*, ed. James P. Piscatori (New York: Cambridge Univ. Press, 1983), 228–229.

37. The standard work on authority and Middle East governments is the older but still quite useful Hudson, *Arab Politics*. See also Bill and Springborg, *Politics in the Middle East* and Fouad Ajami, *The Arab Predicament: Arab Political Thought and Practice since 1967* (New York: Cambridge Univ. Press, 1992). Saddam established and exercised power at home, but without "legitimacy." His legitimacy on the street proved evanescent, and dependent on developments in the crisis and the presence of the West.

38. Gehad Auda, "An Uncertain Response: The Islamic Movement in Egypt," in *Islamic Fundamentalisms*, ed. Piscatori, 109–130; this is noted at 118. See his helpful discussion on the intra-Islamic struggle between the Brothers and the (largely Islamic) Labor party.

39. Lesch, "Contrasting Reactions," 39.

40. Kramer, *MECS* 1990, 197.

41. Ebert, "Gulf War and Aftermath," 85.

42. *FBIS*, 3 August 1990.

43. *FBIS*, 6 August 1990.

44. "Iraqi Invasion Widely Condemned," AP international, 2 August 1990; Ebert, "Gulf War and Aftermath," 88.

45. *SWB*, 4 August 1990.

46. "Rafsanjani: Joining Sides with Iraq Would Be 'Suicidal'," AP international news, 25 January 1991.

47. *SWB*, 9 October 1990.

48. See the discussion in Amatzia Baram, "From Radicalism to Radical Pragmatism: The Shi'ite Fundamentalist Opposition Movements of Iraq," in *Islamic Fundamentalisms*, ed. Piscatori, 37–41. Iraqi opposition groups, both Islamic and secular, met in Damascus in December, hoping that the opportunity was in the offing for real power sharing in a post-Saddam Iraq. The meeting did adopt a twelve-point resolution, calling for a new constitution and a democratic system. But conferees were badly divided, debating such matters as whether to open their conference with the bismallah (noted in Bengio, "Iraq's Shi'a," 56).

49. Quoted in Kramer, *MECS* 1990, 198. Of course, Hamas's position also reflected an intra-Palestinian political contest with the PLO, which will be addressed later in the chapter. Additionally, Hamas was virulently opposed to non-Muslim troops' being brought to Saudi Arabia.

50. The PLO was among those who expressed reservations rather than either approve or disapprove 3036. On 10 August the PLO did reject Resolution 195

permitting the introduction of foreign troops. Yet even then, as Chapter Three notes, some Palestinians at the meeting claimed that the PLO had *not* voted against the resolution but had abstained along with Algeria and Yemen, holding that the vote had been taken in an atmosphere of "indescribable disorder."

51. The articles from both papers appear in *FBIS*, 3 August 1990.

52. See reporting in *FBIS*, 13 August 1990.

53. *FBIS*, 7 August 1990.

54. Wafa Amr, "Jordanians Demonstrate Against U.S.," UPI international, 9 August 1990.

55. *SWB*, 13 August 1990, notes that Republic of Iraq Radio read Saddam's speech at 6:00 P.M. Baghdad time. In fact, the first call for jihad had been made the day before. Shaykh As'ad Bayyud al-Tamimi, leader of the Islamic Jihad Movement, Bayt al-Maqdis, had issued a fatwa on 9 August calling for jihad were Iraq to be attacked and declaring that anyone who fought in the coalition would be an apostate. Tamimi, who had been a *qadi* (judge) in Hebron in the West Bank, had been deported by the Israelis in 1980, and now lived outside Amman. Tamimi claimed credit for the February 1990 attack on a tour bus in Egypt that killed nine Israelis. Throughout the gulf conflict Tamimi proved an ardent supporter of Saddam, urging him to kill Jews. See reporting in *SWB*, 18 April, 11 August, 27 September, and 4 October 1990. See also "Ex-Hebron Kadi—Jihad's Goal: Kill All the Jews," *Jerusalem Post*, 9 April 1990. The demonstration of the five thousand in Amman is noted in Wafa Amr, "Pro-Iraqi Demonstration," UPI International, 11 August 1990.

56. See the informed discussion in Baker, "Islam, Democracy, and the Arab Future," 487–488.

57. Quoted in Lesch, "Contrasting Reactions," 40.

58. Quoted in Ebert, "Gulf War and Aftermath," 85.

59. The entire editorial is in *FBIS*, 8 August 1990.

60. Haddad, "War of Fatwas," 297–299.

61. Ibid., 305. The Islamist whom Haddad quotes, Abd al-Rahman al-Zayd, expressed his views in an article significantly titled "The Role of the Cross in the Crisis of the Gulf" (*dawr al-salib fi azmat al-khalij*). Zayd was convinced of the religious character of the war, one in which President Bush's decisions were informed by American religious leaders (304). He concluded, "After all this, is it possible to separate President Bush's decisions from their religious crusader significance?"

62. Kramer, *MECS* 1990, 197.

63. Ibid., 198.

64. Haddad, "War of Fatwas," 305. Although their statements lacked real exegetical depth, the Iraqi ulama were nonetheless taking a position that comported with what other Islamic jurisprudents would argue. As Chapter Five notes, they declared, "[A]s for seeking the protection of the infidel against the Muslim, even if this was done in accordance with an agreement with the infidels, it is categorically impermissible, because it contravenes definite Islamic rulings which say that the Muslim should not be under the tutelage of the infi-

del, and that whoever permits this is departing from definite rulings and violating the consensus of Muslim scholars." Tendentious though it may be, it yet has merit. See their statement in *SWB*, 15 September 1990.

65. "Saddam Supporters Demonstrate," UPI international, 12 August 1990. Tunisia supported the Arab League vote on 3 August that condemned the invasion, but it did not take part on 10 August when the league approved Resolution 195. It also did not join the coalition, which was probably wise in view of a public that largely supported Saddam.

66. Ibid.

67. Jamal Halaby, "Muslim Demonstrators Back Saddam," AP international news, 18 January 1991.

68. "Sudanese Politicians Join 'Holy War' Call in Gulf," UPI international, 19 September 1990.

69. Linda S. Adams, "Political Liberalization in Jordan: An Analysis of the State's Relationship with the Muslim Brotherhood," *Journal of Church and State* 38 (Summer 1996): 513. Adams provides a helpful context for understanding the nature of that polarization in the years just prior to the 1989 parliamentary elections.

70. See, for instance, Asher Susser, "Jordan," *MECS* 1990, 470–473; as well as Adams, "Political Liberalization in Jordan."

71. *FBIS*, 6 August 1990.

72. Patrick Bishop, "Jordan's Muslims Declare Holy War on U.S.," *Daily Telegraph* (London), 11 August 1990; "Saddam Supporters Demonstrate," UPI international, 12 August 1990; "50,000 Demand Holy War Against U.S., Zionists," AP international news, 31 August 1990.

73. Christopher Lockwood, "The Gulf War: Jordanians Rally Behind Their Close Neighbor," *Daily Telegraph* (London), 31 January 1991.

74. *SWB*, 1 September 1990. I had a similar encounter with an Indian Islamic scholar. While speaking in January 1991 to a group at the University of West Florida, I was interrupted and publicly challenged on whether the Saudis were even Muslims. The challenger stood, taking over the meeting, telling the audience that the Saudis were definitely not Muslims but were, instead, corrupt and licentious.

75. This is the battle in which the meager forces of Imam Hussein, second son of Ali, were defeated in 680. Husayn's tomb is there, an important place of pilgrimage for the Shiʿa. The battle is, for the Shiʿa, an image of the heroic last stand and martyrdom, if necessary.

76. Esposito, "Persian Gulf War," 358, 360.

77. Azzam, "Gulf Crisis," 474; Esposito, "Persian Gulf War," 357.

78. Esposito, "Persian Gulf War," 360. See also reporting in *The Economist*, 26 January 1991.

79. Ebert, "Gulf War and Aftermath," 88.

80. Ibid., 87.

81. See reporting on the parade in "Pro-Iraq Protest in Morocco Draws 300,000 in the Gulf War," AP international news, 3 February 1991; Tom Por-

teous, "Crisis in the Gulf: Moroccans Vent Anger," *The Independent* (London), 4 February 1991.

**CHAPTER SEVEN**

1. Al-Ahram is quoted in *NYT,* 5 August 1990; Huwaidy is quoted in *NYT,* 3 February 1991. Neil MacFarquhar, "Saudi, Egypt, Syria Drawing Up Middle East Blueprint," AP international news, 13 February 1991, quotes the Saudi editor.

2. *SWB,* 1 March 1991 (emphasis added).

3. Quoted in Baker, "Islam, Democracy, and the Arab Future," 497. After the war was over, Muslim Brothers in Jordan and Egypt were the first to announce their disappointment with Saddam, adding, significantly, that they had known his credentials to be suspect, a point we detail later.

4. Quoted in Martin Kramer, *Arab Awakening and Islamic Revival: The Politics of Ideas in the Middle East* (New Brunswick, N.J.: Transaction Publishers, 1996), 275.

5. Khalidi, "Why Some Arabs Support Saddam," 166–167.

6. Quoted in Muhammad Muslih, "The Shift in Palestinian Thinking," *Current History* 91 (January 1992): 22.

7. Significantly, this included Saudi Arabia, where there was considerable pressure toward democratization (discussed below).

8. Quoted in Lockwood, "Jordanians Rally behind Their Close Neighbor."

9. For more on the GNP figures see Chapter Five. The "thawra-tharwa" remark is by Mohamed Sid-Ahmed, cited in Ebert, "Gulf War and Aftermath," (see n. 24 to Chapter Three).

10. See the discussion in Azzam, "Gulf Crisis," 480.

11. Republic of Iraq Radio, 8 August 1990. The text is in *SWB,* 10 August 1990.

12. Cited in Esposito, "Persian Gulf War," 361.

13. Farouk-Sluglett and Sluglett, "Iraq since 1986," 19.

14. Khalidi, "Why Some Arabs Support Saddam," 168–169. Not incidentally, the view that God furnished some Arabs with oil wealth is specifically defended in Tantawi's fifty-page fatwa (discussed in Chapter Six) supporting the coalition. "If you ask about the judgment of Islamic law regarding the distribution of wealth, the answer is: Allah has favored with provisions some people more than others" (Quran 16:71); cited in Haddad, "War of Fatwas," 298.

15. Bengio describes the Ba'thist exposition of imperialism. She points out that in 1973 at a colloquium on Iraqi education curricula, Saddam told those assembled that the central task of education was to define the country's primary enemies for the children and to teach them to hate imperialism (*isti'mar*) (*Saddam's Word,* 127); see the larger discussion at 127–134.

16. Ebert has several examples at the end of "Gulf War and Aftermath." An important study of cartoons and popular culture in the Middle East is Allen Douglas and Fedwa Malti-Douglas, *Arab Comic Strips: Politics of an Emerging Mass Culture* (Bloomington, Ind.: Indiana Univ. Press, 1994). Of particular inter-

est for this analysis is their chapter "Machismo and Arabism: Saddam Husayn as Lone Hero," 46–59.

17. The survey results and concomitant analysis appear in Tareq Y. and Jacqueline S. Ismael, "Arab Politics and the Gulf War: Political Opinion and Political Culture," *Arab Studies Quarterly* 15, no. 1 (Winter 1993): 1–11. Similarly, Dr. Nawal al-Saadawi, a prominent Egyptian sociologist, expressed the view of many Egyptian intellectuals: "I feel there are hidden hands stirring up trouble in the Arab region." Her views and others' appeared in an article on the Gulf crisis significantly subtitled, *"al-muthaqqafun wa al-fannanun al-misriyun yutalibuna bi-insihab quwwat al-ghazw al-amrikiyah"* ("Egyptian Intellectuals and Artists Call for the Withdrawal of the American Invasion Forces"). The article appeared mid-September 1990, indicating that a good part of the elite had already come to view the character of the conflict as significantly altered. "Invasion" may also be rendered "conquest." The article is cited in Ebert, "Gulf War and Aftermath," 87.

18. I argue later that such ascriptions of blame are better seen as different ways of narrating the same event rather than as diverging explanations.

19. Ismael and Ismael, "Arab Politics," 3.

20. Voll, *Islam: Continuity and Change,* 317 (emphasis added).

21. Work by Augustus R. Norton, Eickelman and Piscatori, and John Esposito has prompted much of the thinking here. Specially noted are Norton, "The Future of Civil Society in the Middle East," *Middle East Journal* 47 (Spring 1993): 205–216; and Muslih and Norton, *Political Tides.*

22. Part of the background information here derives from my visits to the region before and after the Gulf War (in 1989, 1990, 1991, 1993, and 1994), which included debriefs with the political staffs at U.S. embassies in Egypt and elsewhere.

23. Eickelman and Piscatori, *Muslim Politics,* 16.

24. For a somewhat similar approach regarding the Palestinians and dual languages, see Johnson, *Islam and the Politics of Meaning.* Writing from the viewpoint of social science rather than history, Johnson describes the Islamic and secular-nationalist lexicographic sets of language symbols in use, especially during the time of the 1936–1939 revolt.

25. Cited in Mansfield, *The Arabs,* 225.

26. Neither nationalism nor Islam seeks a simple recapitulation of the past, although Islamists are often (and wrongly) accused of doing so. For a more balanced view of Islam and modernity, see, for instance, Ahmed and Donnan, eds., *Islam, Globalization, and Postmodernity;* Ibrahim Abu-Rabi', *Intellectual Origins of Islamic Resurgence in the Modern Arab World* (Albany, N.Y.: State Univ. of New York Press, 1996); and Voll, *Islam: Continuity and Change,* especially the chapter "The Resurgence of Islam." Voll argues that many Muslims seek to "Islamize" modern experience. They reject the Western assumption that modernity and democracy are compatible only with secularity.

27. Acceptance of the nation-state system is explored most cogently by James Piscatori in *Islam in a World of Nation-States* (New York: Cambridge

Univ. Press, 1986). Yet there are those who cannot accept any division of the umma, for states of any sort derogate from the sovereignty of God. Such was the view, for instance, of the Egyptian radical Sayyid Qutb, who was put to death by Nasser in 1966. Many radical groups now trace their inspiration to him. The idea of an organizing myth is developed in Zonis, "Leaders and Publics." "Myth" is not used here pejoratively, but refers to the way a cognitive universe is structured.

28. Samuel Huntington, "The Clash of Civilizations?" *Foreign Affairs* 72 (Summer 1993): 22–49. One vigorous critique is Eickelman and Piscatori, *Muslim Politics.* One attempt to critique while finding some merit is Tibi, *Challenge of Fundamentalism.* I find Tibi's approach convincing.

29. Quoted in Scott MacLeod, "In the Wake of 'Desert Storm,'" in *Gulf War Reader,* ed. Sifry and Cerf, 418, 419. Ebert, "Gulf War and Aftermath," abounds with examples of categorical language, as does Kramer, *MECS* 1990.

30. The statement is in *FBIS,* 6 August 1990.

31. Ibid.

32. Cited in Kramer, *MECS* 1990, 200.

33. Lockwood, "Jordanians Rally behind Their Close Neighbor."

34. Ebert, in "Gulf War and Aftermath," 87.

35. Azzam, "Gulf Crisis," 481. Azzam uses "Islamicists" where others would use "Islamists." I have altered the spelling to the latter, more common form. That these ideas could meet in deed and not just in word was evident the next month in Amman during the three-day meeting of the "Conference of Popular Arab Forces." The Arab journalist who covered the event described the scene as George Habash and Nayef Hawatmeh, personae non grata in Jordan since the civil war twenty years earlier, entered the meetings. "Two Marxist Palestinians who were banned from Jordan for 20 years were greeted by loud applause as a conference of *leftists* and *Islamic* groups convened Saturday to demonstrate solidarity with Saddam Hussein" (emphasis added). In December, Iran hosted its "Islamic Conference on Palestine," which drew together a number of Islamic notables but which also included radical leftists like Abu Abbas of the Palestine Liberation Front (PLF) and Ahmed Jibril of the Popular Front for the Liberation of Palestine-General Command (PFLP-GC). Similarly, in April 1991, Khartoum hosted an "Islamic Arab Popular Conference," which reportedly attracted over two hundred participants from fifty-five countries and which "sought to reconcile Islam and Arabism on the basis of their shared repudiation of western hegemony." See the reporting of these conferences in Abdul Jalil Mustafa, "Palestinian Radicals Attend Leftist Conference in Amman," AP international news, 15 September 1990; "Libyan Delegate Calls For Suicide Attacks Against Americans," AP international news, 17 September 1990; Kramer, *MECS* 1990, 185; and Kramer, *MECS* 1991, 182–183.

36. Cited in Meital, "Egypt in the Gulf Crisis," 194.

37. A week after the invasion, an unnamed "senior PLO official in Amman" reported fifty thousand Palestinian fighters in place, ready to defend Iraq. Such reports continued to surface, totaling perhaps hundreds of thousands who de-

clared their preparedness to join in the jihad. These would supplement those in Iraq who had done so. On 3 October 1990, the Iraqi News Agency reported a total of 8,259,516 volunteers had stepped forward within the country. The initial report of Jordanian volunteers is in Wafa Amr, "Palestinians Rally to Saddam's Cause," UPI international, 10 August 1990; that of the 8 million Iraqis is carried in *SWB*, 9 October 1990.

38. Quoted in Kramer, *MECS* 1991, 175.

39. Muhammad Khalifa, *harb al-fatawa*, quoted in Haddad, "War of Fatwas," 306. Haddad cites several such authors and provides excellent commentary in her article, as well as portions of Tantawi's fatwa.

40. Haddad, "War of Fatwas," 309.

41. This was in an address to Islamic leaders; see *SWB*, 11 January 1991.

42. See Fahd's statement in *FBIS*, 13 August 1990.

43. See Mamoun Fandy, "The Hawali Tapes," *NYT*, 24 November 1990.

44. Piscatori, "Religion and Realpolitik," 9–10. The government was forced to monitor preaching at various mosques throughout the kingdom. It also confronted an underground media that circulated tapes and booklets critical of the government and the Western coalition. Overall, the opposition of this sort was small and contained, but it grew after the war. Milton Viorst, "The Storm and the Citadel," *Foreign Affairs* 75 (Jan./Feb.1996): 93–107, describes the enormous social impact of the crisis.

45. See the summary of the petition in Dilip Hiro, *Desert Shield*, 423–424.

46. The quote is in Kupferschmidt, *MECS* 1991, 340. See his discussion at 340–342, and that of Ayalon, *MECS* 1990, 330–331.

47. Khalidi, "Why Some Arabs Support Saddam," 164. For an example of trying to balance censure and moral principle with persuasion, see the transcript of King Hussein's presentation on CNN in September 1990, where he stood "by the principle of the inadmissibility of the acquisition of territory by war" and recognized the sovereignty of the state of Kuwait.

48. Ebert, "Gulf War and Aftermath," 79.

49. Of course there are exceptions. The leader of Islamic Jihad/Bayt al-Maqdis, Shaykh Bayyud al-Tamimi, is one. But then there is the vexing case of Yasir Arafat who had embraced Saddam well before the invasion. Yet Arafat was not entirely predictable, and he certainly faced an extraordinary array of domestic, regional, and international constraints. One agrees with Muhammad Muslih that "throughout the crisis several Arafats were in evidence." See Muslih, "Shift in Palestinian Thinking," 22.

50. The Brotherhood statements are in Kramer, *MECS* 1991, 177, and Kupferschmidt, *MECS* 1991, 355.

51. Kramer, *MECS* 1991, 176.

52. Edward W. Said, "On Linkage, Language, and Identity," *Gulf War Reader*, ed. Sifry and Cerf, 443.

53. Khalidi, "Why Some Arabs Support Saddam," 161, 166.

54. Lesch, "Contrasting Reactions," 47.

55. Kramer, *MECS* 1990, 198.

56. Jon Immanuel and Mathew Seriphs, "Another Imam Ejected for Criticism of Saddam," *Jerusalem Post*, 17 August 1990.

57. See the discussion in Adams, "Political Liberalization in Jordan"; Susser, *MECS* 1990, 457–499; and Susser, "Jordan," *MECS* 1991, 482–519, for further background.

58. Roger Heacock, "From the Mediterranean to the Gulf and Back Again: The Palestinian Intifada and the Gulf War," *Arab Studies Quarterly* 13 (Winter/Spring 1991): 68.

59. I am indebted here especially to Jean-Francois Legrain, "A Defining Moment: Palestinian Islamic Fundamentalism," in *Islamic Fundamentalisms*, ed. Piscatori, 70–87, for this analysis. See also Muslih, "Shift in Palestinian Thinking." This is not to say Hamas, by maintaining a pragmatic posture, approved the coalition. Its denunciations of the foreign forces were bested by none.

60. Over the years, several countries had arrogated the mantle of chief supporter of the Palestinians; Saddam did so quite vigorously in the spring of 1990. The Iranians saw this new crisis as offering an especially promising opportunity to assert their own role. Of course, they approached it in explicitly Islamic terms. For instance, when Iran hosted its "Islamic Conference on Palestine" in December, it not unnaturally termed the intifada the "Islamic uprising in Palestine."

61. The discussion here draws from the articles of Menashri, *MECS* 1990, 350–378, and "Iran," *MECS* 1991, 382–415; Shaul Bakhash, "Iran: War Ended, Hostility Continued," in *Iraq's Road to War*, ed. Baram and Rubin, 219–232; and Said Amir Arjomand, "A Victory for the Pragmatists: The Islamic Fundamentalist Reaction in Iran," in *Islamic Fundamentalisms*, ed. Piscatori, 52–69. The Ahmad Khomeini and Rafsanjani quotes are in Menashri, *MECS* 1991, 401, 402. The level of Iranian support during the March uprising is a contested point. Here, I follow Bakhash. It is obvious, however, that the Iranians would publicly downplay their level of support, whereas Saddam (as he did) would emphasize it. For a contrary view, see Ahmed Hashim, "Iraq, The Pariah State," *Current History* 91 (Jan. 1992): 12–13.

62. Rosemary Hollis, "Inter-Arab Politics and the Gulf War," *Cambridge Review of International Affairs* 5 (Autumn 1991–1992): 21.

63. There are a number of good summaries of the March uprisings. Among them are Hiro, *Desert Shield*, 400–407; Hashim, "Pariah State," 11–16; Khadduri and Ghareeb, *War in the Gulf*, 189–211; and Makiya, *Cruelty and Silence*, 57–104.

64. At the time of the fighting, Ayatollah Abu al-Qasim al-Khoi issued two fatwas, one that called on the people to respect public and private property and to conduct themselves according to the shari'a; and another that called for a nine-member committee of religious figures that would provide at least interim authority. Khadduri and Ghareeb, *War in the Gulf*, 193, discuss the fatwas. Of some controversy is whether Khoi went voluntarily to Baghdad and there announced on television his support for Saddam's drastic measures. That, at least, is the regime's position. His family and other Shi'is claim he was forcibly taken.

The television broadcast aired without sound, so it is impossible to know what Khoi said to Saddam during the appearance. Those listening to the radio said the aged ayatollah asked simply to be left alone. The family claim of a kidnapping seems probable. See the reporting in David Hirst, "Uproar after Iraq Kidnaps Shi'ite Leader," *The Guardian* (London), 22 March 1991; see also Makiya, *Cruelty and Silence*, 73–76.

65. Cited in Hiro, *Desert Shield*, 496, n. 11.

66. Makiya, *Cruelty and Silence*, 59–60.

67. The declaration is reproduced in Hollis, "Inter-Arab Politics and the Gulf War," 23–24.

68. Piscatori, *World of Nation States*, 146–147, 149–150.

69. Mohamed Heikal, *Illusions of Triumph: An Arab View of the Gulf War* (London: HarperCollins, 1992), 333–334.

70. The text is available on-line at www.library.cornell.edu/colldev/mideast /wif.htm The Arabic text is located at *www.library.cornell.edu/colldev /mideast/fatw2.htm*

71. Cited in Bengio, *Saddam's Word*, 133.

### CHAPTER EIGHT

1. Robert Lacey, *The Kingdom: Arabia and the House of Sa'ud* (New York: Avon, 1981), 9.

# BIBLIOGRAPHY

## REFERENCE

BBC *Gulf Crisis Chronology.* Compiled by the BBC World Service. Distributed in the U.S. by Gale Research. Detroit: Gale Research, 1991.

*Conduct of the Persian Gulf War: Final Report to Congress.* Washington, D.C.: Department of Defense, 1992.

Gibb, H. A. R., ed. *The Encyclopaedia of Islam.* 9 vols. New ed. Leiden, Netherlands: Brill, 1960–.

Esposito, John L., ed. *The Oxford Encyclopedia of the Modern Islamic World.* 4 vols. New York: Oxford Univ. Press, 1995.

Glasse, Cyril. *The Concise Encyclopedia of Islam.* San Francisco: HarperCollins, 1991.

Haddad, Yvonne, and John L. Esposito, with Elizabeth Hiel and Hibba Abugideiri. *The Islamic Revival since 1988: A Critical Survey and Bibliography.* Westport, Conn.: Greenwood Press, 1997.

*The Hans Wehr Dictionary of Modern Written Arabic.* Edited by J. M. Cowan. Ithaca, N.Y.: Spoken Language Services, 1976.

Hiro, Dilip. *Dictionary of the Middle East.* New York: St. Martin's, 1996.

*The Holy Quran.* Translation and commentary by A. Yusuf Ali. Brentwood, Md.: Amana, 1983.

*The Middle East and North Africa: 1991.* London: Europa Publications, 1992.

*Middle East Contemporary Survey* (MECS). Edited by Ami Ayalon. Boulder: Westview. Multiple Years.

*The Middle East Military Balance, 1988-89.* Tel Aviv: Tel Aviv University, Jaffee Center for Strategic Studies, 1989.

Orgill, Andrew. *The 1990–91 Gulf War: Crisis, Conflict, Aftermath. An Annotated Bibliography.* London: Mansell Publishing Ltd., 1995.

Reich, Bernard, ed. *Political Leaders of the Contemporary Middle East and North Africa: A Biographical Dictionary.* New York: Greenwood Press, 1990.

Summers, Harry G., Jr. *Persian Gulf War Almanac.* New York: Facts on File, 1995.

*The World Factbook.* Washington, D.C.: Central Intelligence Agency, 1992. Also, on-line version at http://www.cia.gov/cia/publications/factbook/index.html.

## NEWSPAPERS, MAGAZINES, AND BROADCASTS

Associated Press (AP) international news
BBC Summary of World Broadcasts (SWB)
*Daily Telegraph* (London)

The Economist
The Guardian (London)
Foreign Broadcast Information Service (FBIS)
Jerusalem Post
New York Times
Newsweek
Time
United Press International (UPI) international news
U.S. News and World Report
Vital Speeches of the Day
Washington Post

## PRIMARY SOURCES

Aflaq, Michel. *Fi Sabil al-Ba'th [In the Path of the Ba'th].* Beirut: dar al-tale'ah wa al-nashr, 1975.

"Anfal Operations." Iraq Research and Documentation Project, Center for Middle Eastern Studies, Harvard University, internet version. http://fas-www. harvard.edu/~irdp/, 2 April 2001.

Aziz, Tariq. *The Revolution of the New Way.* Milan: Grafis S.p.A, [1977?].

Bengio, Ofra, ed. *Saddam Speaks on the Gulf Crisis: A Collection of Documents.* Tel Aviv: Moshe Dayan Center for Middle Eastern and African Studies, 1992.

Hanna, Sami, and George Gardner, *Arab Socialism: A Documentary Survey.* Leiden, Netherlands: Brill, 1969.

Hussein, Saddam. *Khandaq wahid am khandaqayn fi qadhayya al-jabha al-wataniyya [One Trench or Two Trenches in the Issue of the National Front].* Milan: Grafis, 1977.

———. *Nidaluna wa al-siyasah al-duwaliyah [Our Struggle and International Politics].* Baghdad: dar al-hurriyah lil-taba'ah, 1980.

———. *Saddam Hussein on Current Events in Iraq.* Translated by Khalid Kishtainy. London: Longman, 1977.

———. *The Texts of Letters Exchanged between the Presidents of the Islamic Republic of Iran and the Republic of Iraq, 1990.* Translated by Maryam Daftari. Tehran: Institute for Political and International Studies, 1995.

Ibn Hisham, abd al-Malik. *Sirat rasul Allah.* Translated by Alfred Guillaume as *The Life of Muhammad.* New York: Oxford Univ. Press, 1955.

Jansen, Johannes J. G., trans. *The Neglected Duty: The Creed of Sadat's Assassins and Islamic Resurgence in the Middle East.* New York: Macmillan, 1986.

Karpat, Kemal H., ed. *Political and Social Thought in the Contemporary Middle East.* New York: Praeger, 1982.

Laqueur, Walter, and Barry Rubin, eds. *The Israel-Arab Reader.* New York: Penguin Books, 1984.

Nasser, Gamal Abdul. *Philosophy of the Revolution.* Buffalo, N.Y.: Smith, Keynes, and Marshall, 1959.

Peters, Rudolph. *Jihad in Classical and Modern Islam: A Reader.* Princeton, N.J.: Markus Wiener, 1996.

al-Tabari, abu Ja'far Muhammad. *The Sassanids, the Byzantines, the Lakmids, and Yemen.* Translated by C. E. Bosworth. Vol. 5 of *The History of al-Tabari,* edited by Ihasan Abbas et al. Albany, N.Y.: State Univ. of New York Press, 1999.

## BOOKS

Abu-Amr, Ziad. *Islamic Fundamentalism in the West Bank and Gaza.* Bloomington, Ind.: Indiana Univ. Press, 1994.

Abu Jaber, Kamel. *Arab Ba'th Socialist Party: History, Ideology, and Organization.* Syracuse, N.Y.: Syracuse Univ. Press, 1966.

Abu-Rabi', Ibrahim. *Intellectual Origins of Islamic Resurgence in the Modern Arab World.* Albany, N.Y.: State Univ. of New York Press, 1996.

Aburish, Said. *Saddam Hussein: The Politics of Revenge.* New York: Bloomsbury, 2000.

Ahmed, Akbar, and Hastings Donnan, eds. *Islam, Globalization, and Postmodernity.* New York: Routledge, 1994.

Ajami, Fouad. *The Arab Predicament: Arab Political Thought and Practice since 1967.* New York: Cambridge Univ. Press, 1992.

Arkoun, Mohammed. *Rethinking Islam: Common Questions, Uncommon Answers.* Translated by Robert D. Lee. Boulder, Colo.: Westview Press, 1994.

Barakat, Halim. *The Arab World: Society, Culture, and State.* Berkeley, Calif.: Univ. of California Press, 1993.

Baram, Amatzia. *Culture, History, and Ideology in the Formation of Ba'thist Iraq, 1968–89.* New York: St. Martin's, 1991.

———, and Barry Rubin, eds. *Iraq's Road to War.* New York: St. Martin's Press, 1993.

Barzilai, Gad, Aharon Klieman, and Gil Shidlo, eds. *The Gulf Crisis and Its Global Aftermath.* New York: Routledge, 1993.

Batatu, Hanna. *The Old Social Classes and the Revolutionary Movements of Iraq.* Princeton, N.J.: Princeton Univ. Press, 1978.

Bengio, Ofra. *Saddam's Word: Political Discourse in Iraq.* New York: Oxford Univ. Press, 1998.

Bill, James A., and Robert Springborg. *Politics in the Middle East.* New York: HarperCollins, 1994.

Bulloch, John, and Harvey Morris. *The Gulf War: Its Origins, History, and Consequences.* London: Methuen, 1989.

Campbell, David. *Politics without Principle.* Boulder, Colo.: Lynne Rienner, 1993.

Carpenter, Ted, ed. *America Entangled: The Persian Gulf Crisis.* Washington, D.C.: Cato Institute, 1991.

Chelkowski, Peter, and Robert Pranger, eds. *Ideology and Power in the Middle*

*East: Studies in Honor of George Lenczowski.* Durham, N.C.: Duke Univ. Press, 1988.

Choueiri, Youssef M. *Arab Nationalism: A History.* Oxford: Blackwell Publishers, 2000.

Chubin, Shahram, and Charles Tripp. *Iran and Iraq at War.* Boulder, Colo.: Westview Press, 1988.

Cordesman, Anthony. *After the Storm: The Changing Military Balance in the Middle East.* Boulder, Colo.: Westview Press, 1993.

Darwish, Adel, and Gregory Alexander. *Unholy Babylon: The Secret History of Saddam's War.* London: Victor Gollancz, 1991.

Dawisha, Adeed, ed. *Islam in Foreign Policy.* New York: Cambridge Univ. Press, 1983.

Diggins, John Patrick. *The Lost Soul of American Politics.* New York: Basic Books, 1984.

Doughty, Dick, and Mohammed al-Aydi. *Gaza: Legacy of Occupation.* West Hartford, Conn.: Kumarian Press, 1995.

Douglas, Allen, and Fedwa Malti-Douglas. *Arab Comic Strips: Politics of an Emerging Mass Culture.* Bloomington, Ind.: Indiana Univ. Press, 1994.

Drysdale, Alasdair, and Gerald H. Blake. *The Middle East and North Africa: A Political Geography.* New York: Oxford Univ. Press, 1985.

Eickelman, Dale, and James Piscatori. *Muslim Politics.* Princeton, N.J.: Princeton Univ. Press, 1996.

Eliade, Mircea. *The Sacred and the Profane: The Nature of Religion.* Translated by Willard Trask. New York: Harper and Row, 1961.

Esposito, John L. *Islam and Politics.* Syracuse, N.Y.: Syracuse Univ. Press, 1998.

———. *The Islamic Threat: Myth or Reality?* New York: Oxford Univ. Press, 1992.

———, and John Voll. *Islam and Democracy: Religion, Identity, and Conflict Resolution in the Muslim World.* New York: Oxford Univ. Press, 1996.

Farouk-Sluglett, Marion, and Peter Sluglett. *Iraq since 1958: From Revolution to Dictatorship.* New York: Routledge, 1988.

Fox, Thomas C. *Iraq: Military Victory, Moral Defeat.* Kansas City, Mo.: Sheed and Ward, 1991.

Friedman, Thomas. *From Beirut to Jerusalem.* New York: Anchor Books, 1990.

Fromkin, David. *A Peace to End All Peace.* New York: Holt, 1989.

Geertz, Clifford. *The Interpretation of Cultures.* New York: Basic Books, 1973.

Geyer, Alan, and Barbara Green. *Lines in the Sand: Justice and the Gulf War.* Louisville, Ky.: Westminster/John Knox Press, 1992.

Al-Ghosaibi, Ghazi. *The Gulf Crisis: An Attempt to Understand.* London: Kegan Paul, 1993.

Goldstein, Frank, and Benjamin Findley, eds. *Psychological Operations: Principles and Case Studies.* Maxwell Air Force Base [Montgomery, Ala.]: Air University Press, 1996.

Haim, Sylvia, ed. *Arab Nationalism: An Anthology.* Berkeley, Calif.: Univ. of California Press, 1962.

Heikal, Mohamed. *Illusions of Triumph: An Arab View of the Gulf War.* London: HarperCollins, 1992.

Henderson, Simon. *Instant Empire: Saddam Hussein's Ambition for Iraq.* San Francisco: Mercury House, 1991.

Hinnebusch, Raymond. *Authoritarian Power and State Formation in Ba'thist Syria.* Boulder, Colo.: Westview Press, 1990.

Hiro, Dilip. *Desert Shield to Desert Storm: The Second Gulf War.* London: HarperCollins, 1992.

Hitti, Philip. *History of the Arabs from the Earliest Times to the Present.* New York: St. Martin's Press, 1970.

Hopwood, Derek, Habib Ishow, and Thomas Koszinowski, eds. *Iraq: Power and Society.* Reading, U.K.: Ithaca Press, 1993.

Hourani, Albert. *Arab Thought in the Liberal Age, 1798–1939.* New York: Cambridge University Press, 1983.

———. *A History of the Arab Peoples.* Cambridge, Mass.: Harvard Univ. Press, 1991.

Hudson, Michael C. *Arab Politics: The Search for Legitimacy.* New Haven, Conn.: Yale Univ. Press, 1977.

Ibrahim, Ibrahim, ed. *The Gulf Crisis: Background and Consequences.* Washington, D.C.: Georgetown Univ. Press, 1992.

Iskander, Amir. *Saddam Hussein: The Fighter, the Thinker, and the Man.* Translated by Hassan Selim. Paris: Hachette, 1980.

———. *Saddam hussein: munadilan, wa-mufakirran, wa-insanan [Saddam Husayn: Struggler and Thinker and Man].* Paris: Hachette, 1980.

Ismael, Tareq, and Jacqueline Ismael, eds. *The Gulf War and the New World Order: International Relations of the Middle East.* Gainesville, Fla.: Univ. of Florida Press, 1994.

Johnson, James Turner, and George Weigel. *Just War and the Gulf War.* Washington, D.C.: Ethics and Public Policy Center, 1991.

Johnson, Nels. *Islam and the Politics of Meaning in Palestinian Nationalism.* Boston: Kegan Paul, 1982.

Karsh, Efraim, and Inari Rautsi. *Saddam Hussein: A Political Biography.* New York: Macmillan, 1991.

Kedourie, Elie. *Arabic Political Memoirs and Other Studies.* London: Frank Cass, 1974.

Kelsay, John. *Islam and War: A Study in Comparative Ethics.* Louisville, Ky.: Westminster/John Knox Press, 1993.

———, and James T. Johnson, eds. *Just War and Jihad: Historical and Theoretical Perspectives on War and Peace in Western and Islamic Traditions.* New York: Greenwood Press, 1991.

Kerr, Malcolm. *The Arab Cold War: Gamal 'Abd Al-Nasir and His Rivals, 1958–1970.* 3rd ed. New York: Oxford Univ. Press, 1999.

Khadduri, Majid. *The Gulf War: The Origins and Implications of the Iraq-Iran Conflict.* New York: Oxford Univ. Press, 1988.

———. *Political Trends in the Arab World: The Role of Ideas and Ideals in Politics.* Baltimore: Johns Hopkins Univ. Press, 1970.

———. *Socialist Iraq: A Study in Iraqi Politics since 1968.* Washington, D.C.: Middle East Institute, 1978.

———. *War and Peace in the Law of Islam.* Baltimore: Johns Hopkins Univ. Press, 1955.

———, and Edmund Ghareeb. *War in the Gulf, 1990–91: The Iraq-Kuwait Conflict and Its Implications.* New York: Oxford Univ. Press, 1997.

Kramer, Martin. *Arab Awakening and Islamic Revival: The Politics of Ideas in the Middle East.* New Brunswick, N.J.: Transaction Publishers, 1996.

Lacey, Robert. *The Kingdom: Arabia and the House of Saʿud.* New York: Avon, 1981.

Lenczowski, George. *The Middle East in World Affairs.* Ithaca, N.Y.: Cornell Univ. Press, 1980.

Lewis, Bernard. *The Political Language of Islam.* Chicago: Chicago Univ. Press, 1988.

Makiya, Kanan. *Cruelty and Silence: War, Tyranny, Uprising, and the Arab World.* New York: Norton, 1993.

———. *The Monument: Art, Vulgarity, and Responsibility in Iraq.* Berkeley, Calif.: Univ. of California Press, 1991.

———. *Republic of Fear: The Politics of Modern Iraq.* Berkeley, Calif.: Univ. of California Press, 1998.

Mansfield, Peter. *The Arabs.* New York: Viking Penguin, 1985.

Marr, Phoebe. *The Modern History of Iraq.* Boulder, Colo.: Westview Press, 1985.

Matar, Fuad. *Saddam Hussein: The Man, the Cause, and the Future.* London: Third World Centre, 1981.

Maull, Hanns W., and Otto Pick, eds. *The Gulf War: Regional and International Dimensions.* London: Pinter, 1989.

Milton-Edwards, Beverley. *Islamic Politics in Palestine.* New York: Tauris Academic Studies, 1996.

Morris, Mary. *Regional Dynamics of the Gulf Crisis.* RAND Papers P-7700. Santa Monica, Calif.: RAND Corporation, February 1991.

Musallam, Musallam Ali. *The Iraqi Invasion of Kuwait: Saddam Hussein, His State and International Power Politics.* London: Tauris, 1996.

Muslih, Muhammad, and Augustus R. Norton. *Political Tides in the Arab World.* Ithaca, N.Y.: Foreign Policy Association, 1991.

Nakash, Yitzhak. *The Shiʿis of Iraq.* Princeton, N.J.: Princeton Univ. Press, 1994.

Owen, Roger. *State, Power, and Politics in the Making of the Modern Middle East.* New York: Routledge, 1992.

Peters, Rudolph. *Islam and Colonialism: The Doctrine of Jihad in Modern History.* New York: Mouton, 1979.

Pipes, Daniel. *In the Path of God.* New York: Basic Books, 1983.

Piscatori, James P. *Islam in a World of Nation-States.* New York: Cambridge Univ. Press, 1986.

——, ed. *Islam in the Political Process.* New York: Cambridge Univ. Press, 1983.

——, ed. *Islamic Fundamentalisms and the Gulf Crisis.* Chicago: The Fundamentalism Project, 1991; distributed by Univ. of Chicago Press.

Rabinovitch, Itamar. *Syria under the Ba'th, 1963–66: The Army-Party Symbiosis.* Jerusalem: Israel Universities Press, 1972.

Rashid, Nasser and Esber Shaheen. *Saudi Arabia and the Gulf War.* Joplin, Mo.: International Institute of Technology, 1992.

Renshon, Stanley, ed. *Political Psychology of the Gulf War.* Pittsburgh: Univ. of Pittsburgh Press, 1993.

Rezun, Miron. *Saddam Hussein's Gulf Wars: Ambivalent Stakes in the Middle East.* Westport: Praeger, 1992.

Safran, Nadav. *Saudi Arabia: The Ceaseless Quest for Security.* Ithaca, N.Y.: Cornell Univ. Press, 1988.

Salehi, Fariba. *The Politics of the Gulf War and the Islamic World.* London: Gulf Centre for Strategic Studies, 1991.

Salinger, Pierre, with Eric Laurent. *Secret Dossier: The Hidden Agenda behind the Gulf War.* Translated by Howard Curtis. New York: Penguin, 1991.

Sciolino, Elaine. *The Outlaw State: Saddam Hussein's Quest for Power and the Gulf Crisis.* New York: Wiley, 1991.

Sifry, Micah L., and Christopher Cerf, eds. *The Gulf War Reader.* New York: Random House, 1991.

Smock, David. *Religious Perspectives on War: Christian, Muslim, and Jewish Attitudes toward Force after the Gulf War.* Washington, D.C.: United States Institute of Peace, 1992.

Stoessinger, John G. *Why Nations Go to War.* New York: St. Martin's Press, 1993.

Tibi, Bassam. *The Challenge of Fundamentalism: Political Islam and the New World Disorder.* Berkeley, Calif.: Univ. of California Press, 1998.

Tschirgi, Dan, ed. *The Arab World Today.* Boulder, Colo.: Lynne Rienner, 1994.

U.S. News and World Report. *Triumph without Victory: The Unreported History of the Persian Gulf Conflict.* New York: Times Books, 1992.

Vaux, Kenneth L. *Ethics and the Gulf War: Religion, Rhetoric, and Righteousness.* Boulder, Colo.: Westview Press, 1992.

Voll, John. *Islam: Continuity and Change in the Modern World.* Syracuse, N.Y.: Syracuse Univ. Press, 1994.

Woodward, Bob. *The Commanders.* New York: Simon and Schuster, 1991.

Yergin, Daniel. *The Prize: The Epic Quest for Oil, Money, and Power.* New York: Simon and Schuster, 1991.

Yetiv, Steve. *The Persian Gulf Crisis.* Westport, Conn.: Greenwood Press, 1997.

Zubaida, Sami. *Islam, the People, and the State: Political Ideas and Movements in the Middle East.* New York: Tauris, 1993.

Abd al-Jabar, Faleh. "The Roots of an Adventure." In *The Gulf Between Us: The Gulf War and Beyond,* edited by Victoria Brittain. London: Virago, 1991.

Aburish, Said. PBS Frontline interview, internet version. www.pbs.org /wgbh/pages/frontline/shows/saddam/interviews/aburish.html. 15 September 2000.

Adams, Linda S. "Political Liberalization in Jordan: An Analysis of the State's Relationship with the Muslim Brotherhood." *Journal of Church and State* 38 (Summer 1996): 507–528.

Ahmad, Mumtaz. "The Politics of War: Islamic Fundamentalisms in Pakistan." In *Islamic Fundamentalisms and the Gulf Crisis,* edited by James Piscatori, 155–185. Chicago: The Fundamentalism Project, 1991; distributed by Univ. of Chicago Press.

Ajami, Fouad. "The Summer of Arab Discontent." *Foreign Affairs* 69 (Winter 1990/91): 1–20.

Akins, James. "The New Arabia." *Foreign Affairs* 70 (Summer 1991): 36–49.

Alexander, Ian. "Can Saddam Climb Down?" *National Review* (1 October 1990): 19–20.

Arjomand, Said Amir. "A Victory for the Pragmatists: The Islamic Fundamentalist Reaction in Iran," In *Islamic Fundamentalisms and the Gulf Crisis,* edited by James Piscatori, 52–69. Chicago: The Fundamentalism Project, 1991; distributed by Univ. of Chicago Press.

Auda, Gehad. "An Uncertain Response: The Islamic Movement in Egypt." In *Islamic Fundamentalisms and the Gulf Crisis,* edited by James Piscatori, 109–130. Chicago: The Fundamentalism Project, 1991; distributed by Univ. of Chicago Press.

Ayalon, Ami. "Egypt." *Middle East Contemporary Survey 1990:* 314–349.

Aziz, Tariq. PBS Frontline interview, internet version. www.pbs.org/wgbh /pages/frontline/shows/saddam/interviews/aziz.html. 15 September 2000.

Azzam, Maha. "The Gulf Crisis: Perceptions in the Muslim World." *International Affairs* 67, no. 3 (July 1991): 473–485.

Baker, Raymond. "Islam, Democracy, and the Arab Future." In *The Gulf War and the New World Order,* edited by Tareq Y. Ismael and Jacqueline S. Ismael, 473–501. Gainesville, Fla.: Univ. of Florida Press, 1994.

Bakhash, Shaul. "Iran: War Ended, Hostility Continued." In *Iraq's Road to War,* edited by Amatzia Baram and Barry Rubin, 219–232. New York: St. Martin's Press, 1993.

Al-Bana, Rajib. "The Exploitation of Islam: Saddam's Gulf War Strategy." *Bulletin of the Henry Martyn Institute* (April–June 1991): 63–66.

Baram, Amatzia. "The Iraqi Invasion of Kuwait: Decision Making in Baghdad." In *Iraq's Road to War,* edited by Amatzia Baram and Barry Rubin, 5–36. New York: St. Martin's Press, 1993.

———. "From Radicalism to Radical Pragmatism: The Shi'ite Fundamentalist Opposition Movements of Iraq." In *Islamic Fundamentalisms and the*

*Gulf Crisis*, edited by James Piscatori, 28–51. Chicago: The Fundamentalism Project, 1991; distributed by Univ. of Chicago Press.

———. "Hizb al-da'wah al-islamiyah [The Islamic Call Party]." *Oxford Encyclopedia of the Modern Islamic World*, edited by John L. Esposito. Vol. 2, 121–124. New York: Oxford Univ. Press, 1995.

———. "Mesopotamian Identity in Ba'thi Iraq." *Middle Eastern Studies* 19 (October 1983): 426–455.

———. "Qawmiyya and Wataniyya in Ba'thi Iraq: The Search for a New Balance." *Middle Eastern Studies* 19, no. 2 (1983): 188–200.

———. "Saddam Hussein: A Political Profile." *Jerusalem Quarterly* 17 (Fall 1980): 115–144.

———. "United States Institute of Peace Special Report—Between Impediment and Advantage: Saddam's Iraq." http://www.usip.org/oc/sr/baram/baram .html, 2 April 2001.

Barzilai, Gad, and Elie Rekhess. "Israel." *Middle East Contemporary Survey 1990*, 424–453.

Batatu, Hanna. "Iraq's Underground Shi'a Movements." *Middle East Journal* 35 (Autumn 1981): 578–594.

Bengio, Ofra. "Ba'thi Iraq in Search of Identity: Between Ideology and Praxis." *Orient* 28, no. 4 (1987): 511–518.

———. "Iraq." *Middle East Contemporary Survey 1990*, 379–423.

———. "Iraq's Shi'a and Kurdish Communities: From Resentment to Revolt." In *Iraq's Road to War*, edited by Amatzia Baram and Barry Rubin, 51–68. New York: St. Martin's Press, 1993.

———. "Shi'is and Politics in Ba'thi Iraq." *Middle Eastern Studies* 21, no. 1 (1985): 1–14.

Broder, Jonathan. "Saddam's Bomb." *New York Times Magazine* (1 October 2000): 38–43.

Brown, L. Carl. "Patterns Forged in Time: Middle Eastern Mindsets and the Gulf War." In *Political Psychology of the Gulf War*, edited Stanley Renshon, 3–21. Pittsburgh: Univ. of Pittsburgh, 1993.

Burgat, Francois. "Islamists and the Gulf Crisis." In *The Arab World Today*, ed. Dan Tschirgi, 205–211. Boulder: Lynne Rienner, 1994.

"Chaplains Minister in the Midst of Islam." *Christianity Today* 34 (8 October 90): 68–69.

Conanson, Joe. "The Iraq Lobby: Kissinger, The Business Forum, and Co." In *The Gulf War Reader*, edited by Micah L. Sifry and Christopher Cerf, 79–84. New York: Random House, 1991.

Dawisha, Adeed. "The Gulf War: A Defining Event?" In *The Arab World Today*, ed. Dan Tschirgi, 123–134. Boulder: Lynne Rienner, 1994.

———. "Invoking the Spirit of Arabism: Islam in the Foreign Policy of Saddam's Iraq." In *Islam in Foreign Policy*, edited by Adeed Dawisha. New York: Cambridge Univ. Press, 1983.

———. "The United States in the Middle East.: The Gulf War and Its Aftermath." *Current History* 91 (January 1992): 1–5.

Dessouki, Ali E. Hillal. "Egypt's Response to the Persian Gulf Crisis." *Current History* 91 (January 1992): 34–36.

Doumato, Eleanor Abdullah. "Saudi Arabia." *Oxford Encyclopedia of the Modern Islamic World.* Edited by John L. Esposito. New York: Oxford Univ. Press, 1995.

Ebert, Barbara. "The Gulf War and Its Aftermath: An Assessment of Evolving Arab Responses." *Middle East Policy* 1, no. 4 (1992): 77–95.

Eilts, Hermann F. "The Persian Gulf Crisis: Perspectives and Prospects." *Middle East Journal* 45 (Winter 1991): 7–22.

———. "Saudi Arabia: Traditionalism versus Modernism—A Royal Dilemma?" In *Ideology and Power in the Middle East,* edited by Peter Chelkowski and Robert Pranger, 56–88. Durham, N.C.: Duke Univ. Press, 1988.

Esposito, John. "Jihad In a World of Shattered Dreams." *The World and I* (February 1991): 514–527.

———. "The Persian Gulf War, Islamic Movements, and the New World Order." *Iranian Journal of International Affairs* 5, no. 2 (1993): 340–364.

———, and James P. Piscatori. "Democracy and Islam." *Middle East Journal* 45 (Summer 1991): 427–440.

Farouk-Sluglett, Marion, and Peter Sluglett, "Iraq since 1986: The Strengthening of Saddam." *Middle East Report* (November–December 1990): 19–24.

Frankel, Glenn. "Lines in the Sand." In *The Gulf War Reader,* edited by Micah L. Sifry and Christopher Cerf, 16–20. New York: Random House, 1991.

Friedman, Robert I. "War and Peace in Israel." In *The Gulf War Reader,* eds. Micah L. Sifry and Christopher Cerf, 66–78. New York: Random House, 1991.

Gaier, David W. "Saddam under the Banner of Islam." *Middle East International* 388 (23 November 1990): 19–20.

Geyer, Alan. "Just War, Jihad, and Abuse of Tradition." *Christianity and Crisis* (4 March 1991): 51–53.

"The Glaspie Transcript: Saddam Meets the U.S. Ambassador (July 25, 1990)." In *The Gulf War Reader,* edited by Micah L. Sifry and Christopher Cerf, 122–133. New York: Random House, 1991.

Goldberg, Jacob. "Saudi Arabia," *Middle East Contemporary Survey 1990:* 590–629.

———. "Saudi Arabia." *Middle East Contemporary Survey 1991.*

———. "Saudi Arabia's Desert Storm and Winter Sandstorm." In *The Gulf Crisis and Its Global Aftermath,* eds. Gad Barzilai, et al., 67–86. New York: Routledge, 1993.

Goldstein, Frank, and Daniel Jacobowitz. "PSYOP in Desert Shield/Desert Storm." In *Psychological Operations: Principles and Case Studies,* edited by Frank Goldstein and Benjamin Findley. Maxwell Air Force Base (Montgomery, Ala.): Air University Press, 1996.

Haddad, Yvonne. "Operation Desert Storm and the War of the Fatwas." In *Islamic Legal Interpretations: Muftis and Their Fatwas,* ed. Muhammad Khalid Masud et al., 297–309. Cambridge, Mass.: Harvard Univ. Press, 1996.

Halliday, Fred. "The Gulf War and Its Aftermath: First Reflections." *International Affairs* 67, no. 2 (1991): 223–234.

———. "Historical Antecedents to the Present Crisis." *Rusi Journal* 136 (Autumn 1991): 40–43.

Hashim, Ahmed. "Iraq: The Pariah State." *Current History* 91 (January 1992): 11–16.

Hashmi, Sohail. "The Islamic Ethics of War and Peace." Ph.D. diss., Harvard University, 1996.

Heacock, Roger. "From the Mediterranean to the Gulf and Back Again: The Palestinian Intifada and the Gulf War." *Arab Studies Quarterly* 13 (Winter/Spring 1991): 65–81.

Hehir, J. Bryan. "Baghdad As Target? An Order to be Refused." *Commonweal* 117 (26 October 1990): 602–603.

Hiro, Dilip. "A Few of Our Favorite Kings." In *The Gulf War Reader*, eds. Micah L. Sifry and Christopher Cerf, 408–411. New York: Random House, 1991.

Hitchens, Christopher. "Realpolitik in the Gulf: A Game Gone Tilt." In *The Gulf War Reader*, eds. Micah L. Sifry and Christopher Cerf, 107–118. New York: Random House, 1991.

Hollis, Rosemary. "Inter-Arab Politics and the Gulf War." *Cambridge Review of International Affairs* 5 (Autumn 1991–1992): 16–26.

Hourani, Albert. "Conclusion." In *Islam in the Political Process*, ed. James Piscatori, 226–234. New York: Cambridge Univ. Press, 1983

Huntington, Samuel P. "The Clash of Civilizations?" *Foreign Affairs* 72 (Summer 1993): 22–49.

Ibrahim, Saad Eddin. "Concerns and Challenges." In *Pan-Arabism and Arab Nationalism*, ed. Tawfic Farah, 57–67. Boulder, Colo.: Westview Press, 1987.

Ismael, Tareq Y., and Jacqueline S. Ismael. "Arab Politics and the Gulf War: Political Opinion and Political Culture." *Arab Studies Quarterly* 15, no. 1 (1993): 1–11.

abd al-Jabar, Faleh. "The Roots of an Adventure." In *The Gulf Between Us: The Gulf War and Beyond*, ed. Victoria Brittain, 33–35. London: Virago, 1991.

Kaplan, Robert. "Iraqi Indigestion." *The New Republic* (8 October 1990): 14–15.

Karsh, Efraim. "Survival at All Costs: Saddam Hussein as Crisis Manager." In *The Gulf Crisis and Its Global Aftermath*, edited by Gad Barzilai et al., 51–66. New York: Routledge, 1993.

———, and Inari Rautsi. "Why Saddam invaded Kuwait." *Survival* 33 (January–February 1991): 18–30.

Kelidar, Abbas. "The Wars of Saddam Hussein." *Middle Eastern Studies* 28 (October 1992): 778–798.

Khadduri, Majid. "Harb ("Legal Aspect")." *The Encyclopaedia of Islam.* New ed. Leiden: Brill, 1960.

Khalidi, Rashid. "The Palestinians and the Gulf Crisis." In *The Gulf War Reader*, eds. Micah L. Sifry and Christopher Cerf, 423–430. New York: Random House, 1991.

Khalidi, Walid. "Iraq vs. Kuwait: Claims and Counterclaims." In *The Gulf War Reader*, edited by Micah L. Sifry and Christopher Cerf, 57–65. New York: Random House, 1991.

———. "Why Some Arabs Support Saddam." In *The Gulf War Reader*, edited by Micah L. Sifry and Christopher Cerf, 161–171. New York: Random House, 1991.

Khouri, Rami G. "The Bitter Fruits of War." In *The Gulf War Reader*, eds. Micah L. Sifry and Christopher Cerf, 402–404. New York: Random House, 1991.

Kienle, Eberhard. "Syria, the Kuwait War, and the New World Order." In *The Gulf War and the New World Order: International Relations of the Middle East*, edited by Tareq Ismael and Jacqueline Ismael, 383–398. Gainesville, Fla.: Univ. of Florida Press, 1994.

Knightley, Philip. "Imperial Legacy." In *The Gulf War Reader*, eds. Micah L. Sifry and Christopher Cerf, 3–15. New York: Random House, 1991.

Kondrake, Morton, and Seth Carus, "Neighborhood Bully." *The New Republic* (20 August 1990): 12–15.

Korany, Baghat. "Arab Nationalism." In *The Oxford Encyclopedia of the Modern Islamic World*, edited by John L. Esposito. New York: Oxford Univ. Press, 1995.

Kostiner, Joseph. "Saudi Arabia." *Middle East Contemporary Survey 1991:* 613–640.

Kramer, Martin. "The Invasion of Islam." *Middle East Contemporary Survey 1990:* 177–207.

———. "Islam in the New World Order." *Middle East Contemporary Survey 1991:* 172–208.

Kupferschmidt, Uri M. "Egypt." *Middle East Contemporary Survey 1991:* 337–381.

La Rocque, Gene R. "America's Objectives in the Gulf." In *America Entangled: The Persian Gulf Crisis*, ed. Ted Carpenter, 79–82. Washington, D.C.: Cato Institute, 1991.

Legrain, Jean-Francois. "A Defining Moment: Palestinian Islamic Fundamentalism." In *Islamic Fundamentalisms and the Gulf Crisis*, edited by James Piscatori, 70–87. Chicago: The Fundamentalism Project, 1991; distributed by Univ. of Chicago Press.

Lesch, Ann Mosely. "Contrasting Reactions to the Persian Gulf Crisis." *Middle East Journal* 45 (Winter 1991): 30–50.

Luttwak, Edward. "Agencies of Disorder." In *The Gulf War Reader*, edited by Micah L. Sifry and Christopher Cerf, 290–298. New York: Random House, 1991.

MacLeod, Scott. "In the Wake of 'Desert Storm'". In *The Gulf War Reader*, edited by Micah L. Sifry and Christopher Cerf, 412–422. New York: Random House, 1991.

Maddy-Weitzman, Bruce. "Continuity and Change in the Inter-Arab System."

In *The Gulf Crisis and its Global Aftermath*, edited by Gad Barzilai et al., 33–50. New York: Routledge, 1993.

———. "Inter-Arab Relations." *Middle East Contemporary Survey* 1990: 131–175.

———. "Islam and Arabism." *The Washington Quarterly* 5 (Autumn 1982): 181–189.

Marr, Phoebe. "Iraq: Its Revolutionary Experience under the Ba'th." In *Ideology and Power in the Middle East*, edited by Peter J. Chelkowski and Robert J. Pranger, 185–209. Durham, N.C.: Duke Univ. Press, 1988.

———. "Iraq's Uncertain Future." *Current History* 90 (January 1991): 1–4, 39–42.

Mayer, Ann Elizabeth. "War and Peace in the Islamic Tradition and International Law." In *Just War and Jihad: Historical and Theoretical Perspectives on War and Peace in Western and Islamic Traditions*, edited by John Kelsay and James T. Johnson, 195–226. New York: Greenwood Press, 1991.

Meital, Yoram. "Egypt in the Gulf Crisis." In *Iraq's Road to War*, edited by Amatzia Baram and Barry Rubin, 191–202. New York: St. Martin's Press, 1993.

Menashri, David. "Iran." *Middle East Contemporary Survey* 1990: 350–378.

———. "Iran." *Middle East Contemporary Survey* 1991: 382–415.

Michel, Tom. "Historical Background and Religious Aspects of the Gulf War." *SEDOS* (March 15, 1991): 79–84.

Miller, Judith, and Laurie Mylroie. "The Rise of Saddam Hussein." In *The Gulf War Reader*, edited by Micah L. Sifry and Christopher Cerf, 66–78. New York: Random House, 1991.

Milton-Edwards, Beverley. "A Temporary Alliance with the Crown: The Islamic Response in Jordan." In *Islamic Fundamentalisms and the Gulf Crisis*, edited by James Piscatori, 88–108. Chicago: The Fundamentalism Project, 1991; distributed by Univ. of Chicago Press.

———. "West Bank and Gaza." In *The Oxford Encyclopedia of the Modern Islamic World*, edited by John L. Esposito. New York: Oxford Univ. Press, 1995.

Morrison, Micah. "House of Ghosts." *The American Spectator* 23 (December 1990): 19–21.

Muslih, Muhammad. "The Shift in Palestinian Thinking." *Current History* 91 (January 1992): 22–28.

Norton, Augustus R. "Breaking through the Wall of Fear in the Arab World." *Current History* 91 (January 1992): 37–41.

———. "The Future of Civil Society in the Middle East." *Middle East Journal* 47 (Spring 1993): 205–116.

Pappe, Ilan. "A Modus Vivendi Challenged: The Arabs in Israel and the Gulf War." In *Iraq's Road to War*, eds. Amatzia Baram and Barry Rubin, 163–176. New York: St. Martin's Press, 1993.

Peters, Rudolph. "Jihad." In *The Oxford Encyclopedia of the Modern Islamic World*, edited by John L. Esposito. New York: Oxford Univ. Press, 1995.

Piscatori, James. "Religion and Realpolitik." In *Islamic Fundamentalisms and the Gulf Crisis,* edited by James Piscatori, 1–27. Chicago: The Fundamentalism Project, 1991; distributed by Univ. of Chicago Press.

Pletka, Danielle. "Invasion Drives a Wedge Into the Arab Nation." *Insight on the News* (20 August 1990): 11–13.

———. "Past Glories Shape Destinies of Arabs." *Insight* (4 March 1991): 8–12.

———. "Riding the Anti-Saddam Tide to the Top of the Pyramid." *Insight on the News* (10 December 1990): 26–27.

Post, Jerrold. "The Defining Moment of Saddam's Life." In *Political Psychology of the Gulf War,* edited by Stanley Renshon, 49–66. Pittsburgh: Univ. of Pittsburgh Press, 1993.

Quandt, William. "The Middle East in 1990." *Foreign Affairs* 70 ("America and the World" issue, 1990/91): 49–69.

Reed, Stanley. "Jordan and the Gulf Crisis." *Foreign Affairs* 69 (Winter 1990/91): 21–35.

———. "Jordan: Bitter Refugees." *Business Week* (3 September 1990): 29.

Richman, Sheldon. "Washington's Interventionist Record in the Middle East." In *America Entangled: The Persian Gulf Crisis,* edited by Ted Carpenter, 67–74. Washington, D.C.: Cato Institute, 1991.

Roberts, Hugh. "A Trial of Strength: Algerian Islamism." In *Islamic Fundamentalisms and the Gulf Crisis,* edited by James Piscatori, 131–154. Chicago: The Fundamentalism Project, 1991; distributed by Univ. of Chicago Press.

———. "Jordan: Bitter Refugees." *Business Week* (3 September 1990): 29.

Rodinson, Maxime. "The Mythology of a Conqueror." *Middle East Report* (January/February 1991): 12–13.

Rodman, Peter. "Middle East Diplomacy after the Gulf War." *Foreign Affairs* 70 (Spring 1991): 1–18

Rubin, Berry. "The Gulf Crisis: Origins and Course of Events." *Middle East Contemporary Survey* 1990, 73–97.

Safran, Nadav. "Strike Supporters." *The New Republic* (24 September 1990): 24–26.

Said, Edward W. "On Language, Linkage, and Identity." In *The Gulf War Reader,* edited by Micah L. Sifry and Christopher Cerf, 439–446. New York: Random House, 1991.

Schiff, Ze'ev. "Israel after the War." *Foreign Affairs* 70 (Spring 1991): 19–33.

Schulze, Reinhard. "Muslim World League." In *The Oxford Encyclopedia of the Modern Islamic World,* edited by John L. Esposito. New York: Oxford Univ. Press, 1995.

Simpson, John. "The Aftermath of the Gulf War." *Asian Affairs* 23 (1992): 161–170.

Sluglett, Peter, and Marion Farouk-Sluglett, "Sunnis and Shi'is Revisited." In *Iraq: Power and Society,* edited by Derek Hopwood et al. Reading, U.K.: Ithaca Press, 1993.

El-Solh, Raghid. "The Gulf Crisis and Arab Nationalism." *Peuples Mediterraneens* (January-June 1992): 221–231.

Sonn, Tamara. "Islam and the Political Process in the Arab World: A Post Gulf War Update." *Journal of Developing Societies* 12 (December 1996): 191–204.

Springborg, Robert. "Infitah, Agrarian Transformation, and Elite Consolidation in Contemporary Iraq." *Middle East Journal* 40 (Winter 1986): 33–52.

Susser, Asher. "Jordan." *Middle East Contemporary Survey* 1990: 457–499.

———. "Jordan." *Middle East Contemporary Survey* 1991: 482–519.

Tarver, Heidi. "Words of War: The Persian Gulf Crisis and American Public Discourse." Ph.D. diss., University of California, Berkeley, 1997.

Telhami, Shibley. "Arab Public Opinion and the Gulf War." In *Political Psychology of the Gulf War*, edited by Stanley Renshon, 183–97. Pittsburgh: Univ. of Pittsburgh Press, 1993.

Tripp, Charles. "Domestic Politics in Iraq: Saddam Hussein and the Autocratic Fallacy." In *War and Peace in the Gulf: Domestic Politics and Regional Relations in the 1990s*, eds. Anoushiravan Ehteshami, et al. Reading, UK: Ithaca Press, 1991.

———. "The Iran-Iraq War and the Iraqi State," In *Iraq: Power and Society*, edited by Derek Hopwood et al., 91–115. Reading, UK: Ithaca Press, 1993.

Tyan, E. "Djihad." *The Encyclopaedia of Islam*. New ed. Leiden: Brill, 1960.

"The U.N. Resolutions: The Complete Text." In *The Gulf War Reader*, eds. Micah L. Sifry and Christopher Cerf, 137–156. New York: Random House, 1991.

"U.S. Senators Chat with Saddam (April 12, 1990)." In *The Gulf War Reader*, eds. Micah L. Sifry and Christopher Cerf, 119–121. New York: Random House, 1991.

Viorst, Milton. "The Storm and the Citadel." *Foreign Affairs* 75 (January/February 1996): 93–107

Wall, James. "President Bush Ignores Arab Street Talk." *Christian Century* 107 (22 August 1990): 755–756.

Waas, Murray. "What Washington Gave Saddam for Christmas." In *The Gulf War Reader*, edited by Micah L. Sifry and Christopher Cerf, 85–95. New York: Random House, 1991.

Wiley, Joyce. "Khoi." In *The Oxford Encyclopedia of the Modern Islamic World*, edited by John L. Esposito. New York: Oxford Univ. Press, 1995.

Wright, Robin. "Unexplored Realities." *Middle East Journal* 45 (Winter 1991): 23–29.

Ya'ari, Ehud, and Ina Friedman. "Curses in Verses." *Atlantic* 267 (February 1991): 22–26.

Zonis, Marvin. "Leaders and Publics in the Middle East: Shattering the Key Organizing Myths of Arab Society." In *Political Psychology of the Gulf War*, edited by Stanley Renshon, 269–292. Pittsburgh: Univ. of Pittsburgh, 1993.

# INDEX

Saddam as proponent of, 16
Saddam defended on the basis of, 153
*See also* Arab nationalism; pan-
Arabism
Arab League, 36, 126, 148, 174
Charter (Article 6), 40
Iraq, defender of, 16
Iraq-Kuwait dispute, mediator of,
20–21, 179, 191n20
meeting (28–30 May 1990), 17–19
meeting (3 August 1990), 23, 25, 40
Resolution 3036, 25, 26, 151
meeting (10 August 1990), 23, 25, 39,
40, 96, 103, 105, 123, 134
Resolution 195, 26, 96, 143, 152,
197n13, 217n46
military force of, 13
Arab Maghreb Union (AMU), 192n29
Arab nationalism, 180, 193n40
Ba'thism and, 86, 89
Islam, distinct from, 55, 67
Islam, linked with, 3, 60, 167, 187n4
Kuwait's appeal to, 81
Saddam as advocate of, 19, 208n80
Saddam defended on the basis of, 154
Syrian, 38
umma and, 197n22
*See also* Arabism; pan-Arabism
Arab street, 171, 178, 229n37
Egyptian, 36
Saddam condemned by, 151
Saddam supported by, 31, 34, 140, 149
Saudi, 41
Arafat, Yasir, 159, 172, 215n18, 235n49
intifada and, 33, 86
Israel, relations with, 33–34, 86,
214n10
Palestinian terrorism and, 33, 199n34
PLO "declaration of independence"
and, 87
Saddam, supporter of, 18, 36, 84, 176,
195n51
*ardh* (land), 48
Aref, Abd al-Salam, 57
Argentina, 192n32
*asabiyya* (loyalty to a kinship group),
28

Ashrawi, Hanan, 33, 175
Ashtal, Abdalla Saleh al-, 153
Ashura (Shi'a festival), 46, 211n103,
216n32
Assad, Hafiz al-, 38, 69, 173–174
*as-salaamu aleykum* (peace be with
you), 85
Assyrians, 52
Azaidah, Ahmad al-, 169
Azhar University, al-, 126, 170
Aziz, Tariq, 15, 21, 130, 135, 209n82,
217n46
assassination of, attempted, 62, 68,
72, 209n87
Kuwait, threatening of, 90
oil policies of gulf states, protest
against, 19–20
Azzam, Maha, 169, 234n35

B-52, 1
Babylon, rebuilt by Saddam, 52–53
Babylonians, 52
Badr, Battle of, 71, 114
Baghdad, 8, 9, 61, 163
destruction of, in 1258, 69
founding by al-Mansur, 109
site of conferences during Gulf War,
125–131, 136
Baghdad Betty, 133
Baghdad Summit (1978), 192n32
*baghi* (injustice), 139
Bahrain, 192n29
Baker, James A., III, 135
Bakr, Ahmed Hassan al-, 9, 47, 48
Balfour Declaration, 163
Bandar bin Sultan (Saudi Arabian
prince), 39, 96, 194n46, 195n6,
227n13
Bani-Sadr, Abolhassan, 68
Barakat, Halim, 204n33
Barakat, Tayseer, 109
Baram, Amatzia, 20, 193n41, 204n26,
206n51
Basra, 8–9, 10, 121, 179
Batatu, Hanna, 50
Ba'thism, 47, 50, 78, 91, 120
deficiencies of, 61, 66

Islam and, 53–54, 87, 93, 100, 124
malleability of, 48, 66
Ba'th party, 47, 123, 174–75, 183, 213n137
coalition forces, response to, 101–102, 120
invasion of Kuwait, response to, 94
Islam and, 209n82, 222n123
Shi'a and, 60–63
bay'a (oath of loyalty), 141
Bayt al-Maqdis (Jerusalem), 92, 114
Baz, Osama al-, 21
Bazoft, Farzad, 16, 193n37
Bazzaz, Saad al-, 15, 192n26
BBC, 133
Beg, Mirza Aslam, 157
Begin, Menachem, 193n34
Beit Fajar, 34
Belhadj, Ali, 139
Ben Ali, Zine, 155
Bengio, Ofra, 55, 75, 86, 189n8, 190n13, 205n39, 212n124, 222n123, 232n15
Benjedid, Chadli, 140
Bethlehem, 34
Bilad, Al- (Saudi newspaper), 41
bin Abdul Aziz, Abdullah. See Abdullah bin Abdul Aziz
bin Abdul Aziz, Sultan. See Sultan bin Abdul Aziz
bin Baz, Abd al-Aziz, 144–145, 146, 228n18
bin Ladin, Usamah bin Muhammad, 182
bin Sultan, Bandar. See Bandar bin Sultan
bin Sultan bin Abdul Aziz, Khalid (Saudi prince and lieutenant general), 42
bin Talal, Hassan. See Hassan bin Talal
bismallah (in the name of God), 180, 210n98, 229n48
use by
Ba'th party, 93
Iraqi government, 98, 106, 137
Iraqi military, 121
Iraqi News Agency, 132
PLO, 87

RCC, 70, 91, 210n98
Saddam, 88, 118
Brown, L. Carl, 191n18
Browning, Edmund, 131
Bubiyan, 10, 190n12
Bull, Gerald, 13
Bulloch, John, 61
Bush, George Herbert Walker, 1, 33, 38, 131–132, 181, 187n5, 188n7, 230n61
effigy of, burned, 155
Saddam, letters from, 106, 118, 198n28, 221n96
Saudi Arabia, U.S. troops ordered to, 96
Byzantium, 95, 117, 217n44

Cairo, 18, 23, 25, 133
Cairo conference (1921), 8
Cairo Voice of the Arabs, 133
Carter, Jimmy, 193n34
Ceauşescu, Nicolae, 12
Chadli Benjedid. See Benjedid, Chadli
Chaldean Catholic Church, 131
Charter 91, 213n138
Cheney, Richard (Dick), 39, 96, 173
Christianity, 130–133
Christian Peace Conference, 131
Church of the Holy Sepulchre, 88
Clark, Ramsey, 127
Complete Writings of Saddam Hussein, The, 76
Conference of Popular Arab Forces (September 1990), 234n35
Cox, Percy, 9
Cruise, Tom, 133
Cyprus, 131

Dahuk, 125
Damascus Declaration, 179
dar al-harb (house of war), 99, 209n82
dar al-ifta' (fatwa office), 147
dar al-Islam (house of Islam), 80, 99, 167, 209n82
da'wa (call to embrace Islam), 93, 98, 99, 146, 205n45
da'wa, al- (Islamic Call political party), 58, 61–62, 151, 203n21, 205n45

See also *hizb al-da'wa al-islamiyah*
Dawalibi, Muhammad al-, 126, 136
Dawisha, Adeed, 208n78
*dawla* (state), 54, 138
de Gaulle, Charles, 76
Democratic Front for the Liberation of
Palestine, 36
Desert Shield, 120, 133
Desert Storm, 1, 93, 116, 120
Dhahran, 134, 182
Din Muhammad, Warith al-, 145
Din Rabbani, Burhan al-, 145
Diyala, 125
Djibouti, 25, 26, 97
Dome of the Rock, 110, 113, 220n92
Dulles, John Foster, 193n40
*Dustur, al-* (Jordanian newspaper), 151

*Economist, The* (London), 6, 36
Egypt, 23, 101, 103, 162
ACC, member of, 192n29
coalition forces, response to, 37,
147–148, 152, 228n30
Damascus Declaration and, 179–180
invasion of Kuwait, response to,
36–37, 97, 140, 146–147, 150
Arab League Resolution 3036,
approval of, 25
Arab League Resolution 195,
drafting and approval of, 26
Iraq, sometime ally of, 192n32
Islam and civil society in, 166
PIC, founder of, 216n23
political parties, 150, 152, 169, 229n38
Saddam, appealed to by, 31
Saddam, opposed by, 119, 133
Syria and, 38
ulama, 141
World Islamic Popular Gathering,
member, 127
*See also* Cairo; Mubarak, Hosni;
Muslim Brotherhood (Egypt)
Eickelman, Dale, 83, 166
Eilts, Hermann, 163
Eisenhower, Dwight D., 163
Eliade, Mircea, 51
emirates. *See* United Arab Emirates

Erbakan, Necmettin, 128
Esposito, John, 28

Fadil, Abdullah, 120, 123
Fahd (king of Saudi Arabia), 127, 128,
195n63
Assad and, 39
coalition troops, justification for
calling, 40–43, 143, 145, 147,
172–173
coalition troops, request for, 39, 96,
142–143, 200n58
effigy of, burned, 155
invasion of Kuwait, response to,
24–25, 40–41
Iraq-Kuwait dispute, mediator of, 21
Khomeini, attacked by, 104
Mecca and Medina, protector of, 97,
104–105, 108, 118, 134, 142
noncoalition members, opposed by,
154, 167–168
Saddam, opposed by, 93, 105–107, 116,
117, 132, 134, 137
Saddam's correspondence with,
210n101
*fahl* (large male animal), 140
Faisal I (Hashemite king of Iraq), 46, 60,
107, 201n5
*faridah al-ghaibah, al-* (*The Absent
Duty*), 142
fatwas, 5
bin Baz, issued by, 228n18
bin Ladin, issued by, 182–183
condemning coalition forces and
supporting Iraq, 122, 137
condemning Iraq and supporting
coalition forces, 144, 146, 147, 172
Iranian revolution, supporting, 62
Khoi, issued by, 236n64
problems of contradiction and
authoritativeness, 171
Saddam rejected use of, 55, 59, 138
Tamimi, issued by, 224n152, 230n55
Tantawi, issued by, 232n14
war of, 170
World War I, issued during, 141,
210n100, 227n9

in Najaf (October 1979), 64
declaring Iraq defender of the Arab
    nation (April 1980), 66, 101
to the Arab Cooperation Council
    (23–24 February 1990), 15–16
on the forty-third anniversary of
    the Ba'th (April 1990), 86–87
"fire for Israel" speech (2 April
    1990), 16–17, 86, 94, 176,
    194n46, 214n8
to the Arab Popular Conference
    for Solidarity with Iraq (May
    1990), 87–88
to the Arab League (28–30 May
    1990), 17–18, 195n52
to the Popular Islamic Conference
    (18 June 1990), 88–89
at a symposium honoring Michel
    Aflaq (26 June 1990), 19, 89–90,
    111
17 July Revolution Day (1990), 20,
    136
to Ba'thists, regarding "merger"
    with Kuwait (7 August 1990),
    94
for "The Great Victory Day" over
    Iran (7 August 1990), 94, 119,
    136
justifying the annexation of Kuwait
    (8 August 1990), 29
jihad speech (10 August 1990), 30–
    31, 94–96, 97, 100, 102, 110–112,
    120, 134, 144, 154, 155, 167, 183,
    217n46, 222n124, 230n55
radio address to Iraqi women
    (12 August 1990), 98
second jihad speech (5 September
    1990), 116–117
announcing the *al-hijara* missile
    (9 October 1990), 114
to the World Popular Islamic
    Leadership (December 1990),
    129
to the Popular Islamic Conference
    (11 January 1991), 137
U.S., belief in weakness of, 16
Hussein, Uday, 179, 204n28, 223n125

Hussein I (king of Jordan), 16, 19, 21,
    156, 171
    coalition forces, response to, 35
    invasion of Kuwait, response to, 26,
        34, 176, 199n40, 235n47
Husseini, Faisal, 33, 43
Hussein Ibn Ali (sharif of Mecca), 107,
    141, 163
Huwaidy, Fahmy, 147, 160, 161

*ibadat* (pillars of Islamic practice), 98,
    218n49
*ibdaa'aat* (creative abilities), 55
Ibn Ali, Hussein. *See* Hussein Ibn Ali
Ibn Hisham, 117, 222n111
Ibn Khaldun, 8
Ibn Saud, Abdul Aziz, 104, 107, 142
Ibrahim, Izzat, 22, 72, 88, 90
Ibrahim, Saad Eddin, 187n4
Imam Abbas mosque (Karbala), 179
IMF (International Monetary Fund), 162
imperialism, 13
India, 141
*indimaj* (merger), 197n17
Indonesia, 158
*inkaar* (contestation), 54
International Islamic Front for Jihad
    against the Jews and the Crusaders,
    182
international law, 147, 228n32
intifida, 84, 87, 162, 180, 194n45,
    236n60
    "children of the stones," 71
    invasion of Kuwait linked with, 92
    results, lack of, 33, 86, 198n33
    routinized, 32, 176
*intisab, al-* (clan-based hierarchy),
    205n52
*iqlimiyya* (regionalism), 224n139
Iran, 9, 142, 165, 234n35
    invasion of Kuwait, response to, 122,
    150
Iran-Iraq War, 9, 38, 53, 66–73, 108, 121,
    180
    Iraqi monuments regarding, 45, 121
    jihad, calls to, during, 142
    peace talks, 191n19, 214n11

Popular Islamic Conference and, 125
"Qadisiyya II," 115
Saddam's appeals to Islam during, 83,
85, 112, 122
U.S. policy toward, 164, 177
Iraq, 1, 10, 23, 26, 145, 181
ACC, member of, 192n29
British government, creation of, 8–9,
46
civil society in, 213n138
economy, 10–12
Egypt, sometime ally of, 192n32
flag (new design by Saddam), 138
Gulf War, status during, 29, 46, 88,
99, 110
invasion of Kuwait, response to, 82,
91–92, 150–151, 229n48
Jewish community of, 49
Kuwait, border disputes with, 191n20
media, 223n139
military, 12, 13, 70–71, 110, 138, 146,
190n8
Ministry of Industry and Military
Industrialization, 215n13
National Assembly, 20, 98, 108, 120,
130, 221n96
oil, 11–12, 27, 194n49, 195n57, 215n13
PIC, founder of, 216n23
Revolutionary Command Council
(RCC), 60, 123, 163
bismallah, use of, 70, 210n98
coalition forces, response to, 101,
102
invasion of Kuwait, support for, 29,
91, 100, 119–120, 136, 217n42
Islam, use of, 92
mujahid body, 93
Saddam, deputy chairman of, 47
Saddam, purges by, 49, 63
ulama, 108, 123–127, 146, 220n85,
223n139, 230n64
Iraqi Communist Party, 15
Iraqi News Agency, 132, 235n44
Ishtar, temple and gate (Babylon), 52
Iskander, Amir, 54, 56, 59, 64, 74, 112,
212n119
Islam, 3, 5, 7, 28, 180, 185–186

Arab nationalism and, 167, 187n4
Arab street and, 178
central authority, lack of, 170–171
civil society and, 166
coalition forces condemned according to, 154–159, 160–161, 167–168,
174
by Algerians, 169
by Egyptians, 152–153, 155, 169
by Iranians, 177
by Jordanians, 152, 155, 156–157,
168–169
by Moroccans, 158–159
by Pakistanis, 157
by Saudis, 173
by Tunisians, 155, 161
coalition forces justified according to,
4–6, 126, 148–149, 155
by Egyptians, 146–148, 169, 172
by Saudis, 143–146, 172
Kuwait's appeal to, 81–82
language of politics and, 83, 166–167,
172, 180, 209n82
Saddam, used by, 161, 188n5, 212n124
to attack coalition members, 44,
82, 97–98, 100, 104–108, 116–
119, 122–123, 126–129, 134–135
Iran-Iraq War, during, 66–73, 80,
83, 94
to justify attacking Israel, 114–115
to justify invading Kuwait, 3–6, 19,
41, 46, 80, 90–92, 94, 100–101,
103, 128
linked with Arabism, 87–91, 94–
102, 105, 108, 112, 119–121,
124–125, 136–138, 166–167
to reconcile with Iran, 83–85, 121
to unify Iraq, 53–56, 59–66, 80, 93
Usamah bin Ladin and, 182
See also under Arabism; Arab nationalism; pan-Arabism
Islamic Arab Popular Conference (April
1991), 234n35
Islamic Conference on Palestine
(December 1990), 234n35, 236n60
Islamic Conference Organization (ICO),
25, 126, 144

Lawrence, T. E., 8
Lebanon, 17, 25, 26, 97
  coalition forces, response to, 155–156
Lenin, Vladimir Ilyich, 76
Lesch, Ann Mosely, 17
Levy, David, 34
Libya, 25, 26, 37, 129, 145
  AMU, member of, 192n29
Likud, 33
Luttwak, Edward, 48

M1-A1 (tank), 2
Madani, Abbasi, 129, 139, 169
Mafraq (Jordan), 157
Maghreb, 105, 159
Mahdi, 108, 141
*Majalla, al-* (London-based Arabic
  newsmagazine), 165
Makiya, Kanan, 49, 61, 74, 179, 203n15,
  207n70, 209n84
Maksoud, Clovis, 26–27
Malaysia, 127, 158
Mansur, Abu Jafar abd-Allah al-, 109–
  110
Marduk's gate (Babylon), 52
*marji'* (high-ranking jurist), 58
Marr, Phebe, 205n40
*maru'a* (manliness), 42, 201n63, 227n12
Ma'ruf, Taha, 53
Matar, Fuad, 55, 56, 66, 112, 193n36
Mauritania, 25, 26
  AMU, member of, 192n29
  coalition forces, response to, 156
*mawadda* (friendship), 154
Mecca, 28, 95, 108, 185–186
  Abraha's attack on, 116–117
  Medina and, Fahd as guardian of, 104,
    105, 146
  Medina and, holiest sites of Islam, 31,
    39, 87, 144, 186
  PIC branch, site of, 126, 146
  qibla, 84, 135, 186, 222n112
  Saddam's visit to, 70
  "under the spears of foreigners," 96,
    106, 154
  justification for jihad, 97, 128, 182
Medina, 28, 90

coalition control of as justification
  for jihad, 128
Muhammad's grave, site of, 95
  *See also* Mecca
Middle East Contemporary Survey
  (MECS), 6
*min al-khaleej ila al-muheet* (from the
  gulf to the ocean), 167, 180
Misuari, Nur, 145
Mohtashimi, Ali Akbar, 177
Mongols, 69
Morocco, 24, 25, 26, 97, 105, 162
  AMU, member of, 192n29
  coalition forces, response to, 158–159
  invasion of Kuwait, response to, 150
  *See also* Hassan II
Moro Liberation Front, 145
Morris, Harvey, 61
Mosul, 8–9
"Mother of All Battles" speech (20 Sep-
  tember 1990), 112–113
Mu'awiyah (first Umayyad caliph), 63
Mubarak, Hosni, 81, 169
  coalition forces, response to, 173
  invasion of Kuwait, response to, 24,
    26, 36, 147, 196nn4–5
  mediation of Iraq-Kuwait dispute,
    attempted, 14–15, 20, 21, 173
  Saddam and
    called traitorous by Saddam for
      supporting coalition, 116–117
    rivals for Arab leadership, 18, 31,
      36, 97, 107
Muhammad (prophet of Islam), 28,
  71, 95, 108, 132, 146, 185, 218n51,
  222n112
Muhammad, Husayn Rashid, 122
Muhammad bin Sa'ud University, 173
*muharak asasi* (prime mover), 66
*muharakayn asasiayn* (two prime
  movers), 100
*mujahid* (one who conducts a jihad), 70,
  84, 93, 141, 160, 205n44
*mujtahid* (Islamic jurist formulating
  independent decisions), 55, 62
*mukhabarat* (Iraqi intelligence service),
  127

## DATE DUE

| | | | |
|---|---|---|---|
| | | | |
| | | | |
| | | | |
| | | | |
| | | | |
| | | | |
| | | | |
| | | | |
| | | | |
| | | | |
| | | | |
| | | | |
| | | | |

#47-0108 Peel Off Pressure Sensitive